Composing for Moving Pictures

COMPOSING **FOR MOVING** PICTURES

The Essential Guide

JASON M. GAINES

OXFORD UNIVERSITY PRESS

OXFORD
UNIVERSITY PRESS

Oxford University Press is a department of the
University of Oxford. It furthers the University's objective
of excellence in research, scholarship, and education
by publishing worldwide.

Oxford New York
Auckland Cape Town Dar es Salaam Hong Kong Karachi
Kuala Lumpur Madrid Melbourne Mexico City Nairobi
New Delhi Shanghai Taipei Toronto

With offices in
Argentina Austria Brazil Chile Czech Republic France Greece
Guatemala Hungary Italy Japan Poland Portugal Singapore
South Korea Switzerland Thailand Turkey Ukraine Vietnam

Oxford is a registered trade mark of Oxford University Press
in the UK and certain other countries.

Published in the United States of America by
Oxford University Press
198 Madison Avenue, New York, NY 10016

Library of Congress Cataloging-in-Publication Data
Gaines, Jason M.
Composing for moving pictures: the essential guide/Jason M. Gaines.
pages cm
Includes bibliographical references and index.
ISBN 978-0-19-024092-9 (hardcover : alk. paper); 978-0-19-975477-9 (paperback : alk. paper)
1. Motion picture music—Instruction and study.
2. Composition (Music) 3. Film composers. I. Title.
MT64.M65G35 2014
781.5'4213—dc23 2014032009

9 8 7 6 5 4 3 2 1

Printed in the United States of America
on acid-free paper

For my wonderful, loving and
awe-inspiring wife, Valerie.
You have a remarkable gift to
make the impossible seem possible.

CONTENTS

ACKNOWLEDGMENTS

I WOULD LIKE TO ACKNOWLEDGE and thank Lendell Black for allowing me to use his compositions and video examples in this book. Your friendship has been a true gift. I look forward to the future and all that it brings. I would also like to thank my colleagues Chris Mangum and Robert Brock. Without your support and friendship, this work would not have been possible.

Thank you to my many Logic and composition students throughout North America. Each of you has provided valuable insight to the shape and design of this book. Your contributions are priceless and have inspired me to continue what I love doing—composing and performing music and sharing those experiences with others.

I would like to thank the wonderfully talented composers who agreed to be interviewed for this book: Nathan Barr, Terence Blanchard, David Earl, Steve Horowitz, Paul Lipson, Trevor Morris, and Marc Shaiman. Your work inspires me, and I am humbled by your selfless contribution to this work.

To my parents Arla and Craig Gaines and my sisters Angela Gaines and Alexandra Tinsman—thank you for tirelessly supporting me in the pursuit of my dreams.

Thank you to my dear friends Gianfranco Tornatore and Peter Holsberg. You have been a wealth of inspiration and support throughout this journey.

Finally, I would like to thank my wife, Valerie. You have been unwavering in your support for me. I could not have done any of this without your grace and patience. You inspire me to be better each and every day.

ABOUT THE COMPANION WEBSITE

www.oup.com/us/composingformovingpictures

THE COMPANION WEBSITE provides additional resources to purchasers of the book. The website contains sample template projects, videos, web resources, and audio files that are integral to the topics presented in the book.

1. Any musical examples that have a corresponding audio recording on the website will display the following symbol:
2. Logic Pro X template files allow the reader to actively engage with topics as they are discussed throughout the book. The Logic Pro X template files contain all audio files, MIDI files, software instrument presets and video files required to complete a particular lesson. Concepts that refer to a specific Logic Pro X template file will have display the following symbol:
3. The book references website content to provide further information on topics, as well as links to third-party software applications. The following symbol will designate website content:

PART I

HISTORY, THEORY, AND PRACTICE

CHAPTER 1
A BRIEF HISTORY OF FILM

FILM MUSIC IS DIFFICULT to define because there is no single way to do so. It can serve as an accompaniment or even a character in the film and often both. Film music can establish a time and setting, create and inspire a particular mood, foreshadow things to come, identify a character's thoughts and motives, and generally create a world that audiences can and will relate to. It does all of these things simultaneously, allowing us to forget that we are gazing at a two-dimensional representation of a world that we are not physically inhabiting. We become distracted from the technical aspects of the film whether it is black-and-white, color or silent. Film music aids our transport into another time and place so that we can experience heightened connectivity with the story and characters. Film music shapes our perceptions and adds context to often-vague visual images.

The evolution of film music has been dynamic and arguably as exciting as the character it adds to the films we all have added to our personal history. Film music sits at the intersection of music and film. Even with this obvious relationship, it is important to understand the uniqueness of this position—meaning is created through musical practice and cinematic practice (Kalinak, 2010). As a result, it is arguably fair to say that film music is a hybrid art form that honors both musical and cinematic ideologies. The goal of this short introduction is to provide an engaging overview of film music from its inception to the present day. This chapter will explore why film music is important: music and the silent film, music and early sound with film, classic Hollywood and the post-classic period of the late twentieth century, and forward.

THE IMPORTANCE OF FILM MUSIC

Film music, while written specifically for film, is still simply music at a basic level. The traditional building blocks of music such as tempo, rhythm, tonality, harmony, dynamics, timbre and so on are at the disposal of the composer to create meaning and enhance the experience of the film. Composers use these musical building blocks to create a deep experience with the film.

Interestingly, these musical elements can be used individually or in tandem with other musical elements to evoke emotion and meaning. Listening for all of these elements in a film can be difficult, if not overwhelming, for viewers. Skilled composers understand how and when to use musical elements to set the tone for the film. The music of John Williams has been studied time and time again because of his keen ability to use musical elements as integral components in film.

Jaws (1975) is a classic American thriller directed by Steven Spielberg, with music composed by John Williams. In the story, an enormous, man-eating great white shark terrorizes a quiet summer resort town. Local authorities, with the aid of a marine biologist, are charged with the task of hunting down the shark and returning peace and order to the otherwise sleepy resort town. From a technological standpoint, the film was ahead of its time, and likely a bit too far ahead of its time. Production was plagued with continued delays because of mechanical malfunctions with the movie's star—the great white shark. As a result, Spielberg decided to use William's score to announce the great white shark rather than rely on the mechanical shark. In fact, the shark was rarely seen during the movie but always present in the minds of the viewer thanks to its musical theme.

The character theme for the shark is arguably one of Williams's most famous compositions. He brilliantly used tempo, tonality, and timbre to paint a portrait of the film's villain. The basic theme is simple, but extremely effective. The melody is comprised of two central notes—E and F. These two notes are positioned a half-step away from each other and possess a dissonant relationship. Depending on the context, a half-step harmonic relationship can represent both positive and negative outcomes. Williams used this dissonance to create an extremely dark and ominous mood that seemed to embody the character of the shark. Williams did not stop with the dissonant tonality to announce the presence of the shark; he also employed rhythm and tempo. For example, when the shark was approaching, Williams would signal the distant presence of the shark with the dissonant theme played through rubato quarter notes. When the shark approached and appeared in striking distance, the theme tempo became strict and increasingly faster. While the audience may or may not have known the musical characteristics that supported the intensity of the scene, the end result was still clear.

Musical themes also evoke feelings of pride and nationalism. John Williams was asked to write the music for the *Star Wars* movies, the epic story that follows the rise, fall, and redemption of Anakin Skywalker. In much the same manner as *Jaws*, Williams wrote themes for characters but also for perceived good and evil. For example, the main *Star Wars* theme is highly nationalistic and meant to instill pride, strength, and perseverance to a group of people who are fighting for something that is much bigger than they are. Nationalism is a musical writing style that rose out of Romantic period in the early 1800s and continued into the twentieth century. It was a revolt against social and political norms that impeded societal progress. This period brought new exploration of the humanities and how they can be explored to better the individual as well as society. This enlightenment brought new advances in self-awareness, education, and technology and arguably moved society forward.

Williams knew how to use musical elements and styles to evoke emotion and create an experience that would forever frame a moment in time and context. While there are moments where the absence of music in a film is extremely powerful, it is impossible to deny the importance of film music.

MUSIC AND SILENT FILM

The vast majority of texts that explore music and film begin with the origins of the silent film in the late 1890s through the 1920s. Little was known about how music evolved in this time period until recently. Historians and musicologists have methodically studied musical materials, newspapers, trade journals, and periodicals to better understand the early relationship of music and film. Not surprisingly, they found that film music, as we know it today, was not nearly as evolved (Wierzbicki, 2009). In fact, many early exhibitions of the moving picture were not much more than show booth attractions at fairgrounds, vaudeville shows, and traveling shows. These events were typically noisy and not conducive to a sit-down experience. Music was often used to lure potential patrons to the venue but was not seen as an integral component of the experience (Cook, 2008). During 1894–1905, a number of companies focused on creating and displaying motion pictures in the United States and abroad were established. Hollywood and the culture that it supports would not begin to form until the end of World War I in 1918 (Wierzbicki, 2009).

Thomas Alva Edison is credited as the inventor of the motion-picture camera. This was possible through a collaboration with George Eastman, who had been experimenting with a new type of film made of cellulose nitrate. Edison assigned some of his most brilliant engineers to the collaboration to extend his success from the phonograph in 1877. The result was a Kinetograph (for capturing of moving images) and a Kinetoscope (for playback of recorded, moving images). The first Kinetoscope parlor opened on April 14, 1894, and was seen largely as a parlor trick. The practical uses were somewhat limited for the general public because they could only see the recorded, moving images through a small peephole after paying a nominal fee. Interestingly, Edison's patents for the Kinetograph and Kinetoscope had limited protection in the United States but were free for purchase without the need for licensing outside of the United States. This paved the way for early filmmakers in Europe to exploit and improve upon Edison's invention.

Auguste and Louis Lumière had been in the early film industry in Europe for some time before witnessing Edison's Kinetoscope in Paris. Their family had experience in creating photographic plates and eventually became expert in celluloid film. The brothers had a vision for more commercial motion-picture equipment. They adapted Edison's design and patented the Cinématographe in February 1895. Their iteration of Edison's design included the usage of 35-mm-wide celluloid film that incorporated lessons learned from their experiences with photography—high-speed emulsion that yielded sharper image quality. The frame rate, or frames displayed per second of playback, of the Cinématographe was 16 frames per second (fps). This rate was far lower than Edison's Kinetoscope; however, the Lumière brothers felt the increase in frame sharpness was acceptable. The slower frame rate also offered another benefit. The maximum playback duration of the film increased from thirty seconds with Edison's Kinetoscope to nearly three minutes with the Cinématographe.

The Cinématographe was not bound by the need for electricity. The device was relatively portable and was powered by a simple hand crank. This allowed the Cinématographe to be used in environments that were simply not possible for the Kinetoscope. Also, the image from the Cinématographe could be easily magnified and projected onto a screen. Conversely, Edison's Kinetoscope required that viewers experience playback through a peephole. The Lumière brothers single-handedly changed the way people engage with the moving picture. For the first time, viewers could experience film in an environment that allowed them to focus on the film rather than the delivery mechanism.

The Lumière brothers presented their very first film in a public setting on December 28, 1895, to a modest audience of roughly thirty people, although the

▶ **FIG. 1.1**

The Lumière Brothers. Photofest Asset Locator: WGC000190055

film salon seated a total of one hundred people. By the second showing, word had spread of this new technological innovation, and lines stretched down the street and around the block for the film. The experience was far different than what is expected of modern motion pictures. Audiences were captivated with a twenty-minute program of short films that depicted everyday life including films of workers at the Lumière factory, babies being fed, comic accounts of gardeners in normal work environments, children riding bicycles, women fighting, and a train arriving at a train station (Wierzbicki, 2009). These films would likely not draw large crowds today, especially considering the modern ability to capture video on myriad devices including cellular phones and other mobile devices, but this showing clearly paved the way for audience engagement with film for decades to come.

MUSIC AND EARLY SOUND WITH FILM

Sound became married to film shortly after the groundbreaking innovations from Edison and the Lumière brothers. It is not completely known when the first live performance of music accompanied a film presentation, although it has been reported that a pianist participated in at least a few of the inaugural viewings of the Lumière films. Many scholars believe that music was never intended to be included during the film viewing experience but rather to serve as an interlude between films. For example, in the case of the Lumière brothers' films, a pianist was reported to play during the lull between the changing of the film rolls. Music was meant to be fanfare that preceded the start of the film to frame the experience for the audience.

By some accounts, early film was often described as dull, colorless, soundless, and, as a result, somewhat lifeless to audiences. However, that was not the case with all filmgoers. Audiences were often awestruck by the technological marvel that was unfolding in front of them. They simply could not believe that a technical apparatus was able to replay moments in time on demand (Wierzbicki, 2009). Within a year of the first running of the Lumière brothers' films, music was becoming increasingly incorporated into film performances. Bands, not single pianists, were integrated into the overall performance of the film. In many ways they were regarded as multimedia events because they incorporated multiple ways to excite the senses of the audience. The earliest filmmakers were paving a road through uncharted territory, and business was great.

Music started to become a more integral component of the audience experience. The earliest forms of Foley, the reproduction of everyday sounds in film, began to grow out of the musical interludes that were present in the earliest exhibitions of film. Musicians became a larger part of the audience experience by augmenting on-screen elements with live, musical elements. For example, bands would play nationalistic themes or bugle calls to accompany marching on screen. This had an instant and lasting impact on audiences because the film suddenly sprang to life before their eyes. The interaction between the film and the band was an early form of what is commonly referred to today as source music. Most film historians refer to this music as "diegetic music" to signify that the music is within the film's diegesis, or in other words, narrative (Wierzbicki, 2009).

In the late 1890s, underscore music, which is designed as a foundational component to film, became more commonplace in film exhibitions. The supportive relationship that music played in previous years began to morph into a deeper, symbiotic relationship. Music was beginning to become interweaved into the fabric of film. For example, musical interludes and supportive Foley gave way to musical experiences that were designed to complement, augment, and enhance the audience's experience with film. Interestingly enough, underscore predates the advent of film and film exhibition. Underscore was commonly used in the operas of world-renowned composers such as Beethoven, Mozart, and Wagner. The main difference was that these epic stories of the human experience were performed live in front of an audience. Given the nature of film's immediate engaging qualities, it was only a matter of time before music was asked to play a similar role.

The first decade of music's relationship with film was certainly not managed and was highly experimental. It was not institutionalized, and composers were offered a unique opportunity to explore a medium that was truly new. While many could likely see the potential, few would argue that filmmakers and composers of the late nineteenth century would be able to predict the modern evolution of film and its marriage to music. By 1909, the relationship of music and film had reached a level of ubiquity. The notion of "cue sheets," a manifest of musical components employed in a production, were published in a promotional brochure for the Edison Kinetogram. The publication provided recommendations for how the most recent films for the Edison Kinetogram should be accompanied with music. A list of musical starting and ending points were presented for scenes of the film.

As films grew in length, cues were often accompanied by brief descriptions of what took place in the scene. Wierzbicki (2009) provides the following account of how cues were used in Edison's *Why Girls Leave Home*:

> *The 10-minute film based on a popular 1905 melodrama should be accompanied thusly:*
>
> *At opening, Popular Air.*
>
> *Till second scene, Pizzicato.*
>
> *Till view of the orchestra seats, Regular overture.*
>
> *Till view of the stage is shown, Waltz time.*
>
> *Note—Knock at the door till girl starts to leave home, Home Sweet Home.*
>
> *Till audience applauds, Lively music.*
>
> *Till Act 2, snow scene, Plaintive.*

Till audience applauds, Lively music.
Till Act 3, bridge scene, Pizzicato.
Till gallery applauds, Lively music.
Till Act 4, heroine's home, Plaintive music.
Till hero bursts through the window, Lively, work to climax.
Till next set, girl's return home, Waltz movement.

At this early stage, music cue sheets were somewhat generic and did not refer to original musical works. They were simply meant as guidelines to provide general feelings that would support what audience members were experiencing with the film. Bands could repurpose music from film to film to create a deeper audience experience with little effort. Not surprisingly, this approach is still employed today. The notion of library music is commonplace in film and television. Composers are charged with the task of quickly accompanying cues with musical support. It is not uncommon to hear the same musical samples used in multiple television shows and major motion pictures. Many production studios create musical libraries for various moods and musical styles. For example, complete orchestras have been recorded and sampled for quick and easy use within digital audio workstations to augment prerecorded loops of musical material. Composers were doing much the same thing in the early twentieth century, but without the technological advances provided through modern audio engineering.

The first original musical scores, often referred to as "special music," to accompany film were introduced in the early 1900s. This movement was arguably shepherded by the increasing length of film, ultimately culminating in 60- and 120-minute feature-length films (Kalinak, 2010). Also, film exhibition was a rapidly growing industry. Large theaters began to be built and could accommodate hundreds of people in the audience. Music that accompanied film was critiqued with the film itself. It was becoming clear that the film music industry was not only growing but thriving. In 1914, the American Society of Composers, Authors and Publishers (ASCAP) was formed to protect the rights and intellectual property of its members and to ensure that members received a percentage of royalties generated from their copyrighted works.

ASCAP had a profound impact on the American film industry. Fees were now required for performances in a commercial context. In other words, when music was performed in a theater or other venue, compensation would be awarded to the copyright holder. ASCAP fought tirelessly for the rights of its members and did not shy away from confrontation, if necessary. After a 1917 Supreme Court ruling, it became quite clear that those who used music protected by ASCAP would pay premium penalties if they did not first pay a "music tax" (Wierzbicki, 2009). Film music was beginning to grow into an industry in and of itself. The unfettered relationship between music and film became more formal, especially when increasing amounts of money began to change hands in the new film industry that audiences seemingly could not get enough of.

THE ADVENT OF RECORDED MUSIC AND TALKIES

Following the rise of the full-feature film with large-scale orchestras that began debuting in 1915, film was becoming a global phenomenon. After nearly twenty years of development, sound-on-film recording finally became possible in 1924 through the contributions of Thomas Edison, Augustin Lauste, Tri-Erfon Laboratories, and eventually AT&T's Western Electric. Audiences accepted the new technological breakthrough, and the race was on to create film that incorporated sound, rather than the traditional, silent films. Warner Bros., now a major motion picture studio, was a relatively small studio in the 1920s and began to experiment with sound-on-film recording. AT&T's Western Electric was contracted by Warner Bros. in 1925 to begin experimenting with the notion of sound on film. After nearly a year, their collaborative work yielded the Vitaphone, a system for recording sound to accompany film. The sound itself was not recorded onto the film but rather onto phonograph records that were played back in sync with the film. The discs were roughly 16 inches in diameter and were changed with each reel of film. Warner Bros. marketed and used the Vitaphone in nearly every film from 1926 onward.

The first major release using the Vitaphone system was *Don Juan* in 1926, starring John Barrymore, Mary Orland, and Warner Oland. It debuted on August 6, 1926, at the Warners' Theatre in New York City. Interestingly, the Barrymore family is synonymous with Hollywood, including famous actors John Drew Barrymore and his daughter, Drew Barrymore. While *Don Juan* was the first film to

▶ FIG. 1.2
Vitaphone camera, circa late 1920s early 1930s. Photofest Asset Locator: WGA000772141

use the Vitaphone system, it did not have spoken dialogue. In fact, the big-budget film was not intended to be released with sound accompaniment. It was envisioned to be a silent film. The musical soundtrack was written by William Axt and David Mendoza and recorded and synced to the film for the Vitaphone exhibitions of the film. George Groves, who was working with Vitaphone at the time, was charged with the task of recording the soundtrack for the film. The New York Philharmonic was contracted to perform the soundtrack for the recording.

Following the success of *Don Juan,* Warner Bros. released the *Jazz Singer*, a "talkie" starring Al Jolson, on October 6, 1927, at the Warners' Theatre in New York City. Harry Warner, co-founder of Warner Bros., explained that the Vitaphone was not simply meant to synchronize music with film. It was also meant to deliver spoken dialogue in addition to musical accompaniment (Wierzbicki, 2009). The *Jazz Singer* was met with phenomenal success. Jolson performed six musical selections during the film. While the film was considered to be a success, it was met with some criticism due to the racial undertones. Jolson performed the final musical selection in black face makeup. Further, many of the promotional collateral for the film featured Jolson in blackface makeup. However controversial this was, it did not overshadow the success of the film.

The Jazz Singer was a major milestone in the advancement of the motion picture and forced the hand of other studios, such as Metro-Goldwyn-Mayer (MGM), to catch up to the technological advancement of Warner Bros. The vast majority of studios were simply not capable of recording film and sound simultaneously. A large effort was made to update existing studios for this purpose,

▶ **FIG. 1.3**

The Premier of *The Jazz Singer*, October 6, 1927. Photofest Asset Locator: WGE000068988

but it would take a couple of years for the transition to be complete. Luckily, the transition was complete prior to the Great Depression in 1929. Had this not been the case, Hollywood may not have evolved in the manner that it did.

Not everyone was pleased with the movement to sound in film. International audiences felt that there was a cultural onslaught from the Western world. Many believed that silent movies were a relaxing experience and that recorded sound might hinder the overall moviegoing experience. Musicians in the United States became fearful of losing their employment—that they would be replaced by "canned music" (Wierzbicki, 2009). The Associated Federation of Musicians (AFM) was adamantly against music in film because an increasing number of theaters were being wired for sound, which in turn would decrease employment opportunities for musicians. While the AFM maintained small victories in theaters, it was becoming clear that the world of entertainment was changing. A new era was being ushered in, and there was nothing one could do to stop it.

CLASSIC HOLLYWOOD

While musicians were losing employment opportunities in theaters, they began to find work as full-time staff employees of movie studios. They became an integral component of the moviemaking process, as did carpenters and craftsmen who build sets. Studios employed large orchestras consisting of musicians, composers and arrangers, and conductors. The studio orchestra enabled movie studios to quickly produce musical elements to accompany their new releases. Audiences were enthralled by Jolson's musical selections in the *Jazz Singer*, and movie studios knew this. Newly formed music licensing entities, such as ASCAP, made the prospect of licensing original music somewhat expensive for studios (Wierzbicki, 2009). It became clear to studio executives that original music should be created and existing licenses should be purchased for future use. To that end, Warner Bros. purchased M. Witmark and Sons, a large New York City–based music publisher. This was a brilliant, strategic move because other studios would now have to license previously protected musical material from Warner Bros. This offered a highly effective strategic advantage over the other Hollywood studios.

Historians often define the "classic style" of Hollywood as the period between the late 1930s and the mid-1950s. The manner in which films were made began to change during this period. Movie plots, whether they were thrillers, comedies, or love stories, were meant to take audiences on a new type of journey. In many ways, early films were essentially archives of stage plays. In other words, the manner in which the story was delivered to the audience was very much like a play—long, single shots. Movies that were made in the "classic style" of Hollywood were being made for the film, not the stage. High-profile actors and well-known directors became commonplace in new releases from the film studios. Stories were woven together through multiple scenes that informed the narrative of the film. Multiple versions, or takes, of each scene were shot so that editors could determine the most appropriate version for the final release.

The way in which music was written for film also began to change dramatically during this time period. In early film, music was meant to entertain audiences during interludes between short film exhibitions and to add fanfare to the overall audience experience. It was not uncommon for music to be played at the beginning and end of an exhibition and nothing more. Further, music was often recycled and performed on multiple occasions with different films. Music added to the experience but in no way defined the experience for audience members. This was likely enough for directors of silent film because music was not thought of as something to engage with when viewing a film. It was simply seen as an add-on component of the overall experience. This began to change in the "classic-style" Hollywood films with musical underscore written to specifically complement moods and experiences that mirrored the plot as it unfolded throughout the film.

Music began to take on a defined role and character in film during this period. Composers began to write underscore that subtly mirrored the on-screen elements. The music was meant to be heard but not noticed by the audience members. Leitmotifs, short musical phrases that are associated with an event or character, became more commonplace in film music. Composers used them to subtly create synchronized interplay between the underscore and the film narrative. This new approach to film scoring was demonstrated in Radio-Keith-Orpheum (RKO) Radio Pictures' 1933 film, *King Kong*. The film was directed by Merian C. Cooper, who enlisted the film-scoring talents of Max Steiner. Their work together would arguably shape the next two decades of film music.

▶ FIG. 1.4
Max Steiner conducting the *King Kong* orchestra. Photofest Asset Locator: WGC000278426

Steiner was an accomplished composer at the time he was asked by Cooper to score the music for *King Kong*, but he had never taken on a project of this scale. Cooper envisioned a grand score to complement the larger-than-life story of an enormous gorilla that terrorizes New York City. The story was inspired by his childhood readings of Paul Du Chaillu's 1861 book, *Explorations and Adventures in Equatorial Africa*.

Cooper and Steiner worked very closely together on their shared vision for the film. Cooper made it clear to Steiner that no expense would be spared in regard to the film score for this epic film. Steiner mentions in his biography that Cooper secured nearly $50,000 to ensure that a full orchestra would be available to record Steiner's music. Cooper adapted the film to Steiner's score and vice versa. This was arguably the first time a collaborative relationship of this nature occurred between a director and a film composer.

Steiner was extremely thoughtful in his approach to writing the music for the score. He was deeply inspired by the music of German composer Richard Wagner throughout his career. Steiner employed leitmotifs, a term often linked to Wagner's compositions, throughout the score for *King Kong*. This was the first time that this approach was used in film, although it was common in the opera works of Wagner. Steiner developed leitmotifs for the main characters in the film and referenced them to subtly mirror the events unfolding on screen.

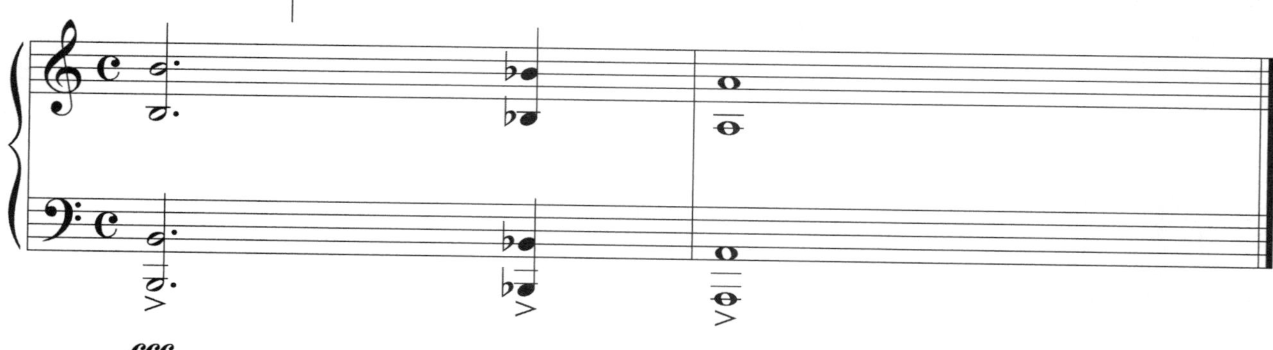

FIG. 1.5
King Kong's leitmotif.

This chromatic theme was written to give the audience a sense of what was about to occur and instill a feeling of terror. It was scored with a full brass section, teamed with low strings to provide an ominous feeling in the audience.

Anne Darrow was the heroine in *King Kong*. This whimsical theme was meant to portray her beauty and grace. It was played in tandem, and sometime at odds, with King Kong's theme. Interestingly, both themes move chromatically from the first note to the second. They are, in a way linked, as they were in

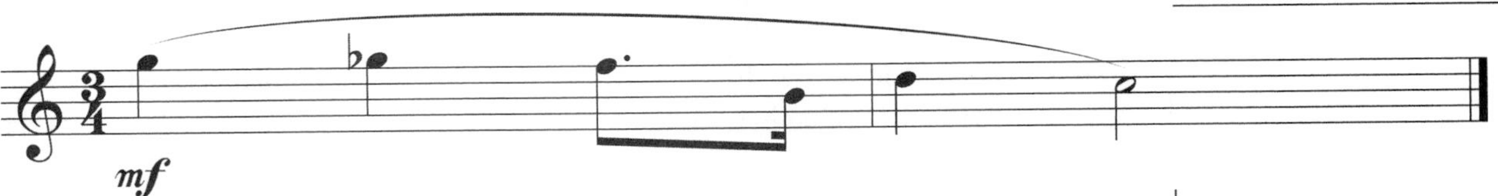

FIG. 1.6
Anne Darrow's leitmotif.

the film. However, the similarity ends there. King Kong's theme falls chromatically throughout, arguably symbolizing a destructive state of being, while Darrow's resolves to the tonic, or first degree of the scale. Darrow's harmonic movement symbolizes purity and grace in stark contrast to King Kong.

Many of the core principals of Steiner's orchestration paved the way for future film composers. He constructed a library of musical tools, largely borrowed from the Western Classical tradition that informed film composition for many decades to come. Steiner epitomized the "classic style" of Hollywood and created a vehicle of expression for future film music. He penned the scores of Hollywood classics such as *Gone with the Wind* (1939) and *Casablanca* (1942) and forever changed the relationship of music and film.

POSTCLASSIC FILM

Postclassic film is often defined as film produced from 1958 and beyond (Wierzbicki, 2009). Hollywood music, as it was known in the past, was nearly nonexistent. This was not to say that lush scores were not being written, they were simply not as commonplace as they were in the classic era of Hollywood. In the postclassic era there was a push to incorporate new sounds and musical styles into the film scores of the time. This could be seen as a rebellion against the predominantly Western Classical approach to film scores from the classic era. Audiences wanted realism—something they could see and feel, such as an onscreen band or radio. The film industry had become a staple of not only American culture but also international culture. Film studios were constantly searching for ways to push the medium forward and to create more engaging experiences for audiences that spanned multiple aspects of popular culture.

The 1960s was arguably one of the most creative times in regard to music and the arts. Multiple genres of music, including jazz, rock and roll, and rhythm and blues, were gaining prominence with audiences in the United States and abroad. Film studios were quick to react. In 1964, United Artists released *A Hard Day's Night*, a film directed by Richard Lester that featured the music of the immensely popular musical group the Beatles.

The film had an estimated budget of $560,000 and made a profit of nearly $2 million. It became quite clear to film studios that music publishing was as big of a business, or even bigger, than film itself. *A Hard Day's Night* was a departure from typical Hollywood releases. It was an experiment in the melding of film, music, and popular culture. In fact, this movie paved the way for music videos that would later become forever embedded in popular culture in the 1980s through the work of Music Television (MTV) and Video Hits One (VH1). United Artists took a risk with this new medium, and it paid off handsomely.

In the early days of film there were few competitors for the attention of audiences. Film maintained a secure role as a primary source of entertainment. This began to change with the advent of television. Audiences were presented with a radically new vehicle for entertainment. Television shows were strikingly similar to the early days of film in that shows were short, usually thirty minutes or less, and music was used to supplement the on-screen performance. Audiences became accustomed to predictable storylines, presentation formats, and the music. The film studios had great involvement in television, so much so that fewer films were being made than in the past. A great deal of time and energy was diverted from the film industry to the television industry (Wierzbicki, 2009).

The 1970s brought a resurgence of the lush movie scores of the 1930s and 1940s. This was due, in part, to the ancillary role music played in television. There was not a lot composers could do in short, thirty-minute programs that we interrupted with commercials several times throughout the broadcast. The large-scale, symphonic sound of the golden age of film began to reemerge with the work of composers such as John Williams. Few would argue that his work in *Jaws* (1975), *Star Wars Episode IV: A New Hope* (1977), and *Superman* (1978) paid tribute to the lush orchestral scores of Max Steiner and others of the 1930s and 1940s.

Technological advances of the late 1970s and early 1980s began to pave the way for a deeper connection between film, music, and various sound effects, including Foley. George Lucas, the director of many films including the *Star Wars* trilogies, was deeply interested in modern advances in film production—specifically, sound design and quality. He enlisted the talents of Ray Dolby, a British-born, Stanford- and Cambridge-educated electrical engineer. Dolby Laboratories, Inc. was conveniently headquartered in the San Francisco Bay area, not far from Lucas. Early sound in film was plagued by an audible hiss that occurred through the recording process to magnetic tape. Dolby and his colleagues were fascinated by the prospect of eliminating noise that resulted from playback and recording from magnetic tape. By the 1970s, his work yielded not only a process for reducing noise in recording and playback but also a process for splitting audio signals over multiple audio channels. This breakthrough paved the way for an incredible aural audience experience while watching film.

Dolby's invention was available in time for Lucas's *Star Wars Episode IV: A New Hope* (1977). The film utilized four-channel sound on 35-mm film that produced an experience like none other. Not to be outdone, Lucas released *Superman* in 1978, which featured five channels of sound where one channel was dedicated to a subwoofer in the rear of the theater (Wierzbicki, 2009). The advances of Dolby surround sound changed the landscape of the moviegoing experience.

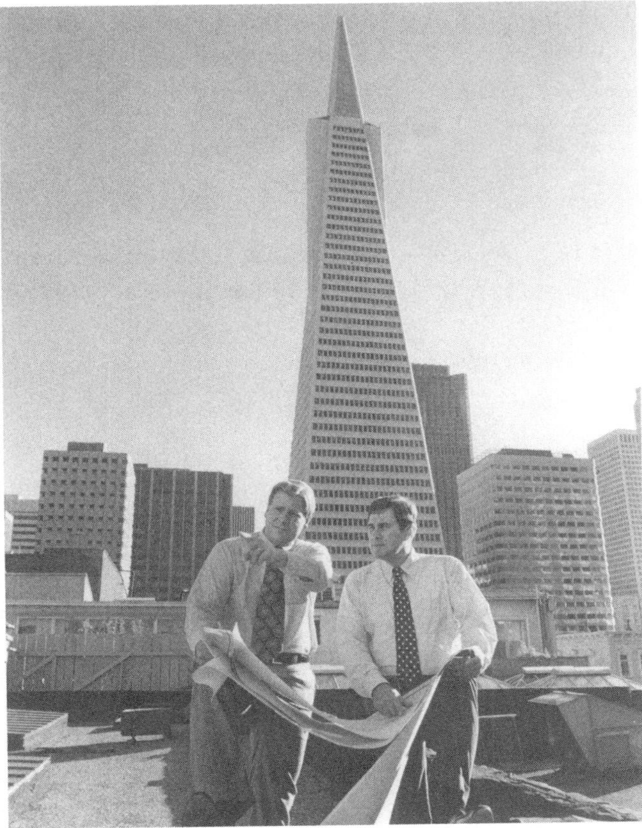

▶ **FIG. 1.7**
Ray Dolby (right), President and founder of Dolby Laboratories, and Bill Jasper, Vice President of Finance of Dolby Laboratories, on the roof of the firm's headquarters in San Francisco, California. Photofest Asset Locator: WGC000554752

Sound appeared in a three-dimensional state and seemed to fly around the room. The improved audio reproduction also made quiet dialog more audible to audience members. It was only a matter of time before other directors wanted to incorporate this new sound technology into their films. Dolby made licensing simple and equipment affordable and reliable. His sound reproduction system soon became the norm in theaters throughout the United States and abroad. The system attracted audiences to theaters because they knew what to expect from a movie that incorporated Dolby sound. The audience felt as it they were in the action because of the three-dimensional effect of surround sound. Film studios began to change their approach to music in film after the advent of the Dolby system. Sound design became increasingly important in the "blockbuster" films of the 1980s and beyond.

The continued relationship between film and music was not always guaranteed from its early beginnings in the 1900s. The relationship did not grow in a consistent, gradual manner. Quite the contrary, there were periods of time where progress was nearly nonexistent and periods such as the golden age of the 1930s and 1940s where film music evolved with rapidity. It would be nearly impossible for one to have predicted the progression of music and film over the last one hundred years, but it will arguably be even more difficult to predict how music and film will evolve over the next one hundred years. The wonderful thing is that we do not have to predict. Based on historical evidence, the evolution of music and film has marched on throughout time and will arguably continue to do so.

REFERENCES

Cook, M. (2008). *A History of Film.* Cambridge, MA: Cambridge University Press.

Kalinak, K. (2010). *Film Music: A Very Short Introduction.* New York: Oxford University Press.

Wierzbicki, J. (2009). *Film Music: A History.* New York: Routledge.

CHAPTER 2
THE DIGITAL AUDIO WORKSTATION

There's no doubt that everything is always an audition in life. Every day that you do a synth mock-up on a cue and play it for the director or producer, it's an audition. It's a double-edged sword though, because with all this stuff, I learned how to write music in a certain style and orchestrate and got to figure it out at my house instead in front of an orchestra [rather than] fail miserably in front of an orchestra. Without all this stuff and the snyth mock-ups that we were suddenly expected to create for the director or producer—don't know how I would have survived without it.

—Marc Shaiman

MUSICIANS AND COMPOSERS are creating music in one of the most interesting, engaging, and advanced eras in history. We have tools at our discretion that frankly have never existed before and have created a fundamental shift in the way we perceive the process of making music. One such tool, the Digital Audio Workstation (DAW), has changed the way music is conceived, performed, recorded, and delivered to clients and consumers. Before we move any further, it is important to explore the following thought: What exactly is a DAW? Anyone who has spent any amount of time with an audio engineer has undoubtedly heard this term before. Even though this term is used frequently in conversation surrounding digital audio recording, a great number of people do not know exactly what this term refers to or what it represents.

For the musician and composer who are new to the notion of creating music with technology, not understanding trade terminology can be somewhat intimidating. For example, this is similar to not knowing basic musical terminology while participating in an orchestra rehearsal. There is no need to be intimidated any longer—a modern DAW is simply the combination of a dedicated software program and specific recording and computer hardware used for the purpose of recording, editing, and producing digital audio. At a very basic level, think of a DAW as modern version of the tape recorder. Before we began using a DAW to record and edit audio, engineers would record audio using tape machines (reel-to-reel recorders). They would then edit this tape the old-fashioned way with razor blades to slice and splice audio. The introduction of the DAW provided virtual tools that allowed editing in a safer and more precise manner.

The DAW has come quite a long way in terms of functionality since it was first introduced in the 1970s. The first DAWs utilized terminal command windows that required inputting of textual commands to edit audio. This process, to many, was counterintuitive and didn't appeal to the large base of musicians and composers who were using pencil and paper to archive their musical ideas. The 1980s was an exciting time for the progression and adoption of the DAW. There were several companies competing to sell software that would allow digital recording with computers. One company in particular, Digidesign, released Sound Designer II. This software helped champion the movement for digital audio recording in studios across the world. Sound Designer II paved the way for Digidesign to release Pro Tools, which has become synonymous with digital audio recording.

Today the DAW is alive and well in the various recording projects that are being explored in home studios, sound stages, and live performance venues throughout the world. This wide-scale adoption is a result of the DAW becoming accessible to a great number of consumers. A cross section of the DAW consumer pool would reveal professional musicians, audio engineers, students, teachers, and enthusiastic novice users.

This eclectic consumer pool is directly related to the large number of DAWs that are present in the marketplace. There truly is something for everyone who is interested in recording digital audio. Students use Apple's GarageBand to record podcasts in classrooms, while professionals can choose from programs such as Digidesign's Pro Tools, Apple's Logic Pro X, Steinberg's Nuendo, Motu's Digital Performer, and Propellerhead's Record. With each passing year, the market for DAWs grows because the choice of software and hardware combinations for consumers parallels this path.

The purpose of this chapter is to introduce you the basic concepts of a digital audio workstation through the lens of Logic Pro X. As mentioned earlier, a number of digital audio workstations are available to musicians and composers. It is common to work with composers who use a different digital audio workstation. It is important to understand the basic concepts and commonalities of each application. You will likely notice many similarities between the major digital audio workstations that are currently available and used by colleagues. Choose the digital audio workstation that you personally feel most comfortable with for daily use and learn to bridge feature differences with a working knowledge of other digital audio workstations. The key is to stay relevant with product offerings to engage and work with colleagues in the field.

INTRODUCTION TO LOGIC PRO X

Project templates are extremely useful when working with a DAW because they are empty projects that have been preconfigured with commonly used tools associated with a particular style of composing, recording, or editing. For example, if you are writing several cues for a television project, it will likely be helpful to create project templates to speed the music creation process. Commonly used instruments and track settings can be preconfigured to save time and frustration when beginning to cultivate a new musical idea.

1. Open your Applications folder and double-click on Logic Pro X.
2. Once Logic Pro X is active and running in the Dock, right-click (or control-click with a single button mouse) on the program icon.
3. Choose Options > Keep in Dock.

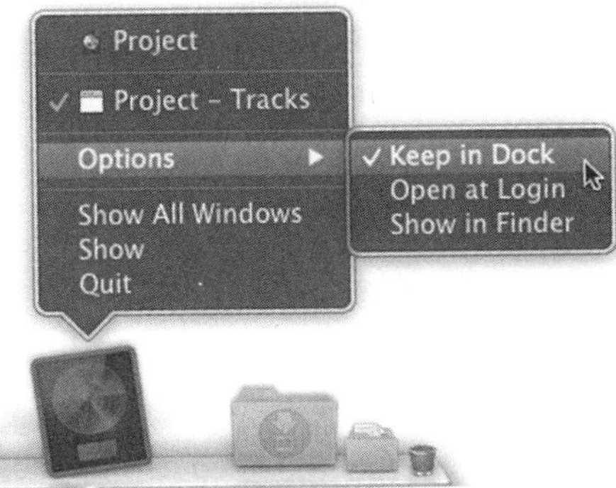

▶ FIG. 2.1

After the initial installation of and first launch of Logic Pro X, the application will search for any Audio Unit (AU) plugins that may be installed on the machine. Logic Pro X will cache these AU plugins and make them available for use from relevant contextual menus. AU plugins are commonly used to extend

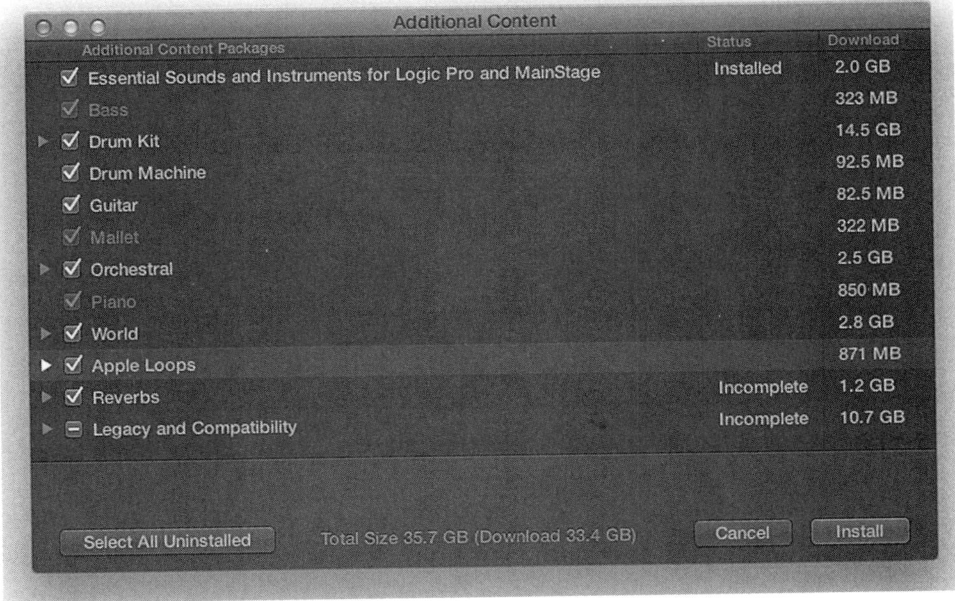

▶ FIG. 2.2

the functionality of a DAW by providing access to new electronic instruments and textures. Currently, Logic Pro X only supports AU plugins. Many third-party plugin developers offer multiple plugin formats to support a wide number of DAWs.

In previous versions of Logic Pro, Apple shipped DVDs that contained additional media, such as sound libraries, software instrument loops, and audio loops. This additional content is now available in the form of a digital download. To download this content, choose Logic Pro X > Download Additional Content from the main menu.

The additional content will likely take a significant amount of time to download because the installation packages are quite large—over 30 GB of data. Once Logic Pro X has downloaded the additional content, it will be available within the application.

PROJECT TEMPLATES

Logic Pro X includes numerous templates that facilitate the creation of music projects. The high-quality templates can be used as a final template for production work or as a starting point for the creation of templates that are more relevant to your personal workflow. They have been preconfigured with commonly used tools that are associated with a particular style of composing, recording, or editing. Again, creating project templates can be used to speed the music creation process by allowing you to define and configure commonly used settings and musical elements.

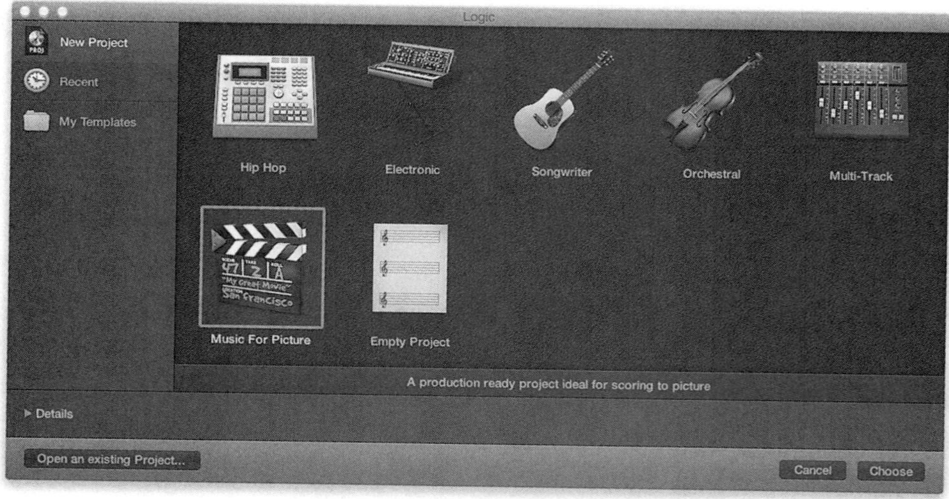

▶ **FIG. 2.3**

To get started, choose the Music for Picture template from the Produce template category. Save the project to the Desktop when prompted by the save dialogue box. This template is simply a starting point to begin creating music. The preconfigured elements may not represent all of the elements you require in a template. For example, you may have several software instruments that you would like to add to this template. We will explore the process of adding and editing settings for Logic Pro X's interface as well as adding tracks and plugins to your template. In the end, you will have experience with the most commonly used elements used in digital audio workstations.

EXPLORING LOGIC PRO X'S USER INTERFACE

▶ FIG. 2.4

1. Control Bar
2. Inspector
3. Tracks Area
4. Smart Controls

CUSTOMIZING THE CONTROL BAR

The control bar is responsible for controlling the playback of your project, but it also displays quite a bit of useful information about your project. The control bar, like many aspects of Logic Pro X, is completely customizable. Control-click anywhere on your control bar and choose Customize Control Bar and Display. A pop-up menu will appear that allows you to customize the feature set of your control bar. The control bar contains four main components: Views, Transport, LCD, and Modes and Functions.

Like many digital audio workstations, Logic Pro X is a highly customizable application. You have the ability to create your own key commands, combine editing windows into user-defined workspace layouts, and customize toolbars. This is helpful because it is best to write music in a familiar and comfortable environment. Technology has matured to a level that allows us to create music in a way that never been done before; however, it is important to make the platform from which we create music as seamless and user-friendly as possible. If you control-click on various aspects of the program, there is a high possibility that you will find shortcuts to program preferences or the ability to customize the interface. This is all in the spirit of modeling a music creation environment that allows you to be comfortable and inspired.

Upon control-clicking on the control bar, you will be presented with a pop-up window. It is possible to select which components will appear in your control bar by selecting of deselecting the relevant checkboxes for each component of the control bar.

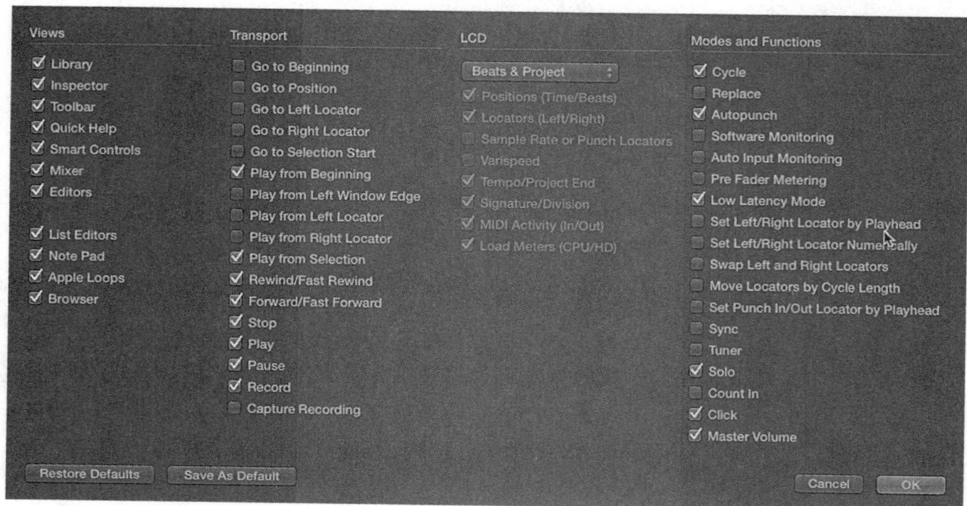

▶ **FIG. 2.5**

Since we are going to be working with video, it is advantageous to select the "Sample Rate or Punch Locators" option to display the current project sample rate in the LCD component of the control bar. To do so, choose Custom from the pop-up window. This will allow you to select "Sample Rate or Punch Locators." This is important because most audio projects for compact discs are recorded at a sample rate of 44,100 Hz, whereas video projects are recorded at a sample rate of 48,000 Hz. Due to the subtle harmonic differences between sample rates, time-consuming problems can occur down the line if different samples rates are used in a single project.

CONTROL BAR COMPONENTS

Logic Pro X provides a comprehensive set of functionality within the control bar. The control can be customized to your liking; however, the default functionality is robust enough for most applications. On the left side of the control bar you will see a group of buttons that represent the views section of the control bar.

▶ FIG. 2.6

The functionality of each button in the views section is explained in the following, from left to right:

1. Library—shows and hides the library.
2. Inspector—provides detailed information for selected items.
3. Toolbar—shows and hides the toolbar.
4. Quick Help—provides in-application access to Logic Pro X support when hovering over a button.
5. Smart Controls—shows and hides smart controls.
6. Mixer—shows and hides the mixer.
7. Editors—shows and hides audio and MIDI editors.

The next section of the control bar, the transport, will likely be familiar to you because it contains playback functionality that is present in a wide variety of media player. The transport also contains functionality specific to Logic Pro X.

▶ FIG. 2.7

The functionality of each button in the transport is listed in the following, from left to right:

1. Play from Beginning
2. Play from Selection
3. Rewind
4. Fast Forward
5. Stop
6. Play
7. Pause
8. Record

The central component of the control bar, the LCD, contains helpful information throughout your project. Clicking on the left side of the LCD can customize the components of the LCD.

There are four LCD presets available for use: Beats and Project, Beats and Time, Beats, and Time. It is also possible to customize the transport. Choose custom for the pop-up menu. This will allow you to display available functionality in the LCD.

► **FIG. 2.8**

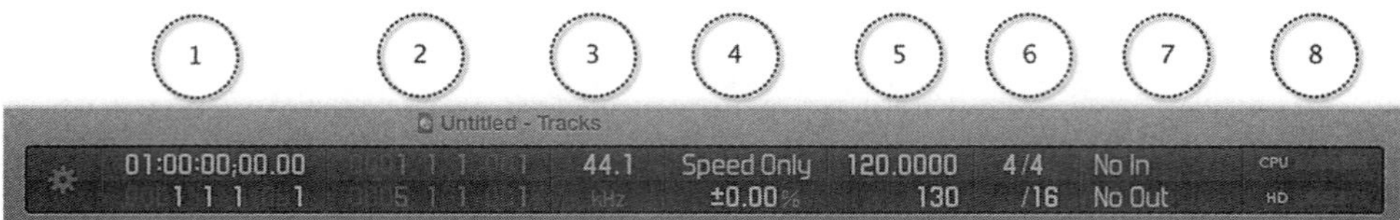

► **FIG. 2.9**

1. Positions (Time/Beats)—This section displays your current position in both SMPTE timecode (top number) as well as musical time (bottom number). In Logic Pro X, SMPTE is displayed in hours, minutes, seconds, frames, and subframes. Musical time is represented in bars, beats, divisions of beats (eighth note, sixteenth note, etc.), and ticks. SMPTE timecode is gold standard measurement for aligning musical elements to on-screen elements in film and television projects.

Tip: A tick is a division of a bar. One tick is equal to 1/3840 of a bar. Ticks will be discussed in depth in a later chapter.

2. Locators (Left/Right)—This section defines the length and location of the project's locators. Locators outline the beginning and ending of a section, cycle region, or skip cycle region. These sections will be described in greater detail later.
3. Sample Rate or Punch Locators—This section allows you to choose the project sample rate, as well as set punch locators.
4. Varispeed—This section provides a way to speed up or slow down the entire project, similar to the original varispeed feature of tape machines. The most practical use for this option is checking how a project might sound at a faster or slower tempo, or practicing or recording a performance at a lower speed.
5. Tempo/Project End—This section provides a way to set the tempo of the project and the length of the project.
6. Signature/Division—The top number displays the time signature of the project, in this case 4/4, also known as common time. The bottom number displays the resolution of divisions that are used and displayed in the tracks area. In this case, sixteenth notes are utilized as a resolution in the control bar and the tracks area.

7. MIDI Activity (In/Out)—This section displays incoming and outgoing MIDI data. MIDI will be discussed in a later chapter.
8. Load Meters (CPU/HD)—This section displays the amount of CPU resources that Logic Pro X is accessing, as well as hard disk bandwidth.

The last section, Modes and Functions, contains the following options, from left to right:

▶ FIG. 2.10

1. Cycle
2. Autopunch
3. Low Latency Mode
4. Varispeed
5. Solo
6. Click

EDITING TOOLS

Logic Pro X contains a vast number of tools that enable you to quickly manipulate musical elements in your audio project—the left-click tool and the command-click editing tools. You can select the function of these editing tools by toggling the tool bar in the control bar.

▶ FIG. 2.11

Notice that the left-click tool and the command-click tools share the same editing tools. This is because you can assign an editing tool to your mouse cursor (left-click) but also have a secondary editing tool available that is invoked when the command key is pressed. This allows you to quickly move between editing tools during your music creation workflow.

In addition to the left-click tool and the command-click tools, there is a third editing tool. It is possible to assign an editing tool to your right mouse button (right-click button). This additional editing tool can be enabled in the editing tab of the Logic Pro X general preferences window. Navigate to Logic Pro X > Preferences > General > Editing Tab.

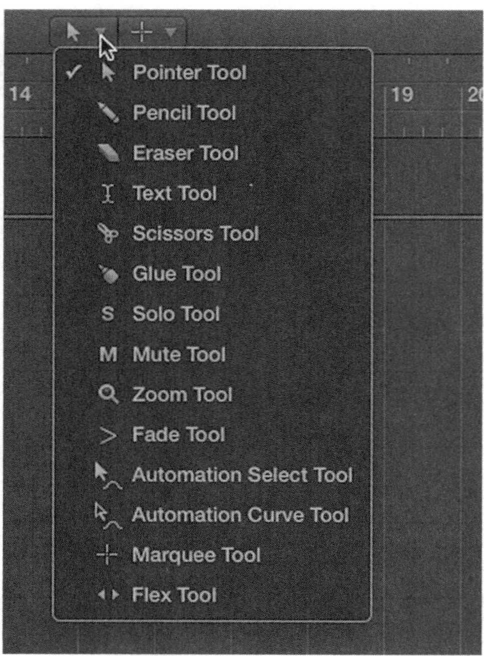

▶ **FIG. 2.12**
The left-click editing tool.

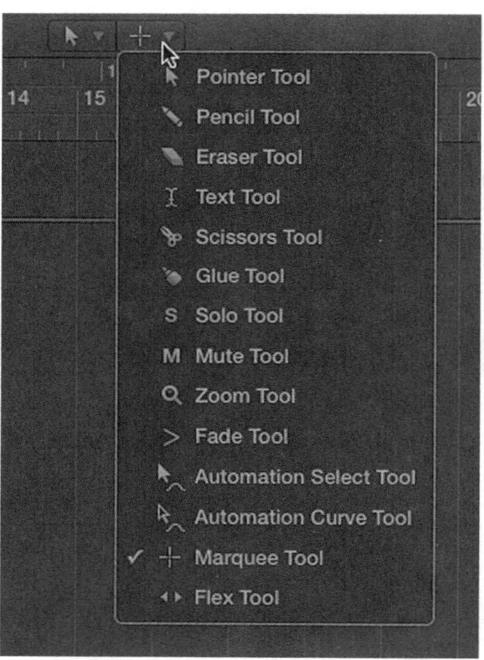

 **FIG. 2.13**
The command-click editing tool.

When you enable the right mouse button to be used as an editing tool, you are provided a third pop-up menu to the right of the left-click and command-click editing tools in the toolbar. In combination with the left-click and command-click editing tools, the right mouse button editing tool can dramatically speed project editing. Keep in mind that all of the tools discussed up to this point exist solely for the purpose of creating music with a digital audio workstation. The best editing workflow is one that you do not have to spend

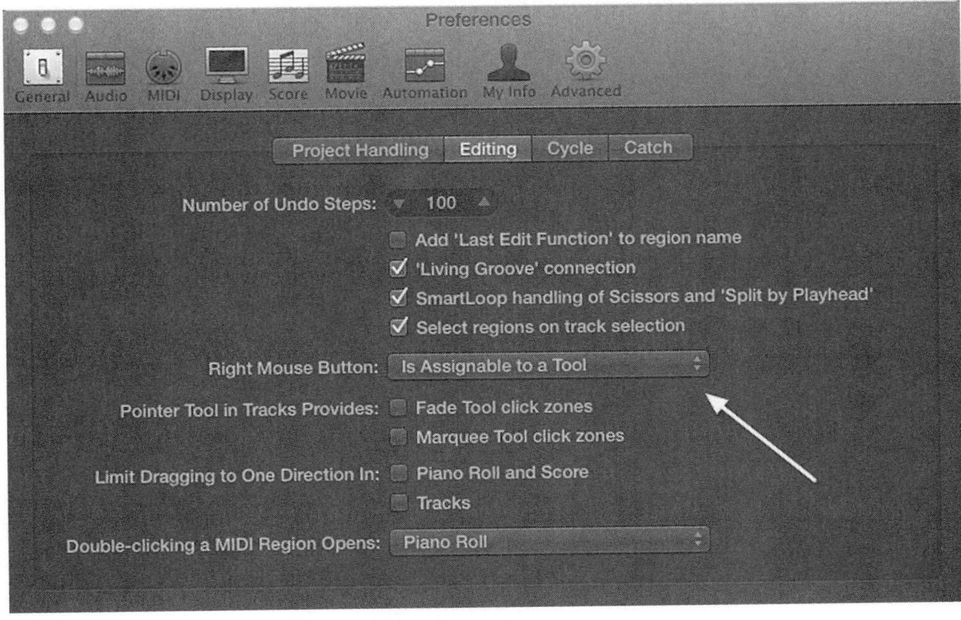

▶ **FIG. 2.14**

time thinking about. Try to design your music creation workspace in a manner that allows you to spend the bulk of your time doing what you do best—creating music.

TRACKS AND TRACK COMPONENTS

Since we are working with a Digital Audio Workstation, it only makes sense that we understand how our audio and MIDI data is manipulated in the workspace. Like any other DAW, Logic Pro X organizes audio and MIDI data on tracks. This approach allows you to separate, organize, and work with data in an extremely efficient manner. For example, it is possible to record four trumpet players on four individual tracks. This will allow you to manipulate the timbre, volume, and other aspects of each performer individually.

▶ **FIG. 2.15**

In the illustration you notice that we have an audio track that contains four audio regions. Regions are a graphic representation of a section of audio that is being used in the tracks area. Some refer to these as clips of audio. Regardless of how they are referred to, they are essentially the portion of the audio file that is currently being used in the tracks area of the project.

Directly to the right of the track name there are four buttons on the tracker header in Logic Pro X's default configuration:

M—Allows you to mute the entire track, excluding it from playback.

S—Allows you to solo this track. Essentially, all other tracks are silenced to allow the sole playback of this track.

R—Arms or enables your track to record audio.

I—Monitors your audio input.

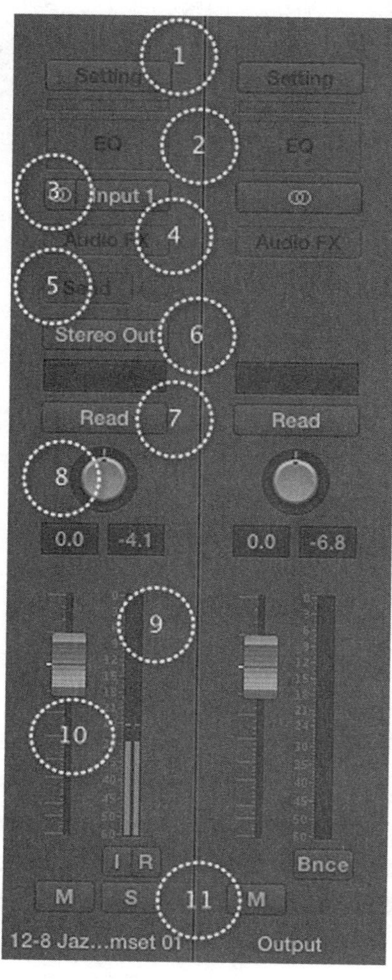

▶ **FIG. 2.16**

1. Channel Strip Settings—Clicking and holding on this button will produce a dropdown menu that offers settings specific to this channel strip.
2. EQ—Clicking in this box will enable channel strip equalization (EQ), allowing you to manipulate EQ settings for this track. EQ settings can dramatically change the characteristic of your track. A musician's sound character can be determined and adjusted by EQ manipulation.
3. Input—Displays your current input (microphone input, etc.).
4. Effects Slots—Effects slots exist for the purpose of enabling high-quality digital signal processing (DSP) plugins on a channel strip. DSP plugins provide extended functionality to alter sound. For example, reverb is typically added through the use of a DSP plugin.

5. Sends—Send slots allow you to send audio information to auxiliary tracks or buses.
6. Output—Displays your current output.
7. Automation Modes—Provides a method for automating parameter changes.
8. Panning Knob—Enables the adjustment of audio location in the stereo spectrum.
9. Level Meter—Displays your volume level and allows you to quickly identify metering problems.
10. Fader—Controls the volume level of audio on the channel strip.
11. Mute, Solo, Input, and Record Enable buttons—Provide the same functionality as similar buttons on the track header.

ADDING ADDITIONAL TRACKS

Audio tracks are extremely important in a musical project. They hold all of the musical data that form your musical project. Individual tracks are often created for individual instruments.

▶ FIG. 2.17

1. Click on the small plus sign at the top of the track row.
2. A New Tracks dialogue box appears.

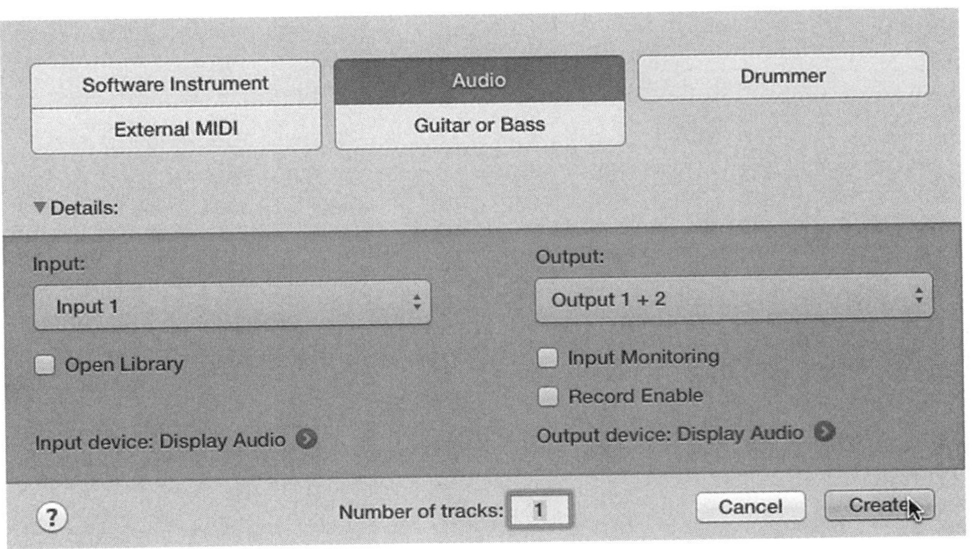

▶ FIG. 2.18

3. Choose the number of tracks you wish to add.
4. Click create.

REORDERING TRACKS

Organization is extremely important in any large project, and this is no exception when working with musical projects. It is common to order tracks in groups to quickly view a specific section of instruments you are using (e.g., violin section). These instruments may not have been added in sequential order. Fortunately, it is easy to reorder tracks in Logic Pro X. This will organize your musical project by instrument type. This is helpful when viewing and editing various sections of music.

▶ FIG. 2.19

Position your pointer tool over the track you wish to move. The pointer changes into a hand that will enable dragging of tracks. Click and hold the track with the hand and drag the track to the desired position.

RENAMING TRACKS

Continuing with the larger theme of organization, naming tracks is an essential first step in any audio project. It can be difficult to navigate through a large audio project if tracks are not named properly. A great deal of valuable time can be lost trying to sort through a long list of unnamed or improperly named audio or MIDI tracks.

▶ FIG. 2.20

Tracks can be easily renamed by double-clicking on the track name. The pointer tool changes into a text tool, signifying the ability to type in a new name for the track. When a track name is changed anywhere in the application (mixer, channel strip, track header, etc.), the name updates in all locations.

▶ **FIG. 2.21**

When a track name is no longer fully visible in the track header because of length, Logic Pro X will truncate the full title. To view the full title, move the pointer tool to the right edge of the track header. The pointer will change into a resize pointer that enables the resizing of the horizontal length of the track header.

▶ **FIG. 2.22**

CHANGING TRACK SIZE

When working with a single track, it might be helpful to make that track larger for easier viewing. For example, increasing the size of a trumpet track will increase the size of the waveform in the Tracks area. This will reveal more of the waveform and can be helpful when searching for musical cues. For example, high notes played by a trumpet will be apparent in the waveform because they will likely be louder and more visually bulbous in the waveform.

▶ **FIG. 2.23**

Position the pointer tool in the lower left-hand corner of the track. The pointer tool will change into a resize tool that will enable the resizing of the track. This view can be extremely helpful when reading waveforms on audio tracks. Notice that more of the waveform is visible in the Tracks area.

▶ FIG. 2.24

To return the track (and any other tracks that may have been resized) to the default track size, Shift-click in the lower left-hand corner of any track.

DELETING TRACKS

A typical audio project can contain quite a few audio and MIDI tracks. Some tracks contain musical ideas that for one reason or another are not used in the project. In the spirit of organizing your audio project, it can be helpful to delete tracks that are not being used in the project.

▶ FIG. 2.25

Position the pointer tool over the track you would like to delete. Click the track to select it. Press the delete key on your keyboard. The track has now been deleted.

▶ FIG. 2.26

Depending on your keyboard make and model, there may be two separate delete keys present on your keyboard, one near F12 and the other in the center block of keys between your main typing keys and your number pad. Either key will delete tracks as expected. Deleting tracks one by one can be time consuming if the audio project contains many tracks. Logic Pro X can detect which tracks are being used and which are not. This is determined by search for audio or MIDI content on the track. If the track does not contain audio or MIDI content, Logic Pro X will consider that track to be unused. To delete unused tracks, simply choose Track > Delete Unused Tracks from Logic Pro X's main menu.

THE BROWSERS AREA

The modern Digital Audio Workstation offers far more functionality today than it ever has. Where early iterations were limited to audio editing, modern DAWs offer advanced audio editing and MIDI editing and are often preloaded with thousands of samples and loops to use as building blocks in order to foster musical ideas and to speed mockup delivery to clients.

Logic Pro X, like many other modern DAWs, provides a great deal of audio and MIDI content to use royalty-free in projects. In fact, this content can be heard in various projects that span independent film productions, major studio recordings, and everything in between. Artists such as Herbie Hancock, Carlos Santana, Christina Aguilera, and many others use DAWs audio and MIDI content in their musical projects.

Click on the Browsers button in the upper right corner of your workspace.

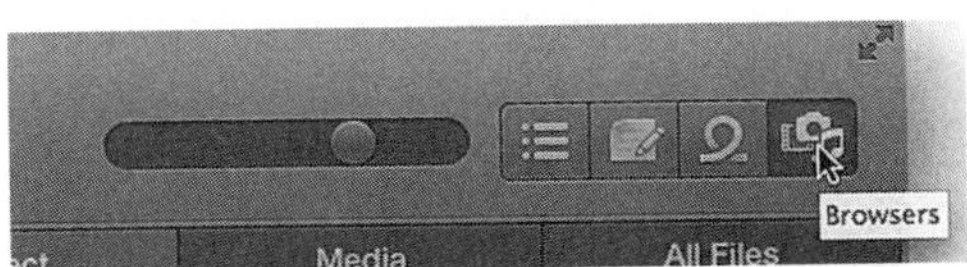

▶ **FIG. 2.27**

The Browsers area is revealed and contains three components: Project, Media, and All Files. Take a moment to familiarize yourself with each section. We will discuss the project area next.

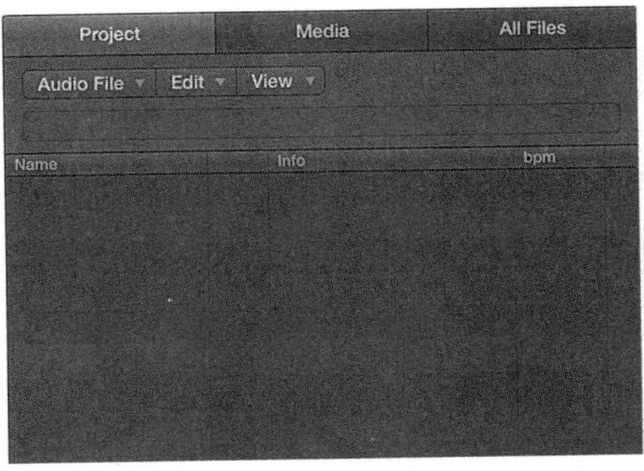

▶ **FIG. 2.28**

THE PROJECT AREA

When you think of the word project, what comes to mind? Most likely, you think of all of the audio and MIDI that is contained in your project. Logic Pro X uses the project area to organize audio. Simply, the project area in Logic Pro X contains all of the audio content that is used in your musical project.

The Project area provides a great deal of helpful information to the user:

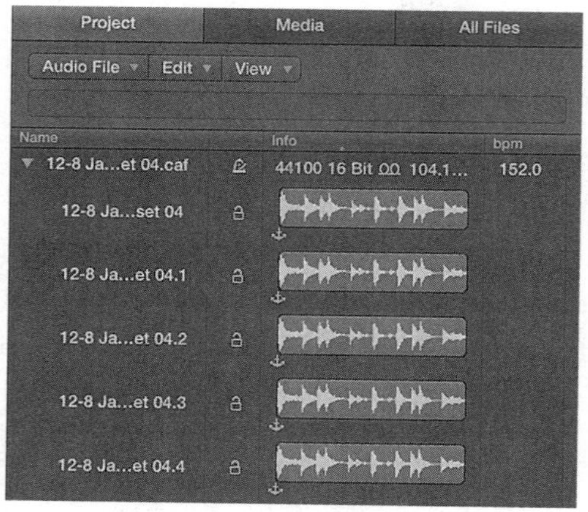

▶ FIG. 2.29

- The name of the audio file
- The name(s) of the audio regions that represent the audio file
- The sample rate of the audio file
- The bit depth of the audio file
- Whether or not the audio file is mono, stereo, or compressed
- The file size of the audio file

This project area shows that there is one audio file being used in this project, "12-8 Jazzy Drumset 04.caf." You'll notice that five similar names are listed underneath the main audio file name. This is because there are five copies or instances of this particular audio file being used in the tracks area of the project.

▶ FIG. 2.30

A closer examination reveals that each individual region is named to correspond with the name in the project area. While this naming convention works in most circumstances, there are times that renaming individual regions may come in handy. It is possible to rename the regions in the project audio browser in much the same manner as renaming tracks.

Double-click on a region name in the Project audio browser to change the name of the region. Once the name has been changed, the new names will automatically update in the Arrange window.

▶ FIG. 2.31

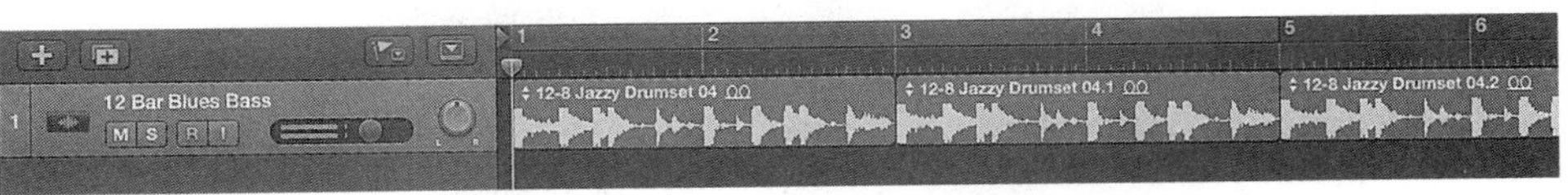

▶ FIG. 2.32

You may have noticed that the file in the project area possesses a .caf file extension. CAF is an acronym that stands for Core Audio Format. Apple uses this file extension for loops that are included with Logic Pro X.

APPLE LOOPS AREA

Logic Pro X provides a great deal of audio and MIDI content that is royalty-free and available for use in projects. These loops can augment or provide the foundation for audio projects in varying stages of development. Loops are frequently used in audio projects for film and television because they often help develop a characteristic sound that is representative of the project as well as the composer. We will explore loop creation in depth in a later chapter.

▶ FIG. 2.33

The Apple Loops area allows you to search in several ways for audio and MIDI content. There is a search box that allows you to specify desired results. In this case, "Trumpet."

▶ FIG. 2.34

Search results appear in the bottom half of the loop browser. The results section denotes tempo, key, duration, and the relevance to your search query. You can also tag the loop as a favorite for quick access in the future.

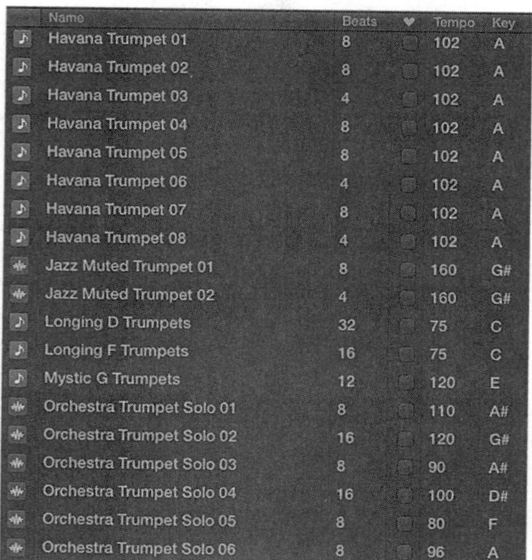

Name	Beats	♥	Tempo	Key
Havana Trumpet 01	8		102	A
Havana Trumpet 02	8		102	A
Havana Trumpet 03	4		102	A
Havana Trumpet 04	8		102	A
Havana Trumpet 05	8		102	A
Havana Trumpet 06	4		102	A
Havana Trumpet 07	8		102	A
Havana Trumpet 08	4		102	A
Jazz Muted Trumpet 01	8		160	G#
Jazz Muted Trumpet 02	4		160	G#
Longing D Trumpets	32		75	C
Longing F Trumpets	16		75	C
Mystic G Trumpets	12		120	E
Orchestra Trumpet Solo 01	8		110	A#
Orchestra Trumpet Solo 02	16		120	G#
Orchestra Trumpet Solo 03	8		90	A#
Orchestra Trumpet Solo 04	16		100	D#
Orchestra Trumpet Solo 05	8		80	F
Orchestra Trumpet Solo 06	8		96	A

▶ **FIG. 2.35**

It is also possible to filter search results by time signature and by major or minor tonalities (scale).

▶ **FIG. 2.36**

THE LIBRARY

The library is an invaluable component of the views area in the control bar. It contains channel strip presets of audio and software instruments to aid in shaping the sound of your audio project. For example, if you recorded a guitar player and want to change the characteristic of their sound, you would likely begin the transformation with a channel strip preset. Essentially, channel strip presets load EQ ad DSP plugins to alter the original signal of the track.

▶ **FIG. 2.37**

Audio Channel Strip Presets

When selecting a library component to be applied to an audio track, Logic Pro X will load all of the relevant Digital Signal Processing (DSP) plugins onto the track that create the desired sound quality.

1. Se lect an audio track in the tracks area.
2. Select the Library button in the views are of the control bar to reveal the Library, if needed.
3. Search for "American Metal" in the Library search field.
4. Double-click the "American Metal" preset.

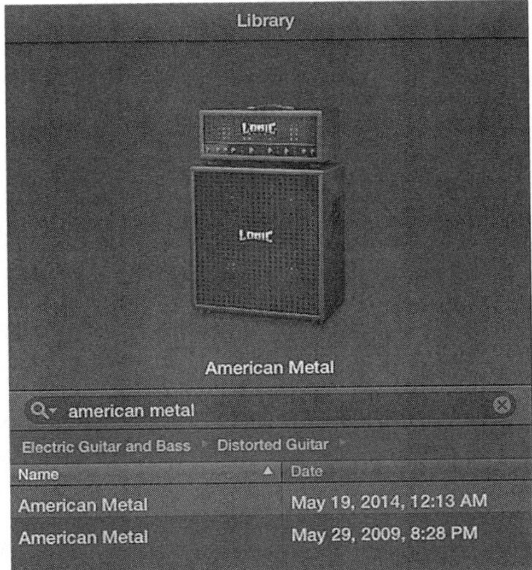

▶ **FIG. 2.38**

When a preset is selected, the relevant Digital Signal Processing (DSP) plugins are applied to the currently selected channel strip in the tracks area. This includes relevant EQ. Any audio recorded or placed on this track will by processed by the plugins and EQ settings from the channel strip preset.

The track header is also renamed with the name of the selected preset. Double-clicking on the track header name and typing in the desired name will quickly change this.

It is not necessary to visit the library in the media and lists area to select a channel strip preset. The presets are available on the channel strip as well.

Software Instrument Tracks

Software instrument presets are particularly interesting because like audio channel strip presets they load DSP plugins and EQ settings. In addition, software instrument presets load a software instrument that can be triggered by a multitude of supported MIDI controllers. In fact, Logic Pro X does not require a third-party MIDI controller—there is one built right into the application. To view the keyboard choose Window > Show Typing Keyboard. This is particularly helpful when a physical MIDI controller is not available, like traveling on a train or plane.

Since the musical typing keyboard has a limited range, it will likely be necessary to change the range when entering MIDI information. Octaves are selected with the Z and X keys on the keyboard.

▶ **FIG. 2.39**

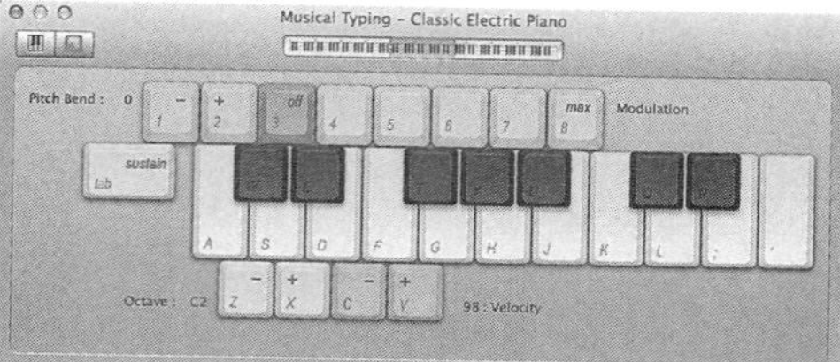

▶ **FIG. 2.40**

The velocity MIDI parameter relates to how hard a note is "hit" while being recorded. It is similar to a marcato marking. Laptop keyboards are not touch sensitive and as a result are not able to record velocity parameters. Velocity can be changed with the C and V keys on the keyboard.

Let's create a software instrument. Create a new track by clicking on the small plus sign at the top of your track row and choose to create one Software Instrument.

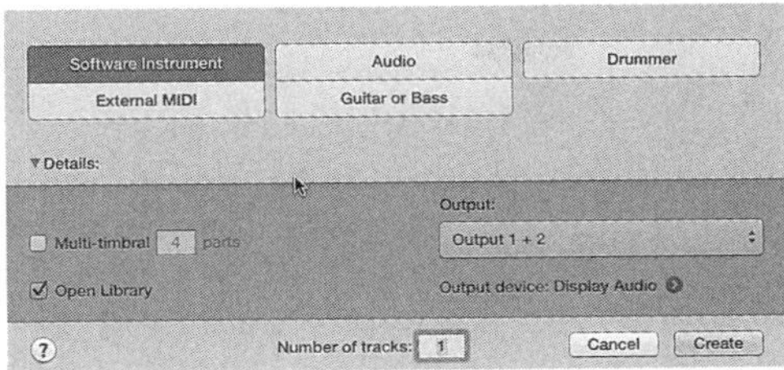

▶ FIG. 2.41

Logic Pro X will create a software instrument track with the default software instrument, Classic Electronic Piano. This is the default software instrument that is loaded when creating a new software instrument track. Navigate to the Library in the control bar and search for "blues." Select the "Classic Blues 01" preset from the Library.

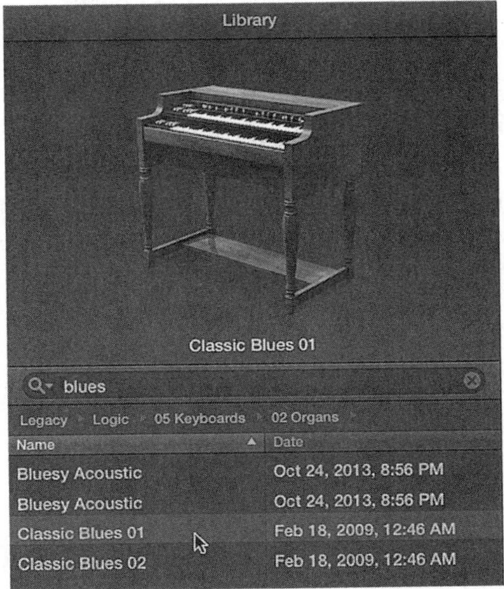

▶ FIG. 2.42

Like the audio channel strip presets, the relevant Digital Signal Processing (DSP) plugins are applied to the currently selected channel strip in the tracks area. The track is renamed with the name of the preset being used. The default name can be changed to something more appropriate by double-clicking on the name of the track and providing a new name.

Create Software Instrument Presets

Once the channel strip preset has been chosen, the necessary software instrument and DSP plugin is loaded onto the track. The software instrument presets are the combination of a software instrument, DSP plugins, and EQ settings. It is possible to edit these presets to create new software instrument presets. This is extremely helpful when building a library of sounds that help shape the sound of a composer and/or a project.

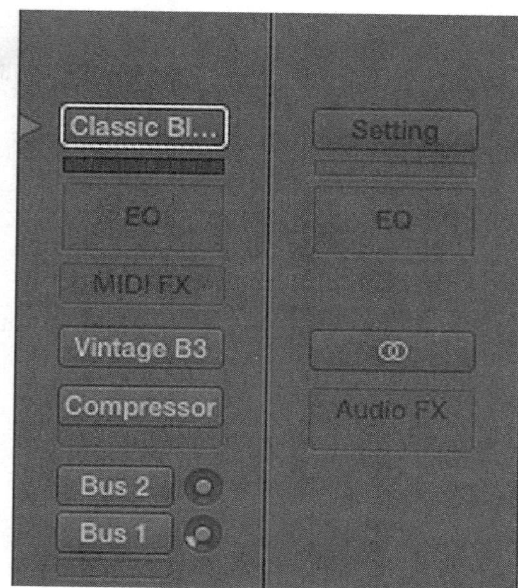

▶ **FIG. 2.43**

Double-click on the Vintage B3 software instrument in the channel strip and the software instrument will open in a floating window.

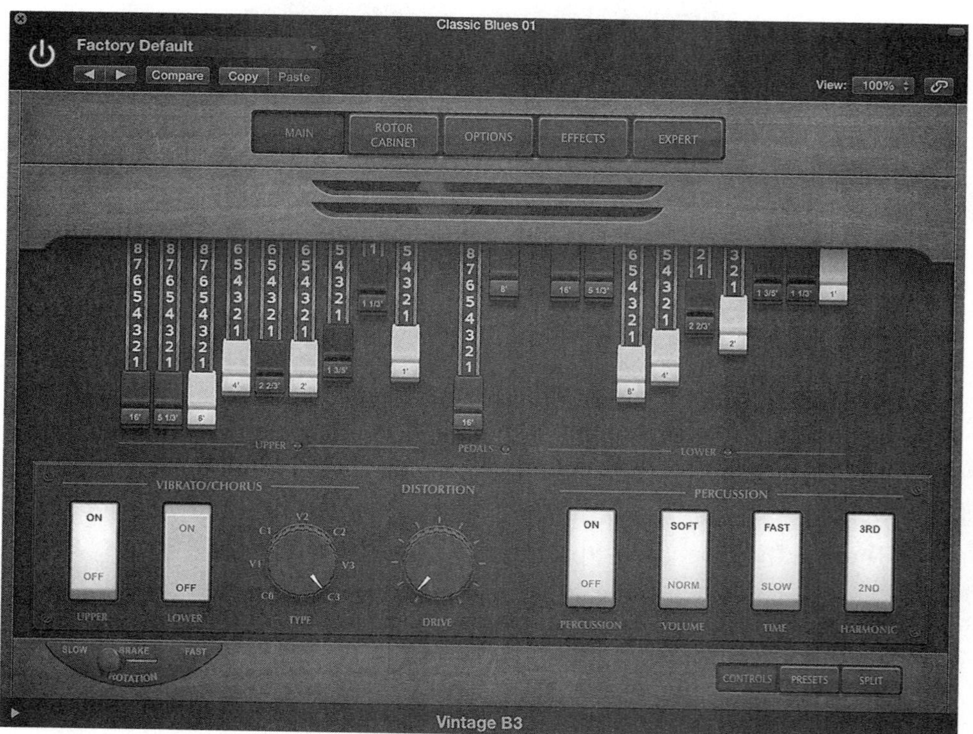

▶ **FIG. 2.44**

Each software instrument contains various presets that can be customized and saved as a new preset. Select the preset menu. From this pop-up window it is possible to load a preset or save any changes made as a new preset.

Software instrument presets are a fantastic way to expand the library of tools at your disposal and help shape the sound of your musical project. The most memorable music written for film and television has a character all its own. The

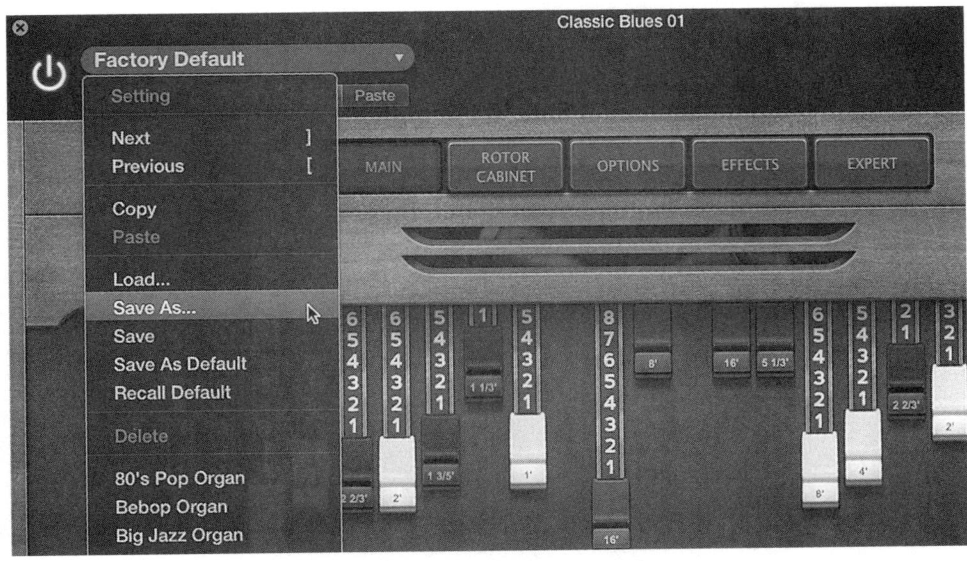

▶ **FIG. 2.45**

essence of this unique quality allows the listener to deeply connect the music with on-screen elements. In a sense the music becomes a character in the story.

Add DSP Plugins to Channel Strips

The combination of custom software instruments presets and the careful use of DSP plugins can produce exciting results that can define the voice of a composer. The greatest composers, arrangers, and orchestrators are flexible and have the ability to craft music in myriad styles. However, their personal voice and style is not lost across genres. This is partially due to the choices they make in orchestration. The creation of software instrument channel strip presets can help shape the voice of new and experienced composers, arrangers, and orchestrators.

1. If the Vintage B3 software instrument is closed, double-click it in the channel strip to reopen it.
2. Spend some time working with some of the various presets that exist in the software instrument.
3. Change some of the default parameters in the Vintage B3.
4. Save the changes as a new preset within the software instrument.
5. Click on the empty slot beneath the compressor plugin on the channel strip that contains the Vintage B3 software instrument.
6. Choose Reverb > Space Designer > Stereo. This will load a reverb plugin onto the channel strip. Another empty slot is placed below the newly created Space Designer plugin.

The sounds of the Vintage B3 preset will sound different because of the addition of the reverb plugin. Adding additional DSP plugins to the channel strip

▶ FIG. 2.46

can further alter the sound. In a sense, you are creating a web of sound through the use of plugins. This common technique is frequently used to enhance and alter music ideas.

Changing the Order of DSP Plugins

The order in which plugins are placed on a channel strip can deeply impact the finished sound from the channel strip. This is because Logic Pro X processes the audio on the channel strip with a plugin in order. Think of this concept as ingredients in a recipe. There is a specific order in which ingredients are added to dish. While there are many ways to cook a dish, certain chefs develop an identifiable characteristic in the way they combine and experiment with ingredients. This analogy extends to working with DSP plugins.

In the example above, the audio will be compressed with the Compressor plugin and then processed with reverb by the Space Designer plugin. This may or not produce a sound that is pleasing to you. Fortunately, Logic Pro X allows you to change the order in which audio is processed by DSP plugins.

1. Navigate to the channel strip that contains the Vintage B3 software instrument and the two DSP plugins (Compressor and Space Designer).
2. Drag the Space Designer above the Compressor plugin on the channel strip.

▶ FIG. 2.47

The signal of the Vintage B3 will now be processed by the reverb plugin before being compressed by the compressor plugin. Subtle changes to the processing order can dramatically enhance your audio projects and help to define a sound that is characteristic of the project and your work as a whole.

Save Channel Strip as a Preset

Once the channel strip has been populated with a software instrument and a desired set of DSP plugins, it can be saved for future use. These presets can be later used to apply similar processing to other audio tracks to create a consistent sound throughout your audio project.

Click and hold on the current preset name in the channel strip.

▶ FIG. 2.48

Navigate to "Save Channel Strip Setting as" from the pop-up window.

▶ **FIG. 2.49**

Name the preset and use the default save location.

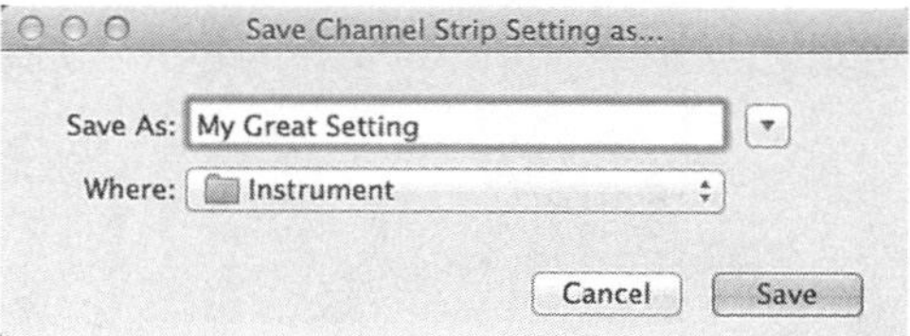

▶ **FIG. 2.50**

The name of the preset in the channel strip will update to reflect that newly created channel strip preset.

▶ **FIG. 2.51**

Backing Up User-Created Presets

When working with computers it is highly recommended, if not essential, to back up information that can act as the gatekeeper between you and your finished projects. The necessity to archive data applies to every computer user, but backups are rarely performed. This is a professional responsibility for those who use computers to deliver digital content to clients on a professional level.

Navigate to/Users/*Your User Account Name*/Library/Application Support/Logic/.

This folder contains the user specific data files for Channel Strip Settings, Data Management Settings, Key Commands, Plug-in Settings, and Sampler Instruments. Open the Channel Strip Settings folder. There are two folders: Instrument and Track. The channel strip preset that was created earlier in this chapter should be present in the Instrument folder.

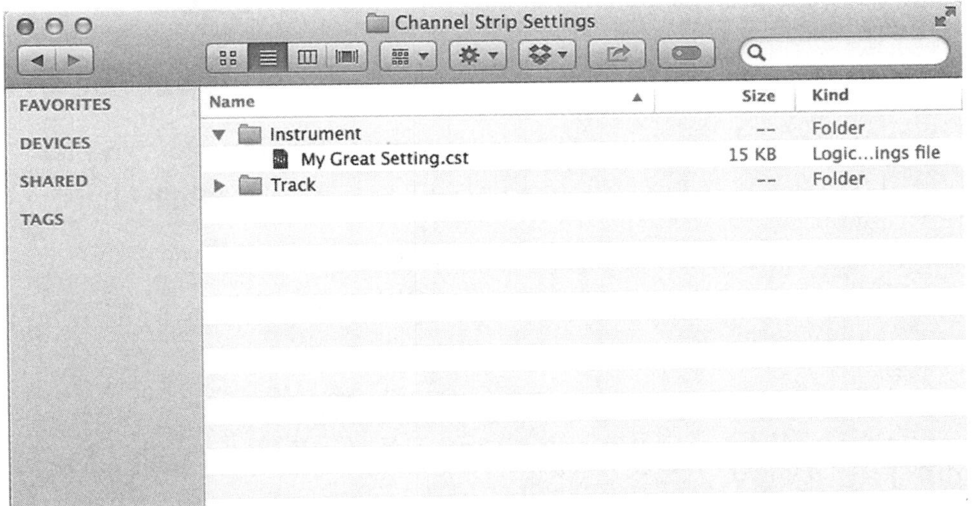

▶ **FIG. 2.52**

These files can be burned to a compact disc or copied to an external volume, such as a flash drive or hard drive. Archiving and backup techniques are discussed in greater detail in a later chapter.

ALL FILES SECTION OF THE BROWSERS AREA

The all files section, as the name suggests, allows you to browse through your computer to find relevant audio files to add to your project. Think of it as an integrated version of the OS X Finder.

1. Navigation—Allows you to navigate back and forth through folders and drive volumes.
2. Current Viewing Location—Displays the folder level that is being currently viewed.

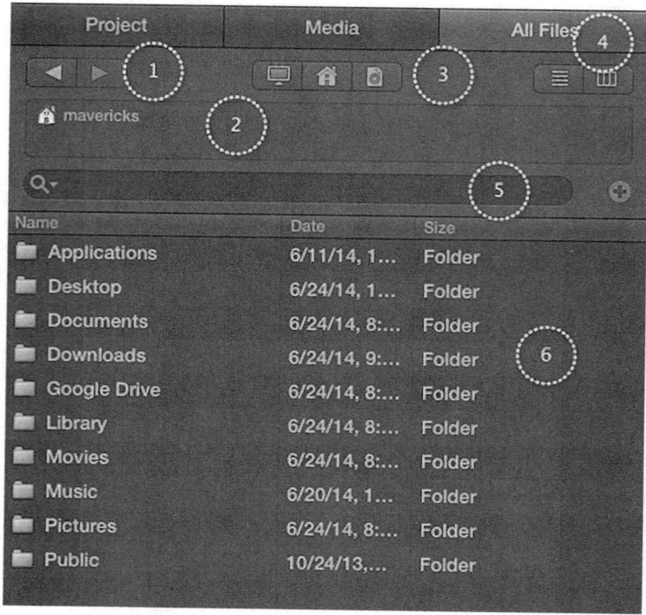

▶ **FIG. 2.53**

3. Computer View—Displays hard drives and volumes attached to your computer. Home View—Displays files and folders that reside in your user account. Project View—Displays files that reside within the current project.
4. Toggles view between list and column view.
5. Search box to filter file results.
6. File results list.

ADDING FILES TO THE PROJECT SECTION OF THE BROWSERS AREA

Logic Pro X is considered to be a drag and drop program. Essentially, this means that audio can be dragged from anywhere (i.e., Desktop, Flash drive, hard drive) into the tracks area in Logic. The musical elements will be copied into the project folder. While this option is helpful and convenient, it is important to be able to import audio into the Project section of the browsers area without placing media directly in the Tracks area.

To proceed with this section, download the project files from the companion website.

1. Create a new Logic Pro X project. From the menu bar, choose File > New.
2. Choose Empty Project. If a Logic Pro X project is open you will be prompted with options to save and close the current project.
3. When prompted to create audio tracks from the new tracks dialogue box, choose ten stereo audio tracks.

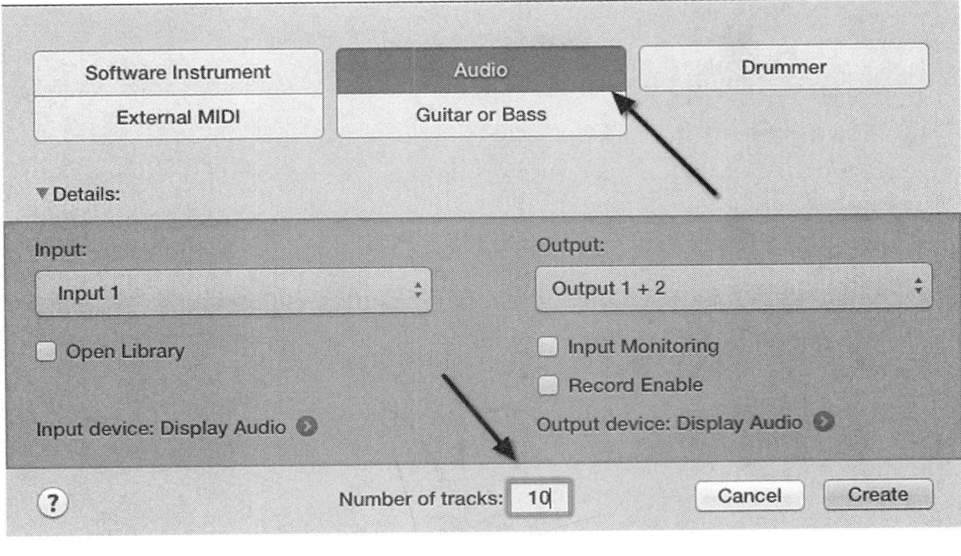

▶ **FIG. 2.54**

▶ **FIG. 2.55**

4. Rename the tracks in the following order:
   1. Guitar
   2. Synth Organ
   3. Bass
   4. FX Loop
   5. SFX
   6. Pad
   7. Shaker

8. Tambourine
9. Drums 1
10. Drums 2

5. Navigate to the Project section of the browsers Area.
6. Choose Audio File > Add Audio File from the local menu bar.
7. Navigate to the audio files that were downloaded from the companion website.
8. Click Add All. The files are added into the lower pane of the window.
9. Click Done. If prompted to change the sample rate of the project, click Change Project.

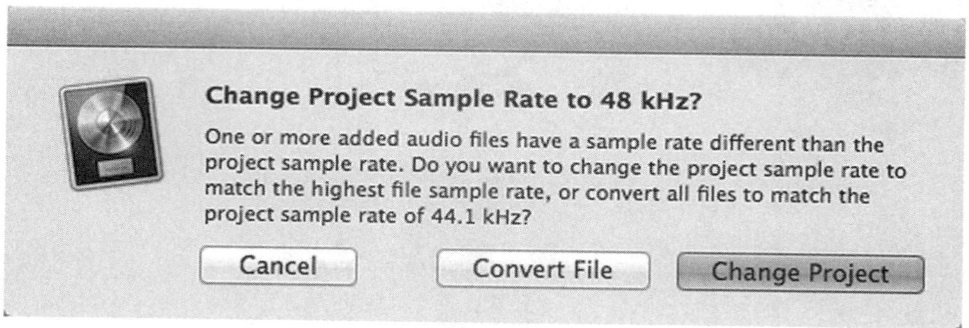

Change Project Sample Rate to 48 kHz?
One or more added audio files have a sample rate different than the project sample rate. Do you want to change the project sample rate to match the highest file sample rate, or convert all files to match the project sample rate of 44.1 kHz?
Cancel
Convert File
Change Project

▶ FIG. 2.56

The audio files that were imported were exported from a project that was recorded at a sample rate of 48 kHz. The default sample rate for Logic Pro X is 44.1 kHz. Logic Pro X is attempting to match sample rates to prevent any potential problems in the project. Sample rates will be discussed in greater depth in another chapter.

ADDING FILES TO THE TRACKS AREA

The Project section of the browsers area contains ten audio files whose names match those of the tracks listed in the track row.

1. Starting with the Guitar track, drag Guitar.aif into the tracks area.
2. Use the help tag to drag the audio 1 1 1 1. Logic divides the tracks area into bars, beats, divisions of beats (1/4, 1/8, 1/16 notes, etc.) and ticks (1/3840 of a bar). By dragging to 1 1 1 1, you are dragging to bar 1, the first beat of bar 1, the first division of beat 1 and the first tick of beat 1.

▶ FIG. 2.57

3. If prompted to import tempo and marker information, click Yes. These audio files were exported from a previous project that contained a specific tempo and track markers. Logic Pro X will restore that information, if possible.

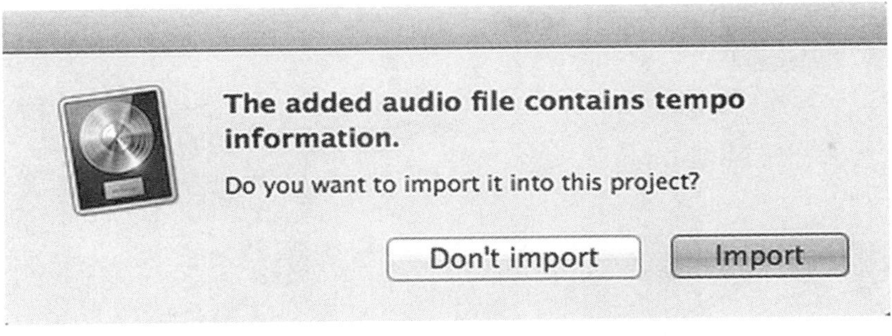
The added audio file contains tempo information.
Do you want to import it into this project?
Don't import
Import

▶ FIG. 2.58

4. Drag the remaining files in the Project section of the browsers area to each track with the corresponding name.

5. Press the Space Bar to begin playback. A finished version of the project is provided on the companion website for reference.

▶ FIG. 2.59

Regardless of the size and scope of a project, the ability to navigate the project quickly and efficiently is extremely important. Logic Pro X offers several ways of navigating the project to quickly view portions of the project in more detail.

ZOOMING INDIVIDUAL REGIONS

Hold down the control and option keys simultaneously. The Pointer tool turns into a Zoom tool. Logic Pro X allows functions to be assigned to custom key commands. The Zoom tool key command cannot be changed or customized. While holding the control and option keys, drag a small section around the second waveform on the Guitar track.

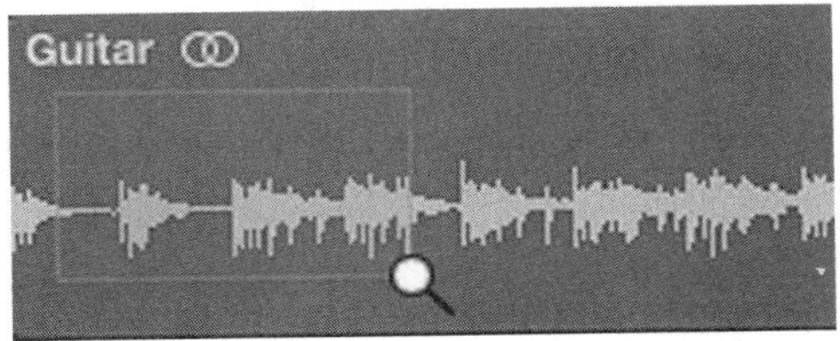
Guitar

▶ FIG. 2.60

Logic Pro X will zoom on the selected part of the region.

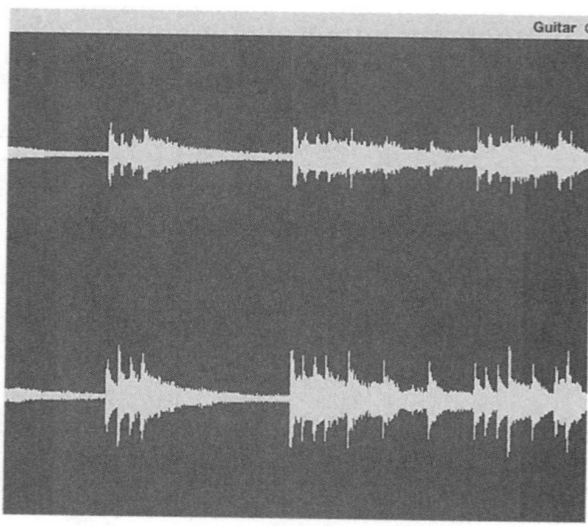

▶ FIG. 2.61

To return to the previous zoom level, simultaneously hold control and option, then click anywhere in the Tracks area.

ZOOMING PROJECT VIEW

While zooming in on individual regions may helpful in certain situations, it is also helpful change the zoom level of the entire project. This includes anything that is placed in the Tracks area—tracks, audio regions, MIDI regions.

It is first necessary to show the toolbar by clicking the toolbar button in the control bar. Notice the two sliders. They control the zoom level horizontally and vertically.

▶ FIG. 2.62

Experiment with the zoom levels to get a feel for the function of the sliders. Sliders and tool bars provide a great deal of functionality in an application but can be cumbersome to use because they require the user to move to separate areas of the graphical user environment. Key commands often provide the same functionality (or even more in some cases) than tool bars and sliders.

Logic Pro X has a default set of key command for zooming audio and MIDI regions:

Horizontal Zoom In: Command–Right Arrow
Horizontal Zoom Out: Command–Left Arrow
Vertical Zoom In: Command–Down Arrow
Vertical Zoom Out: Command–Up Arrow

You should now have a basic understanding of how to interact with Logic Pro X's interface, track handling, and file handling. Throughout this book we will explore recording and editing audio and MIDI, Loop creation, working with movie files, basic project mixing, client delivery and collaboration, and best practices and troubleshooting.

CHAPTER 3
RECORDING AND EDITING AUDIO

And music is sort of revealing truth. When you compose, you're freezing pieces of truth together as best you can. When you're composing or you're playing music, you're revealing something that is ultimately already there.

—*Marc Shaiman*

SAMPLE RATES

WITH THE RISE OF DIGITAL AUDIO WORKSTATIONS, knowledge of audio-sampling rates has become increasingly important for musicians and composers who produce digital media. Sampling audio is the process of capturing an analog signal as a digital signal—in other words, converting analog signals into digital signals. Sample rates correspond to the number of audio samples taken during one second. This process is necessary to edit and manipulate audio in a digital audio workstation. The two most common sample rates are 44.1 kHz (44,100 Hz) and 48 kHz (48,000 Hz), resulting in 44,100 or 48,000 samples per second. When recording audio into your musical project, you are converting the analog signal from the microphone or amplifier into a digital signal.

Film and television audio projects require the sample rate to be set at 48 kHz. This sample rate was chosen because of video frame rate (frames per second) requirements. Video editors have several frame rates to negotiate—NTSC (29.97 fps), PAL (25 fps), 24 fps, and 30 fps. The 48 kHz delivers a consistent 22 kHz frequency response sample rate that is compatible with these frame rates. Audio projects that are destined for compact discs utilize a 44.1 kHz sample rate. This difference seems subtle enough but can cause potentially disastrous results because there is a distinct tonal difference between audio recorded at 44.1 kHz and audio recorded at 48kHz. Many modern digital audio workstations will warn the end user if there are sample rate incompatibilities, but it is important to be cognizant of the current sample rate of a project.

Audio engineers will frequently record at higher sample rates to attempt to capture more audio information, resulting in an arguably more accurate depiction of the recorded audio. These higher sample rates are not chosen arbitrarily; they are directly proportional to the final sample rate destination. Audio projects destined for nonvideo playback are often recorded at 88.2 kHz or 176.4 kHz. These higher sample rates are chosen because they are multiples of 44.1 kHz and are symmetrically compatible as a result. Audio projects that are destined for video and film can be recorded at higher samples rates such as 96 kHz and 192 kHz because they are symmetrically compatible with 48 kHz. When the projects are bounced, or exported to a playable audio file, they will be downscaled to the final 44.1 kHz or 48 kHz sample rate. The process of downscaling the audio project is known as dithering.

CHANGING SAMPLE RATES IN LOGIC PRO X

Within Logic Pro X, navigate to File > Project Settings > Audio. Choose the desired project sample rate from the audio settings pane.

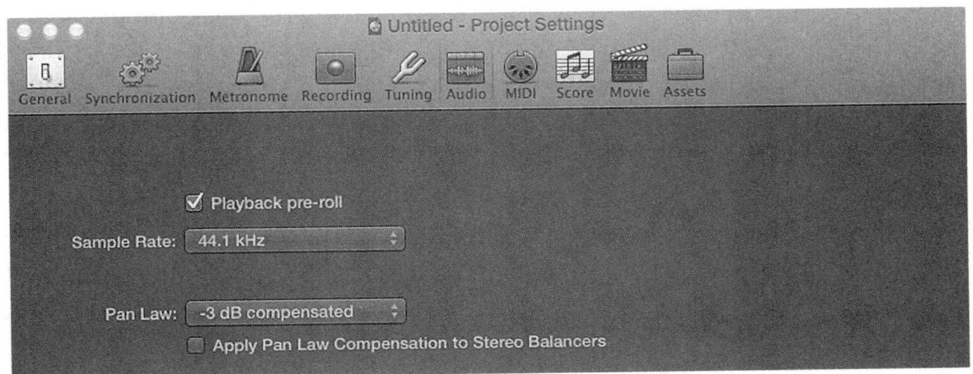

▶ **FIG. 3.1**

The sample rate is a project-based setting that Logic Pro X stores within the project template file rather than a global preference for the program. Instead of creating a global sample rate change for all projects, Logic Pro X will use the sample rate that is set on a per-project basis. However, it should be noted that the default sample rate is 44.1 kHz. Sample rates for music and film projects should be set to 48 kHz or a sample rate that is directly proportional, such as 96 kHz or 192 kHz.

It is helpful to have the sample rate of a project displayed in the control bar along with time and playback controls.

Control-click (or right-click) anywhere on the control bar and choose customize Control bar and Display. Select Sample Rate or Punch Locators. The current project sample rate will be displayed in the control bar.

The project sample rate can also be changed from the control bar once "Sample Rate or Punch Locators" is enabled. This is helpful when you are working with film and video projects where the sample rate is required to be 48 kHz.

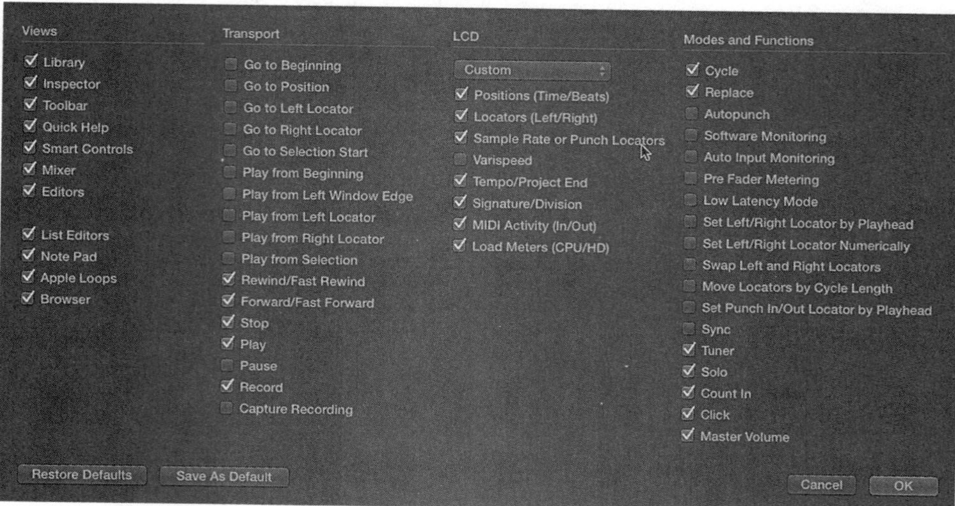

▶ **FIG. 3.2**

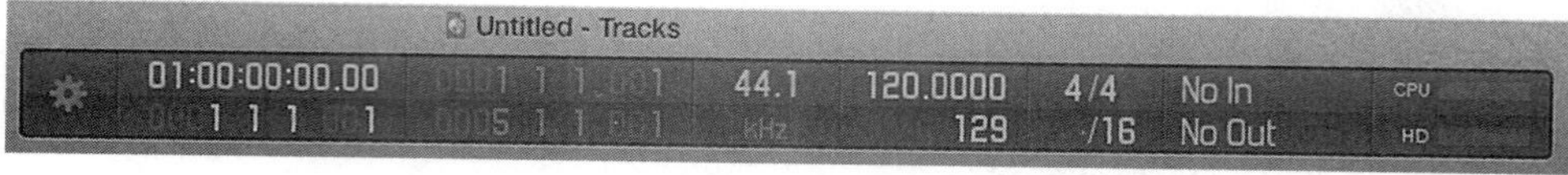

▶ **FIG. 3.3**

Displaying the sample rate in the control bar can prevent problems down the road because it is always clear which sample rate is being utilized in the audio project.

RESAMPLING AUDIO FILES

If audio was recorded at an incompatible sample rate, it can easily be resampled to utilize the proper sample rate. This will prevent needless rerecording of audio content for your musical project. It would be a shame to have to rerecord an impeccable performance.

Download the project audio files from the companion website and unzip the project to the Desktop.

Navigate to the Project Audio Browser in the Browsers area. Notice that the sample rate of the audio file is 44.1 kHz. This sample rate is incompatible with the project sample rate of 48 kHz. This audio file will need to be resampled to 48 kHz.

▶ **FIG. 3.4**

Select Drum Set.aif audio file. Choose Audio File > Copy/Convert File(s).

▶ **FIG. 3.5**

Rename the file to "Drum Set 48 kHz.aif" and change the sample rate to 48 kHz, if needed.

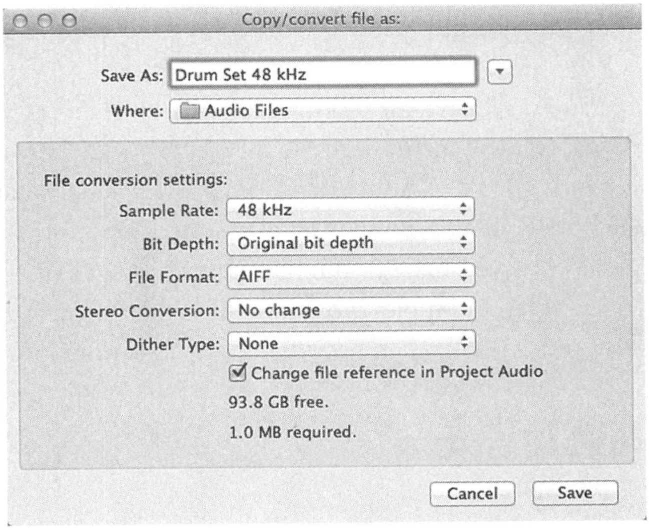

Copy/convert file as:

Save As: Drum Set 48 kHz

Where: Audio Files

File conversion settings:

Sample Rate: 48 kHz

Bit Depth: Original bit depth

File Format: AIFF

Stereo Conversion: No change

Dither Type: None

☑ Change file reference in Project Audio

93.8 GB free.

1.0 MB required.

Cancel Save

▶ FIG. 3.6

Click Save. The audio file will now be resampled to 48 kHz and will be placed in the same position in the Tracks area. This audio file will now be compatible for playback in film and television projects.

RECORDING FILE TYPES

Most digital audio workstations have the ability to choose a destination file format for the delivery of content. The two most commonly used file formats are the Audio Interchange File Format (AIFF, sometimes referred to as AIF) and Waveform Audio File Format (WAV, sometimes referred to as WAVE). Both AIFF and WAV files are members of the pulse code modulation (PCM)

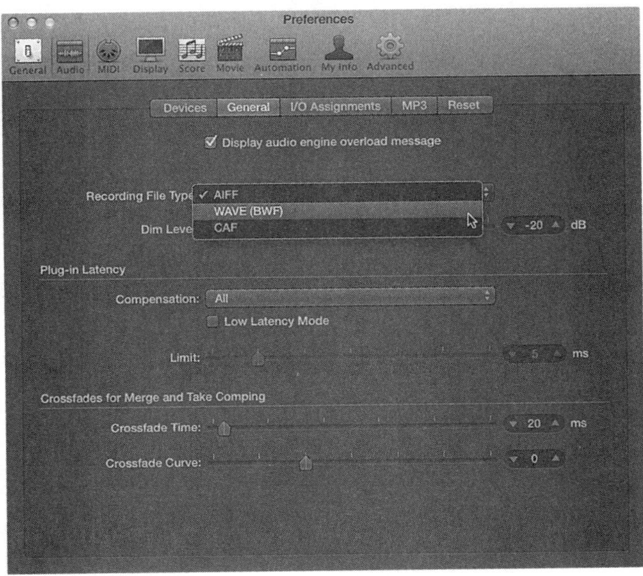

▶ FIG. 3.7

family. The destination format should be determined before the final delivery of the project. Typically, either format is acceptable, but it is important to check with your client to ensure that the music you are sending is in an acceptable format. Changing the default file format for recording musical content is quick and simple.

Open Logic Pro X and navigate to Logic Pro X > Preferences > Audio. Click on the General tab. Choose the desired file format from the pop-up menu.

Notice that that Logic Pro X supports three different file format types for recording—AIFF, WAVE (BWF), and CAF. The BWF symbolizes that the WAVE file is a Broadcast WAVE file. Core Audio File Format (CAF) is a high-quality file format that was invented by Apple, Inc. More information on Broadcast WAVE file and the Core Audio Format can be found at the following locations:

RECORDING SETTINGS

For the most part, the process of recording musical content in a digital audio workstation is relatively straightforward once it has been configured properly. If the proper configuration has been completed, the only need is to focus on creating musical content for your project.

Open Logic Pro X and navigate to Logic Pro X > Preferences > Audio and click on the I/O Buffer Size pop-up menu.

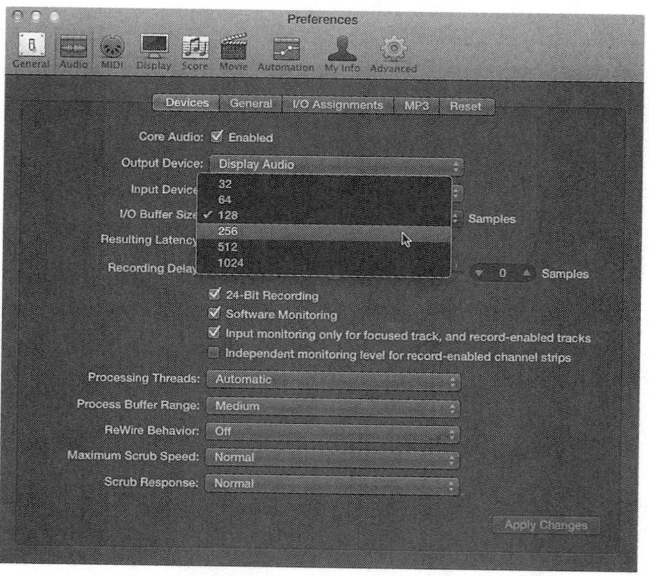

▶ FIG. 3.8

Notice there are several buffer settings. The buffer size directly relates to CPU performance and latency (delay in the round trip of an audio signal). Generally, a higher buffer setting creates more latency in the audio signal flow but reduces load on the CPU. Conversely, a lower buffer setting produces less latency in the audio signal flow but increases load on the CPU. The following analogy describes buffer setting and its impact on CPU load and latency.

Imagine that you live in a small village that is conveniently built on the bank of a small river. The only way to bring water into the village is through the use of workers with various sizes of buckets. When a worker walks to the river with a large bucket (large buffer setting), it will take quite a bit of time to fill the bucket because of its large size. There will not be a steady stream of water because there is quite a bit of time waiting for the bucket to fill. The worker (CPU) is not working very hard because he is spending most of his time waiting for the bucket to fill up. When a worker walks to the river with a small bucket (small buffer setting), he will be returning to the village rather quickly because it does not take a great deal of time to fill up the smaller bucket. This is good news for the village because it will have a steady stream of water, but the worker has to work much harder because he is making frequent trips to and from the river.

Buffer sizes are often chosen based upon the current stage of the project—recording, mixing, and mastering. When recording, a near-zero latency environment is preferred because headphone latency can be distracting for musicians in the studio. When mixing and mastering, latency is not as much of a problem. A higher buffer setting is optimal for this stage because processor intensive DSP plugins and software instruments can utilize the CPU. It is important to note that there is no perfect buffer setting. The optimal setting is going to be specific to the recording situation and the hardware (computer, audio interface type and connection) used in the project. Trial and error will be the best manner in which to find a buffer setting that is appropriate for the project.

FRAME RATE SETTINGS

When working with film and video it is important to be aware of the frame rate of the film or video that you are writing music for. On-screen motion is accomplished through the playback of thousands of individual pictures, referred to as frames. Most digital audio workstations support several formats when working with film and video, including drop and nondrop frame rates. Knowledge of frame rates is important because musicians do not typically work with this sort of timing mechanism; they work with varying tempi, bars, and beats. It is best to communicate with the filmmaker to determine the frame rate used in the film.

To set frame rate settings in Logic Pro X, create a new, empty project. Navigate to File > Project Settings > Synchronization.

Choose the relevant frame rate from the pop-up menu.

- 24 fps: Film, high-definition video
- 25 fps: PAL video/television broadcasts
- 30 fps (drop frame): NTSC video/television broadcast; rarely used
- 30 fps: High-definition video; early black-and-white NTSC video
- 29.97 fps (drop frame): NTSC video/television broadcasts

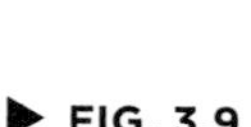

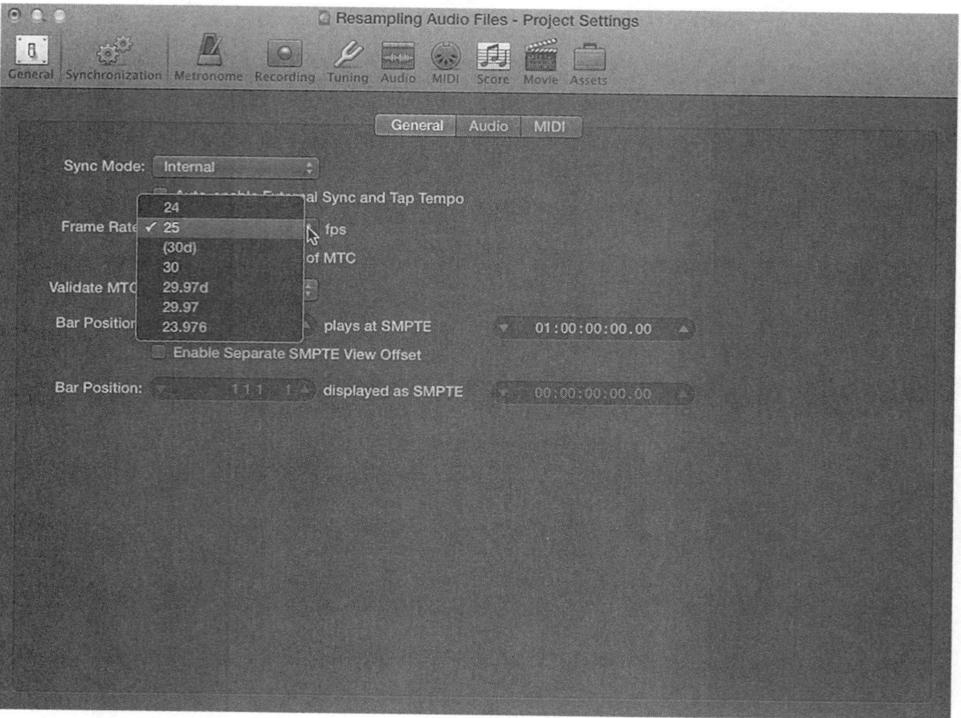

▶ **FIG. 3.9**

- 29.97 fps: Standard definition NTSC
- 23.976 fps: 24 fps running at 99.9 percent, which facilitates easier transfer of film to NTSC video

It is common to receive a proxy video when sketching and creating musical projects. In essence, a proxy video is a lower-quality video file that is smaller in file size and requires less disk bandwidth to play back. This preserves system resources for the musical project itself.

UTILIZING SECONDARY DRIVES FOR RECORDING

All computers have some form of main, long-term storage. This storage is often a hard disk, also known as a hard drive. In recent years, solid-state drives (SSDs) have been introduced into the consumer marketplace. While SSDs are quite a bit faster than traditional spinning platter hard disks, the storage capacity and price point generally make hard disks a better option for the majority of consumers.

There have been quite a few advancements in hard disk technology over the past decade. Users have enjoyed consistently increasing storage capacities as well as improved read and write speeds. These improvements have been of great benefit to audio professionals, but even with these improvements hard disks struggle to meet the critical demands of media professionals.

The use of multiple hard drives is a technique that many media professionals employ to split the increasing workload of media projects across multiple hard drives. It is common for media professionals to employ a dedicated hard disk to run the computer operating system and a dedicated hard disk for media, such as video and audio. The technique of using multiple hard drives increases the computer's ability to handle digital media because the total disk streaming bandwidth is increased with each added drive. In fact, many audio professionals use more than two drives. A third drive is often added to host various third-party software instruments. Multiple hard drives can be added to the machine via empty internal drive bays or through external drive enclosures that utilize USB, FireWire, External SATA (eSATA), or Thunderbolt connections.

Drives should be formatted properly before use as a secondary media drive. Even if a drive appears to be formatted and readable by the operating system, it will most likely need to be reformatted before use. Drive manufacturers often format hard disks with a FAT32 file system before shipping them to consumer outlets. FAT32, for the most part, is suitable for general use but can be problematic for media professionals. FAT32 has a single file size limitation of 4 GB. Large media files can easily surpass this threshold. Every major operating system has native read and write support of the FAT32 file system. The same cannot be said for Apple's HFS+, Microsoft's NTFS and various formatting schemes for Linux distributions—ext2, ext3, etc. Third-party drivers are required for interoperability. See Chapter 9 for information on drive formatting and partitioning.

Once the secondary drive is properly portioned and formatted, it is fairly simple to employ the secondary drive for recording.

Open Logic Pro X and create a new, empty project and choose two stereo audio tracks from the new tracks dialog box.

Choose File > Save As. If necessary, click the disclosure triangle in the Save dialog box to reveal advanced save settings. Choose the secondary drive as the save destination for the Logic Pro X project, in this case, the "Data" drive. Ensure that all files are included in the project by selecting all of the check boxes.

Logic Pro X will now use the secondary drive to receive audio information that streams from the audio interface. In fact, projects that were not created on the secondary drive can be moved to the secondary drive. This simple step can significantly increase performance of the digital audio workstation.

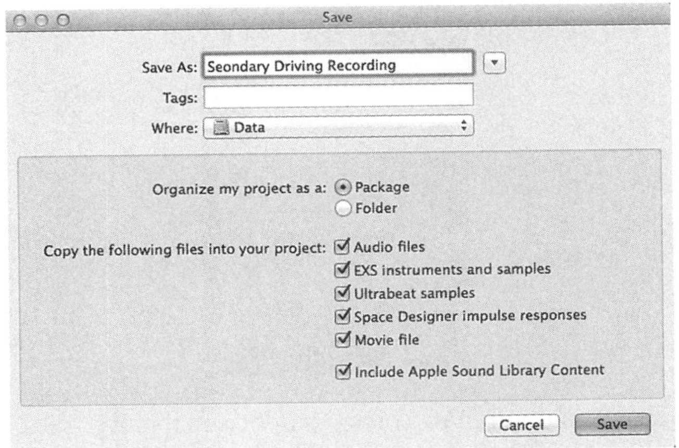

▶ **FIG. 3.10**

RECORDING SINGLE TRACKS

Modern digital audio workstations have made the process of recording extremely simple. The most difficult part of recording is the actual setup of recording—program settings, microphone level configuration, placement, etc.

Download the project audio files from the companion website and unzip the project to the Desktop.

Open the "Secondary Drive Recording" project and verify that the track is using input 1 from the channel strip.

▶ FIG. 3.11

Select the R button on the Vox track header to enable the track for recording.

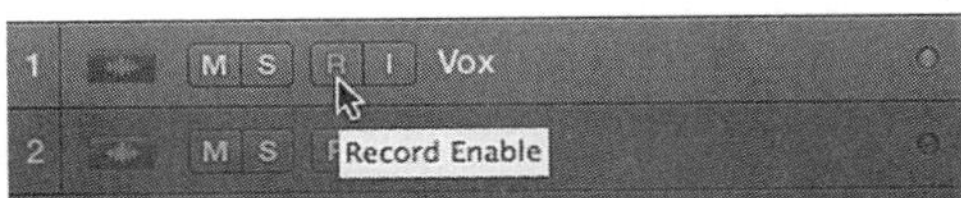

▶ FIG. 3.12

The color of the R button will change to red and begin blinking to indicate the track has been enabled for recording.

Note: If you are working on a laptop, it is important to use headphones to prevent a feedback loop from occurring. If headphones are not available, press the mute key on the keyboard to prevent the feedback loop from occurring.

Press the record button in the control bar to begin recording. Notice that only the track that is record-enabled will record audio data.

▶ FIG. 3.13

The audio waveform will become visible on the track as audio is captured.

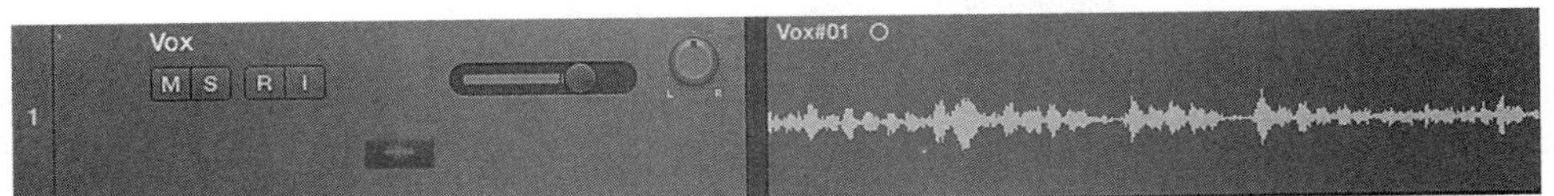

▶ FIG. 3.14

RECORDING MULTIPLE TRACKS

Most recording projects contain more that one track of audio. This is even true in projects that to seem to possess a single audio track, such as a public service announcement. Likely, there are several audio tracks used to create a single composite track.

Change the input on the channel strip for Vox 2 to input 2. This ensures that each track will have its own input.

Delete any audio that was previously recorded on the Vox track by selecting the waveform and pressing the delete key. Press the R button on both the Vox and Vox 2 tracks. Press the record button in the control bar. Both tracks will now record simultaneously.

Note: The total number of tracks that can be simultaneously recorded is dependent on the number of available inputs on your audio interface.

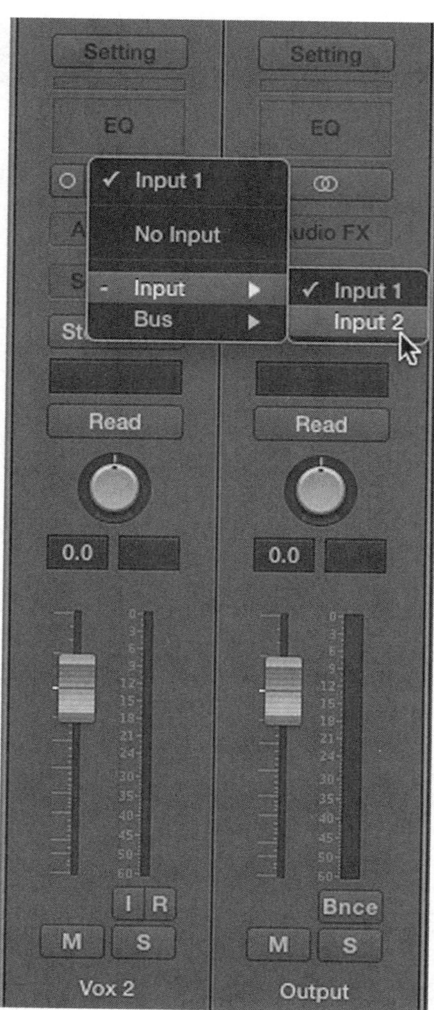

▶ FIG. 3.15

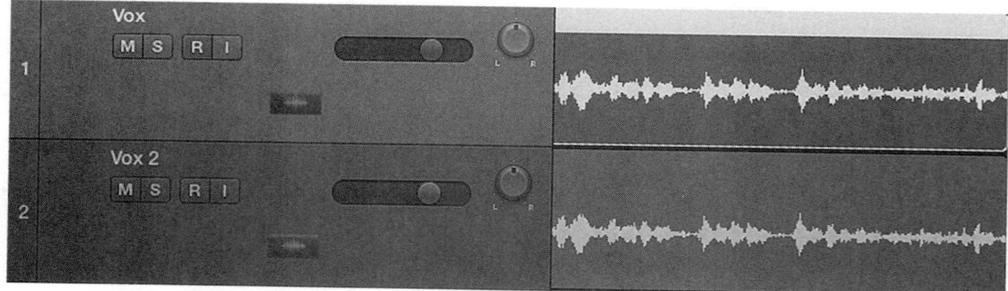

▶ FIG. 3.16

RECORDING IN GROUPS

If there are multiple tracks in an audio project, it can be quite cumbersome to record-enable several tracks one by one. Fortunately, this workflow can be streamlined through the use of groups. Essentially, once tracks are assigned to a group the entire group can be record-enabled at once. This can be particularly helpful when recording large groups of instruments or instruments that utilize more than one microphone, such as drum sets.

Choose Window > Open Mixer or press Command–2. Select both tracks by dragging across the bottom of the tracks in the mixer.

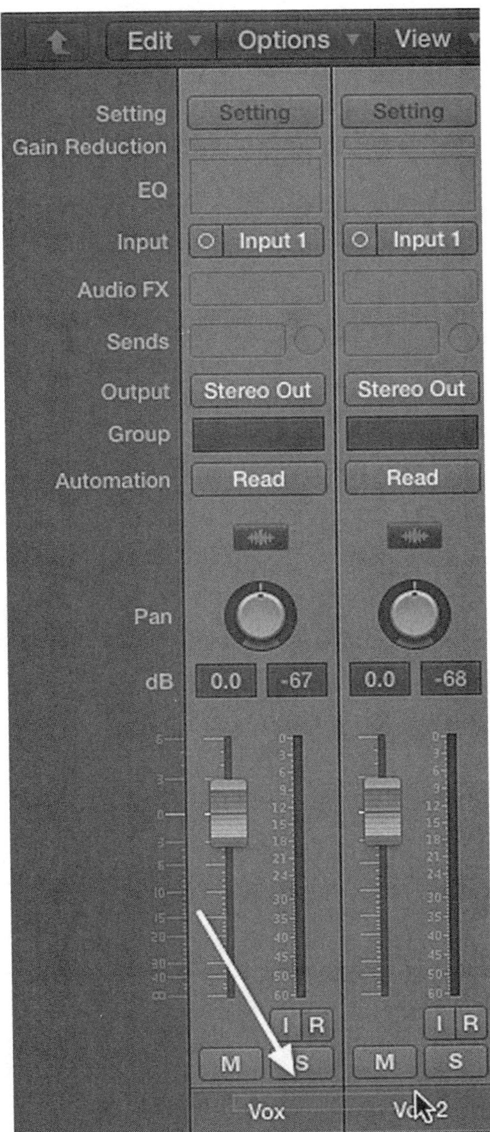

▶ FIG. 3.17

Once the tracks are selected, click and hold on the channel strip's group slot above the panning knob.

▶ FIG. 3.18

Assign the two tracks to group 1 by selecting the group from the pop-up menu.

▶ FIG. 3.19

The grey space now denotes the number of the group the track is assigned to, in this case, group 1. Open Group Settings by double-clicking on the group number in the grey rectangular space.

▶ FIG. 3.20

In the Group Settings, select Record. This will allow all of the tracks in the group to be record-enabled at the same time.

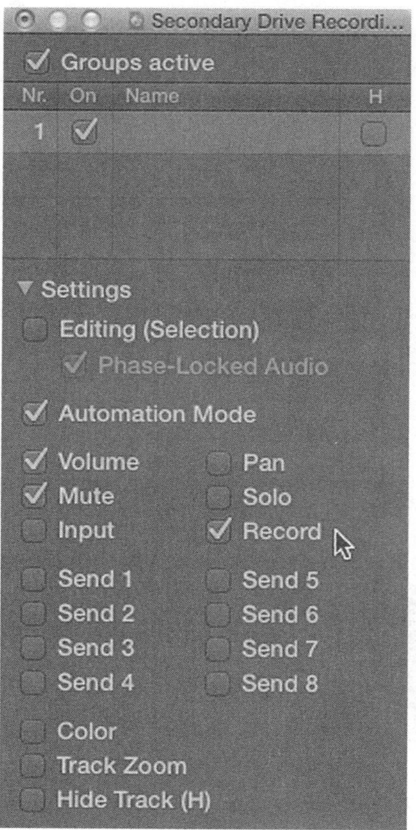

▶ FIG. 3.21

Once you have selected the record option, close the Group Settings window. Click the record-enable button on one track. Notice that both tracks become record-enabled at the same time.

To turn off the group features, choose Options > Disable Groups from the Mixer's local menu or press Shift–G.

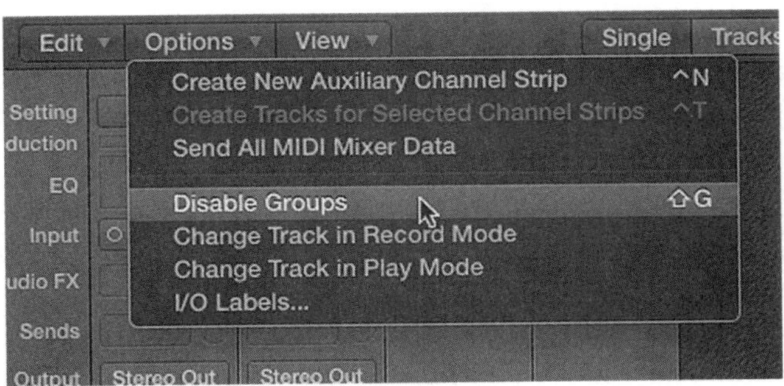

▶ FIG. 3.22

CYCLE RECORDING

Cycle recording is a functionality that is built into most digital audio workstations. At the most basic level, cycle recording allows you to record a predetermined section of music with multiple passes. There is no set length for how long a section can be, but cycle recording generally works best with small sections of music—4 bars, 8 bars, etc. Lengths that are longer than this begin to obviate the benefits of cycle recording. Typically, cycle recording is used to create composite tracks of the multiple recorded passes. For example, it is possible to record a bass player continuously performing an 8-bar section of music. Pieces of each pass can be combined to create a composite performance of the takes.

Cycle recording is implemented in roughly the same manner in most digital audio workstations. A section of music can be selected in the menu bar of the application to create a cycle region. In Logic Pro X, when a cycle region is created a yellow bar appears in the menu bar. Also, the default playback starting point changes from the current location of the play head to the beginning of the cycle region.

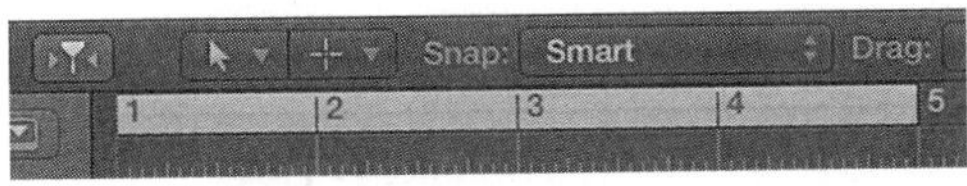

▶ FIG. 3.23

In the case above, a cycle region has been created that begins at bar 1 and ends at the end of bar 4. This 4-bar section will cycle during playback and recording. It is quite easy to create a cycle region in Logic Pro X. Simply drag from left to right in the upper part of the ruler. Cycle regions can also be created via the control bar. This approach is often quicker and more accurate that dragging a selection in the ruler.

Examine the numbers in the control bar directly to the right of the SMPTE timecode section. These numbers detail information about the current cycle region. The top grouping of numbers denote the location of the left locator, while the bottom grouping of numbers denote the location of the right locator. Again, in this case, a cycle region beginning on bar 3 and ends at the end of bar 6.

▶ FIG. 3.24

To change the location of the left and right locators of the cycle region, double-click on the locator you wish to change. The pointer tool turns into a text tool.

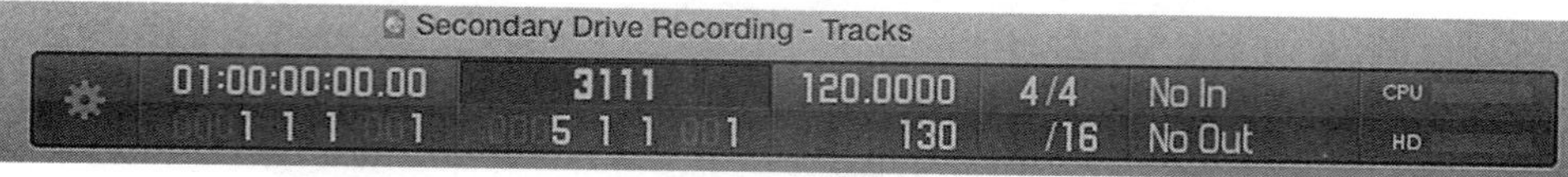

▶ FIG. 3.25

3 1 1 1 represents the exact location of the left locator in bars, beats, divisions of beats, and ticks (1/3840 of a bar). In this case the left locator is at the first beat, first division of the beat, and the first tick of the third bar. It is not necessary to type in the beat, division, and tick locations if they will be at the beginning of the bar. In other words, to change the left locator to begin at bar 4, it would only be necessary to type in a single 4 instead of 4 1 1 1. Logic Pro X assumes the values for beats, divisions, and ticks will default to the beginning of the bar unless specified.

Set up a cycle region from bar 1 through the end of bar 2 in the Secondary Drive Recording Project that was created earlier in this chapter. If the project wasn't created, it can be obtained from Book Files > Secondary Drive Recording. Begin recording on Audio 1. Record several passes of the cycle region.

When you have finished recording, you'll notice that there are multiple tracks nested onto one audio track. These are the multiple takes that were recorded with each pass of the cycle region. The takes can be edited so that the best pieces of each take are combined in a single composite take. This is known as creating a comp take.

Creating a comp take is as simple as dragging over the section you would like to keep, taking pieces from different tracks. Your pointer tool will turn into a comp tool when you mouse over the grouping of takes. Drag over each section you would like to be included in the comp take.

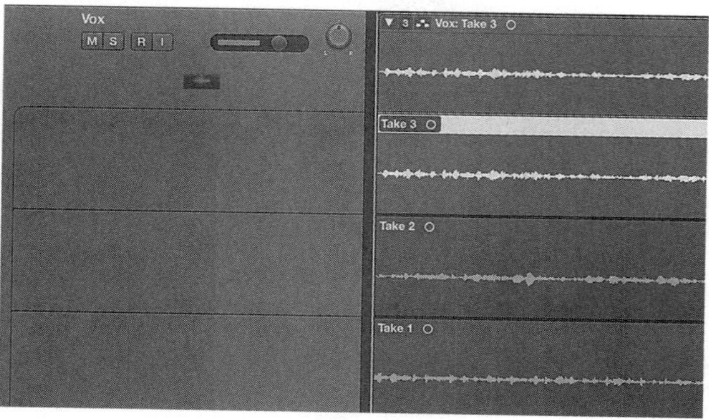

▶ FIG. 3.26

▶ FIG. 3.27

During playback, only the sections that have been chosen when creating the comp take will play. The overview track at the top signifies where the composite pieces have been divided and merged by displaying a white line at each break point.

When you are finished editing your comp take, press the Take folder button in the upper left corner of the audio take.

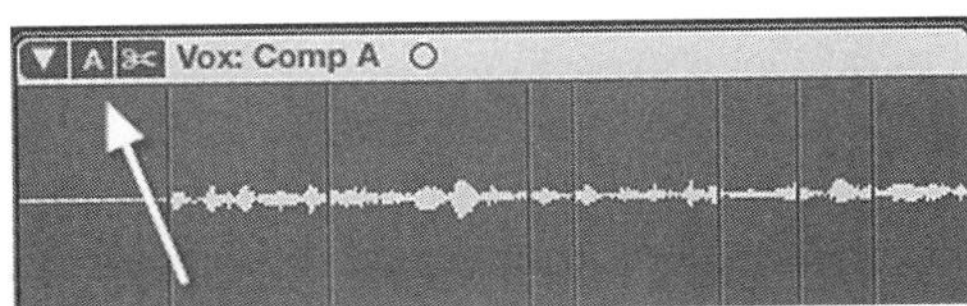

▶ FIG. 3.28

Choose flatten and merge. This will create a new, single audio file with the pieces of the comp take flattened together.

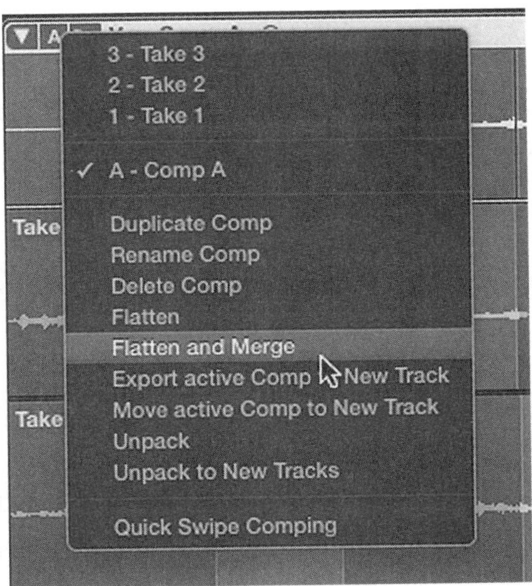

▶ FIG. 3.29

A number of other options in the menu include creating new comp takes and exporting comp takes to new tracks. Try experimenting with creating alternate comp takes by using the Duplicate Comp option. This allows you to explore new ways of combining the track without losing any previous work that you may have done.

DYNAMICALLY EDITING AUDIO

For the most part, recording and editing audio is a static process. Traditionally, once the audio has been recorded it is extremely difficult to manipulate tempo information. This is because audio contains many elements, such as complex harmonic tonal signatures and formants, which must be manipulated in parallel in order to edit the waveform. There are several third-party plugins, most notably Celemony's Melodyne plugin, that can perform these complex actions. Logic Pro X has built-in audio editing tools that allow you to manipulate audio in much the same way that MIDI can be manipulated. It is possible to quantize audio regions to ensure the performance snaps to Logic Pro X's time grid. In other words, a performance that was not recorded in strict time can be forced to play with a strict tempo. For example, a drum performance that was not recorded in strict time can be manipulated to play against a strict, metronomic marking.

TIME STRETCHING AND DIGITAL AUDIO MANIPULATION

Time stretching allows musicians and composers to literally stretch the value of a pitch or series of pitches in a recording. This can be particularly helpful if a grouping of trumpets needs to hold a cadenza slightly longer or if a musical section would benefit if the vocalist held a note for a longer duration. This is often the case in film and television projects where it is imperative to sync the music with on-screen elements. There are several software applications that can accomplish this task, and there will likely be more in the future. For the purposes of this book, we'll explore the time-stretching features in Logic Pro X, simply known as Flex Time.

Flex Time can be easily enabled at any time while you are editing audio. It is available from the tools menu and can be utilized as a left-click or command-click tool. Choosing the tool is quite easy. Simply choose the tool from the tools menu in the upper in the toolbar.

Once the Flex tool has been chosen, notice that your left-click tool turns in the Flex Tool when you mouse over an audio region.

Once you have chosen the Flex Tool as either your left-click or command-click tool, editing audio could not be simpler. Identify the portion of the audio file that you would like to lengthen or shorten and drag the waveform. If Flex Time has not been previously used on this audio region, Logic Pro X will need to index, or map, the transients that exist in the audio file. You will be presented with a window to choose the Flex Mode that will index the audio file. This technique is an invaluable addition to your professional workflow when writing and editing music for

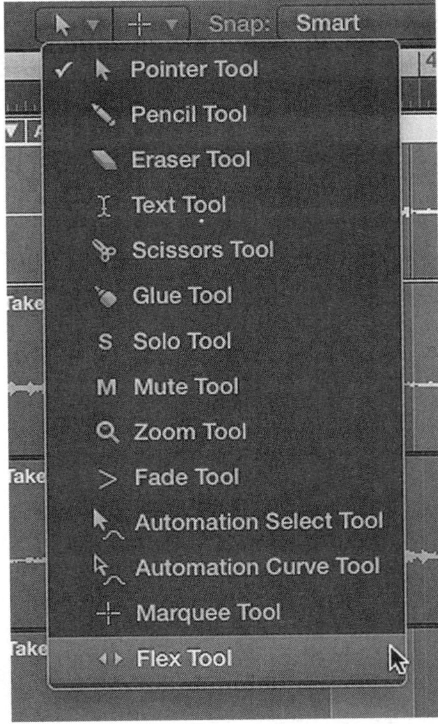

▶ **FIG. 3.30**

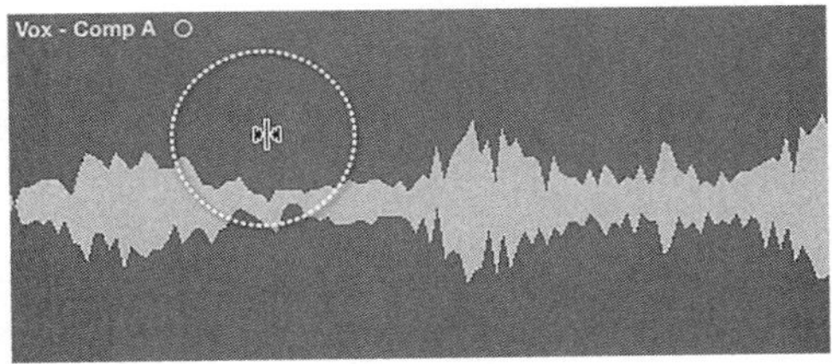

▶ **FIG. 3.31**

film and television because musical elements can be lengthened or shortened to sync with visual cues in the film. It is not uncommon to write music to a specific version of a film and be asked to adapt music to future versions.

There are seven Flex Modes for you to choose from:

- Automatic (Polyphonic)
- Monophonic
- Slicing
- Rhythmic
- Polyphonic
- Speed (FX)
- Tempophone (FX)

Once you choose the Flex Mode that is appropriate for the audio file, the audio file will be mapped based on the algorithm used in the Flex mode. You can see the results of the mapping by enabling Flex View. This can be accomplished by choosing Flex View from the local View menu or by pressing Command–F.

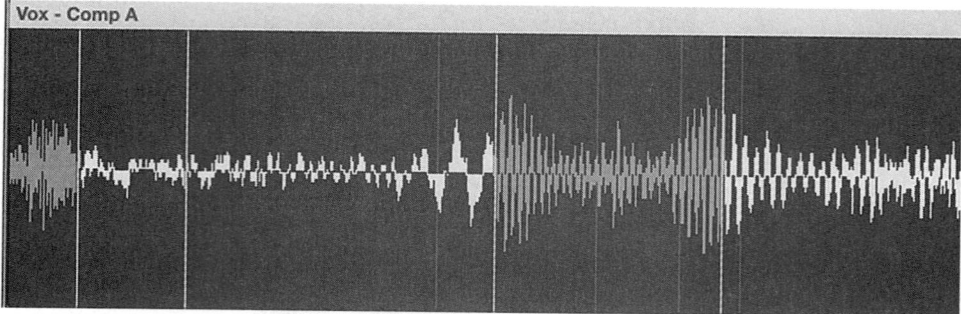

▶ **FIG. 3.32**

The white vertical lines indicate how the audio file was mapped to the Flex Mode chosen. Clicking on the white line will result in the creation of a Flex marker.

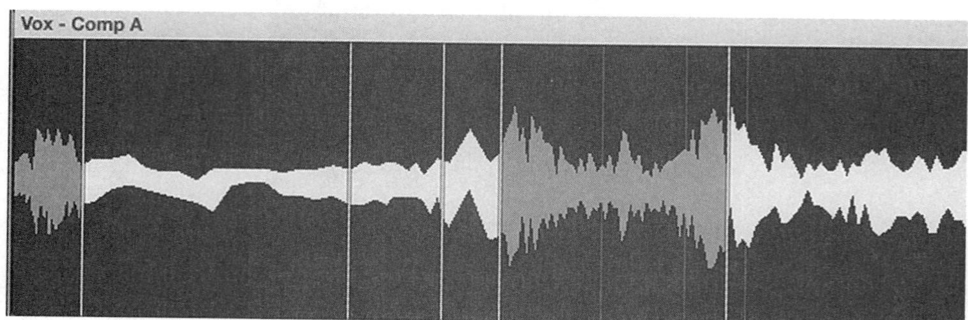

▶ **FIG. 3.33**

Essentially, each section of the waveform can be partitioned so that it can be individually manipulated to fit with within a certain length of time. To lengthen or shorten a part of the waveform, drag the flex marker closer or farther away from the other flex marker.

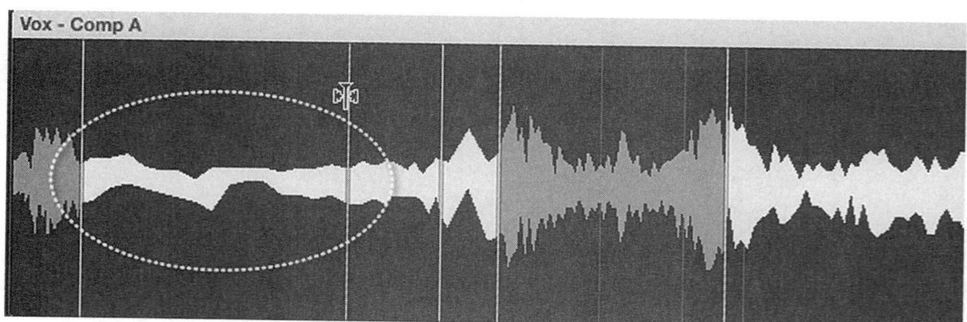

▶ **FIG. 3.34**

In this case the section between the two flex markers has been lengthened. The pitch of the audio file will remain the same. Only the duration of that section will be altered. Previously, creating edits such as this was timely, if not impossible. This technique can be extremely helpful to make a section of music breathe more and come to life by more closely matching the character of the music with the visual cues in the film. When music for film and television is written well, it complements the on-screen visual cues and becomes an additional character in the story.

QUANTIZING AUDIO REGIONS

Quantizing is a term that is usually reserved for conversations that involve MIDI data. It is easy to quantize MIDI performances because MIDI information is simply data. MIDI data only informs the electronic instrument what to play, when to play it, and how to play it. Audio data has been more problematic in regard to quantizing because it is not informing an electronic instrument what to play; it is the performance. There is more involved when manipulating an audio performance because you are not just changing timing information by moving around data, you are moving the whole performance itself—transients, room tone, performance inflections, and so on. Imagine trying to tell a trumpet when and how to play after they have already finished the recording, especially weeks later when you are editing your film project!

Flex Time allows you to quantize audio regions in much the same way you would quantize a MIDI region. This is a somewhat amazing feat because you have the ability to utilize audio files that may have been unusable before. For

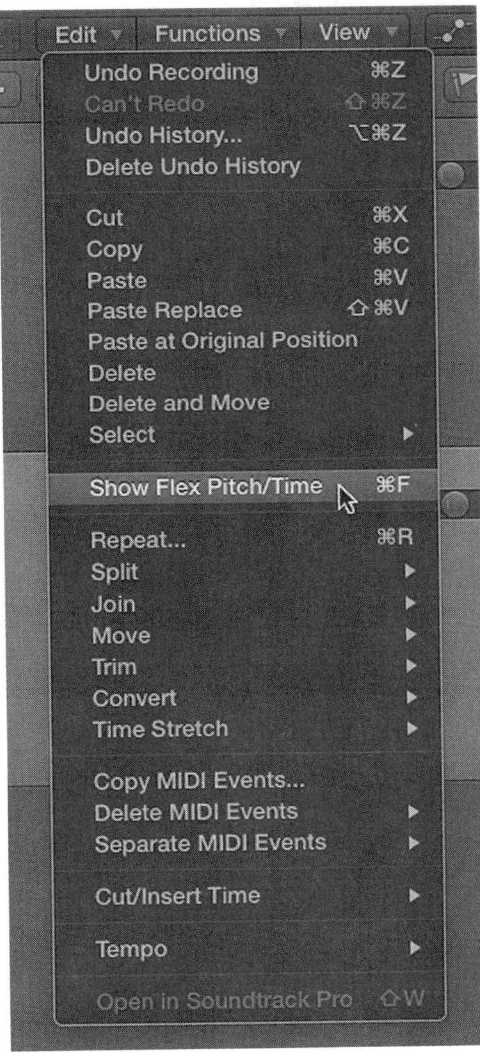

▶ **FIG. 3.35**

example, a percussionist may have played out of tempo during a recording session that rendered the take useless. That out-of-time performance can now be quantized to play back seamlessly with the time grid of the project. The resurrected performance may add the necessary ingredient to complement a film or television project.

In order to quantize a percussion sound, it must be first mapped by enabling flex view. To enable flex view on an audio file, simply choose Edit > Show/Hide Flex Pitch/Time from the local menu in the Tracks area. This can also be achieved by pressing Command–F.

Once Flex view has been enabled, you will notice that a pop-up menu has appeared on each audio track.

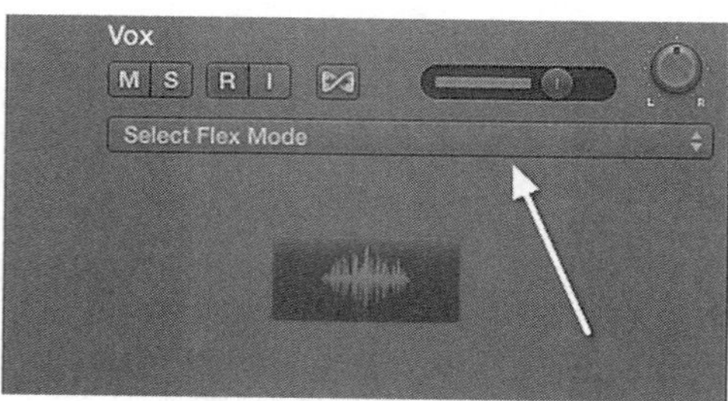

▶ FIG. 3.36

Choose the Flex mode that is appropriate to your needs from the pop-up menu. Once the Flex mode is enabled, transient markers will appear on the waveform. These transients allow the Flex time mode to quantize the audio file.

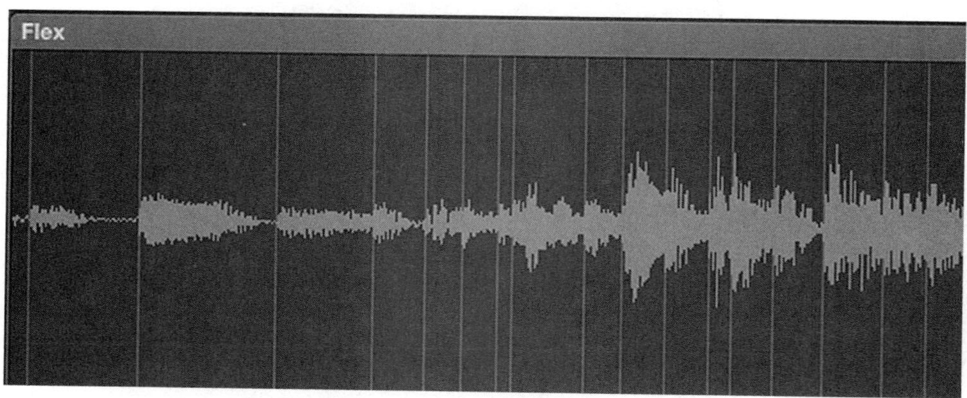

▶ FIG. 3.37

Quantizing will allow you to snap performances to divisions of beats. In other words, you can snap a musical performance to play back in strict time. This is extremely important when trying to sync music to on-screen elements. To enable quantizing after you have chosen a Flex mode, navigate to the region parameter box in the upper-left corner of the Tracks area. There is a pop-up menu to choose the desired snapping division for quantization.

Choose the desired quantizing settings, or snapping division, from the pop-up menu. Once you have selected the quantizing settings, the audio file in

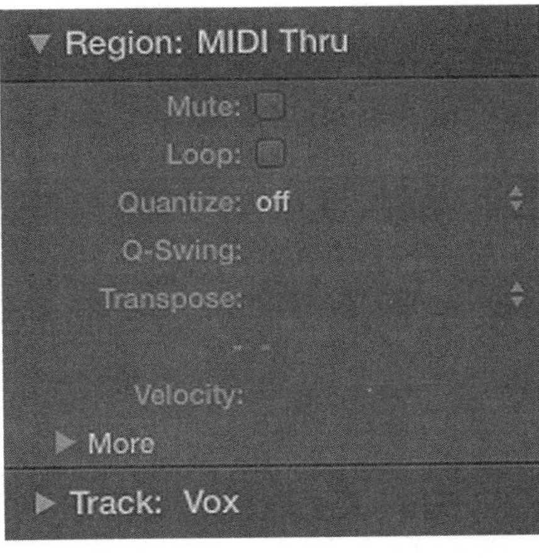

▶ FIG. 3.38

the Arrange will update to reflect your choice. You may need to experiment to achieve the optimal result. For example, using a 1/16 note setting on a musical passage that contains 1/32 notes may not provide optimal results. It might be helpful to experiment with different Flex mode settings, such as rhythmic, polyphonic, and so on.

EXPORTING TO AAF FORMATS

Logic Pro X is a wonderful digital audio workstation, but it is certainly not the only digital audio workstation. Several top-notch software applications are present in the market, all of which possess various strengths that may aid you in the process of finishing your film and television project. Most digital audio workstations do not support native exchange of proprietary file formats. For example, Pro Tools cannot natively open a Logic Pro X project or vice versa. Fortunately, it is possible to move musical projects between digital audio workstations through the use Advanced Authoring Format (AAF) exports and imports. This is a common technique when collaborating on film and television projects with other composers.

AAF is frequently used to move projects from Logic Pro X to Pro Tools and Nuendo. Essentially, all of the audio files are packaged in a format that each digital audio workstation can understand. Keep in mind that MIDI instruments and software instruments must be bounced in place to audio files prior to export. This is because the collaborating composer may not possess the same software instrument or MIDI instrument on their computer.

AAF EXPORT

AAF files are similar to Open Media Framework (OMF) files in the sense that they provide a way to move audio projects between digital audio workstations. Previous versions of Logic Pro allowed for OMF and AAF export functions; however, Logic Pro X only provides AAF importing and exporting features.

Video editors tend to prefer AAF files because they preserve the time position of audio clips as well as references to tracks and volume automation information.

Download the project audio files from the companion website and unzip the project to the Desktop.

Open the AAF Export Project and Choose File > Export > Project as AAF File.

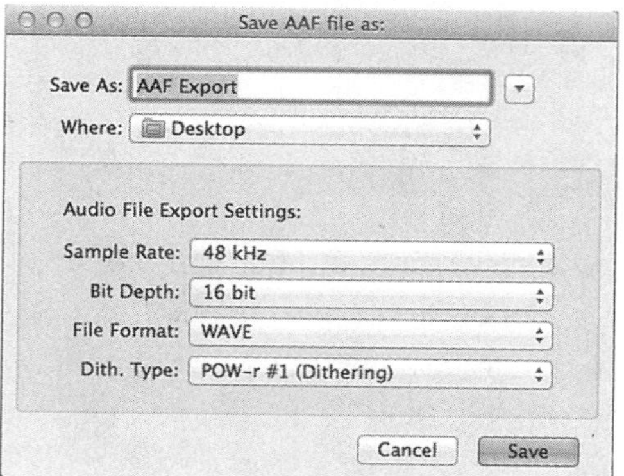

▶ FIG. 3.39

Choose the following settings:

Sample rate: 48 KHz
Bit Depth: 16 Bit
File Format: WAVE
Dithering type POW-r #1

When you have finished choosing the appropriate settings, click Save. Logic Pro X will now export the audio project as an AAF project. You will now notice that there are two elements to your AAF project in the in the export location (in this case, the Desktop): the AAF template file and an audio files folder that the AAF template file references. It is necessary to have both elements available when importing an AAF project into another digital audio workstation.

CHAPTER 4
RECORDING AND EDITING MIDI

But the thing is, it's really about the manipulation of ideas. That's what it is. The MIDI mock-up thing—that's over with. We still do that, but that's not the sole intent for having all this gear. . . . For me it's actually to do production work.

—*Terence Blanchard*

MIDI HAS EXISTED for over a quarter of a century and is arguably one of the most important tools in the modern musician's tool kit. MIDI allows composers and musicians to create musical projects with musical sounds that were previously not available. MIDI sequencers were instrumental in the evolution of nearly every musical style for the past thirty years. In fact, the use of MIDI is not limited to any particular musical genre. It can be found in funk, rock, rhythm and blues (R&B), hip hop, and popular music. MIDI performances can be frequently heard in projects for film and television due to the inherent flexibility of modern MIDI instruments. MIDI performances are easy to capture, edit, and enhance to quickly adapt to change that may be required in tight release schedules that are often associated with film and television projects.

MIDI has evolved substantially since its inception. Initially, MIDI data were used to trigger electronic sounds that were meant to emulate physical instruments. These emulations were of varying quality and in some cases were extremely poor. Brass instruments were particularly difficult to emulate. Despite these deficiencies, MIDI became a popular choice for musicians and composers because musical scores could be played back via electronic instruments and provide a rough glimpse of the final sound of the project. The quality of MIDI instruments has continuously improved over the past few decades. It can be difficult to discern an audible difference between live and MIDI instruments in certain circumstances. This progress comes with the blow of a double-edged sword. Composers are able to make a living despite consistently shrinking production budgets at the cost of performance opportunities for instrumentalists.

The MIDI mockup became popular when writing music for film and television for several reasons, but particularly because music could be presented to production staff and approved before musicians were called into the studio for a recording session. Any changes that needed to be made to the score could be done prior to the final recording session to prevent the need for multiple recording sessions. It was also a benefit to composers because they had a better idea of what their music would sound like when it was eventually recorded. Generally speaking, if a MIDI mockup were acceptable, the final project recorded with live musicians would sound even better.

MIDI CONTROLLERS

MIDI controllers are often confused with musical keyboards because they look and seemingly function in much the same manner as a musical keyboard. However, in their simplest form, MIDI controllers are simply tools that send MIDI data to digital audio workstations. MIDI controllers do not send musical information to a sequencer; they send raw data to the sequencer that triggers musicals sounds that are mapped to respond to specific MIDI data. In a way, MIDI controllers are no different than other human interface devices (HIDs). QWERTY keyboards send data to a computer operating system that is interpreted as keystrokes. Mice translate raw movement data into tracking information for pointers and user interface elements on a screen. In the end, these devices interpret data we provide, through our actions, into events. MIDI controllers present the first level of interaction between musicians and digital audio workstations.

Modern MIDI controllers take on many shapes and forms. MIDI controllers are often designed to look and feel like pianos, but that paradigm is continuously shifting. A number of MIDI device manufacturers have created MIDI controllers that are based on new and exciting input methods, such as touch-sensitive touch pads that map finger movements to MIDI controller data. These new controller interface designs are meant to allow musicians to engage with MIDI instruments in a new and exciting way to bolster new and exciting musical ideas.

Logic Pro X has a built-in MIDI controller that enables the QWERTY keyboard to be used as a MIDI controller when an external MIDI controller is not available. It is invoked by choosing Window > Show Musical Typing from the global menu bar. A floating MIDI controller will appear within Logic Pro X's editing environment. This is a handy tool when inputting MIDI data in locations where a traditional MIDI controller may not be practical—for example, planes, trains, and automobiles.

Many external MIDI controllers are sensitive to how hard keys are pressed on the controller. This MIDI data, known as velocity, is used to adjust accentuation during playback. This is similar to musical emphasis, commonly referred

▶ **FIG. 4.1**

to as marcato markings, in live performance. Since a QWERTY keyboard on a computer is not sensitive to keystroke pressure, the Musical Typing Keyboard cannot determine the velocity, or musical emphasis, of the note. To solve this problem, Logic Pro X records static velocity data when touch data is not available. The default velocity input from the Musical Typing Keyboard is 98 and can be decreased by pressing the C key and increased by pressing the V key. This allows musicians who do not have access to a MIDI controller that supports velocity to record musical emphasis into their musical project.

Many MIDI controllers on the market today rely on generic class-compliant drivers that enable installation without the need for additional software drivers. Essentially, these drivers allow musicians to connect MIDI controllers and audio recording equipment to their machine with little or no effort. Generally speaking, MIDI controllers do not require additional drivers, as most are class-compliant devices. Class-compliant driver packages ship preinstalled with a most computer operating systems. Windows and Macintosh computers take advantage of the preinstalled class compliant drivers. However, class-compliant compatibility is somewhat fragmented with Linux distributions. There are many distributions, or versions, of the Linux operating system. Each distribution contains varying software packages and may or may not include class-compliant drivers for MIDI and Audio devices. Historically, this has not been an issue for musicians and composers because the overwhelming majority of them use Windows or Macintosh operating systems.

RECORDING MIDI

MIDI performances create extremely flexible working situations for musicians who are composing for film and television. This is largely due to the fact that MIDI controllers can trigger a multitude of instruments. A single composer can orchestrate and perform and entire piece with strikingly realistic instrumental samples. In fact, the quality of modern software instruments rivals live musicians. That is not to say that software instruments are superior to live musicians, simply that the quality gap between the two is diminishing. There is one fact that will always remain true: MIDI performances provide musicians with great opportunities to explore orchestration with instruments that may not be readily available to them.

Recording MIDI data is similar to the process of recording audio. A track must be record-enabled to receive the MIDI data. Since MIDI data does not create sound, software or virtual instruments must be instantiated to play back the data. A number of digital audio workstations include high-quality software instruments that can be heard in myriad projects that span film, television, and popular music. A number of third-party companies maintain an impressive catalog of software instruments. The Vienna Symphonic Library and the various libraries from Native Instruments and IK Multimedia are a few examples of high-quality third-party software libraries. Virtual instruments come in various formats: Audio Units (AU) and Virtual Studio Technology (VST). Logic Pro X natively uses AU plugins, and Pro Tools natively uses VST plugins. Most manufacturers create both AU and VST versions of virtual instrument packages for your convenience. Let's explore recording MIDI data into a Logic Pro X project.

Open Logic Pro X and create a new, empty project. Choose two software instrument tracks from the new tracks dialog box.

▶ FIG. 4.2

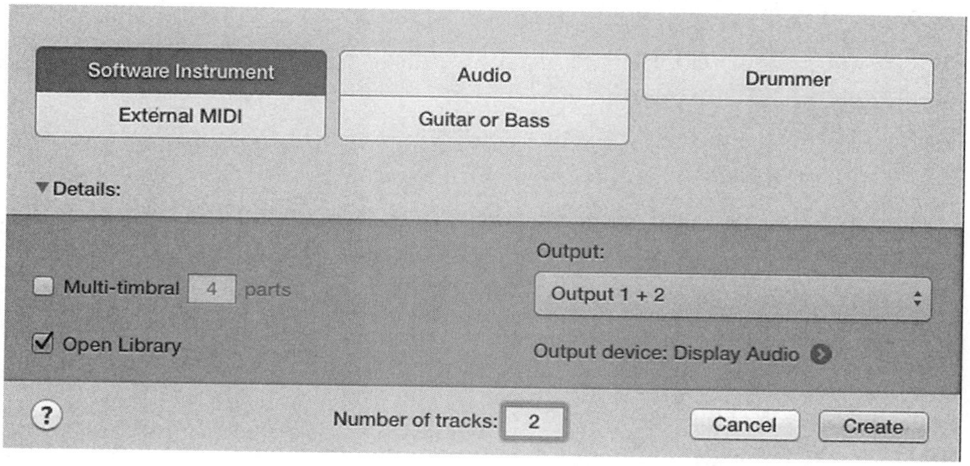

Choose File > Save As and choose the save location to the Desktop, including all assets. Name the project "MIDI Recording."

Rename track 1 to Piano and track 2 to Strings.

▶ FIG. 4.3

Select track 1 and press the Library button in the control bar. Choose Legacy > Logic> 02 Acoustic Pianos > Bösendorfer Piano Club.

Notice that that I/O slot is populated with the EXS24 sampler. There are also two DSP plugins loaded: Channel EQ and Space Designer. All of these components create the preset for the Bösendorfer piano.

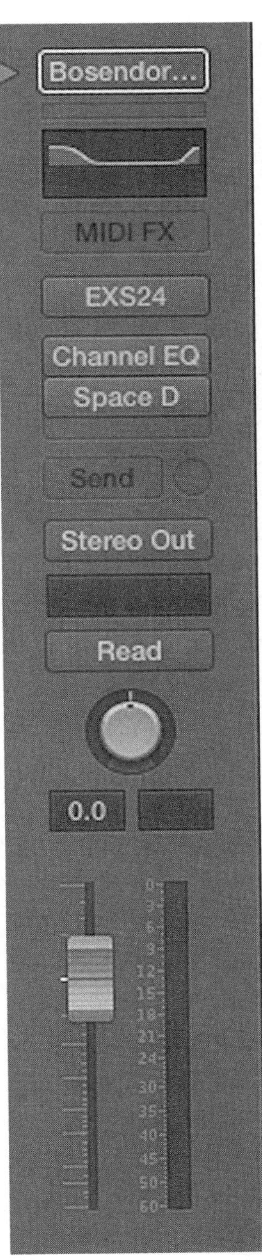

▶ **FIG. 4.4**

Play a few notes on any connected MIDI controller (if a MIDI controller is not available, use the Musical Typing Keyboard). If you are familiar with the sound of a physical Bösendorfer piano, you will most likely be pleased with the virtual representation of that instrument.

One of the lesser known and exciting features of Logic Pro X is the ability to capture MIDI performances as MIDI data. In other words, if playback is enabled, Logic Pro X can salvage any performance that was performed but not recorded. In a sense, Logic Pro X is always recording MIDI data even when not in record mode. The functionality to capture a MIDI performance as a recording is only available by key command. This feature can be extremely helpful when sketching ideas during movie playback but not recording. You will never have to worry about losing a musical idea.

Navigate to Logic Pro X > Preferences > Key Commands. Type "capture" in the search box.

Select Capture as Recording and click the Learn by Key Label button. Logic Pro X will learn the desired key command for the functionality.

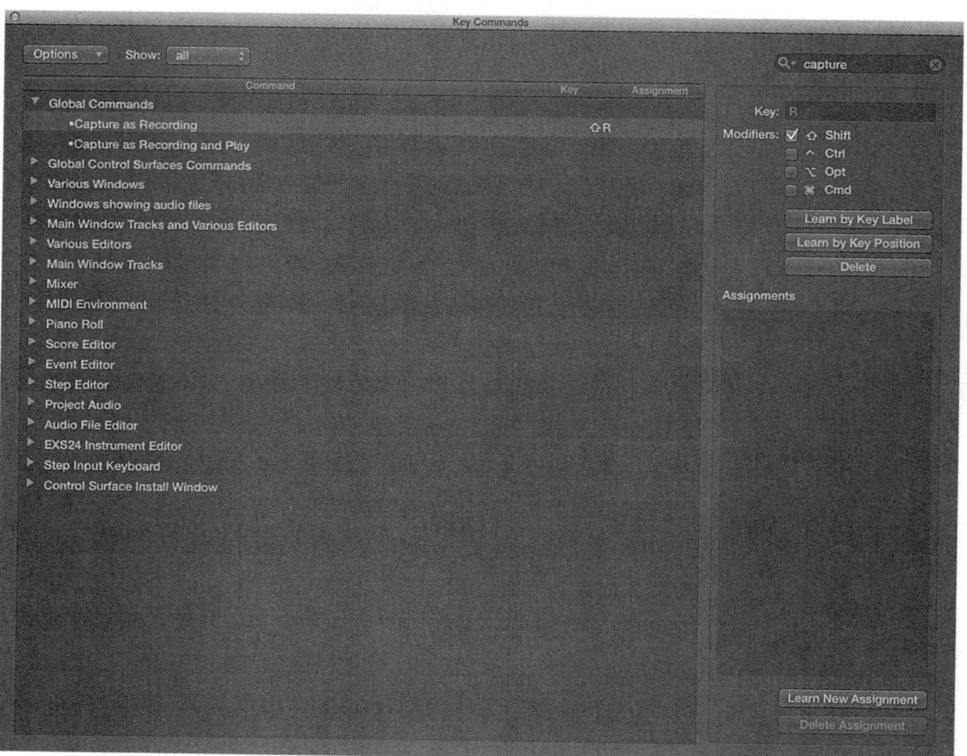

▶ **FIG. 4.5**

Press Control, Command, and M at the same time. Logic Pro X will learn the key Command and use Control–Command–M as the trigger for Capture as Recording.

Note: This is only a suggested key command. You can choose whichever key command you prefer.

Start playback and play a musical passage on your MIDI controller or Musical Typing Keyboard.When finished, press Control–Command–M to capture the performance as MIDI data.

Notice that your previous performance has now been added to the Tracks area on the Piano track. Again, this feature can be invaluable when sketching musical ideas during movie playback while not in record mode.

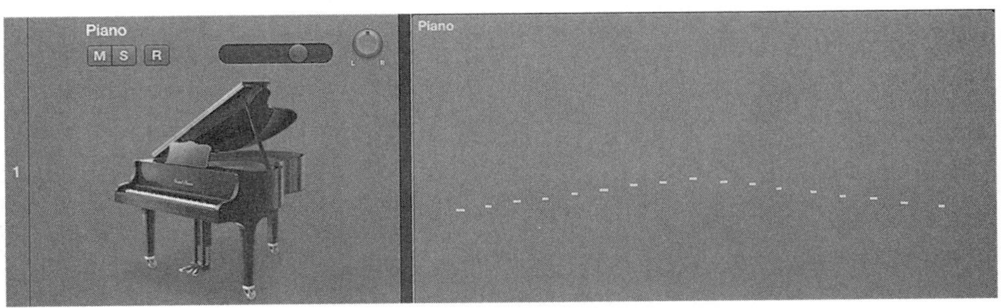

▶ FIG. 4.6

COPYING MIDI DATA TO CREATE LAYERED INSTRUMENTS

MIDI data is widely popular with musicians and composers because it is extremely flexible. Sine MIDI data is just that—data—it can be manipulated in various ways. One of the most common ways MIDI data is manipulated is through copying and layering. This technique allows you to build large orchestral passages by copying and pasting MIDI data to other instruments. Imagine being able to quickly create a full orchestral string section that originated from a single MIDI passage.

Select the MIDI region that was recorded in the last lesson. If MIDI data wasn't recorded, record a small MIDI region on the Piano track.

Hold down the Option key and drag the MIDI region to the Strings track.

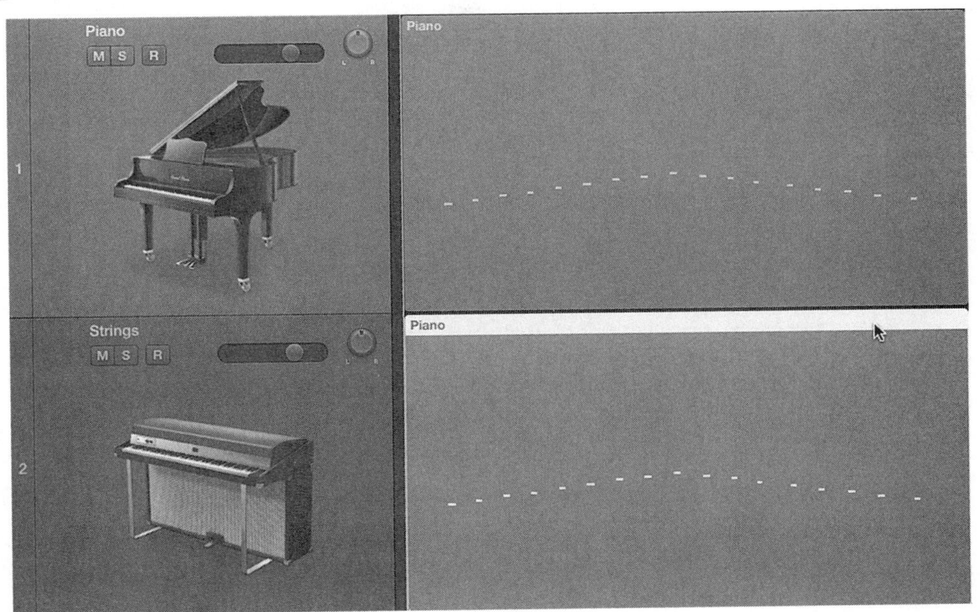

▶ FIG. 4.7

Select track 2 and press the Library button in the control bar. Choose Legacy> Logic> 07 Pop Strings > Warm String Section.

Notice that that I/O slot is populated with the EXS24 sampler. There are also three DSP plugins loaded: Compressor, Exciter, and Space Designer. All of these components create the preset for the Warm String Section.

▶ **FIG. 4.8**

Start the project playback. Notice that the string section mirrors the playback of the piano track. This technique can be used in myriad ways. You are only limited by your imagination. Composers often use this technique to layer percussive events on melodic events to strengthen the composition.

Since the musical information is MIDI data, it can easily be manipulated in any number of ways. MIDI data can be cut, copied, and pasted in a similar way to text in a Microsoft Word document. This is an invaluable technique for quickly strengthening melodic passages. For example, the string track in the previous lesson can be augmented with additional voices. Copying and pasting the melodic information to another voice in the Piano Roll will create additional melodic layers in the MIDI region.

Select the MIDI region on the strings track. Choose Window > Open Piano Roll from the global menu bar. The MIDI data for the strings track in now displayed in the Piano Roll editor. Select the strings MIDI data by dragging around it.

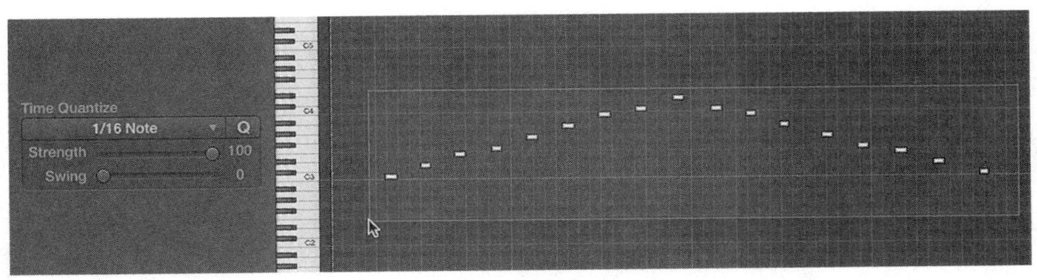

▶ **FIG. 4.9**

Note: Your MIDI recording may look different than the MIDI recording above.

With the MIDI notes selected, press and hold on the selected notes, press the Option key, and drag the selected group up or down. This results in the MIDI data being copied to create a polyphonic musical passage.

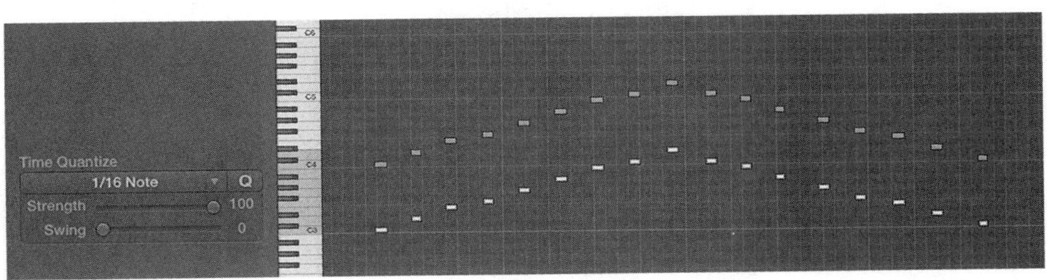

▶ **FIG. 4.10**

In the example above, the data has been copied to add a second voice that sounds exactly one octave above the originally recorded passage. This technique can save a great deal of time, but it is important to be mindful of the harmonic structure of the overall composition. Copying symmetrically up an octave will not change the harmonic structure of the composition, but copying up a major third certainly will. If a C Major scale were recorded and then copied up a major third, the resulting harmonic structure would be E Major over C Major. This will change the C Major tonal center and likely not yield the desired harmonic outcome. In the end, great care must be taken to preserve the intended tonal structure of the composition.

RECORDING MULTIPLE LAYERED INSTRUMENTS

MIDI data can easily be copied between tracks within the Piano Roll, but MIDI data can also be recorded to multiple MIDI tracks simultaneously. This technique saves a great deal of time when working with film and television projects.

You can create layered, textural instruments without having to copy and paste MIDI data.

Delete any MIDI data that exists on the Piano and Strings tracks and create two new software instruments tracks.

Select track 3 and press the Library button in the control bar. Choose Legacy > Logic > 08 > Pop Horns > Funk Horn Section.

Select track 4, then choose Legacy > Logic> 08 > Pop Horns > Soprano Sax.

Arm each track for recording by selecting pressing Control key and selecting R on the track header of each track. Press the Record button in the control bar and begin recording with your external MIDI controller or the Musical Typing Keyboard.

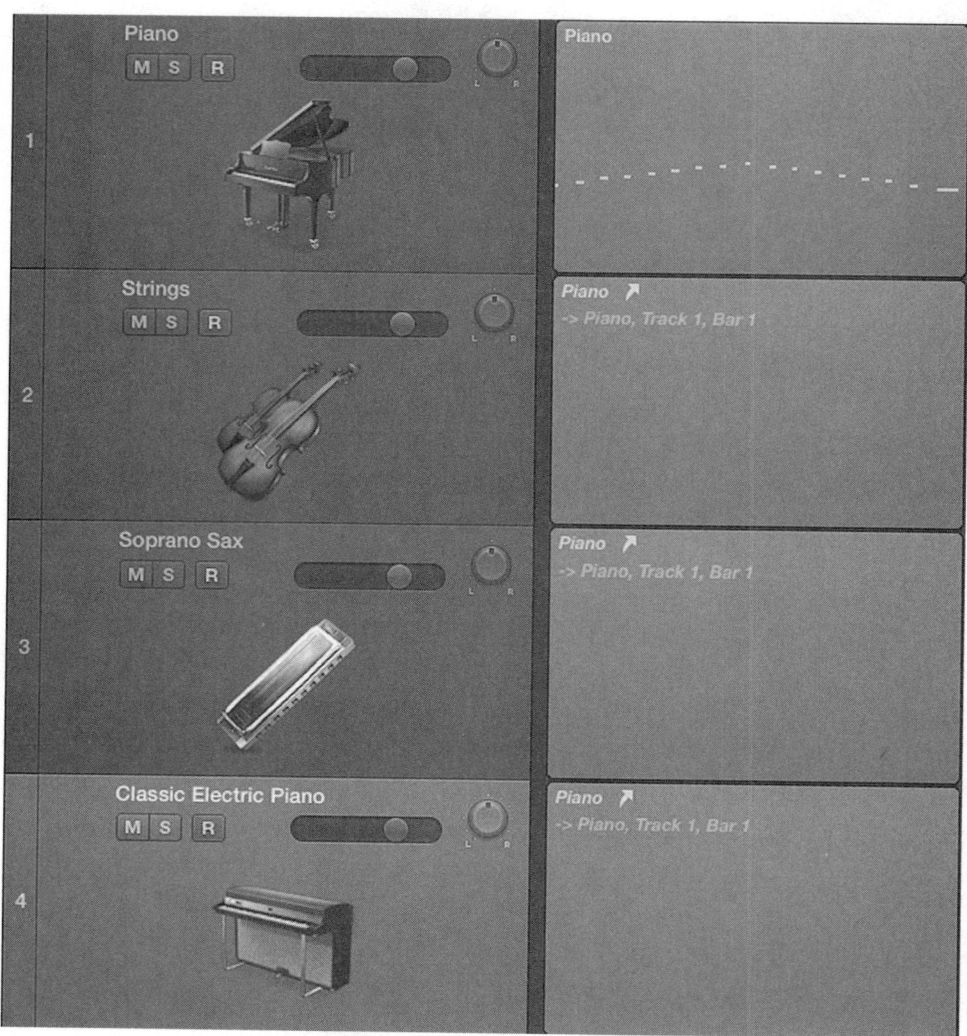

▶ **FIG. 4.11**

Notice that only the first track selected prior to recording contains MIDI data. The other tracks use aliases. Essentially, an alias is an object that points to, or uses, another object's data. In other words, each track that is using an alias is referencing MIDI data from another track. If the data changes on the track that contains the MIDI data, all of the other alias tracks will reference that newly updated MIDI data. Aliases are useful when creating layered instruments because they allow you to quickly create large orchestral passages while only writing one piece of MIDI data. The MIDI data will propagate to all of the other instruments through the alias.

It is also possible to directly copy MIDI data to another track rather than creating an alias to the original MIDI data. This is helpful if you would like to have layered instruments that do not update from the original MIDI data. In other words, each MIDI track will be autonomous from one another.

Select the software instrument track that contains the original MIDI data (for reference, track 1 from the previous screenshot contains the MIDI data).

Select the MIDI region on the Tracks area and choose Region > Repeat Regions (Command–R).

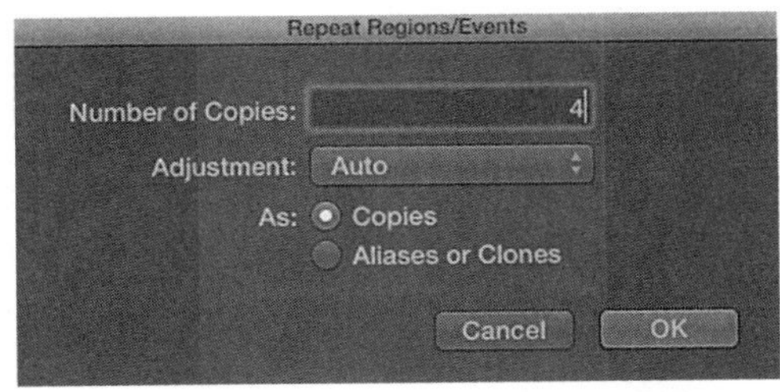

▶ FIG. 4.12

Choose four copies and click OK.

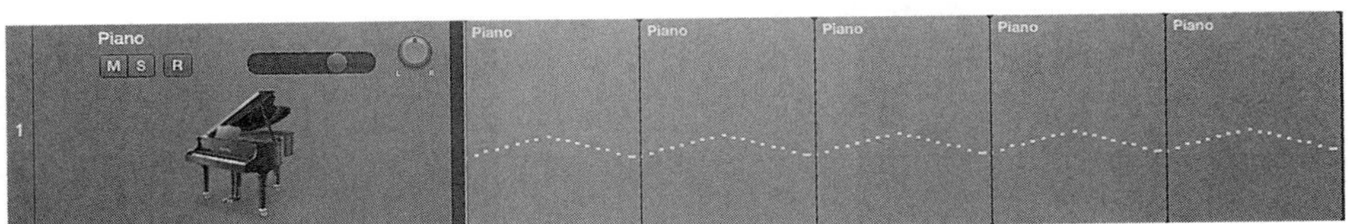

▶ FIG. 4.13

Four copies of the original MIDI data are created. It is important to note that these new MIDI regions are copies of the original, not aliases or clones. This means that each copy can be edited individually. This is helpful for creating musical passages that are similar to the original MIDI data but can contain differences that are specific to each instrument.

PROGRAMMING MIDI REGIONS

MIDI passages can be directly recorded into a sequencer much like audio is recorded in a digital audio workstation. This is one of the most common input methods for MIDI data. Most musicians and composers who work with MIDI likely do not think they are programmers, but in reality they are. One of the most powerful aspects of MIDI is the ability to program a musical passage without having to perform in real time. This allows musicians and composers to be musically productive in environments where the may not have access to a recording studio or a MIDI controller.

To get started, we'll need to create a blank MIDI region on a software instrument track in the Tracks area. Select the Pencil tool from the left-click tool menu. Click on bar 1 of a software instrument track to create a blank MIDI region.

Drag the MIDI region from the lower right corner to stretch the region length to two bars.

▶ **FIG. 4.14**

Select the MIDI region and choose Window > Open Piano Roll from the global menu bar. This Piano Roll editor will open. This editor can also be opened by key command (Command–4).

Once the Piano Roll editor opens in a new window, you'll see that it is empty. You now have an empty canvas to begin creating musical ideas.

Choose the Pencil tool from the Piano Roll's left-click tool menu.

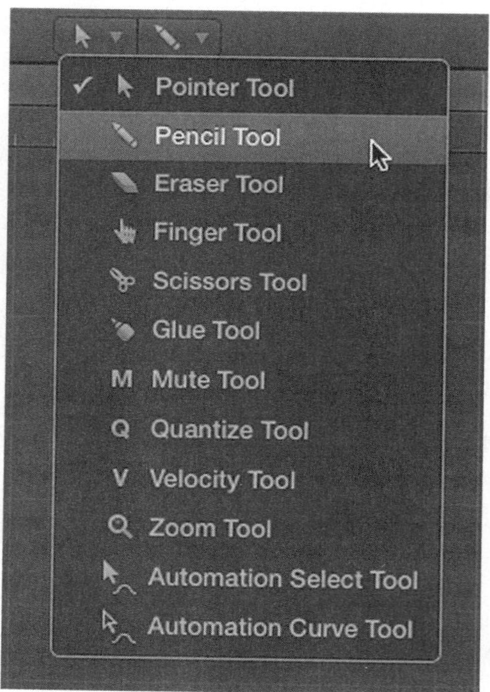

▶ **FIG. 4.15**

To being inputting MIDI data, simply click on the desired note. A note guide is available on the left side of the Piano Roll editor in the form of a piano that denotes octaves.

It is possible to change note lengths by dragging from the lower right corner of the MIDI note after is has been entered into the Piano Roll editor. Logic Pro

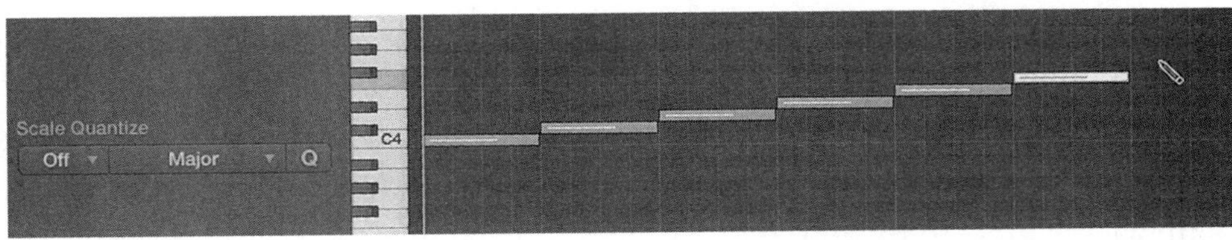

▶ FIG. 4.16

X will remember the last length that you change and will make that the new default note entry length.

CREATING DRUM SETS IN CYCLE RECORD MODE

Drum set recording is often challenging for musicians who do not physically play the drums or who do not have access to a drum set. MIDI drums sets can be programmed manually with the pencil tool or recorded in cycle record mode. This allows you to record a different component of the drum set with each pass—essentially, building a drum set piece by piece. MIDI drum sets have become extremely common in professional projects and can be heard in many facets of the music industry.

Create a new software instrument in your Logic Pro X project. Mute all other tracks in the project.

Tip: It is possible to mute or solo multiple tracks by dragging up or down across the track headers in Logic Pro X. Conversely, it is possible to disable muting or soloing on multiple tracks by holding down the option key while pressing on a mute or solo button on the track header.

Name the newly created track Drum Cycle. Select track 5 and press the Library button in the control bar and choose Legacy > Logic > 04 > Drums & Percussion > 02 Electronic Drum Kits > Roland TR-808 Kit. The software instrument track will be populated with all of the necessary components to reproduce the desired sound: Channel EQ, Compressor, and the EXS24 software instrument.

There is likely a cycle region area set up beginning at bar 1 and ending at the beginning of bar 5. To turn on cycle mode, press the C key. If a cycle region is not present, drag left to right in the bar ruler to create a cycle region. At this point a 4-bar cycle should be present. Cycle mode is enabled when the cycle region is highlighted green in the bar ruler.

When recording drums in cycle mode, the key concept is to record one aspect of the drum set on each pass of the cycle. In fact, the drum set components to not need to be recorded in a particular sequence.

Position the play head at the beginning of the project. Press the record button in the control bar to begin recording. With each pass of the cycle record a different aspect of the drum set.

Note: MIDI drum sets are programmed to utilize a specific octave on the MIDI controller. This is usually octave 0.

When you are satisfied with your recording, preview your newly created drum set region.

Depending on your keyboard performance skills, you may or may not have recorded the performance with proper metronomic timing. Fortunately, it is somewhat simple to fix tempo fluctuations during performance. Since MIDI is just data, it can be manipulated in many ways, including quantizing the performance. Quantizing is the process of taking a MIDI region and snapping the MIDI notes to the closest division of a beat (1/8, 1/16, 1/32, 1/64, etc.). Different quantizing settings are more appropriate in certain situations. For example, if a drum region utilizes a double-time snare pattern, it would likely be more appropriate to quantize to a 1/32 note or a 1/64 note.

Select the drum set region that you recorded. A black bar is present at the top of a region when selected.

Navigate to the region parameter box in the upper left corner of Logic Pro X. It will display the name of the preset used, in this case, the Roland TR-808 Kit.

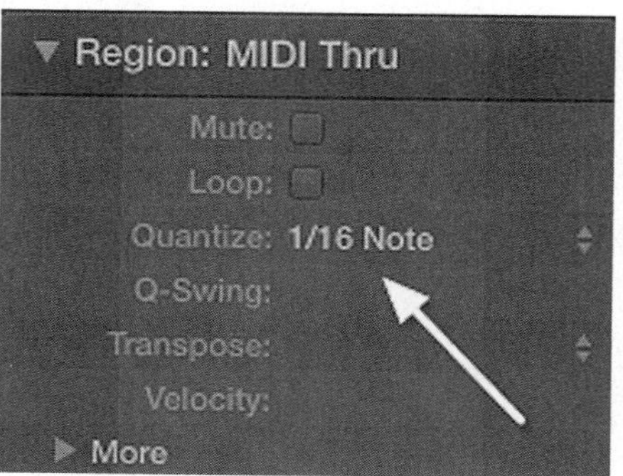

▶ **FIG. 4.17**

Select the Quantize pop-up menu and choose 1/16. Notice the MIDI notes in your region shift ever so slightly in one direction or another. Logic Pro X is re-aligning the MIDI notes to play back in sync with the selected quantizing division and the tempo that you chose in the control bar. Experiment with different quantize settings to experience how the various quantize settings affect your MIDI region.

Logic Pro X possess quantization settings that strictly snap to the chosen beat division and quantization settings that attempt to emulate a looser feel. This is all done in an attempt to make the music sound more human.

Select the Quantize pop-up menu and choose the 1/16 Swing A setting. Notice that the performance plays slightly behind the beat, similar to the feel of a jazz performance.

Quantizing a MIDI region is a great way to ensure that the MIDI region plays appropriately, but sometimes it is helpful to create default quantization settings so that all newly created MIDI regions will adhere to a particular quantization setting. This can be assigned at the global level so that all newly recorded MIDI data will be quantized when recorded.

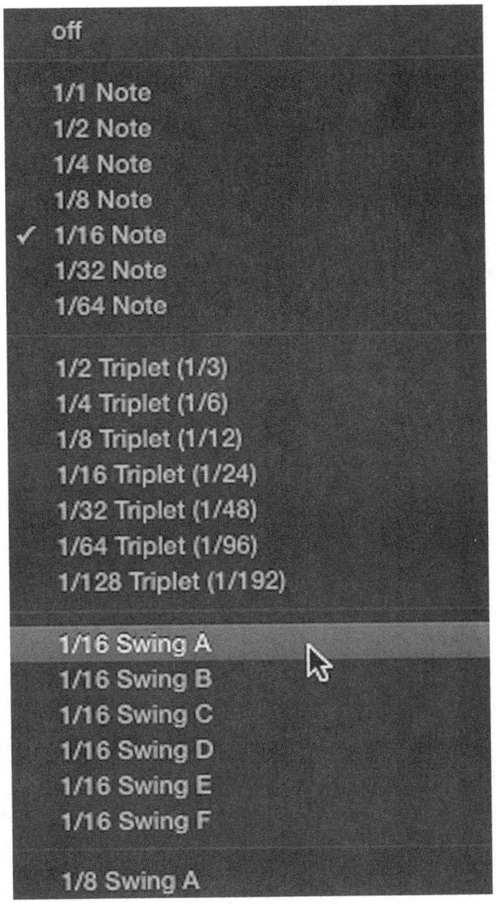

off
1/1 Note
1/2 Note
1/4 Note
1/8 Note
✓ 1/16 Note
1/32 Note
1/64 Note
1/2 Triplet (1/3)
1/4 Triplet (1/6)
1/8 Triplet (1/12)
1/16 Triplet (1/24)
1/32 Triplet (1/48)
1/64 Triplet (1/96)
1/128 Triplet (1/192)
1/16 Swing A
1/16 Swing B
1/16 Swing C
1/16 Swing D
1/16 Swing E
1/16 Swing F
1/8 Swing A

▶ **FIG. 4.18**

Note: MIDI data can still be individually quantized at the region level despite global quantization settings.

Delete any MIDI information that exists on the Roland TR-808 kit track. Select any area in the gray background of the Tracks area. Choose 1/16 from the quantize pop up menu in the inspector. A global quantization has now been set. Any MIDI data recorded will use this quantization level.

Global quantization levels can be extremely helpful when recording MIDI, but they lock the performance recording into a specified quantization level. 1/16 may work perfectly well for a performance that does not incorporate performance elements that are faster than a sixteenth note. This may not always be true throughout the project. For example, a MIDI drum set may include musical elements such as a snare that never play faster than a sixteenth note. However, the same drum set performance may include cymbal with 1/32 note passages. In a case such as this, it would be helpful to record the varying drum set elements on different tracks. Once isolated, each MIDI region can be individually quantized at the region level to ensure that the proper quantization setting is used.

SEPARATING MIDI REGIONS BY NOTE PITCH

Recording in cycle mode is a wonderful way to build drum sets pass by pass. Typically, the drum set is recorded on the same track, which limits the available sounds to those in the software instrument used to record the drum set unless the data is later moved to another software instrument track. However, this approach does not provide the flexibility to use the snare sound from one software instrument and the kick sound from another instrument. Multiple sounds cannot be used because the MIDI data are nested together in a single MIDI region. Separating MIDI note messages into new MIDI regions will allow you to mix and match drum set sounds from varying software instruments.

Navigate to the Apple Loops area in the control bar. Select the All Drums button in the Loop browser.

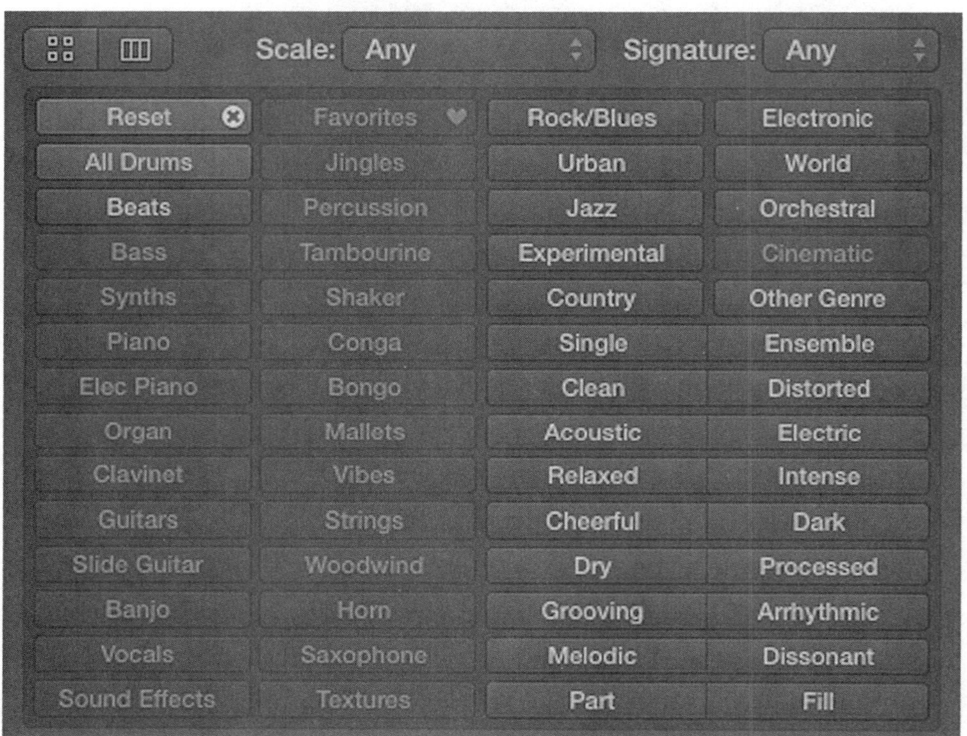

▶ FIG. 4.19

Choose 2-Step Balancing Beat 01 from the search results in the bottom pane of the Loop browser. Drag the loop into the Tracks area. The Tracks area will create a new track with the relevant software instrument and plugins required for playback.

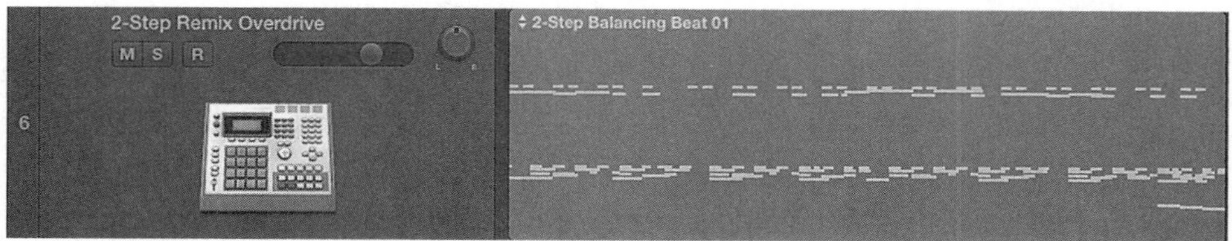

▶ FIG. 4.20

The MIDI region that was created contains quite a bit of MIDI data. Each piece of MIDI data is associated with a particular MIDI note message. Each note voice range can be separated onto an individual track in a separate MIDI region.

Select the 2-Step Balancing Beat 01 MIDI region and choose Edit > Separate MIDI Events > By Note Pitch from the Tracks area's local menu bar.

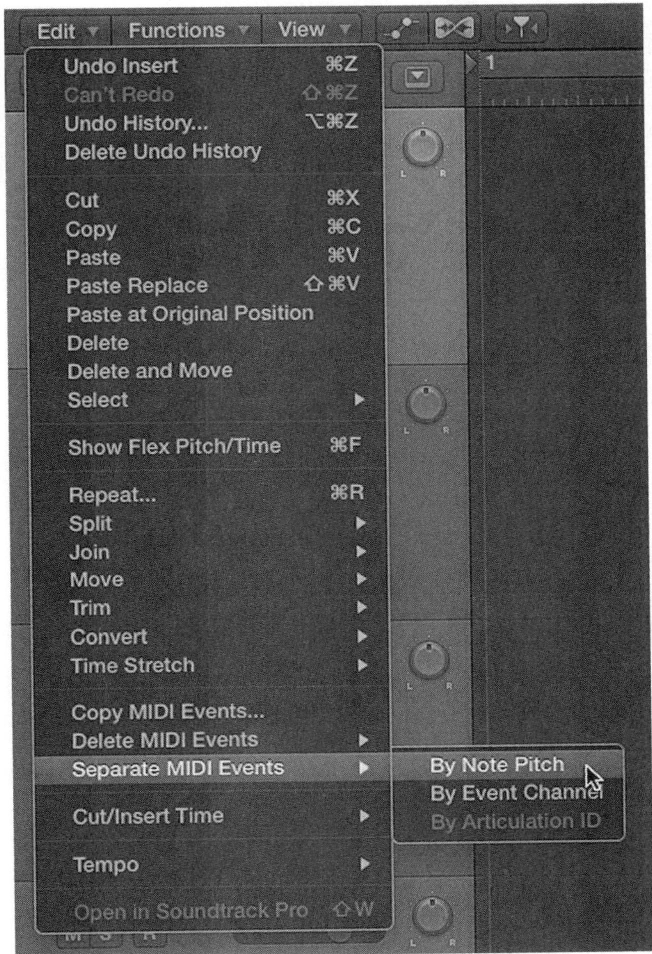

▶ FIG. 4.21

Logic Pro X will separate the MIDI data by note pitch and create new tracks and regions for each note pitch. This results in each portion of the drum being isolated onto separate tracks. Since the MIDI data has been isolated, it can be copied to a nonpercussion track for textural enhancement, as well. This results in harmonic doubling of rhythmic elements. Portions of the drum set that do not need to be isolated can be merged together again to optimize track space in the Tracks area. Selected specific regions can be done by holding the Shift key while selecting regions—in this case, tracks 7, 9, 15, and 20.

Choose Edit > Join > Regions from the Tracks area's local menu bar.

The MIDI regions are now merged back into one MIDI region, with the exception of the MIDI regions that were deselected. The deselected MIDI regions

▶ **FIG. 4.22**

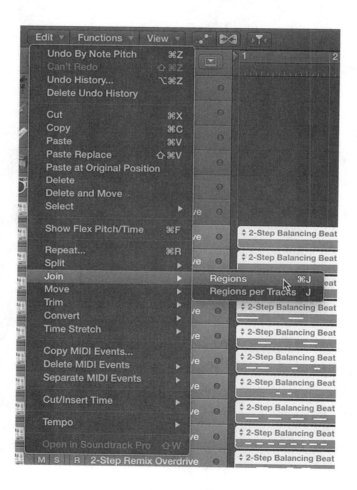

▶ **FIG. 4.23**

can easily be copied to another software instrument track for rhythmic layering or can be moved entirely to another track to change the software instrument used for playback.

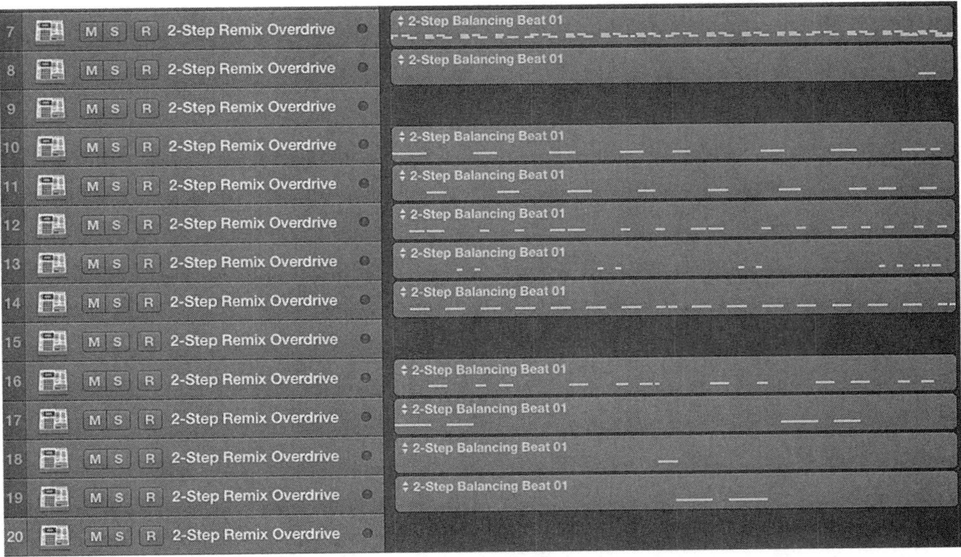

▶ FIG. 4.24

HUMANIZING MIDI PLAYBACK

MIDI is an extremely flexible music-making tool, but programmed MIDI performances sometimes leave much to be desired when compared to live performances. While there are several factors that contribute to this, the main factor is humanistic feel. MIDI data is performed based on a timing grid that is extremely precise, down to 1/3840 of a bar of music. Humans are nowhere near as accurate as computers. These imperfections contribute to the overall experience of music. Some of the best "mistakes" create extremely powerful musical passages.

Logic Pro X possesses deeply powerful MIDI creation and editing tools. One of those tools, the Transform window, can humanize a MIDI region in order to make MIDI playback more human-like.

Choose File > New from Logic Pro X's global menu bar. If prompted, save and close the currently open project.

Create four software instrument tracks. Select track 1 and navigate to the Apple Loops area in the control bar. Select All Drums and choose the "Beachside Drumset 01" loop. When you have located the loop, drag the loop to bar 1 of track 1.

▶ FIG. 4.25

Drag left to right in the upper part of the bar ruler to create a cycle region beginning and ending at the beginning of bar 3. This can also be accomplished by typing the bar number in the control bar.

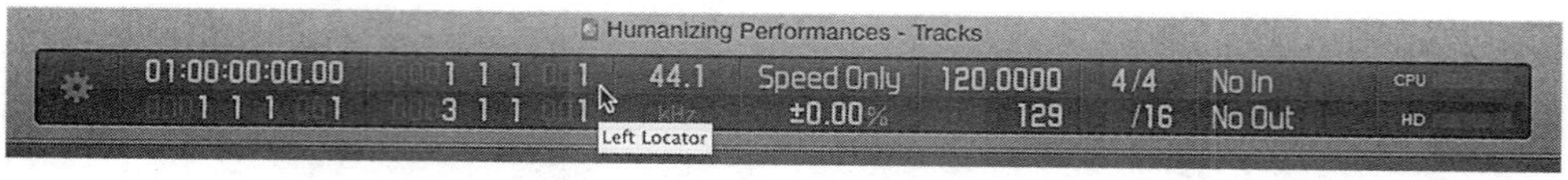

▶ **FIG. 4.26**

Change the tempo in the control bar from 120 beats per minute to 90 beats per minute.

Select the MIDI region and choose Window > Open Piano Roll. The Piano Roll MIDI editor will open in a new window and display the contents of the Beachside Drumset 01 MIDI region.

The drum set region is a relatively simplistic drum loop made up of kick drum, rim shot, and high hat cymbal sounds. The region can be divided into two sections: tempo anchor elements and ornamentation. In the case of this region, the kick and rim shot sounds act as metronomic anchors, while the high hat provides ornamentation. This drum loop sounds somewhat stiff because the MIDI data snaps tightly to the time grid in Logic Pro X.

The rigidity of the drum loop can be reduced by slightly altering the placement of the MIDI data as is relates to the time grid. As much as we may wish, humans are certainly not perfect and cannot play music with the same precision of a metronomic time grid. In order for our MIDI performances to sound as human as possible, it is important to alter the MIDI data so that is does not sound so rigidly perfect.

In the Piano Roll editor, select the high hat cymbal sound by selecting the related note on the piano at the left side of the window. All of the MIDI notes in the row will be selected. With the MIDI notes selected, choose Functions > MIDI Transform > Humanize.

▶ **FIG. 4.27**

The Transform window will open with the Humanize preset initialized. The Humanize window provides excellent tools for randomizing velocity, note length, and note position for a grouping of selected MIDI data. By default, the

Humanize preset will randomize note position by plus or minus 10 ticks, randomize velocity (how hard a note is hit) by plus or minus 10 MIDI values (scale of 0–127), and randomize note length by plus or minus 10 ticks. (One tick is equal to 1/3840 of a bar.) As you can imagine, these randomizations will be subtle, but will potentially add humanistic playback characteristics to the MIDI performance.

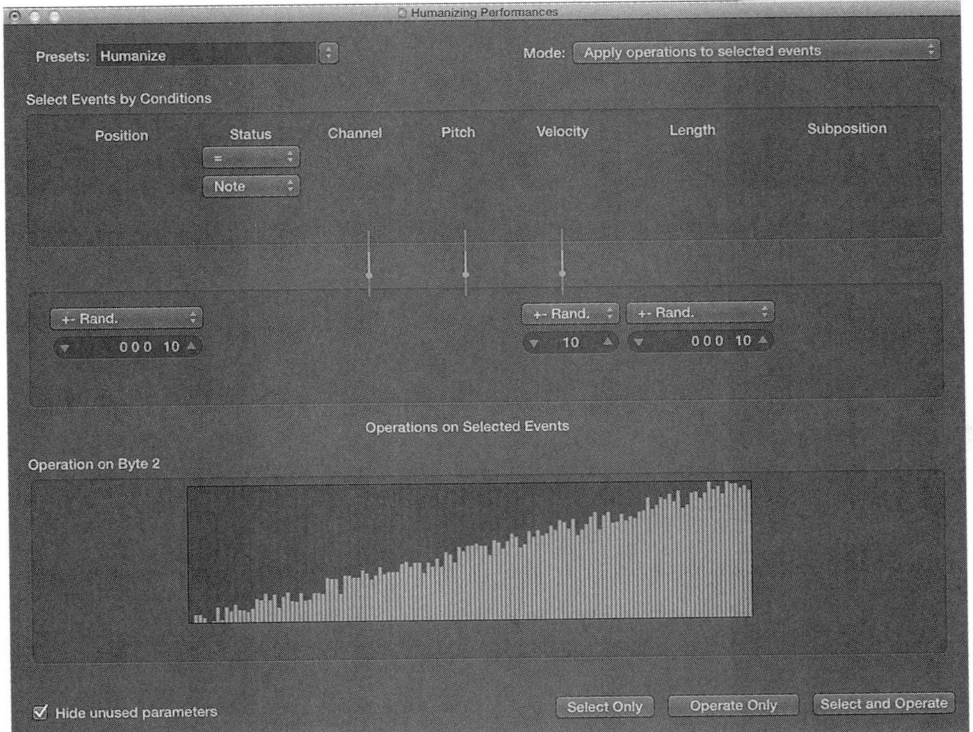

▶ FIG. 4.28

At the bottom of the Transform window there are three buttons: Select Only, Operate Only, and Select and Operate. The functionality of each button is as follows:

- Select Only: Select all of the MIDI notes in the MIDI region that is present in the Piano Roll editor.
- Operate Only: Perform the humanizing randomizations on only the notes that are selected in the Piano Roll editor.
- Selecta and Operate: All MIDI notes present in the Piano Roll editor will be selected and subject to the randomizations of the Transform window's Humanize preset.

Ensuring that only the high hat cymbal notes are selected in the Piano Roll editor, press the Operate Only button in the Transform window. Notice that only the selected MIDI notes in the Piano Roll editor are affected by the Humanize present.

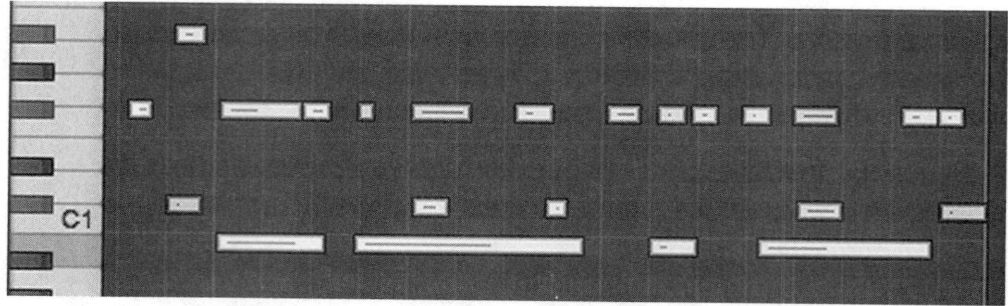

▶ **FIG. 4.29**

The changes to the original MIDI data are slight but can make the difference between a drum set that sounds programmed and a drum set that sounds more lifelike. Notice that only the high hat cymbal sounds were altered. This choice was deliberate because the kick drum and rim shot sounds provide a solid tempo foundation that the variations of the high hat cymbal float upon. The variations in the high hat cymbal would not be as clear without a frame of reference that is created by the unwavering tempo set forth by the kick drum and rim shot.

CHAPTER 5

TO LOOP OR NOT TO LOOP—AN EXPLORATION OF LOOPS, BEDS, AND FOLEY

For me, it's a challenge that you have to approach by what you are actually seeing on the screen, what you are actually hearing, and trying to push yourself as a musician to not just rewrite or imitate yourself. You have to constantly question yourself and be willing to try new things out.

—Steve Horowitz

MUSICIANS AND COMPOSERS are continually exploring new and innovative ways to add character to the music they create for film and television. This approach can take many forms including new and unexpected melodic and harmonic elements, interesting rhythmic elements, and sound effects. When music was first married to film it was common to have music performed in front of the moving picture in a theater. In an attempt to make the performance more exciting, sound effects were added to augment the experience of the theater-going public. The live performance aspect of the film experience was unique, and many people would visit the theater multiple times to see how the experience would change from one performance to the next.

The role and responsibility of the composer has become significantly more complex as the profession matured. It is common to have multiple teams of musicians working on a film project. A unique subset of composers, sound designers, copyists, and editors work tirelessly to shape music that will create the perfect atmosphere for a film. While the core principle has largely remained the same, there are new tools available that aid musicians who are creating music for film, television, and other mediums.

Musical loops have existed for quite a while in music. They have taken the form of repetitive percussion elements in rhythm and blues compositions and extend to musical samples that are used in popular music and hip hop. Essentially, a musical loop is a symmetrical piece of musical content. Imagine a 4-bar drum sequence that can be played consecutively multiple times and sound as if it is a continuous performance because the starting and end points seamlessly mesh. While any instrument can be used to create a loop, drum sets are commonly used for loop content. There are some who believe that musical loops are a new phenomenon, a byproduct of the digital age, and have diminished the level of musicality within various genres of music. While musical loops are popular and may have increased in popularity due to the increased use of digital audio workstations, it is not necessarily accurate to say loops have diminished the quality of music. In fact, repetition is one of the core principles of music—state a theme, develop the theme, and restate the theme.

We wouldn't have the 8- and 12-bar blues forms if we didn't use loops. We wouldn't have call-and-response improvisation if the notion of repetition and imitation did not exist. It is arguable to say that we wouldn't have music, as we know it today, without utilizing some aspect of looping in composition. Nearly every style of music uses loops in one way or another. Looping has been deeply embedded in the fabric of our musical culture for some time.

The purpose of this chapter is to explore loop creation in Logic Pro X. Through the loop-creation process you will be able to determine the most appropriate type of loop to create for your musical project. The two most common loop types are audio loops and MIDI loops, often referred to as software instrument loops in the Logic Pro X user community. Both loop types have distinct strengths that will enable you to create engaging musical content for your musical project.

THE LOOP BROWSER REVISITED

Like many other digital audio workstations, Logic Pro X is an extremely flexible music creation tool for film and television because it contains thousands of loops, sound effects, and music beds that are freely available for use in professional projects. It is likely that you have heard a musical project created with loops in film, major television shows and specials, and popular music. Artists such as Usher, Rihanna, Radiohead, and Jay-Z have used loops in Top 40 musical projects. Loops are often used as base content for musical composition, and it is common to use a loop as a drone, or background texture, in a professional project. These drones help create a "mood" that is representative of the film scene. For example, a dirge-like guitar loop may be used as the thematic base of a composition to convey sadness in a film or television scene. The standard audio content that is included with Logic Pro X and other applications is of high quality, but the real benefit is that these applications can be extended with user-created audio content, as well as audio content that is purchased from a third-party vendor.

Just as in cultivating a musical idea, there are no set rules for employing loops. However, loops can be particularly beneficial for creating static musical elements that are used as musical building blocks. Rhythm section elements such as bass, harmonic, and percussion instruments are typically used when employing loops. However, loops are not limited to rhythm section elements. It is common to loops brass, woodwind, and brass elements as well. Think of a loop as being more than a symmetrical pattern; they are musical building blocks that can add great texture and presence to an already fantastic piece of music.

To get started viewing and working with loops, open Logic Pro X and create a new project. In this case, we'll create a project with eight software instrument tracks. Select the first track and navigate to the Apple Loops area.

The Loop browser can display a large amount of data. It is important to understand the filters that are available to focus search to ensure that search results are relevant.

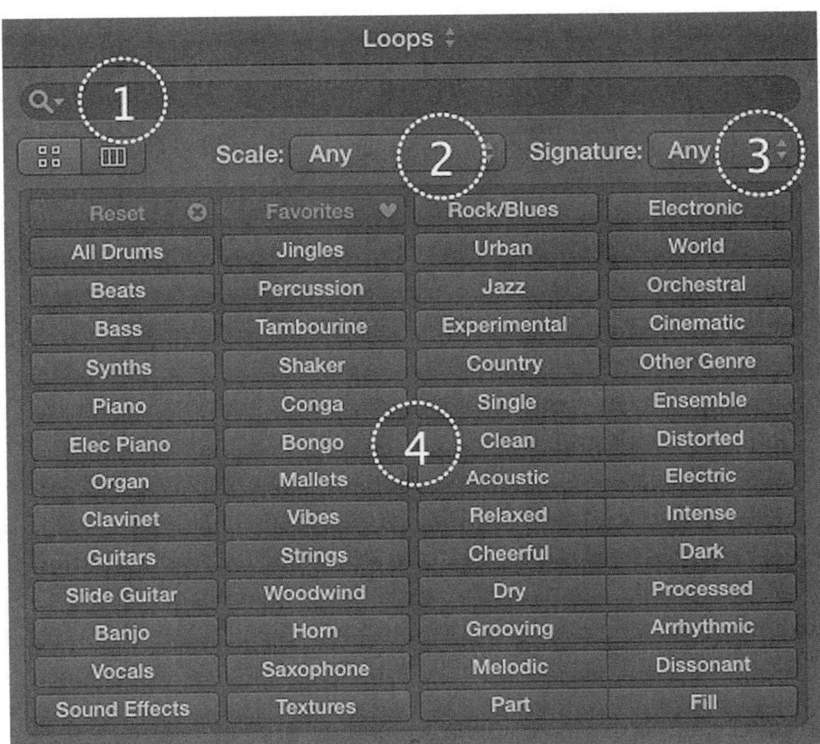

▶ **FIG. 5.1**

1. Search: Loops, sound effects, and beds can be searched for via keywords that are associated with the audio content. The keywords are associated through metadata that is attached to the audio content in the tagging process.
2. Scale: Search results can be limited to scales that are major, minor, neither, or good for both. Depending on where the loop or bed starts melodically, it may be possible for the loop to be used in a major tonality or a relative minor tonality.
3. Signature: Loops can be searched for by key signature. Common time, or 4/4, is the default search parameter; however, there are other various time signatures available such as 7/8 and 9/8. The time signature specifies how many beats are present in a bar of music and what type of note division will equal 1 beat. For example, the 4/4 time signature contains 4 beats in every measure and every quarter note will be given

1 beat. The 7/8 time signature contains 7 beats of music in every measure and each eighth note will be given 1 beat.

4. Button View: The loop browser possesses several ways to search for loop content for use in your musical projects. If you would like to limit your search to jazz percussion, simply press the jazz button and the percussion button to limit your search.

Search for a loop by selecting the following parameters in the music view: Acoustic, Grooving, and Guitars.

▶ **FIG. 5.2**

Upon selecting the search parameters, search results will appear in the lower portion of the loop browser. There is quite a bit of helpful information that is provided in the search results: tempo, key signature, total number of beats in the loop, search relevance, and favorites. You can quickly determine if the loop meets the criteria of your project and save the loop as a favorite for quick access in the future.

Tempo is extremely important when working with projects that are meant to sync with moving objects in a film. On-screen elements often dictate the tempo of your project because they rhythmically move across the viewing stage. Tempo can be determined by manually with a watch by counting the perceived tempo of moving objects. For example, a spinning windmill spins in tempo. A group of children walking in lockstep down a school hallway walk in tempo. There are also a number of applications available to help your determine tempo by tapping an indicator in the application. This is often referred to as "tap tempo." There are a number of free and paid applications available in Apple's iTunes music store. Many of the applications can be purchased for iPhone and iPad mobile devices. One stellar example is Tap/Tempo by Benjamin Jaeger.

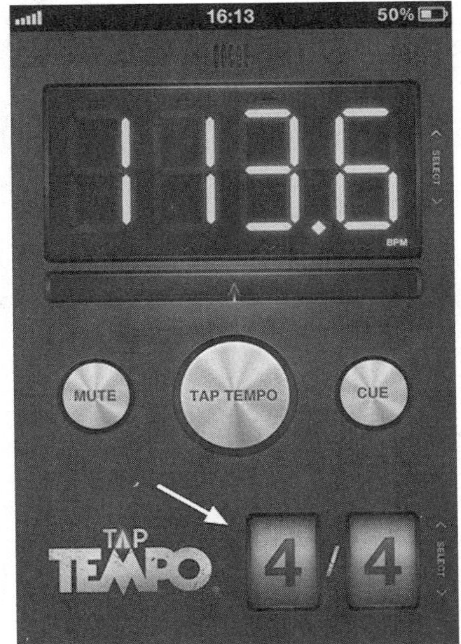

▶ **FIG. 5.3**

Tap/Tempo allows you to tap the tempo you observe while watching on-screen elements move across the stage by simply tapping the "Tap Tempo" button. If you have a particular metronomic meter setting in mind such as 6/8 or 7/4, this can be changed in the lower right corner of the application. Sadly, tempo is often not given the importance it deserves when writing musical passages in general. The tempo of a composition is arguably as important as harmony and orchestration. Think of tempo as another character in the musical story—all of the elements must work together to tell the tale.

Loops are extremely flexible because they often have the ability to adjust to tonality and tempo changes. For example, if a project is set in the key of C Major with a tempo of 120 beats per minute and a desired loop was recorded in D Major at a tempo of 140 beats per minute, Logic Pro X will be able to automatically adjust the loop to the tonality and tempo of the project. If the relationship between the original tempo and key is somewhat close, the end result will be undetectable. You may notice an audio artifact, or noticeable distortion of audio, the farther away you move from the original key and tempo of the loop. Tempo and harmonic adjustment provide a great amount of flexibility when working with film and television projects because on-screen elements may vary slightly between scenes, requiring slightly different tempo settings.

In regard to Logic Pro X, there are two types of Apple loops: blue Apple loops (audio loops) and green Apple loops (Software Instrument loops), which are hybrid audio/MIDI loops. Software instrument loops can be placed on a software instrument track or on an audio track. If they are placed on a software

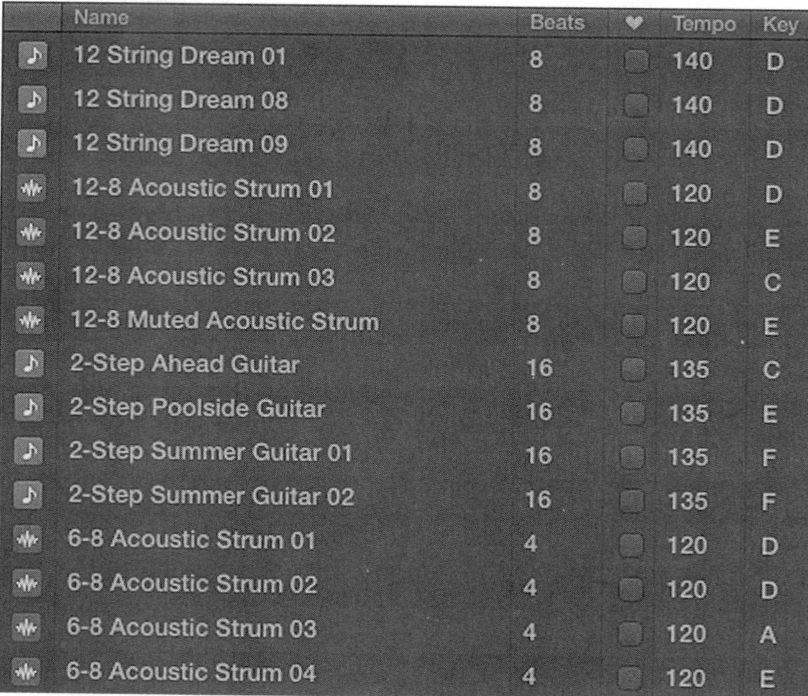

	Name	Beats	♥	Tempo	Key
	12 String Dream 01	8		140	D
	12 String Dream 08	8		140	D
	12 String Dream 09	8		140	D
	12-8 Acoustic Strum 01	8		120	D
	12-8 Acoustic Strum 02	8		120	E
	12-8 Acoustic Strum 03	8		120	C
	12-8 Muted Acoustic Strum	8		120	E
	2-Step Ahead Guitar	16		135	C
	2-Step Poolside Guitar	16		135	E
	2-Step Summer Guitar 01	16		135	F
	2-Step Summer Guitar 02	16		135	F
	6-8 Acoustic Strum 01	4		120	D
	6-8 Acoustic Strum 02	4		120	D
	6-8 Acoustic Strum 03	4		120	A
	6-8 Acoustic Strum 04	4		120	E

▶ **FIG. 5.4**

instrument track, the relevant software instrument and DSP plugins will load. The loop will be played back using MIDI data. If the software instrument loop is placed on an audio track, a waveform will be used for playback. MIDI use has become increasingly popular with composers for film and television.

Drag 12 String Dream 08 to the first software instrument track in your project.

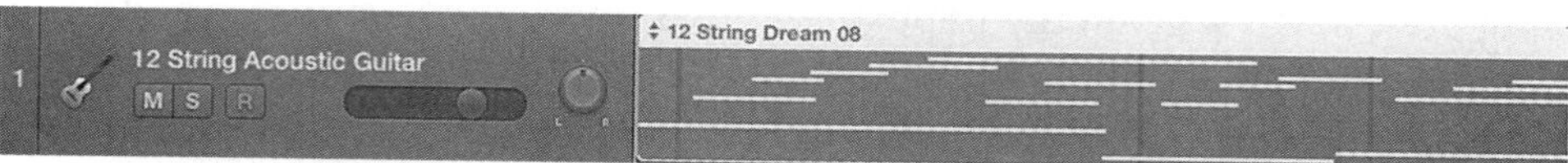

▶ **FIG. 5.5**

The appropriate software instrument and DSP plugins required to produce the Apple loop are loaded on the track and channel strip. Start playback to preview the loop you placed on the software instrument track in the Tracks area.

Create a new audio track by pressing the new tracks button above the first software instrument track. Rearrange the audio track so that is resides directly below the software instrument track. Drag 12 String Dream 08 loop from the Loop browser to the newly created audio track underneath the software instrument track. Notice that the loop is converted into a waveform, rather than MIDI data.

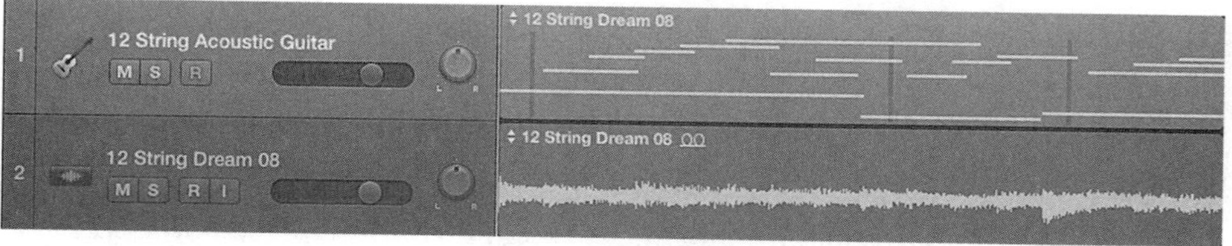

▶ **FIG. 5.6**

Start playback and listen for any similarities or differences in the two tracks. You will notice that the two tracks sound identical. The only difference is that one loop is played back through a software instrument track and the other loop is played back through an audio track.

In most cases, using a software instrument loop provides more flexibility than an audio loop. This is because software instrument loops can be easily manipulated and edited because they are essentially MIDI loops that are played back in real time by a software instrument. Nearly every aspect of the performance can be edited including pitch, rhythm, velocity, and harmonic structure. Audio loops cannot be edited in the same manner but do offer some benefit over software instrument loops.

Audio loops are transportable between digital audio workstations. If you would like to share audio files with someone who does not possess the software instrument used to create the audio loop, you are able to share an audio loop in various formats such as WAV, AIFF, CAF, AAC, and MP3. Higher quality PCM-based audio files are preferred over compressed audio formats. Audio files also preserve CPU usage in large projects. It is much easier for a digital audio workstation to stream audio from a hard drive than it is to render a software instrument and the DSP plugins required to create the desired sound in real time. CPU preservation can quickly become a necessity when working with a film or television project that is utilizing numerous software instruments. In this case, audio loops will free necessary processing power.

MIDI loops can be easily converted into an audio loop within Logic Pro X. This is accomplished through the bounce in place feature. To convert a MIDI loop into an audio loop, right-click on a MIDI region in the Arrange area.

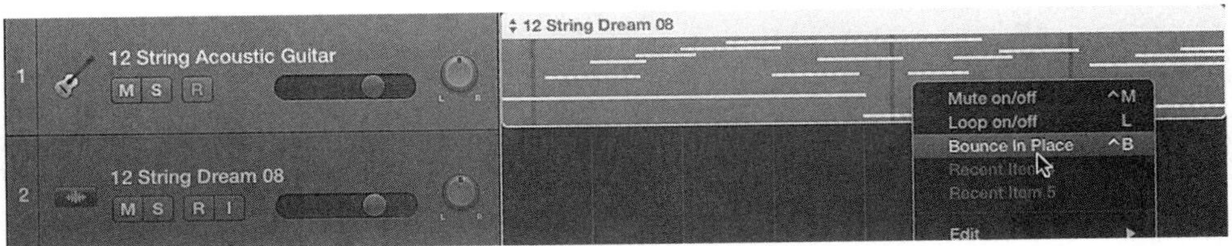

▶ FIG. 5.7

You are presented with several options in the contextual menu. Choose Bounce In Place.

By default, Logic Pro X will bounce, or convert, the MIDI loop into an audio loop on a separate track and mute the original MIDI loop. You can choose to leave the original MIDI loop untouched or delete it entirely when the bounce process has been completed. If you are using this process to free CPU cycles, you will likely want to delete the original software instrument track from the project once the bounce process has been completed.

Note: Logic Pro X continues to allocate RAM to the software instrument track even if the track is not being used.

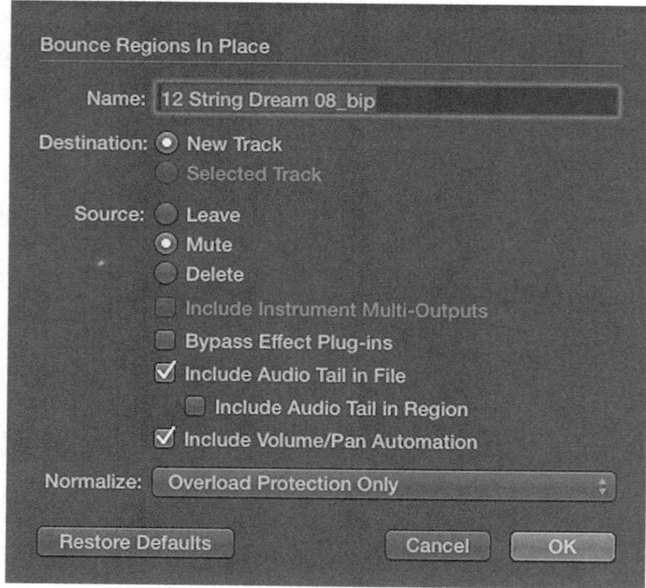

▶ FIG. 5.8

Once the bounce process has finished, the MIDI loop is converted into an audio loop and placed on a new track in the Tracks area. If using the default settings, the original MIDI loop will be muted and remain in the project. The loop name will be appended with "_bip" that signified it was bounced in place.

▶ FIG. 5.9

This loop can be shared with users who are using different digital audio workstations, such as Pro Tools, Nuendo, and Digital Performer.

Note: The newly created audio loop will be placed in the Audio Files folder within the project folder or package for convenient access.

CREATING AUDIO APPLE LOOPS

In recent years, many digital audio workstations have evolved to include robust sample libraries that represent myriad styles of musical building blocks. It is common for a modern sample library to include several thousand loops, sound beds, and pads for use in audio projects. These sound libraries are invaluable for musicians and composers who need to sketch a mockup project or quickly build a final project. The quality of sample libraries has increased dramatically, and many final audio, film and television projects include loops in some fashion. In fact, you will likely not notice that loops are being used because the quality of the parent library is so high. Loops have allowed single composers to create lush orchestral scores with minimal financial overheard. While many projects can be augmented by off-the-shelf loops, sound beds, and pads, it is advantageous to build a sample library that is specific to a particular project or representative of a personal sound. These libraries help to define the character of a film and television project and identify a musical personality that is representative of the composer or the project at hand. Again, musical loops are another character in the overall story of the musical accompaniment.

Apple loops are loops that have been created with the Apple Loops Utility. Loops created by this utility will adjust to tempo and key signature changes. Further, they are searchable through the loop browser in Logic Pro X. Searching is performed with the aid of metadata (data about data), which describes the type of loop that it is. Metadata is attached to the loop during the loop creation process in the Apple Loops Utility. Metadata directly relates to tagging functionality in the loop browser, which allows you to essentially group loops into categories. For example, loops of a similar sound or genre can be tagged into a category for quick reference while working on a project. Working in categories of sound will aid you in creating and developing the musical character of the composition. An Apple loop does not have to be a traditional loop in the sense that is possesses a symmetrical start and end point. The loop can be a sound bed, such as rolling waves or generic traffic noise.

Download and unzip the audio files for the Apple Loops Utility lesson from the companion website. Create a new audio track in Logic Pro X and drag the "Drum Track" audio file into the Tracks area.

To create an Apple loop, simply select the Drums Tracks loop in the Tracks area in Logic Pro X and choose Functions > Open in Apple Loops Utility from the Tracks area's local menu.

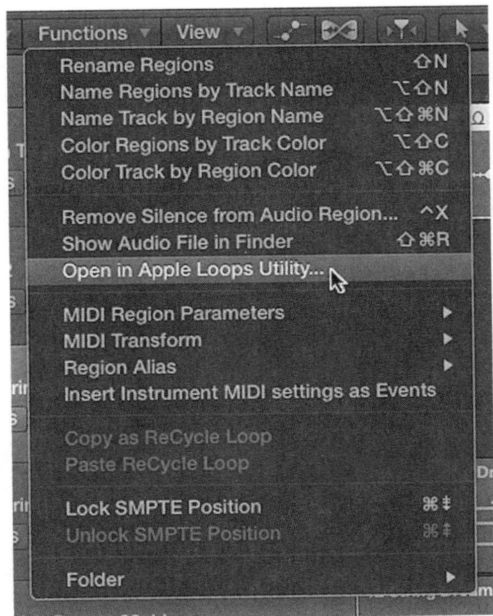

▶ FIG. 5.10

Once the Apple Loops Utility launches, you'll be presented with the main interface of the application. There are several sections available on the Tags tab of the Apple Loops Utility.

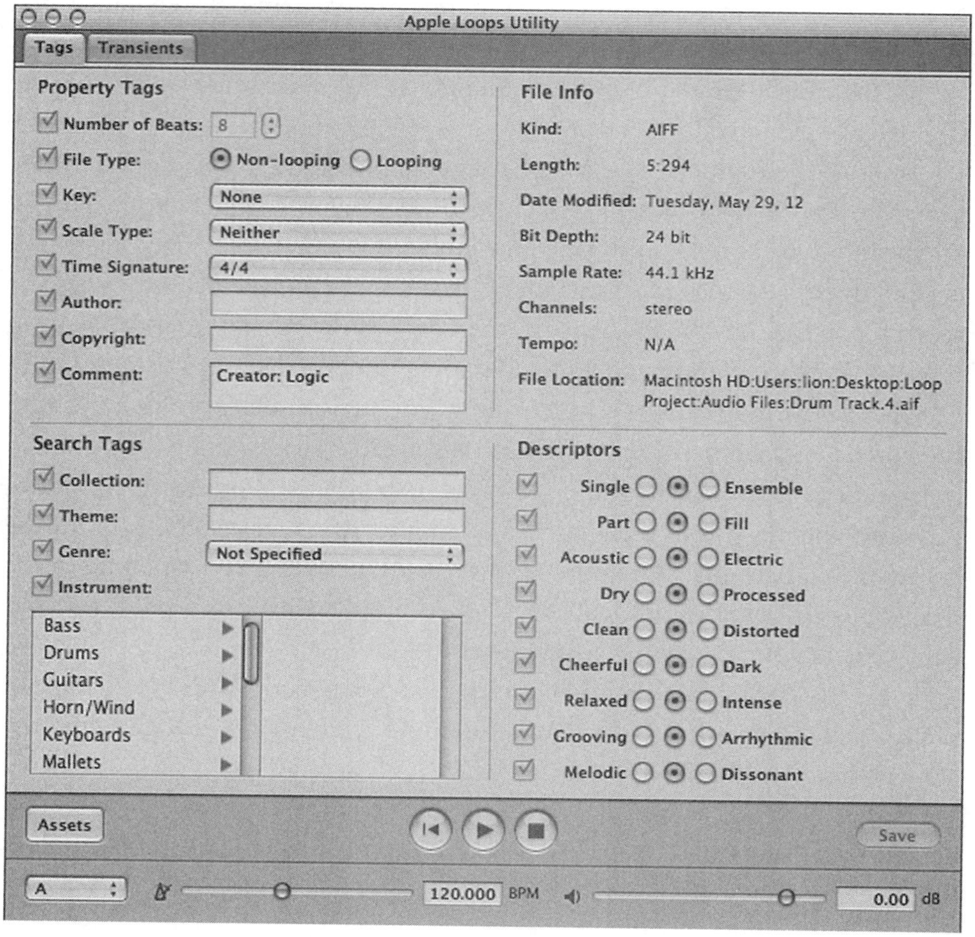

▶ FIG. 5.11

Property Tags—allows you to specify whether is file is looping or nonlooping, scale type (major, minor, both, neither), time signature, and author information.

Search Tags—allows you to provide a collection name, theme name, genre, and instrument type for the loop. For example, the loop can be provided a theme name for a particular film or television project.

File Info—provides detailed information about the audio file used for the loop, including kind, length, bit depth, sample rate, and length. Remember to use 48 kHz for audio files that are slated for film and television projects.

Descriptors—allows you to provide description tags to the loop. These descriptors correspond to search parameters in the loop browser's music view. The descriptor tags are particularly important when assigning categories to loops. Again, these categories can represent a sound or mood that can be used during a project.

The transients tab allows you to have greater control over how the loop will adjust to the tempo of the project. Musical project for film and television often require several tempo changes to sync the music to on-screen elements. Transients are used to map the audio file and ultimately facilitate a digital audio workstation's ability to adjust the tempo and tonality of a loop. Typically, transients relate to the most common amplitude changes, or peaks, in an audio file. The pulse, or beat, of an audio file aligns with the transient locations.

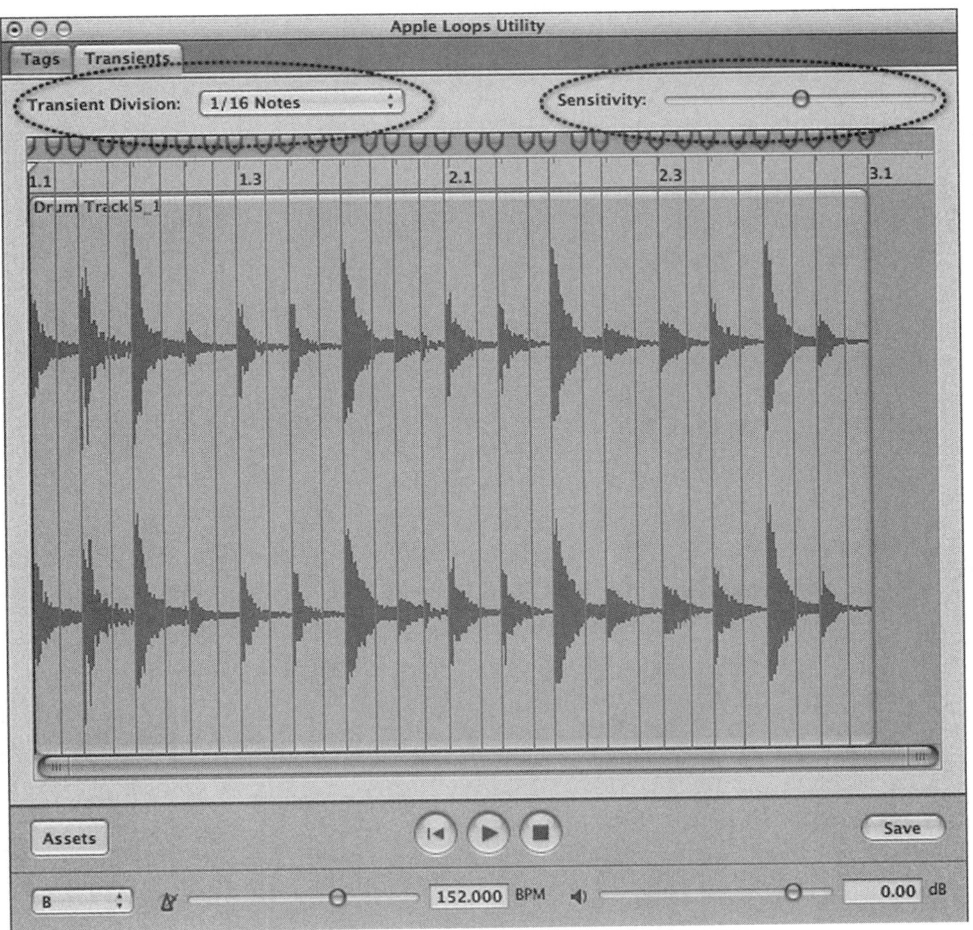

▶ **FIG. 5.12**

The Apple Loops Utility can adjust the number of transients that are added in the audio file by allowing you to choose the division of the beat they placed on—an 8th note, 16th note, and so on. There is no right or wrong choice in regard to the division setting used in this section. The rhythmic character of the loop will dictate the division you choose. For example, if the loop contains elements that are played at a 32nd note, it may be best to use a 32nd note division when adding transients.

There are times when transients occur at points in the audio file that are not necessarily a beat value. Transients are added based on the amplitude of the audio file. The Apple Loops Utility will consider points in the audio file with higher amplitude as transients. You can adjust transient detection sensitivity by dragging the sensitivity slider. Dragging right will increase the sensitivity of the transient detection.

Finally, there are times when transients are falsely detected and need to be removed. This typically happens when a transient is placed at a point that is not representative of higher amplitude. This added transient marker can cause problems when speeding up or slowing down the loop in an audio project.

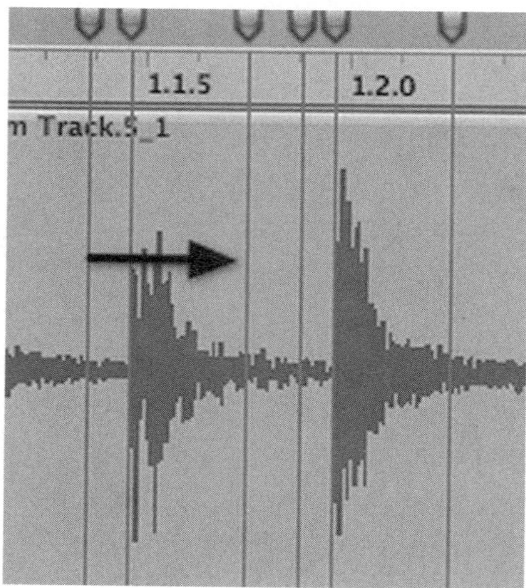

▶ FIG. 5.13

In order to remove the transient, simply select the transient marker in the beat ruler and press the delete key on your keyboard.

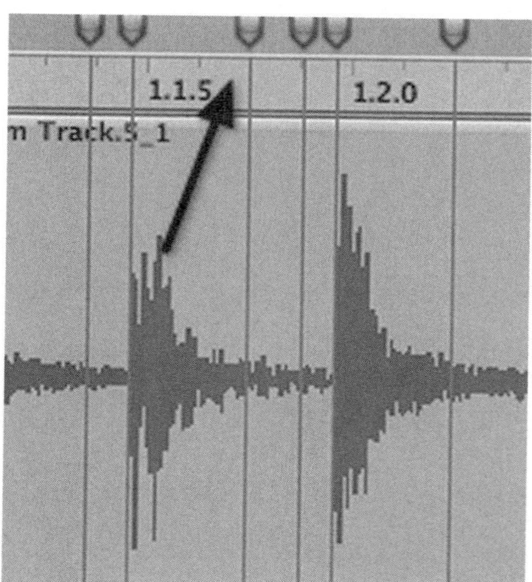

▶ FIG. 5.14

The transients will be deleted from the loop and they will not be used as a reference point to speed up or slow down the loop during playback.

When you have finished tagging your loop and have removed any unnecessary transients, click the save button in the lower right of the Apple Loops Utility.

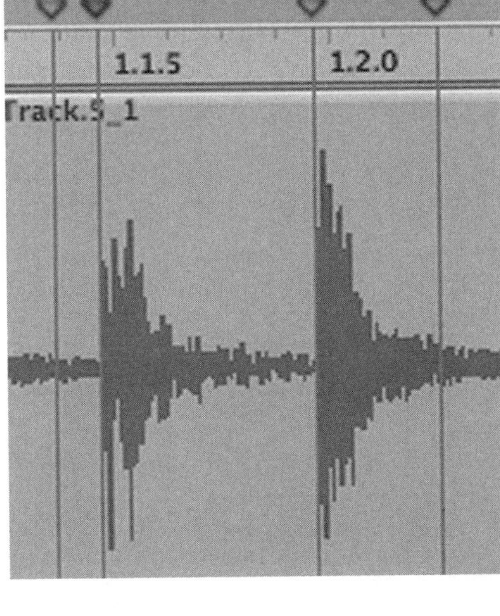

▶ FIG. 5.15

Close the Apple Loops Utility to return to Logic Pro X. You are now on your way to building a library of loops to augment and enhance your musical project.

All that is left in the loop creation process is adding your loop to Logic Pro X's Apple Loops library. This will ensure that your loop is available at all times through the loop browser in Logic Pro X. It is recommended that you rename your loop before adding it to the Apple Loops library to properly describe the contents of the loop. For example, if the loop is a drum loop meant for a specific film or television project, it might be best to name the file with the name of the project and the type of instrument (i.e., xfilmproject-drums). It can be helpful to label audio and MIDI regions in an audio project to describe the musical content of the loop—background music, name of the instrument, sound effects type, etc.

Show the toolbar and navigate to the Tracks area of the audio project and choose the text tool for the left-click tool. Click on the region header to rename the audio region after selecting the text tool.

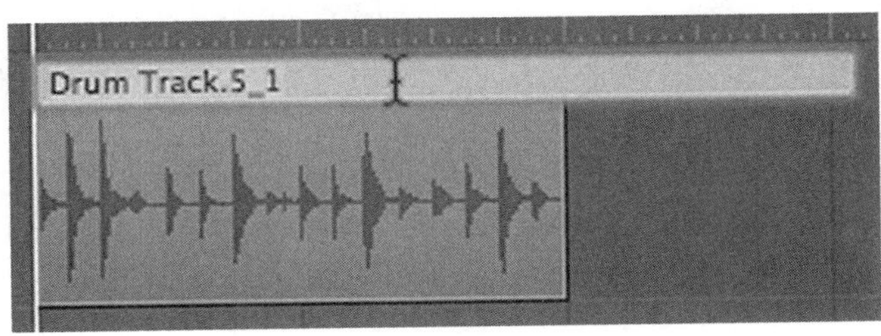

▶ FIG. 5.16

Type in the desired name for the audio region and press the return key on your keyboard to save the new region name. As mentioned previously, try naming the loop with something that is relevant to the project. Once you have renamed the audio loop, it is possible to add the loop to the Apple loops library by dragging the loop into the Loop browser or by selecting the loop and choosing File > Export > Region to Loop Library.

You will be presented with a dialog box to provide a name for your loop and other information that will allow you to search for the loop once it has been added to your Apple Loops Library. Tagging is extremely important because you can quickly find the loop through a search of the loop browser. Also, if you have a large library that caters to a particular sound or mood, it is helpful to search by category to find loops that may enhance the project. This can be a dramatic timesaving tool when under tight production deadlines. Film and television productions are notorious for strict delivery timeframes.

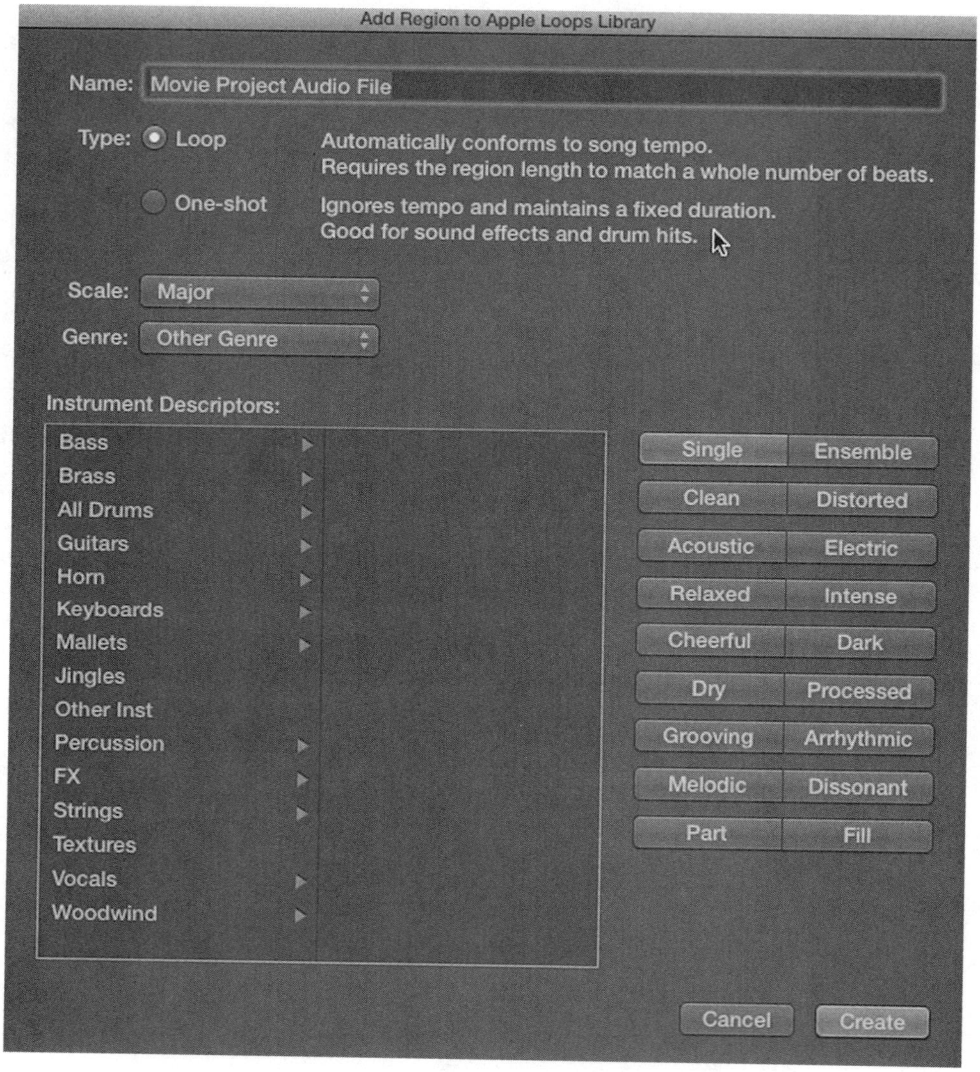

▶ **FIG. 5.17**

If you are adding a sound effect to the loops library, such as waves crashing on beach, choose the One-shot option. Logic Pro X will play One-shot loops without referencing tempo information. This is helpful for audio loops that do not adhere to strict tempo. In other words, these loops do not adjust to tempo changes. This is helpful when working with on-screen elements because the sound of a wave crashing on the beach will likely not be synced to the tempo of the composition You also have the option to choose the key, genre, instrument descriptors, and search categories.

Note: If you do not choose a key in the dialog box, Logic Pro X will assume that the loop was recorded in the key of C Major.

It is important to tag your loop appropriately so that it will accurately appear in searches in the loop browser. Time is of the essence when meeting production deadlines. Each of the categories in this dialog box mirrors the search categories that are available in the Loop browser. When you have finished naming and tagging your loop, press the create button. Logic Pro X will examine the number of beats in the loop, bounce the loop, and add it to the Apple Loops Library.

Once is has been added to the Apple Loops library, you will be able to search for the loop just as you would for any other loop in the Loop browser.

CREATING MIDI APPLE LOOPS

MIDI instruments have become increasingly popular over the past few decades as the quality of the instruments has improved to sound more realistic and lifelike. They have augmented the tools available to create engaging musical projects for film. A number of software instruments are included with many digital audio workstations, as well as a robust community of third-party developers that extend their native capabilities. Within Logic Pro X, the Apple Loops library contains thousands of royalty-free loops, sounds beds and pads, and Foley for use in audio projects. Many of these musical and textural artifacts are in an audio format such as the Audio Interchange File Format (AIFF) or the Core Audio Format (CAF). There are also a great number of these musical and textural artifacts in MIDI format. It is possible to create MIDI loops in much the same manner as an audio loop is created. They offer similar benefits as audio loops by adding character and uniqueness to the musical library that creates the foundation for your film project. Further, MIDI loops help to expand the orchestration possibilities in your film and television project, especially considering many of us do not have access to a studio string section in our living room!

The process of creating MIDI loops that can to be added to the Apple Loops library is similar to the process of creating audio loops. A MIDI loop can be created by recording into Logic Pro X via a MIDI controller or created manually in a MIDI editor such as the Piano Roll, Step Editor, or Ultrabeat. MIDI files that were created in separate MIDI editor can be imported as well. MIDI loops are architecturally different than audio loops because MIDI loops are simply data that instructs the related software instrument what to play. In other words, audio loops represent a recorded waveform, whereas MIDI loops represent data required to replicate the MIDI performance via a software instrument.

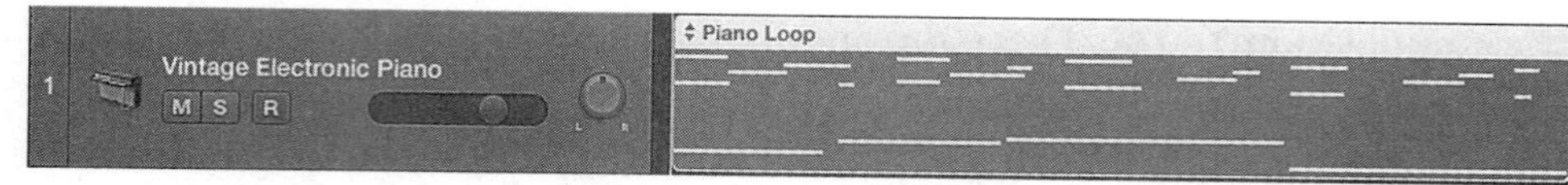

▶ **FIG. 5.18**

The loop shown represents MIDI data that details note value, note duration, note velocity, and so on. It requires that a software instrument be instantiated for playback. In this case, the Vintage Electronic Piano software instrument is loaded onto the track that the loop resides on. The MIDI loop will use the sound library from the Vintage Electronic Piano for playback.

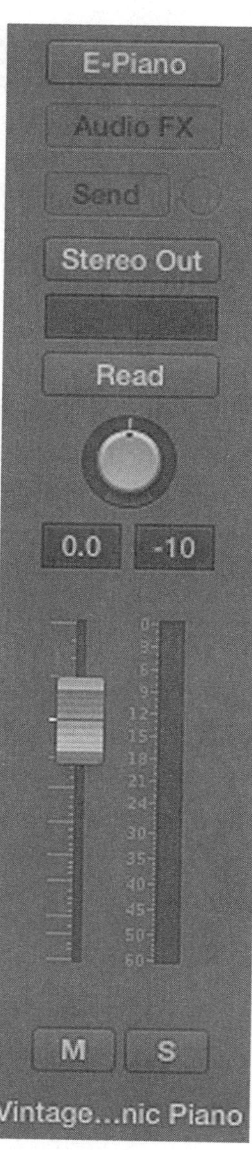

▶ **FIG. 5.19**

Since this is not an audio loop, there is no need to open the loop in the Apple Loops Utility for the purpose of tagging and editing transients. MIDI loops can be added to the Apple Loops Library directly by choosing File > Export > Region to Loop Library or by dragging the MIDI loop directly into the Apple Loops Library. Once you have started the process of adding the MIDI loop to the Apple Loops Library, you will be presented with a dialog box to provide details about the MIDI Loop.

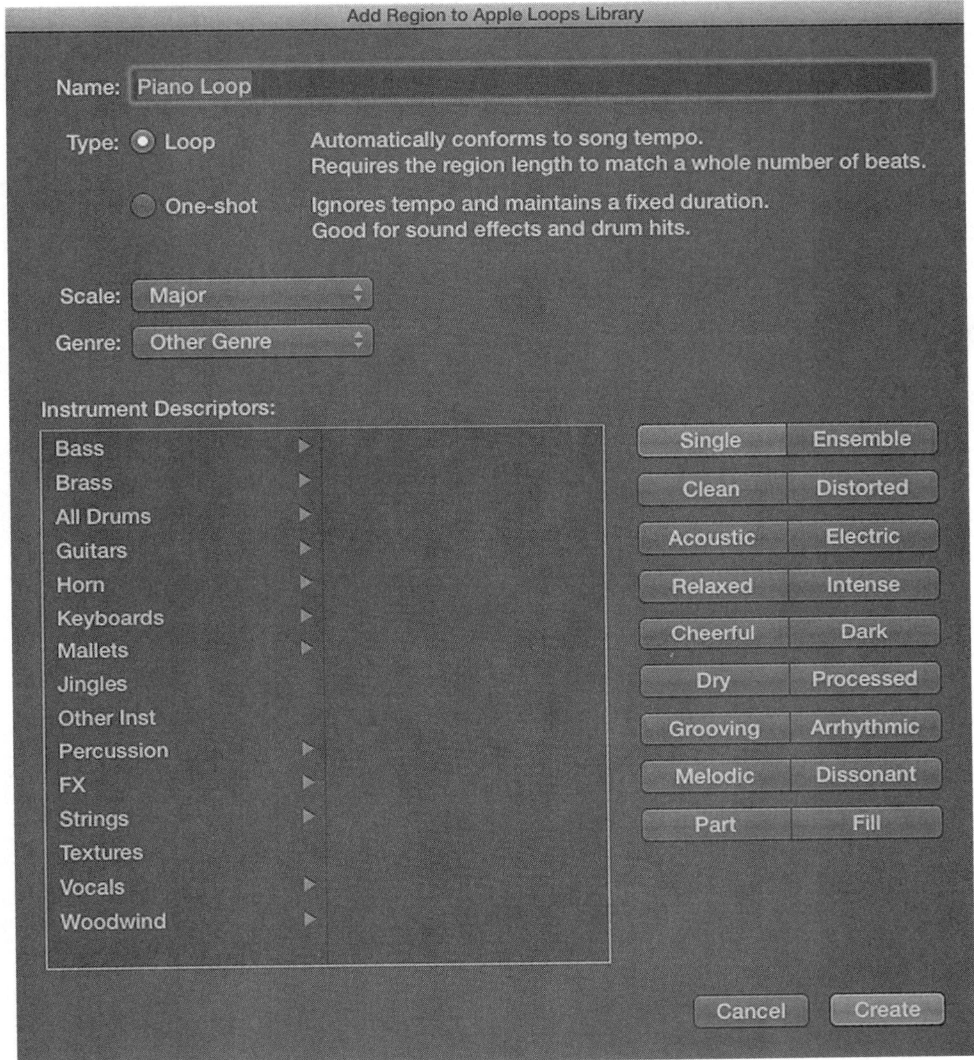

▶ **FIG. 5.20**

The options available when adding a MIDI loop are identical to the options available when adding an audio loop. You are able provide a name for your loop and other information that will allow you to search for the loop once it has been added to your Apple Loops Library. Each of the categories in this dialog box mirrors the search categories that are available in the Loop browser. When you have finished naming and tagging your loop, press the create button.

The MIDI loop will be added to the Apple Loops Library once the import process has completed. It is now possible to search for the Apple Loop via the loop browser.

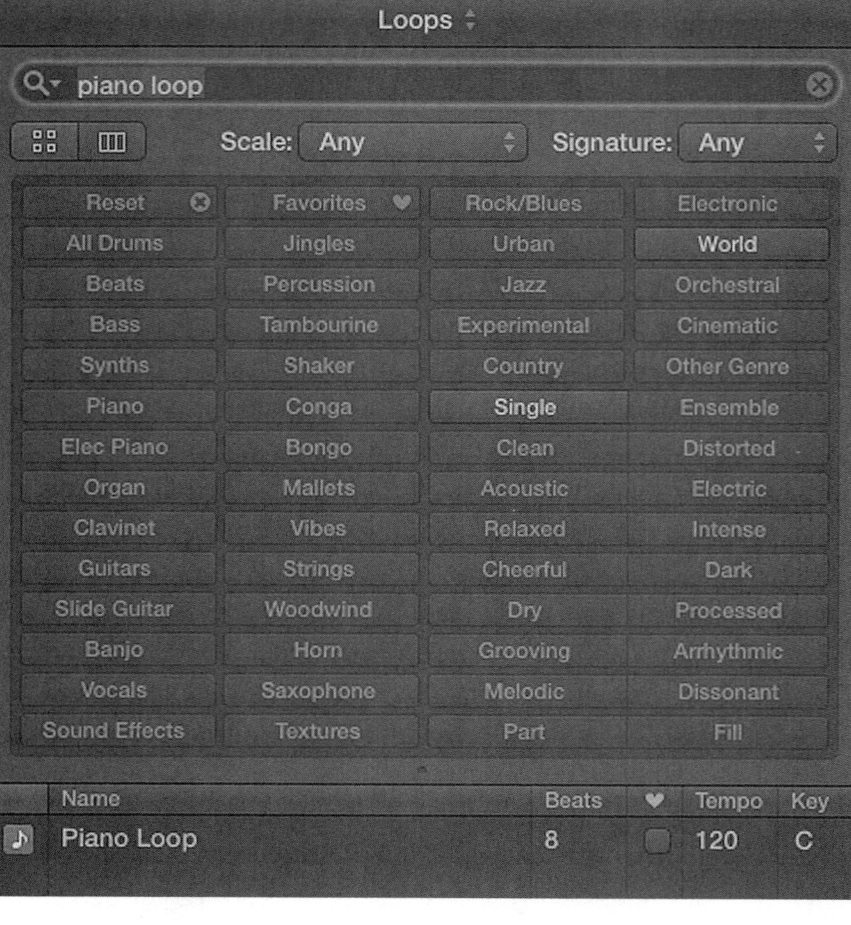

▶ **FIG. 5.21**

The loop browser will show the tempo, tonal center, or key signature and the number of beats present in the loop. A preview of the loop is possible upon clicking the loop in the loop browser. Notice that the loop plays back with the same software instrument it was created with, in this case, the Vintage Electronic Piano.

To recap, MIDI loops are often referred to as software instrument loops or hybrid loops. Software instrument loops are extremely flexible because they can be placed on a software instrument track and/or an audio track. If a software instrument loop is placed on an audio track, the loop will be represented as a waveform and can be edited in a manner that is consistent with editing audio files. If a software instrument loop is placed on a software instrument track, the relevant software instrument will be instantiated and the loop will be represented as MIDI data.

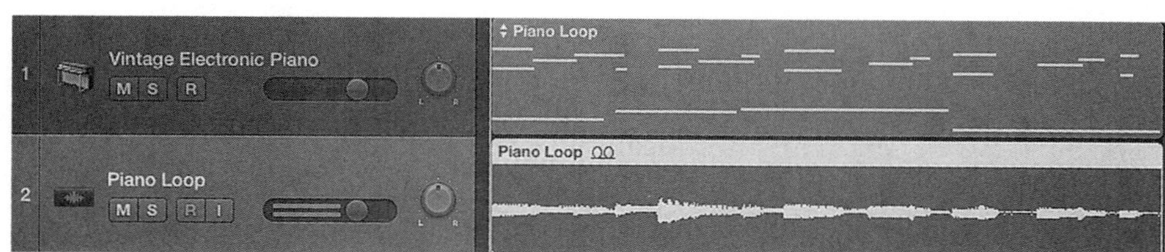

▶ **FIG. 5.22**

Each approach yields the same aural result. The listener will not be able to discern any noticeable difference between the software instrument version and the audio version of the loop. In certain instances it may be easier to use either the audio or the software instrument version of the software instrument loop when editing a project.

BACKING UP AND RESTORING LOOPS LIBRARIES

Creating a loops library that exemplifies a unique personal sound takes time and great effort. Loops libraries are the corner stone of any audio project. It is important to safeguard the library that you have spent time cultivating. Logic Pro X organizes user created loops into a specific location on your hard drive that can be easily moved to another computer or a secondary hard drive to protect the library and/or to preserve space on the startup disk. Logic Pro X stores user created loops in the Library folder of the user account. This is done to ensure that only the user who created the loop will have access to use the loop. Loops that are shared with all users of the computer are stored in the Library folder at the root level of the hard drive. All computer users have access to this Library folder.

Open the startup hard drive on your desktop, likely entitled Macintosh HD, and navigate to your user account folder that resides in the Users folder. Several folders reside in your user account folder, including the Library folder. Open the Library folder and navigate to the Audio folder. Logic Pro X stores all user created loops in the User Loops folder in the Apple Loops folder. For example, the path to this folder would be:

Your_User_Account_Name/Library/Audio/Apple Loops/User Loops/

As of Mac OS X 10.7, Apple hid the Library folder from users to protect user-specific application data and settings. To navigate to this folder via the Finder application, Choose Go > Go to Folder from the Finder's menu. You will be presented with a text box to signify the desired folder location.

Type in the following path:

~/Library/Audio/Apple Loops/User Loops/

Note: The tilde is a shortcut that represents the name of your user account.

The loops that reside in this folder can be backed up onto another drive to preserve data in the event of a hardware failure. User loops can also be permanently moved to another drive location and linked back to the default User Loops folder through the use of a symbolic link. The loops will reside on another drive and a symbolic link will create a pathway from the default User Loops

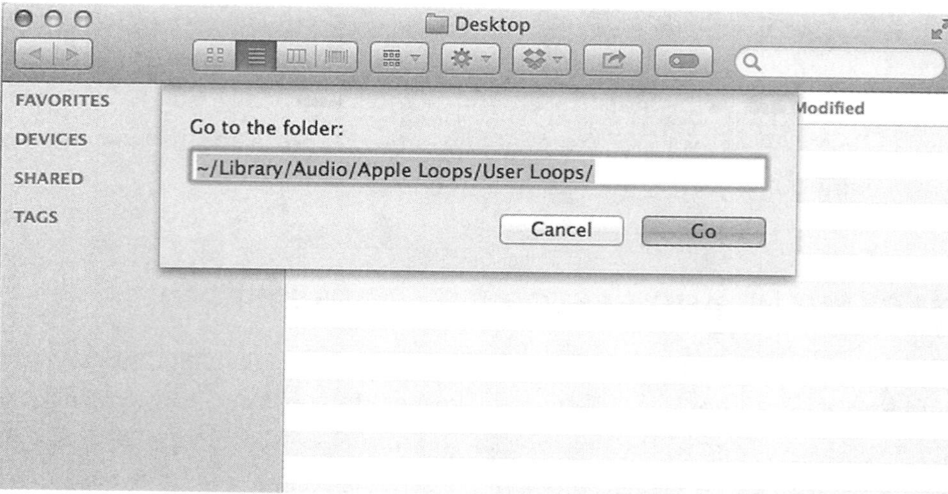

▶ **FIG. 5.23**

folder to the folder on the secondary drive. In other words, the symbolic link points to another location where the data resides. This commonly used practice provides greater flexibility in regard to storage and helps to spread required bandwidth resources needed by the digital audio workstation across multiple hard drives.

Symbolic links can be created through the Command Line Interface (CLI), known as the Terminal application, by using the following command:

ln –s/path/to/original/path/to/link/location

It is not necessary to use the CLI in order to create a symbolic link. This can be accomplished by using a contextual menu service made available by a third-party software developer, Nick Zitzmann, entitled SymbolicLinker. Once the service is installed, the service initiates a contextual menu item that creates symbolic links for any file or folder of your choosing. Simply right-click on the item and choose Services > Make Symbolic Link from the contextual menu.

The service will create a symbolic link in the same directory as the file or folder. The file name of the symbolic link will be appended with "symlink" to differentiate between the original file or folder and the resulting symbolic link. In the case of "test folder" the symbolic link would be entitled "test folder symlink."

The process of migrating user loops to a secondary hard drive begins with copying the User Loops folder to another hard drive.

Once the User Loops folder has been copied to the secondary hard drive, it is safe to delete the original User Loops folder that resides in the Apple Loops folder. Right-click on the User Loops folder on the secondary hard drive and choose Services > Make Symbolic Link. A symbolic link entitled "User Loops symlink" will appear on the drive alongside the User Loops folder. It is necessary to drag the newly created symbolic link into the Apple Loops folder on the primary hard drive.

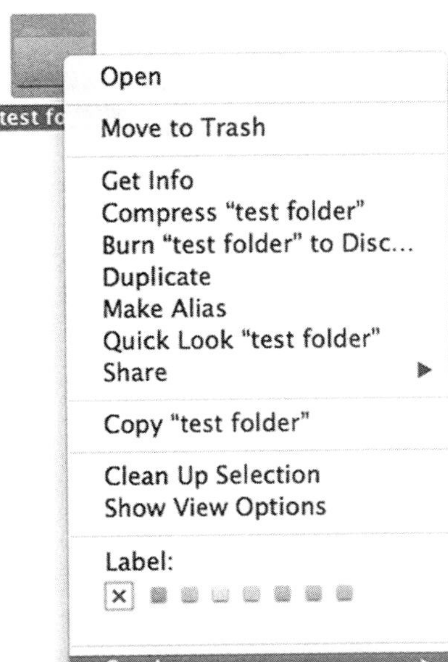

▶ **FIG. 5.24**

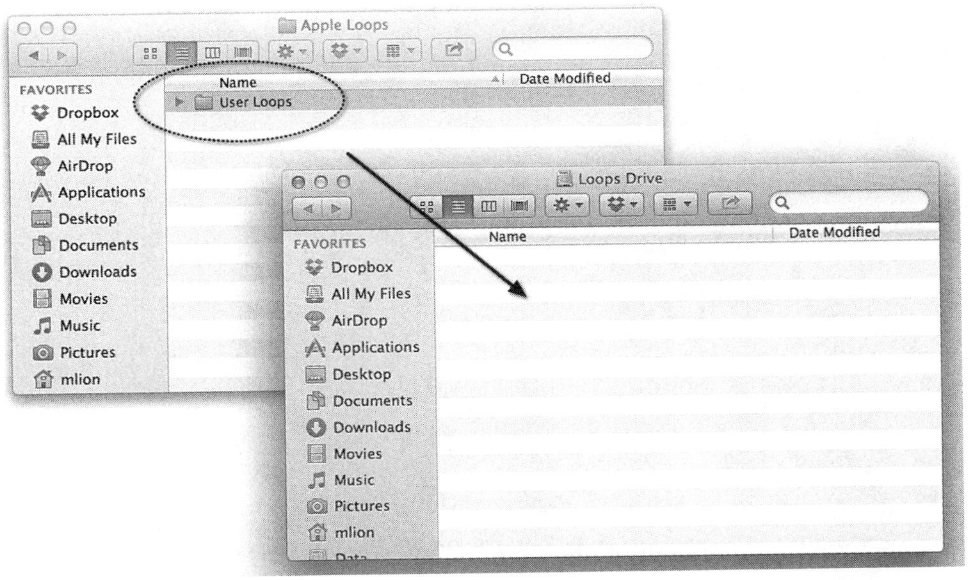

▶ **FIG. 5.25**

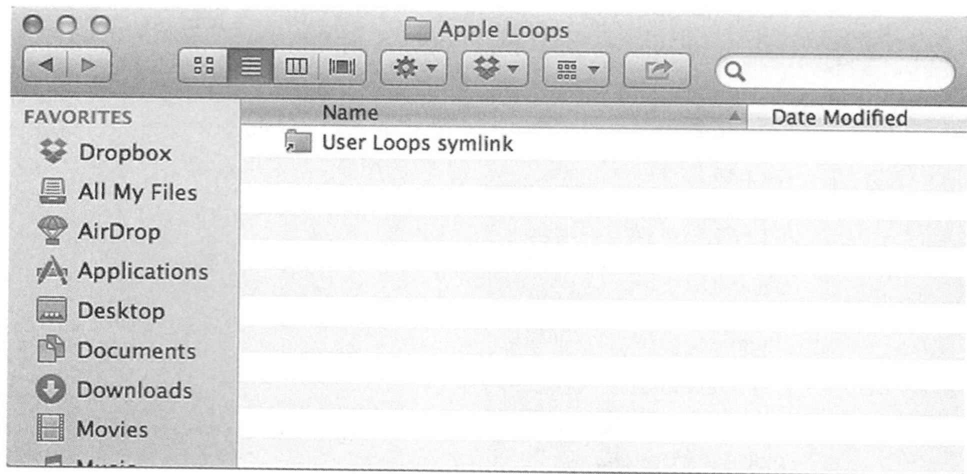

▶ FIG. 5.26

Once the symbolic link has been copied to the primary drive, select the symbolic link and press the enter key to rename it. The symbolic link must be named in the same manner as the original folder in order for it to work properly with applications that are expecting a particular naming convention. In this case, the symbolic link should be renamed to "User Loops" rather than "User Loops symlink." Once the symbolic link has been renamed, it will behave in the same manner as the original folder. The only difference is that the User Loops folder now resides on another hard drive.

This technique can also be used to transport and utilize loops on another computer workstation. Simply back up the user's loops folder and move the

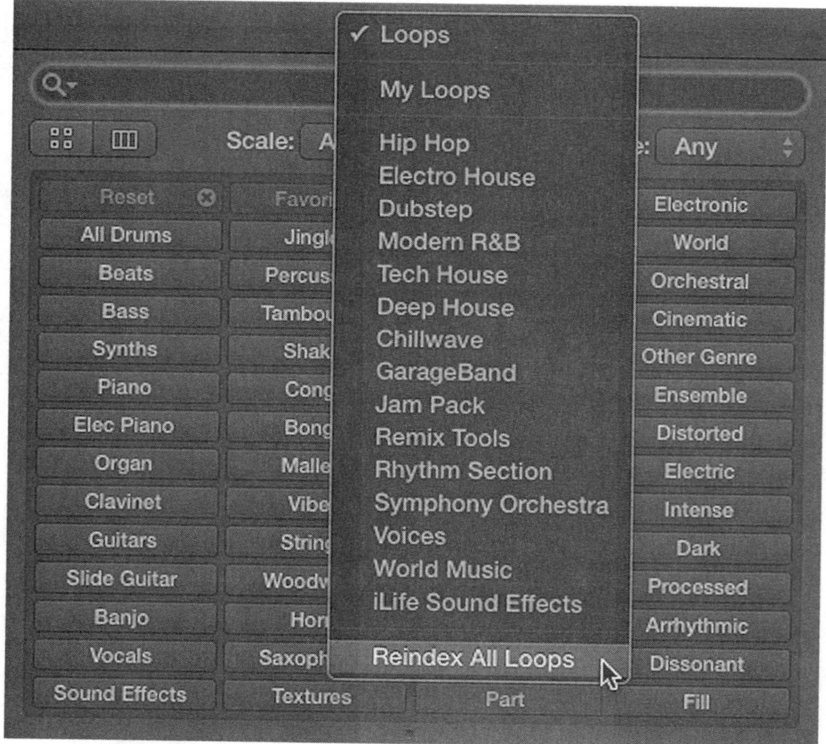

▶ FIG. 5.27

symbolic link from the external hard drive to the User Loops folder on the computer. Logic Pro X will now use the user loops that reside on the external hard drive rather the user loops that exist on the primary hard drive. Logic Pro X will need to rebuild its Apple Loops Library database to incorporate the loops on the external hard drive. Navigate to the Loops tab of the Apple Loops area in Logic Pro X. Click Loops at the top of the Loop Browser, then choose Reindex All Loops from the pop-up menu.

When the indexing process has completed, Logic Pro X will be able to utilize the loops that reside on the external hard drive. You now have extended the capabilities of your computer in an effort to make the compositional process more streamlined and efficient in regard to your loop management.

CHAPTER 6
WORKING WITH VIDEOS

It took me a long time to understand that the time I spend away from composing during a project is as important as the time I spend actually composing. My mind is always working through ideas whether I know it or not, and what on one afternoon seems an insurmountable proble, is often easily fixed that evening after some time away from the studio.

—*Nathan Barr*

WRITING MUSIC FOR FILM is a deeply collaborative process that involves a great number of professionals working with media elements to produce a single, cohesive piece of work. Music professionals often work in different locations and share content throughout the creative process. Nonlinear editing applications have revolutionized the way we work with media because they allow us to create high-quality, engaging content in a quick and efficient manner. When working in nonlinear editing environments it is essential that timing references be consistently handled to ensure synchronization of musical and visual elements in the film. Computer workstations have greatly simplified the process of writing music for film and television because audio and video elements can be utilized simultaneously within a nonlinear editing application. Music and audio elements can be seamlessly locked to on-screen visual elements in a video clip. The use of nonlinear editing applications greatly increases the speed, efficiency and creativity of media professionals.

PROXY VIDEO FILES

We live in a world where high-definition media is commonplace and is expected by consumers. Standard definition televisions are considered obsolete and are rarely sold in consumer electronics stores. Typically, the high-definition video classification refers to devices that are capable of displaying a progressive signal at either 720 horizontal scan lines or 1080 horizontal scan lines. This is commonly referred to as 720p or 1080p, where "p" represents progressive scan. The transition away from standard definition television began late in the twentieth century with 720p devices, with 1080p devices following shortly thereafter. 1080p has been widely adopted, but 720p is still commonly used in many consumer devices.

High-definition video provides a superior experience over standard definition video but yields far greater file sizes and requires increased disk bandwidth to accommodate the signal. It is important to be cognizant of the increased disk bandwidth requirement when writing music to a video clip within a digital audio workstation (DAW). The DAW is likely using a great deal of system resources to utilize third-party software instruments, digital signal processing (DSP), and stream audio and MIDI data from the hard drive. Incorporating a large video file into the workflow will decrease DAW performance. Proxy video files are commonly used to preserve system resources when working in a DAW.

Proxy videos files are reasonably high-quality media files, but have a much smaller file size when compared to native media shot by high-definition cameras. The smaller footprint diminishes the amount of system resources required to play the file. Also, uploading a proxy video file to a local or remote server to disseminate to collaborators will be much quicker due to the small file size. Proxy video files can be easily created in many nonlinear video applications such as Final Cut Pro, Avid Media Composer, and Adobe Premier by transcoding the original high-quality video clip into an optimized proxy video file.

VIDEO FRAME RATES

Logic Pro X is works closely with QuickTime, a powerful video playback and editing platform in OS X. QuickTime works hand-in-hand with Logic Pro X when working with video. Logic Pro X can accept any video format the QuickTime supports including, mov and m4v file formats. It is important to gather information about the video file you wish to use with your audio project prior to opening the video file in Logic Pro X. Timing reference information, such as the video frame rate, is crucial when setting up synchronization settings within Logic Pro X. QuickTime can provide this information in a quick and easy way.

Download and unzip the sample movie files from the companion website. Navigate to the Applications folder and open QuickTime Player.app. Choose File > Open File from the QuickTime Player menu.

Open the Left Right End Scene video file. Once the video has loaded in the QuickTime Player application, it is possible to gather timing reference information to use within in Logic Pro X.

Choose Window > Show Movie Inspector from the QuickTime Player menu, or use the Command–I key command.

The inspector provides relevant information about the video that includes format, frames per second (fps), data size, data rate, and the size of the video. This

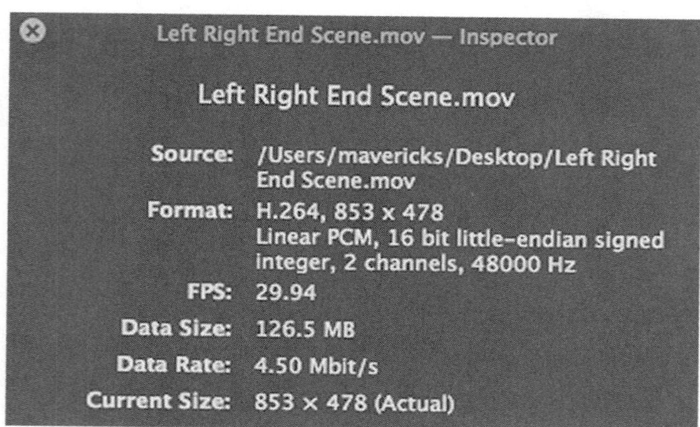

▶ **FIG. 6.1**

information will be used to inform frame rate synchronization settings within Logic Pro X. Common frame rates include NTSC (29.97 fps) and PAL (25 fps).

FRAME RATE SYNCHRONIZATION SETTINGS

In order for Logic Pro X to adequately handle video files, it must know the frame rate of the video to properly synchronize audio information with video information. This is accomplished through the project-based synchronization settings.

Navigate to File > Project Settings > Synchronization. The General tab contains options for configuring project-based video sync settings, including sync mode, frame rate, and SMPTE start position.

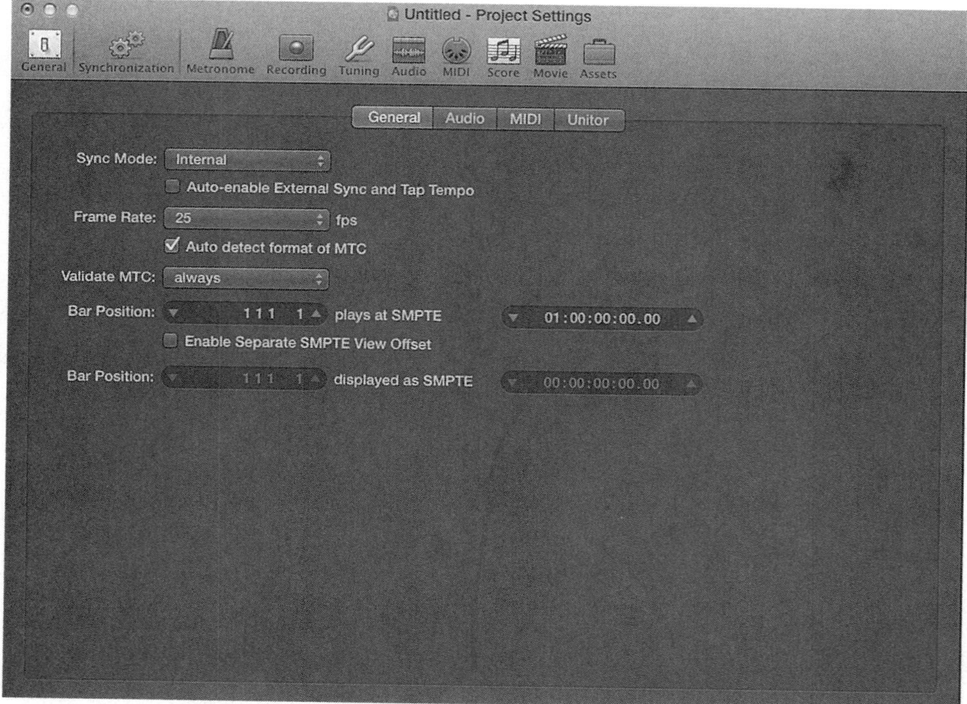

▶ **FIG. 6.2**

Choose the desired frame rate from the pop-up menu. Logic Pro X Natively supports the following frame rates:

- 24 fps: Film and high definition (HD) video.
- 25 fps: Phase Alternating Line (PAL). Analog television color encoding system that is commonly used outside of the United States.
- 30 fps (drop frame): National Television System Committee (NTSC). NTSC video broadcast that is rarely used.
- 30 fps: High-definition video.
- 29.97 (drop frame): NTSC video and television broadcasts.
- 29.97: Standard definition NTSC
- 23.976: 24 fps running at 99.9 percent, which facilitates easier transfer of film to NTSC video

If the "Auto detect format of MTC" checkbox is selected, Logic Pro X will attempt to analyze the incoming time code and automatically set the appropriate frame rate. The MTC standard does not allow for a distinction between 29.97 fps and 30 fps frame rates. Logic Pro X will interpret the frame rate as approximately 30 fps and set the frame rate as either 29.97 fps (drop frame) or 30 fps (nondrop). This interpretation will likely be correct because both frame rates are standards.

CHANGING PROJECT SAMPLE RATES

There are a number of sample rates commonly used in recording audio. Generally speaking, the various sample rates derive from two main sample rates: 44.1 kHz (44, 100 Hz) and 48 kHz (48, 000 Hz). Typically, 44.1 kHz is used for compact disc (CD) projects and 48 kHz is used for video projects. It is common to record at multiples of these sample rates to increase the number of audio samples taken per second. For example, it is possible to record and CD project at 44.1 kHz, 88.2 kHz, or 176.4 kHz, and it is possible to record audio for a video project at 48 kHz, 96 kHz, or 192 kHz.

It is important to be cognizant of the sample rate setting when working with video files in audio projects. The sample rate of the audio project should be changed from 44.1 kHz to 48 kHz (or multiples of 48 kHz) to be compatible with the video file.

Navigate to File > Project Settings > Audio.

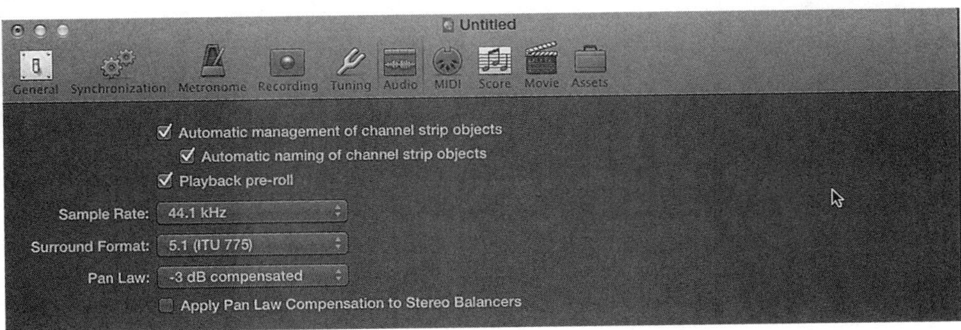

▶ **FIG. 6.3**

Change the project sample rate from 44.1 kHz to 48 kHz by selecting 48 kHz from the pop-up menu. All audio that is recorded in this project will be recorded at 48 kHz. It is advantageous to display the current project sample rate in the control bar for quick access to sample rate settings. Right-click on the control bar and choose Customize Control bar Bar and Display.

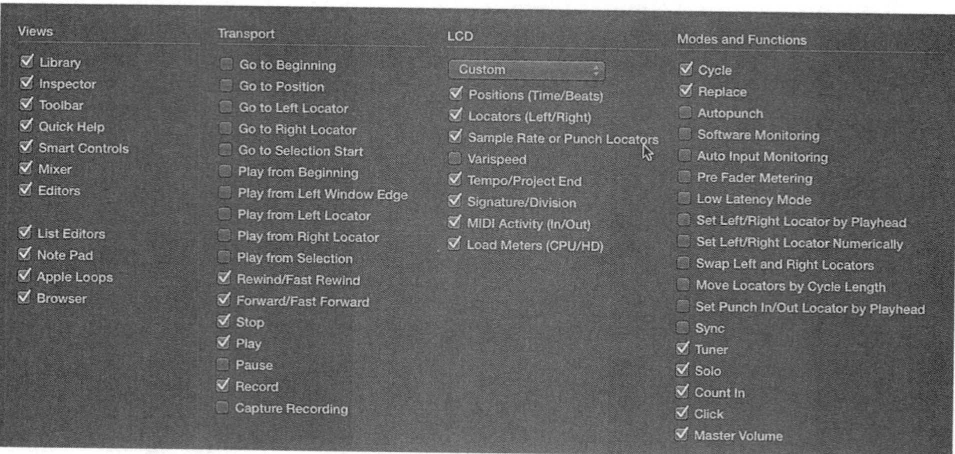

▶ FIG. 6.4

Choose to display Sample Rate or Punch Locators. Logic Pro X will now display the current sample rate, in this case 48 kHz, in the control bar for quick review and access.

OPENING VIDEO FILES IN LOGIC PRO X

Once the frame rate of the video has been determined, it is necessary to open the video in Logic Pro X, adjust synchronization settings, and enable the movie track. Logic Pro X utilizes Global Tracks to control settings that affect the entire project. To view Global tracks, click the Show/Hide Global tracks button in the Tracks area.

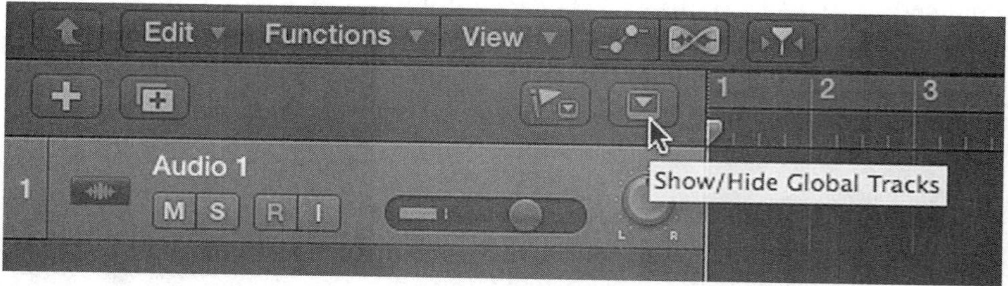

▶ FIG. 6.5

By default, Logic Pro X displays the Arrangement, Marker, Signature, and Tempo Global tracks above the track listing. There are other Global Tracks, such as the movie track, available for use in your project.

Open Logic Pro X and create a new project with a single audio track. Right-click on the Global Tracks area and choose Configure Global Tracks.

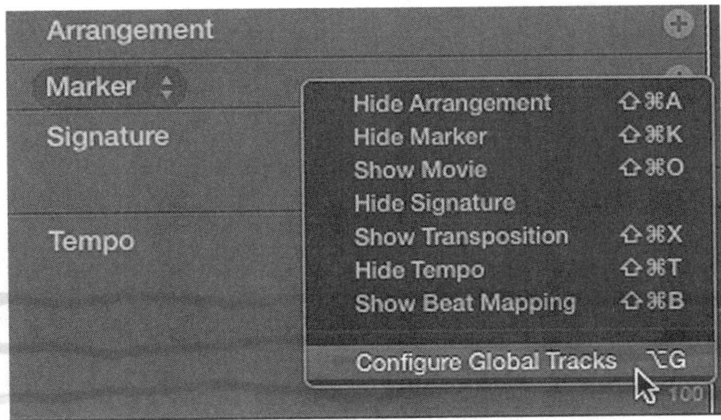

▶ FIG. 6.6

Once the movie track has been enabled, it will be displayed alongside the other Global tracks in the Tracks area. Mouse over the title of the movie track and click the title to open a file.

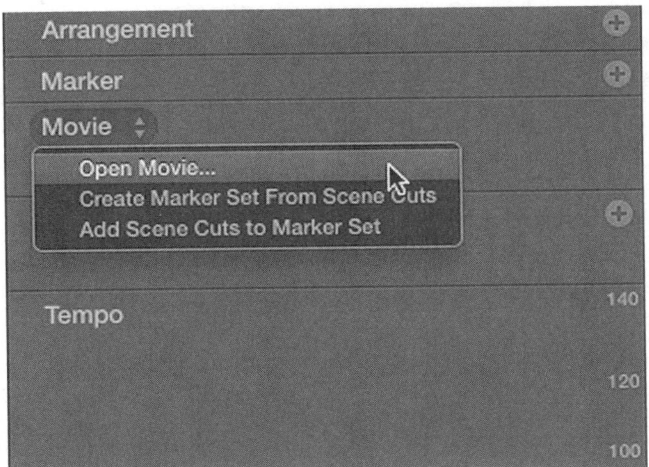

▶ FIG. 6.7

Navigate to your Desktop and open the Left Right End Scene that was downloaded from the companion website. Logic Pro X will prompt you to import the video and accompanying audio track.

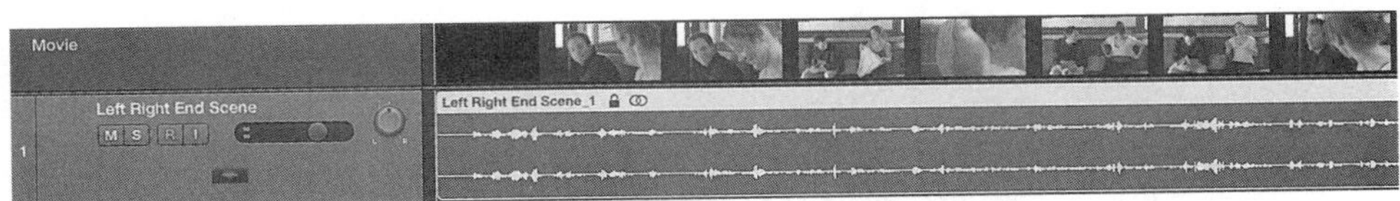

▶ FIG. 6.8

Once the audio and video has been loaded, video thumbnails will display on the movie track in the Global Tracks area. The audio from the video has been imported into the Logic Pro X project directly underneath the video thumbnails. It is common for proxy videos to include temporary music and vocal dialog. This audio track may be distracting during the composition process. The audio can be muted at the track level by selecting the mute (M) button on the track header.

When creating music for a new sequence, you will likely want to mute the audio track that was included with the proxy video. It can be easy to be influenced by music that may have been used before. It is important to watch the video in an environment that is free from distraction in order to better prepare yourself to write music that is appropriate and relevant for the video. You should be keenly aware of on-screen elements during the initial viewing of the scene. These elements include the natural rhythmic pacing of objects (moving cars, walking characters, flying birds, etc.), general mood, and color scheme. All of these elements should be considered throughout the compositional process.

SMPTE TIMECODE

SMPTE timecode refers to a set of time standards that are defined and managed by the Society of Motion Picture and Television Engineers. SMPTE is widely used today to synchronize audio, MIDI, video, and film. Timecode is displayed in the format 00:00:00:00:00, representing hours, minutes, seconds, frames, and subframes, respectively. SMPTE timecode provides a common time structure that offers a level of consistency between various hardware and software components. Think of SMPTE timecode as a common timing language that prevents timing inconsistencies between hardware and software from occurring.

Logic Pro X is application that is designed to be a tool for music composition, creation, and performance. Every aspect of the user interface is designed with music in mind. This is true of the bar ruler as well. As the name suggests, the bar ruler is a measurement tool that displays the location of musical elements in the Tracks area by bars, beats, and divisions of beats. The bar ruler is an invaluable tool when working with musical passages but can quickly lose its relevance when writing musical elements that are required to be measured by SMPTE timecode rather than musical bars. Fortunately, the bar ruler can be customized to predominantly show SMPTE timecode rather than musical bars.

Choose View > Secondary Ruler from the Track's area menu.

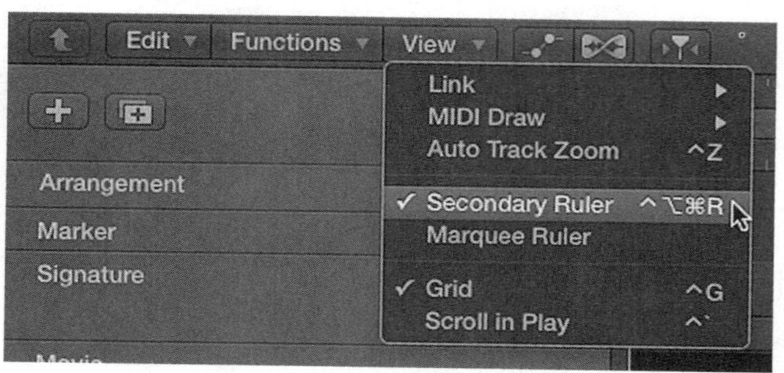

▶ **FIG. 6.9**

The bar ruler now displays SMPTE timecode. This is extremely important when aligning musical elements to timecode rather than musical bars. After all, the on-screen elements are not moving in musical time. We must adapt to the natural tempo of the scene. The music you write will need to be synced directly to specific events in time. It is helpful to display a large, floating SMPTE timecode window on a second monitor to quickly see where musical elements line up with SMPTE timecode. Click on the transport in the control bar and choose Open Giant Time Display.

▶ FIG. 6.10

Logic Pro X will open a resizable SMPTE window that can be moved to a secondary monitor for quick reference when placing audio elements in your project.

▶ FIG. 6.11

Again, SMPTE timecode is displayed in hours, minutes, seconds, frames, and subframes. Other DAWs also use SMPTE timecode to sync elements in your project. Logic Pro X uses the same industry standards adopted by other software and vendors, such as Avid, Propellerhead Software, Focusrite, and Apogee. This ensures compatibility between various computer and hardware configurations.

ADDING MUSICAL TRACKS TO VIDEO PROJECTS

Music has become an integral component of the cinematic experience. In many ways, music takes on the role of a character in the film, which deeply adds to the overall experience. Music can also augment the character through theme music. Wilhelm Richard Wagner was famous for his use of Leitmotifs, or short recurring musical passages, to represent characters and events in time in his compositions. The musical themes are often augmented or morphed throughout the composition to symbolize the character's experience with change throughout the story. This approach has been borrowed time and time again by film composers to present a wide range of emotion to moviegoers. A wonderful example of recurring musical themes associated with musical characters is represented in the Star Wars films, scored by John Williams. Each character is associated with a recurring theme that beautifully introduces the character into the scene, often before the actor appears on-screen.

Adding musical tracks to your film project is the first step to building your musical interpretation of the film. Many musicians and composers use software instruments to begin building their compositions before going into a recording session with live musicians. This approach saves time and money and allows the composer to ensure that the music is appropriate and approved before entering the recording studio.

To add tracks to your music project in Logic Pro X, press the New Tracks button directly above the Global Tracks area.

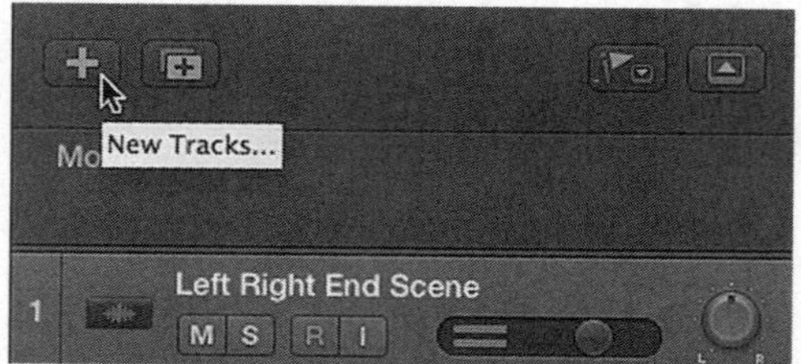

▶ FIG. 6.12

Choose to create and add eight new software instrument tracks to your musical project. Again, software instrument or MIDI tracks allow you to add virtual instruments to your project that can be used in the final project delivery or serve as a mockup for approval before entering into a recording session. There are a number of high-quality software instruments built into Logic Pro X, as well as a robust community of third-party software instruments. Some of the most notable third-party software instruments include the offerings from the Vienna Symphonic Library, Native Instruments, Spectrasonics, Propellerhead, and Toontrack.

Software instruments extend the native functionality of Logic Pro X and other DAWs by incorporating vast libraries of sound to augment and enhance your musical project.

Software instruments can be added to a software instrument track by clicking and holding on the instrument slot of the software instrument track.

You will be presented with a pop-up window that details the available software instruments on your computer.

Logic Pro X has eighteen high-quality software instruments. They are listed in the top portion of the pop-up window. Third-party software instruments, such as Spectrasonics Omnispehere, appear under AU Instruments in the lower portion of the pop-up window. Once you choose the desired software instrument, it will be loaded onto the software instrument track.

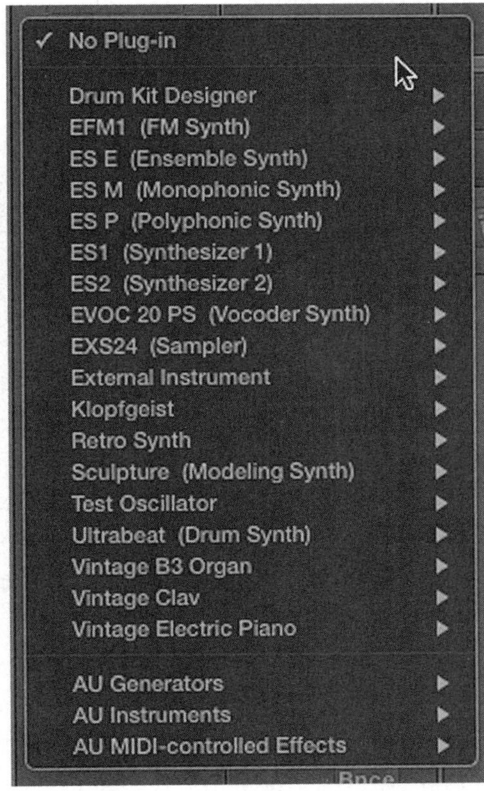

▶ **FIG. 6.13**

USING FOLEY IN MUSICAL PROJECTS

Foley is the reproduction of everyday sound effects for use in film, television, radio, and video game projects. Essentially, Foley tracks include any sound that is not recorded dialog, such as door openings and closings and many others. We are accustomed to viewing films that have accompanying Foley tracks. In fact, if we viewed a film that did not contain a Foley track, it would likely be difficult to make an emotional connection with the film and its characters. We are trained to expect Foley, the secondary film soundtrack of a film.

Foley art became popular in the early part of the twentieth century as films became more popular with the public viewing audience. The term Foley refers to Jack Donovan Foley (1891–196), who is widely recognized as the forefather of Foley art. New and exciting career paths in the film industry became available with the increase in the popularity of film. Foley artists, recording engineers who specialize in recording ambient sound for film, were suddenly in demand by film studios to record sound effects that on-set microphones were not able to capture.

Jack Donovan Foley developed myriad techniques for emulating real-world sounds through trial and error and creative thinking. Many of these techniques are still in use by Foley experts today. Notable tricks include using flapping gloves to represent bird wings flapping in the air, using gelatin and hand soap to create squishing sounds, and coconut shells to represent the sound of a horse running. Logic Pro X contains a number of high-quality Foley samples that can be freely used in any project.

Navigate to the Apple Loops area in the control bar and change the view to column view. Click on Foley in the Loops browser.

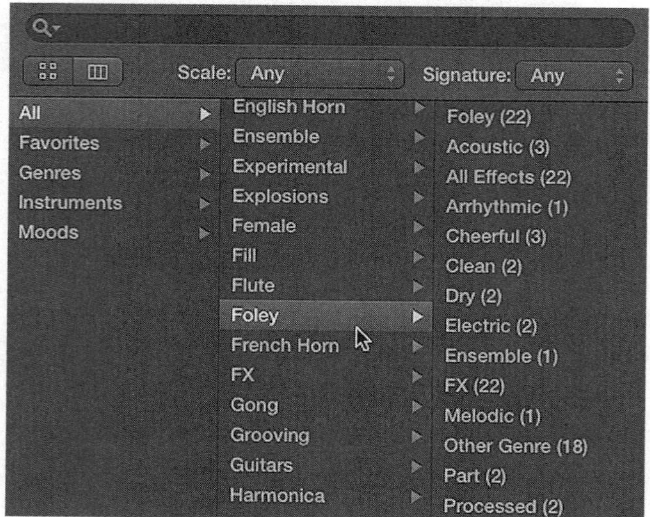

▶ **FIG. 6.14**

There are a number of Foley artifacts to choose from such as camera noises and computer printers to enhance your project. A number of musicians and composers are called upon to write music as well as do sound design for a film project. Sound design covers a vast scope of musical work including music composition, Foley recording and design, and mixing and mastering a project.

SPOTTING FOLEY

Precise timing is required when working with sound effects. Foley must be synchronized with time, not musical bars. Dragging an audio region to a precise location in the Tracks area can be difficult because audio regions generally snap to bars, beats, or divisions of beats, depending on your zoom level. This is problematic because if Foley is not closely aligned with the on-screen elements, the desired effect can be lost.

Fortunately, Logic Pro X offers a solution for spotting Foley, or any audio for that matter, to a particular location in the Tracks area. This is accomplished by enabling the pickup clock key command within Logic Pro X.

Navigate to the key commands windows by choosing Logic Pro X > Key Commands > Edit from the main menu or by simply pressing Option–K.

Choose Options > Expand All to reveal all of the available key commands in Logic Pro X. Type "pickup" in the search box and press enter.

Select Pickup Clock (Move Event to Playhead Position). Notice that the function has been assigned to the semicolon key.

This key command allows you to move audio to the current location of the playhead. In the example above, a door opening sound was added to the film at the exact time a character is walking through the door. The character entrance

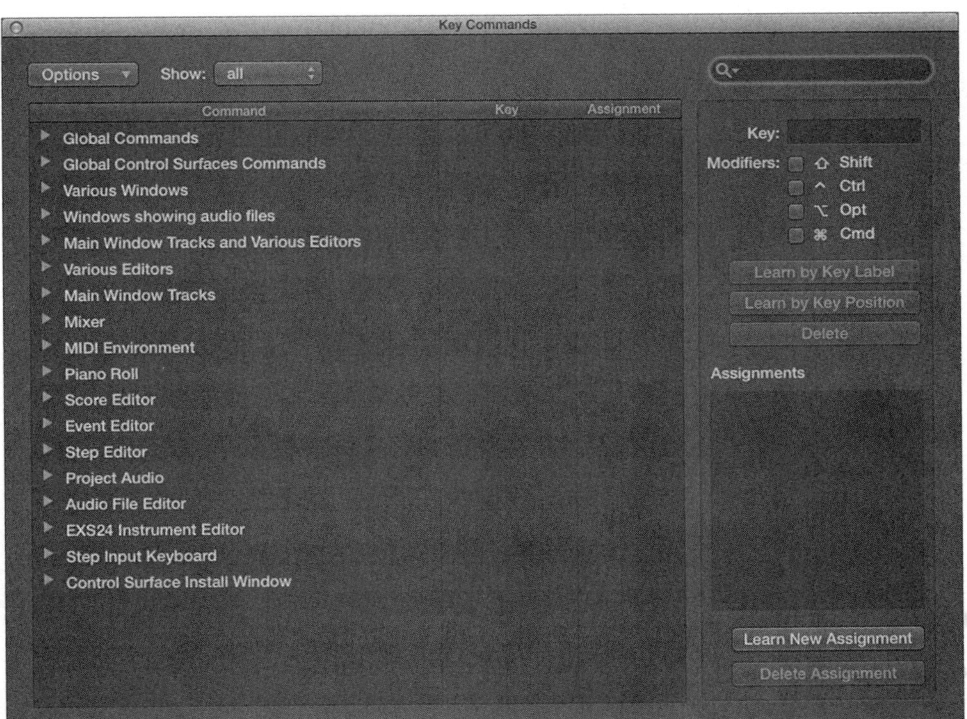

▶ FIG. 6.15

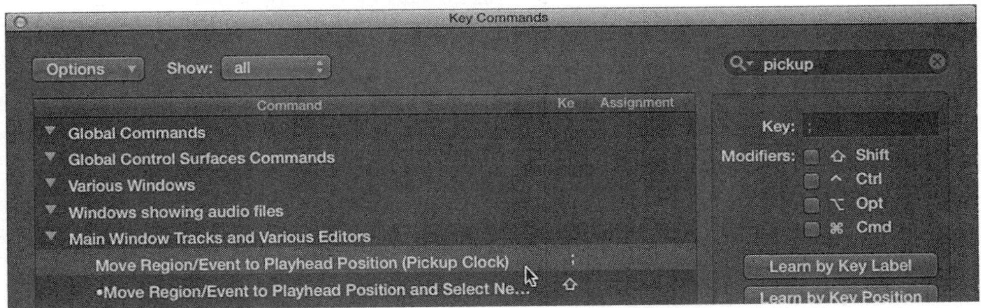

▶ FIG. 6.16

▶ FIG. 6.17

is not synchronized to musical time and should not be; however, the audio file still needs to be linked to Logic Pro X's time grid. The pickup clock key command allows you to place audio in the Tracks area in a manner that is synchronized with on-screen elements, not necessarily musical time represented in bars, beats, and divisions of beats.

SCENE CUTS AND SCENE MARKERS

Music is a wonderful companion to film because it augments the on-screen action and arguably creates a more engaging experience for viewers. Music can dynamically shift moods to represent the sentiment of a particular scene. Modern films are an aggregate of hundreds or even thousands of individual shots that are organized into scenes and woven together to create a story. Throughout the course of a film, scenes quickly change, and it is important to adjust the music soundtrack accordingly to convey the appropriate mood. Composers often look for natural breaks, referred to as scene cuts, in the film to insert musical transitions.

It is important to be aware of scene cuts when writing for film because they dictate the overall flow of a particular scene. For example, the intensity of a conversation between two characters in a film can be conveyed by the speed and frequency of cuts that focus on each character. It is possible to manually identify scene cuts in Logic Pro X, as well as scan the film and automatically detect scene cuts.

Choose Create Marker Set from Scene Cuts on the Global Movie track. Logic Pro X will create scene markers wherever is detects a cuts in the video. The scene markers will appear in the bar ruler once Logic Pro X has scanned the video file.

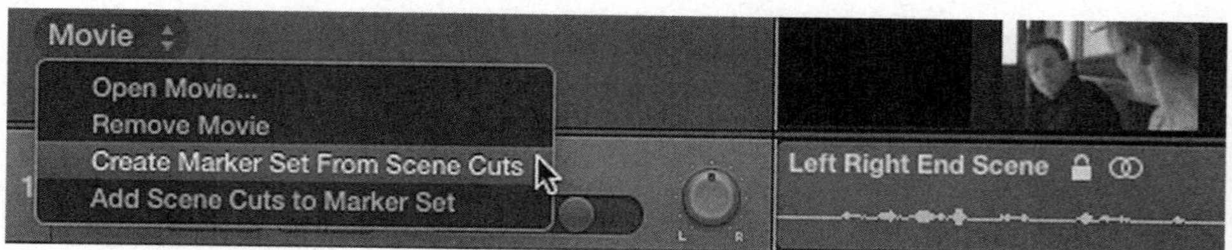

▶ **FIG. 6.18**

Navigate to the Lists Editors area in the control bar and choose select the Marker tab. Notice the scene markers are listed in under markers.

Scene markers clearly define where Logic Pro X detected scene cuts. There is one problem with this approach—Logic Pro X locks scene markers to their current SMPTE position. In other words, the scene marker cannot be moved from the position provided in the detection process. It is necessary to convert scene markers into standard markers if you would like to move the start position of the marker to accommodate a musical passage entrance.

Press Command–A to select all of the scene markers. Choose Options > Convert to Standard Marker.

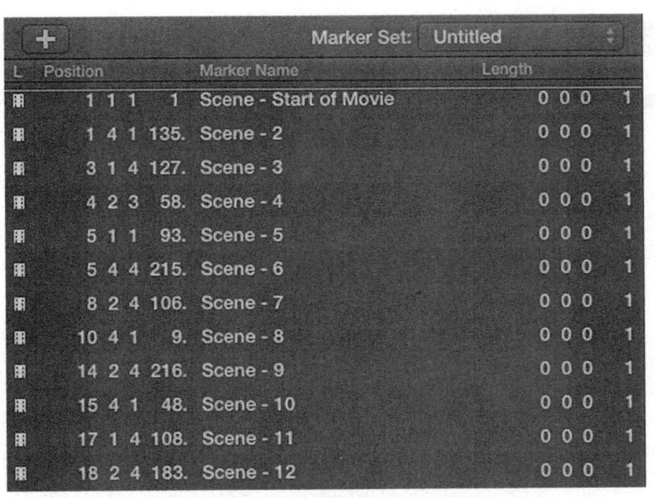

▶ **FIG. 6.19**

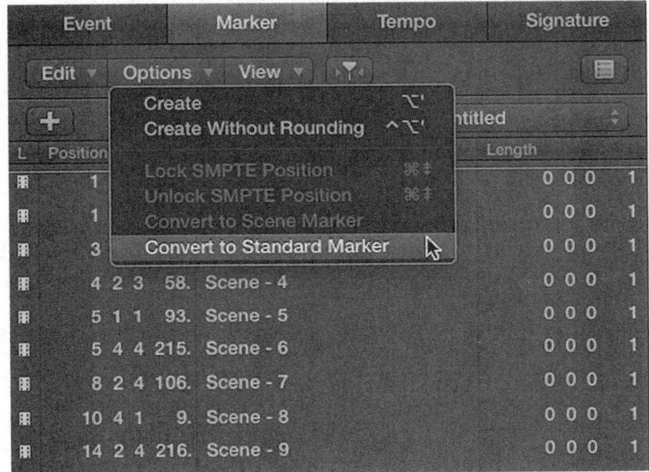

▶ **FIG. 6.20**

Every marker will be converted to a standard marker, enabling it to move its start position. This allows you to place music in a start position that will be more realistic-sounding to the audience.

To view Markers in the Tracks area, simply choose to show the Marker Global Track.

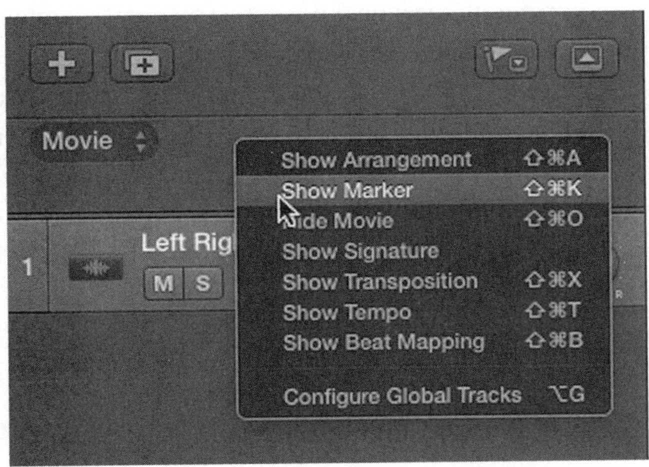

▶ **FIG. 6.21**

RENAMING AND COLORING MARKERS

Markers are an invaluable tool for identifying and organizing musical phrases in a DAW. Similar or repeating musical passages can be colored and named for quick and easy identification. This will undoubtedly speed up your workflow and make your writing process more directed and efficient.

Navigate to the Lists Editors area in the control bar and choose select the Marker tab.

Select the scene you would like to rename. In the lower portion of the Marker pane, select the marker text. Provide a new name for your marker. The new marker name will be updated in the Marker pane, as well as the marker in the bar ruler.

▶ FIG. 6.22

To change the color of the marker, choose View > Colors from Logic Pro X's main menu. You will be presented with a color palette window. Simply select the marker you would like to add color to and then select the color from the color palette window. Your marker will be represented with the color you selected from the color palette window.

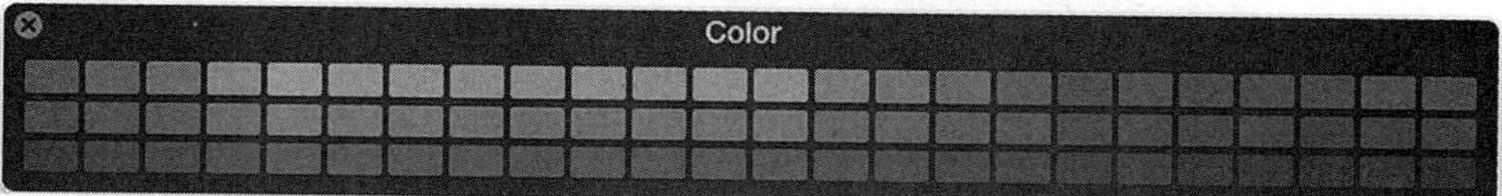

▶ FIG. 6.23

EXPORTING MUSICAL PROJECTS TO VIDEO

Writing music for film and television is an iterative process that often involves several rounds of review before final approval is given to finalize the project or schedule a recording session with live musicians. It is common to use low-resolution proxy videos throughout the music review process. This is primarily due to their small file size and inherent ability to be shared via the Internet and cloud-based solutions, such as Dropbox, in a relatively quick manner. DAWs that possess the capability to handle video files will more than likely have the ability to export audio projects back to the original video.

To export your musical project to a video file within Logic Pro X, choose File > Movie > Export Audio to Movie.

You will be presented with a Sound Settings window to choose the audio format and quality of music to export to your video.

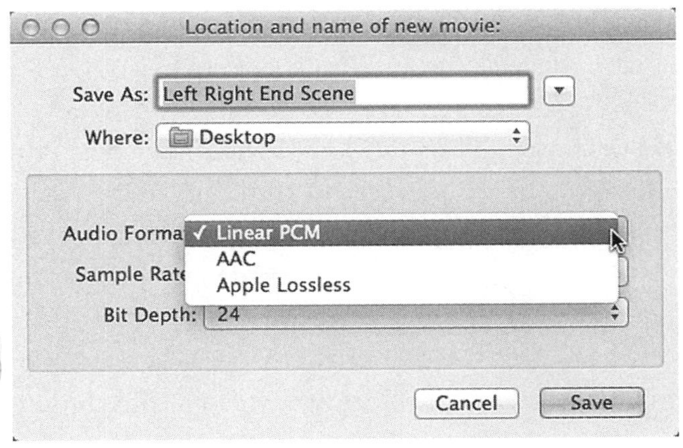

▶ **FIG. 6.24**

Generally speaking, you will likely want to change the format type of the audio you are be exporting. The default format is from the Pulse Code Modulation (PCM) family. These are high-quality audio files that are larger in file size than lossy file types such as Advanced Audio Coding (AAC) files. AAC files are commonly used for digital distribution due the highly efficient encoding scheme. AAC is the successor to the MPEG-1, Layer III file (MP3) file because it achieves similar audio quality at smaller file sizes.

Depending on the delivery method, it may be best to choose an audio format that will yield a smaller footprint. This will speed the transmission of the video file through an Internet connection. Video files should never be sent via email because your provider or the recipient's provider will likely reject the email due to attachment size limitations.

Choose to save the export to your Desktop by selecting the Desktop in the pop-up window or by simply pressing Command–D. This handy key command changes the save location of any save dialog box to the Desktop. Naming conventions are extremely important when sending files for review. Try using a naming convention such as *year-month-day-filename*, for example, 2014-1-1-myfile. This

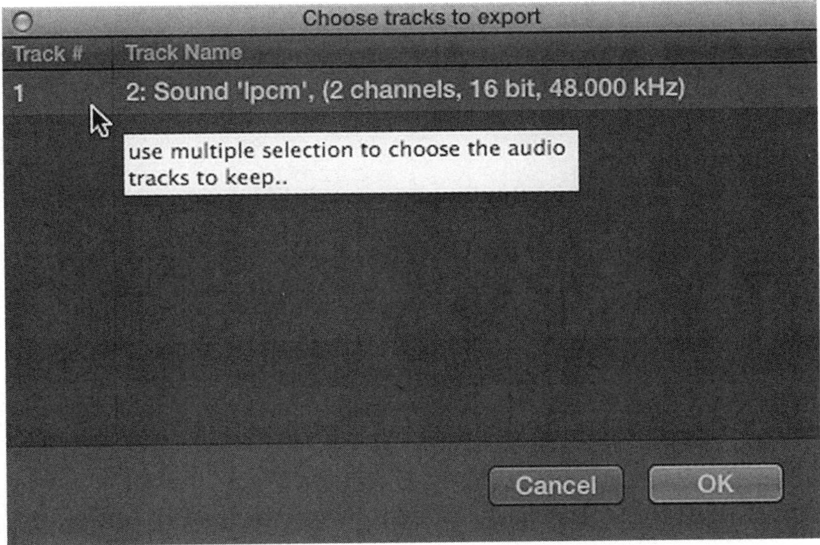

▶ **FIG. 6.25**

naming convention is helpful when sending files to collaborators because the files will automatically be sorted in Windows Explorer or OS X's Finder application when viewing files in list view.

Once you have chosen a save location for your file, Logic Pro X will present a final option to configure audio tracks to send back to the video file.

If you imported the audio from the video at the beginning of the project, that audio will be sent along with your musical composition to the video. Simply delete the original audio track to remove the audio content that was originally sent with the video. Click OK to initiate the audio export. Logic Pro X will bounce the audio project and create a new video at the chosen save location. The video can now be sent to collaborators for review.

CHAPTER 7
MUSIC CREATION ON MOBILE DEVICES AND AN INTRODUCTION TO BASIC MIXING

The biggest thing we have to do after creating a theme is to create an adaptive score through dynamic submixing of the tracks. Dave wrote this beautiful huge piece of music for this one game level, and we ended up extending it from two to three minutes of music into this big twenty-minute piece because of our dynamic mixing. When we were implementing the music into the game, it was all real time, control driven. Meaning that if an enemy were close to you, it would trigger a certain series of submixes. Or if you were, in the case of Iron Man, flying high, and it's an altitude-based parameter, you've actually changed the submix to adapt.

—Paul Lipson

CREATING MUSIC AND MIXING WITH MOBILE DEVICES

THE LOOK AND FEEL of recording environments has changed dramatically since the advent of the DAW. It is now possible to produce high-quality audio projects outside of the traditional recording studio. Musicians and composers can create and capture beautiful musical projects in a nontraditional home studio, with a laptop on a plane or with minimal mobile device equipment during a live performance. The tools required to work with digital audio have become smaller in size and are more efficient. Mobile devices are arguably approaching feature parity with traditional DAWs.

Audio hardware manufacturers are releasing products that are inspired by and designed to complement mobile devices. Apogee electronics recently released an iOS-compatible version of its popular Duet audio interface. Musicians can now record in the field with a professional audio interface that complements the small form factor of an iPhone or iPad. The audio project can be created and mixed in GarageBand for iOS and exported to Logic Pro X for further processing. There are other DAWs for iOS, including Cubasis and Auria. Apogee has made available a companion app that allows you to set microphone levels that are connected to the Duet audio interface.

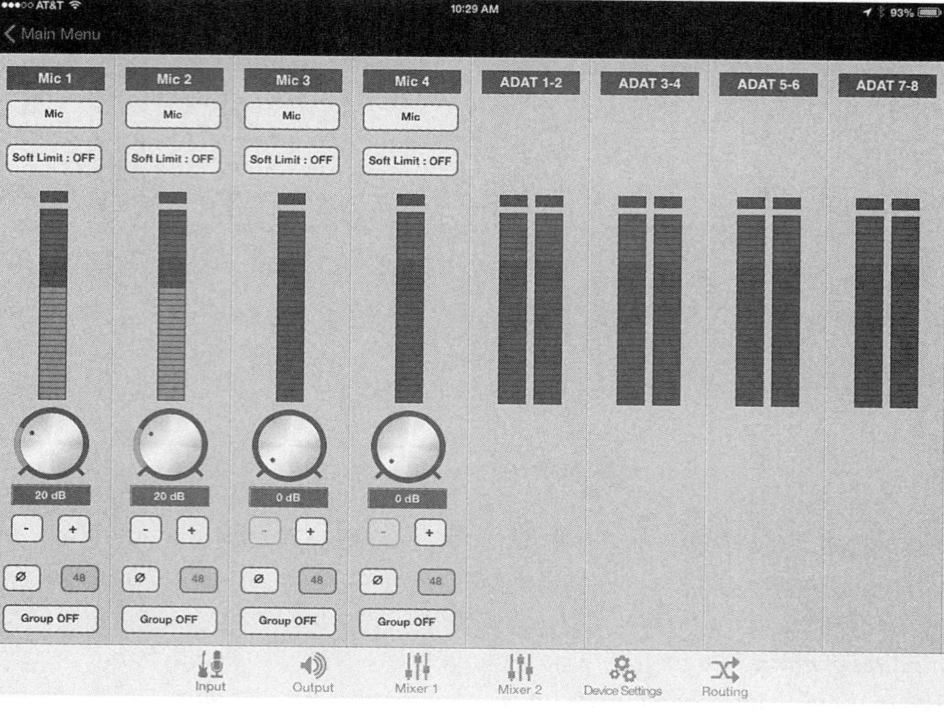

▶ **FIG. 7.1**

The Maestro app is a universal app that runs on both the iPhone and the iPad. It controls the physical inputs on the Duet for Mac and iPad. It can also control the panning or balance of audio tracks on the audio interface. As mentioned before, there are a number of audio and MIDI applications that are compatible with the Apogee Duet for Mac and iPad. For our purposes, we will focus on GarageBand for iOS due to its seamless compatibility with Logic Pro X.

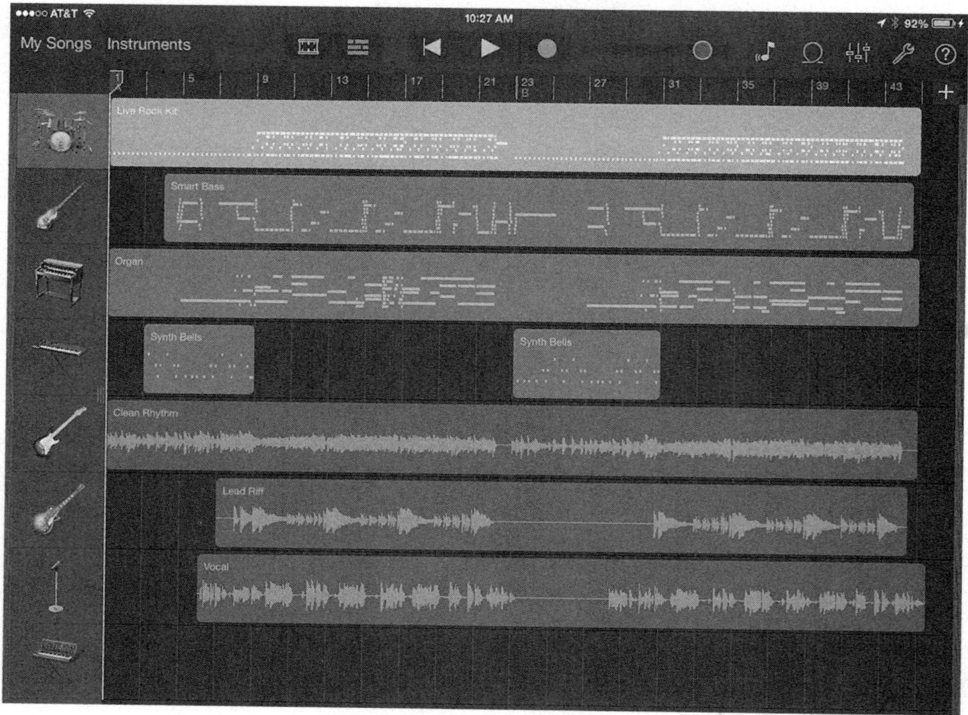

▶ **FIG. 7.2**

At first glance, GarageBand for iOS is instantly familiar to anyone who has ever worked with a DAW. Audio and MIDI information is separated into tracks to facilitate easy editing of each individual musical instrument. Common recording, playback, and mixing features are available within the application. While GarageBand for iOS is not as feature-rich as computer-based DAWs, there is certainly enough to begin working through a musical thought. For example, when working with the Apogee Duet for iPad and Mac, one can record live instruments and vocals that are of professional quality. Live instrumental recordings can be created in tandem with software instruments in much the same manner as a traditional DAW. The portability of this setup makes capturing valuable thoughts much easier and flexible. A more advanced sketch of the musical thought can be captured before moving your workflow to a traditional computer-based DAW.

Basic mixing tools are available in GargeBand for iOS. Simply swipe the track listing area to the right to show the track controls. Each track has a mute button, solo button, and volume slider.

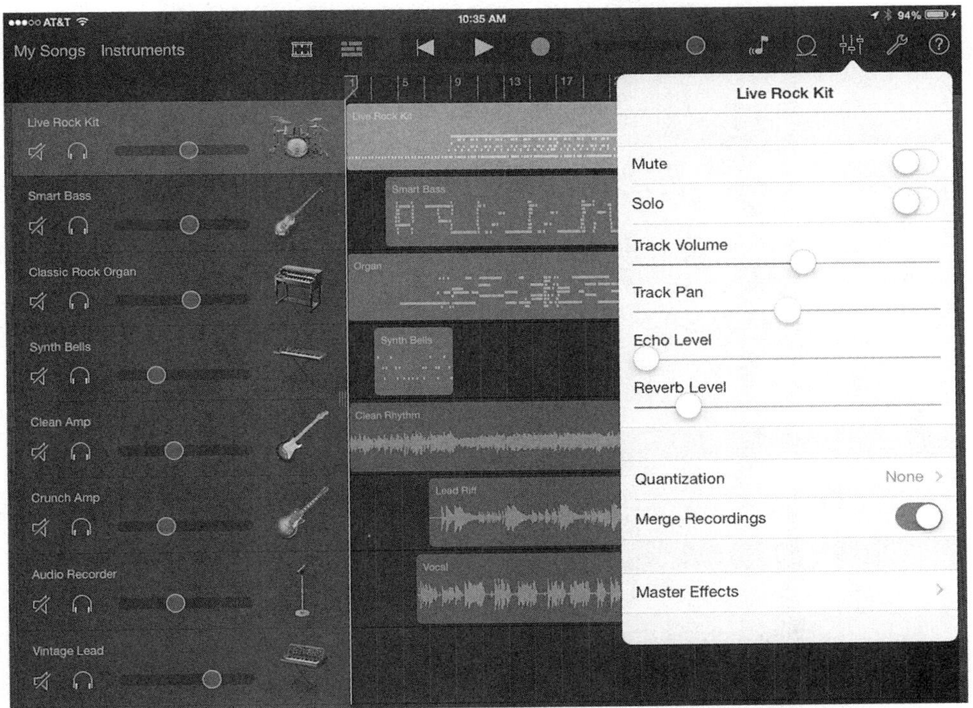

▶ **FIG. 7.3**

More advanced mixing features can be found by pressing the track information button in the toolbar. In addition to muting, soloing, and track volume, it is possible to alter track panning, reverb, and quantization levels from this view.

Musical inspiration can happen anywhere but, unfortunately, rarely occurs when you are close to a DAW or have access to staff paper and a pencil. Mobile devices have become invaluable tools in music creation because they approach the power of a DAW in a small, lightweight package that is easily transported.

The ability to capture musical idea at any time has offered a great deal of flexibility for the modern musician. Musical projects can be started on any number of mobile devices and seamlessly continued on a DAW, where you have even greater access to software instruments and DSP plugins, at a later time. It certainly is an exciting time to be a musician and composer.

EXPORTING AND IMPORTING GARAGEBAND FOR iOS PROJECTS

GarageBand for iOS provides a unique, mobile toolkit for starting musical projects. Once you have begun your music project, moving it a more feature-rich DAW like Logic Pro X is a quick and easy process.

Press the My Songs button in GarageBand for iOS. Then press the press the share button to reveal sharing options.

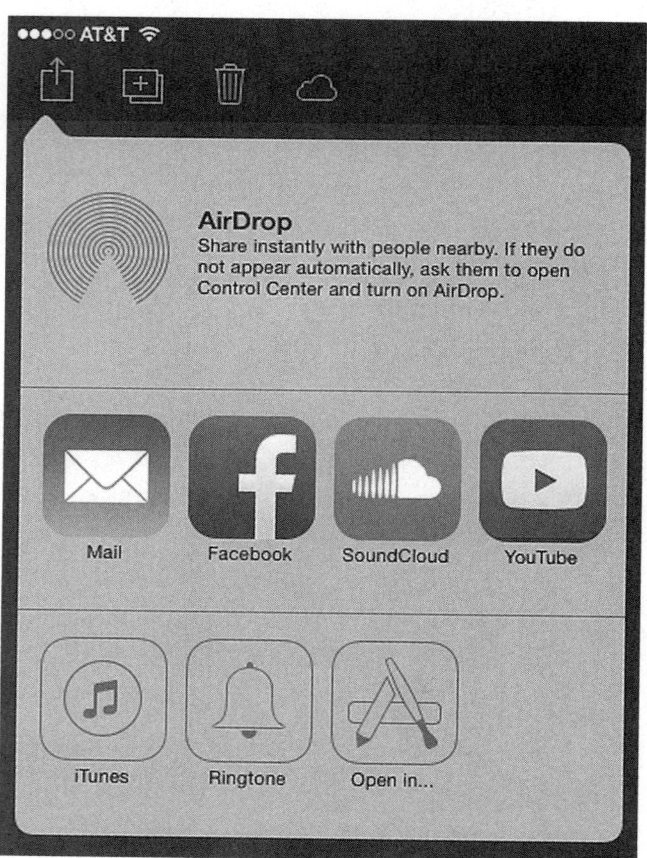

▶ FIG. 7.4

Select the project you would like to export and choose Share Song Via iTunes. You will be prompted to choose the sharing format. Choose to send your project to iTunes as a GarageBand project.

Open iTunes on your computer and select your iOS device in the iTunes sidebar. Select Apps from the iTunes menu and scroll down to reveal the App File Sharing Pane.

Cancel
Choose Format
Send "Export to Logic Pro" to iTunes as:

iTunes
Tap to send your song as a stereo file to the iTunes File Sharing area on your Mac or PC.
When you sync your device with a Mac or PC, locate the File Sharing area under the 'Apps' tab in iTunes, then click GarageBand to see your exported song.

The apps listed below can transfer documents between your iPad and this computer.

GarageBand
Today 10:30 AM
Tap to copy the multi-track GarageBand project to send to a Mac or another iOS device.
When you sync your device with a Mac, locate the File Sharing area under the 'Apps' tab in iTunes then click the GarageBand icon to see your exported song.

▶ FIG. 7.5

▶ FIG. 7.6

Select GarageBand from the Apps pane and any available GarageBand documents for export will be displayed in the list. In this particular case, there is one file entitled, Export to Logic Pro.band.

Drag the file from iTunes to your Desktop. Right-click (or Control-Click) on the file on your Desktop and choose Open With > Logic Pro X.

Logic Pro X will now attempt to open the GarageBand file. You may be prompted to download a compatibility update. This update provides all of the necessary software instruments required to provide full compatibility with GarageBand projects created on iOS. You will be prompted to save the GarageBand project as a Logic Pro X project. Choose the save the newly created Logic Pro X project on your Desktop.

Once you have successfully converted your GarageBand project and saved it as a Logic Pro X project, you will be free to continue building the musical idea that was started on your mobile device.

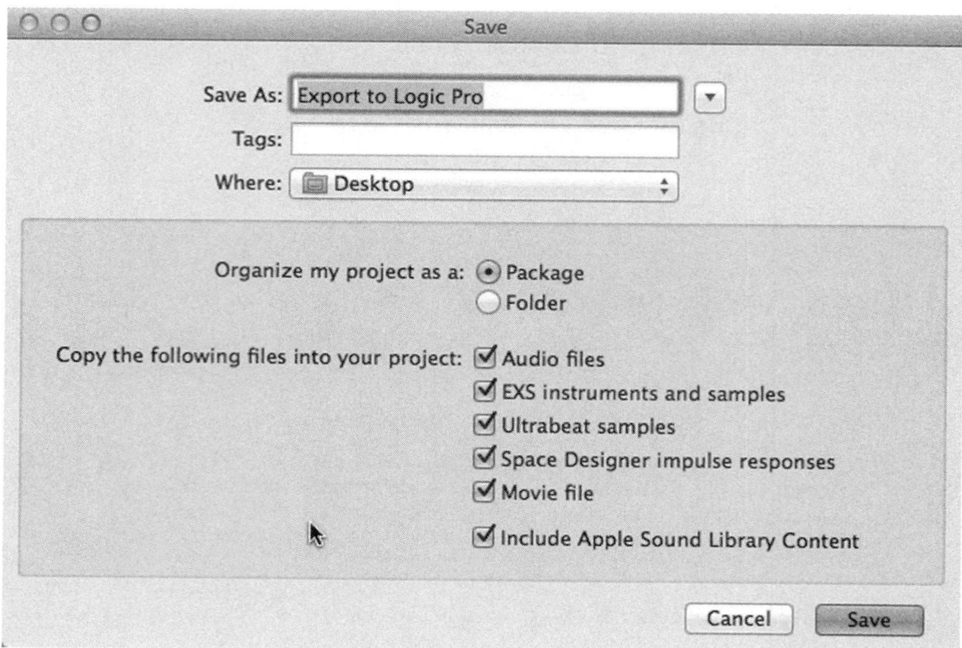

▶ FIG. 7.7

BUSES AND AUXILIARY TRACKS

Signal flow, or the flow of audio information through a digital audio workstation (DAW) and/or outboard audio gear, is an extremely important concept to understand when working with digital audio. The manner and order in which audio flows through software-based and hardware-based effects can have a significant effect on the final sound of your music. For example, the order in which a guitar sound is processed with either hardware-based or software-based reverb, compression, and delay effects can change the overall sonic character of the instrument.

Processing digital audio in real time can be an extremely taxing process for your computer's system resources. It is a common practice for digital audio to be processed in batches to limit the use of system resources. In other words, if you want to use a reverb effect on four separate tracks of trumpet performance, you will want to process all of the trumpet tracks at once rather than processing each track individually. Each instance of the reverb plugin will use valuable system resources. Also, it is quicker to use a single instance of reverb to process all four audio tracks rather than instantiate four individual reverb plugins.

This technique requires that you use a bus to batch process audio. Think of a bus as a virtual cable that is used to send audio signals from one channel strip to another. Essentially, when you use a bus, you send the output of a channel strip to the input of another. In the example of the four trumpet tracks, each individual trumpet channel strip's output would be sent to the same input of another channel strip. This receiving channel strip can be a Bus channel strip or an Auxiliary channel strip. Plugins are placed on the receiving channel strip so that you only instantiate one plugin, rather than four in the case of the trumpet channel strips. Logic Pro X provides sixty-four permanent buses for use at any time.

To send your audio to another channel strip via a bus, simply click and hold the output of the channel strip you would like to send via a bus.

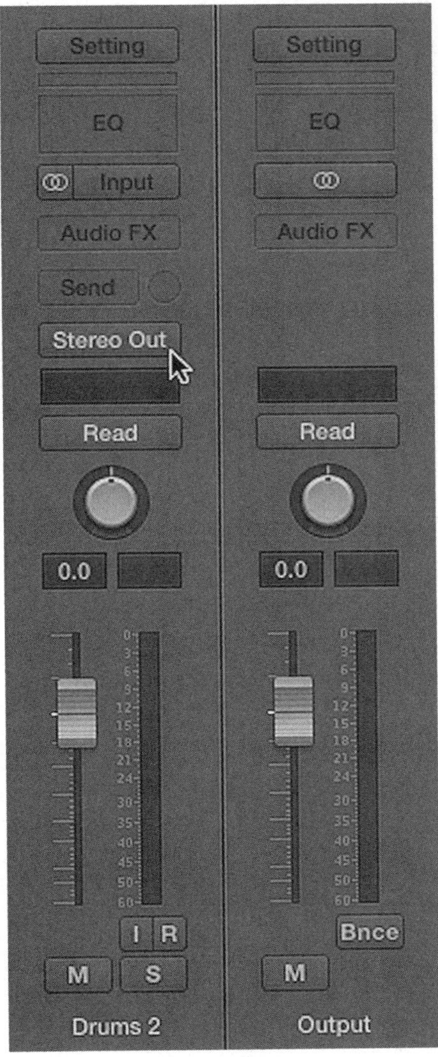

▶ **FIG. 7.8**

Choose the bus you would like to use. Remember, there are sixty-four buses to choose from. They all provide the same functionality.

Once the bus has been selected, an auxiliary track will be created in the mixer (Fig. 7.9). Essentially, the bus sends the audio information from the track to the auxiliary track. DSP plugins should be added on the auxiliary track so that any audio or MIDI data that is sent to it will be processed by the DSP plugin.

Notice that the input of the auxiliary track in the bus that was chosen as the output of the audio track (Fig. 7.10). The process of adding DSP plugins to an auxiliary track is exactly the same as adding DSP plugins to an audio of software instrument track. Simply click and hold on the inserts slot and choose the desired DSP plugin.

At this point, it is best to rename you auxiliary track so that you can easily identify the purpose of the auxiliary track. For example, if the main purpose of

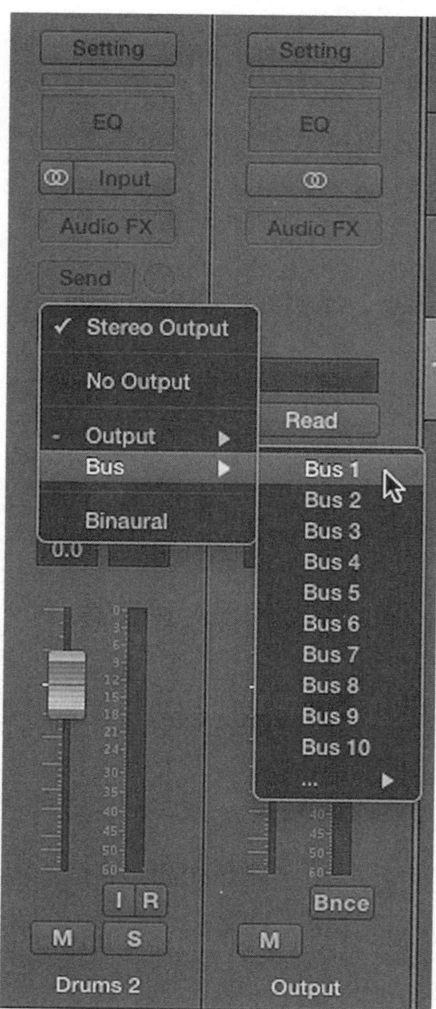

▶ **FIG. 7.9**

the auxiliary track is add reverb to a grouping of tracks, simply name the auxiliary track "Reverb" (Fig. 7.11). To process additional tracks of audio with the auxiliary track, simply choose the bus as the output for those tracks.

It is important to discuss signal flow within Logic Pro X. Signal flow describes the path that audio signals travel on through the DAW. In the case of Logic Pro X, audio signals travel from left to right in the mixer (Fig. 7.12).

CREATING STEM TRACKS TO TRANSPORT AUDIO

Stem tracks are often requested when working with digital audio because they allow you to send a set of premixed tracks that can be used within another digital audio workstation or nonlinear video editing application, such as Final Cut Pro, Premier Pro, or Avid Media Composer. Stems are essentially a grouping of tracks that have been premixed into a single track, or stem. Auxiliary tracks are typically used to create stem tracks within Logic Pro X. Examples of famous stem tracks include the complete recordings of the Beatles from *Abbey Road*.

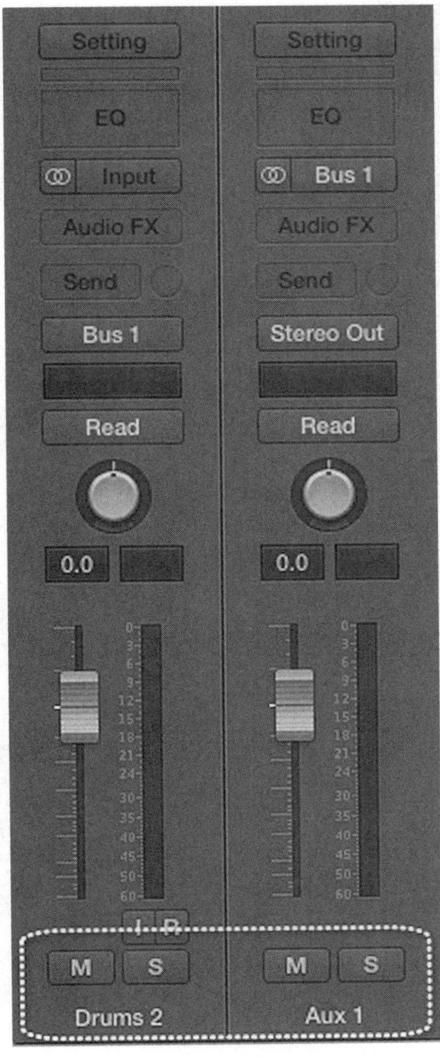

▶ **FIG. 7.10**

Stems allow musicians and composers to use prerecorded music to augment and enhance their current musical project.

The first step in creating stem tracks is to decide which tracks you would like to export as stem files. Musician will often choose to send groupings of instruments, such as a rhythm section or a part of a rhythm section, to another musician, composer, or producer to be used in another digital DAW. In this case we will export an entire project as stem files so they can be used in another application.

To begin choosing which tracks you would like to export as stem files, open the mixer within Logic Pro X (Fig. 7.13). This can be achieved by to Window > Open Mixer in the menu bar.

In order to export tracks as stem files, they need to be assigned to a bus. This will create an auxiliary track that will be used to facilitate the export process. Tracks can be exported via an auxiliary track individually or as a group. For example, you may choose to export all of the microphones assigned to a drum set recording as a single stem. Conversely, you may also want to export each individual

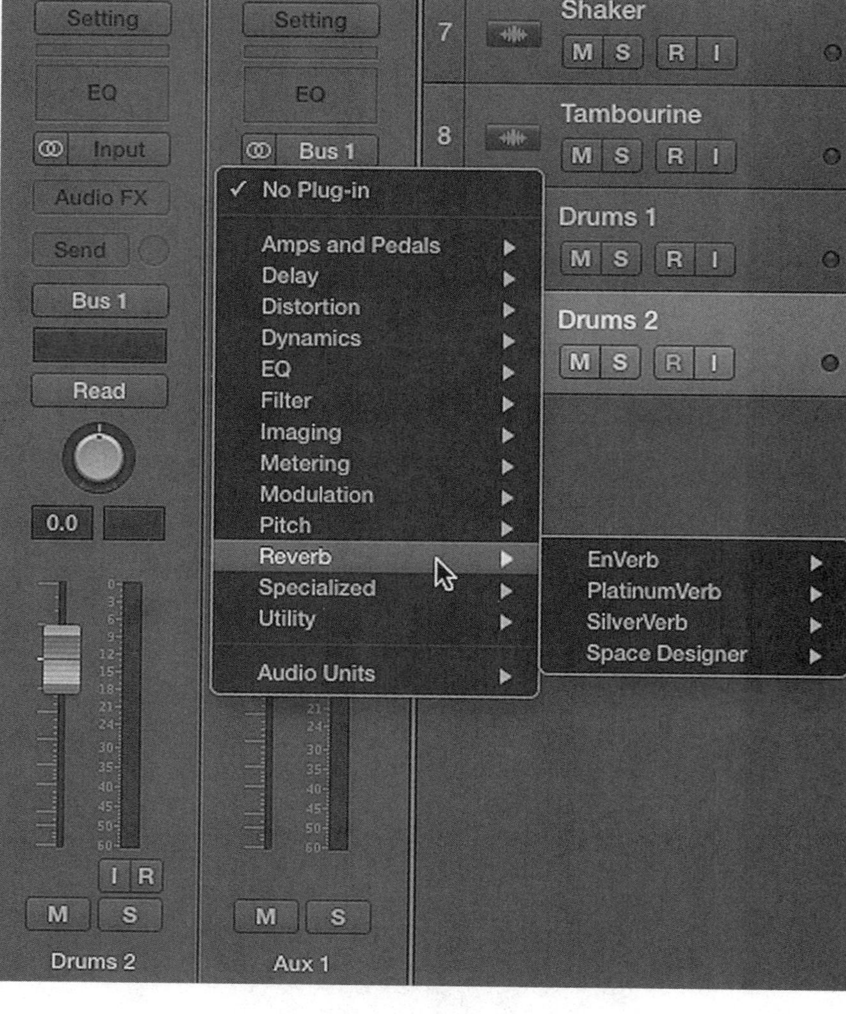

▶ **FIG. 7.11**

microphone of the drum set recording as an individual stem. Whatever your export preference is, you have the flexibility to export as a group or individual tracks. To assign the tracks to a bus, simply lasso around the desired tracks to select them. Let's start by grouping our drum tracks (tracks 9 and 10) by assigning them to a bus. In the mixer, select the two tracks by dragging, or lassoing, across them.

Once you have the two tracks selected, click and hold the next available send slot on one of the tracks and choose the first available bus—in this case, bus 1 (Fig. 7.14). The tracks will now be assigned to bus 1 and a new auxiliary track will be created the right of the tracks in the mixer. Rename the auxiliary track with a name that describes the grouping, for example, "drum set."

To create more track groups, repeat the same procedure mentioned before. You may wish to create groups for other instrument groups, such as brass, saxophones, etc. (Fig. 7.15). Creating auxiliary tracks for individual tracks is done in much the same way. Instead of grouping tracks together, simply choose an individual track and assign it to a bus. A new auxiliary track will be created for the track.

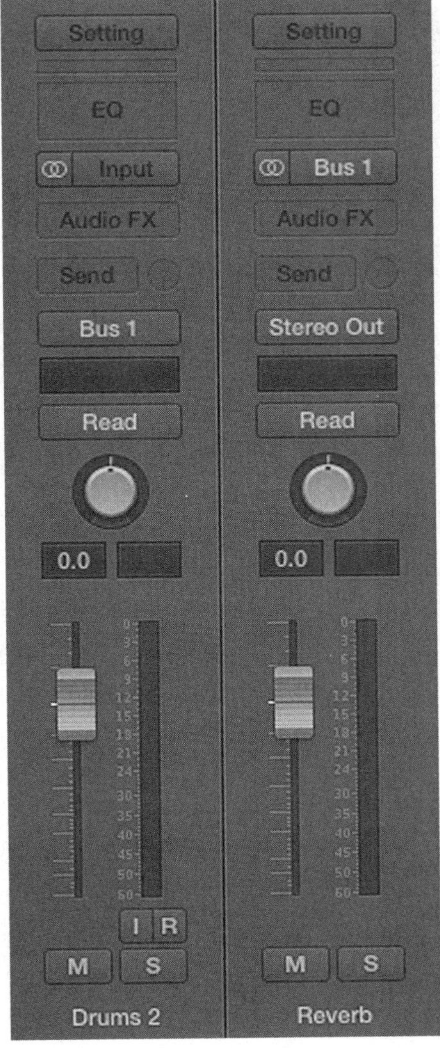

▶ FIG. 7.12

The next step in the stem track creation process is to add the newly created auxiliary tracks to the Tracks area so that they can be individually exported as audio files. Select the auxiliary tracks that you would like exported as stem files and choose Options > Create Arrange Tracks for Selected Channel Strips in the mixer's menu bar.

The track or tracks will now be added to the Tracks area's tracks listing (Fig. 7.16). It is now necessary to create a small empty region on the track to facilitate the export process. Draw an empty region on the auxiliary track with the Pencil tool.

When you are ready to export your tracks, choose File > Export All Tracks as Audio Files from Logic Pro X's menu bar. Each track in your Tracks area, including the auxiliary tracks, will be exported as audio files (Fig. 7.17). These files are ready to be sent to your collaborator.

AUTOMATING TRACKS

When working with multiple tracks in an audio project, it is often necessary to automate changes that you may wish to make to a track, such as volume, panning,

▶ **FIG. 7.13**

EQ, and plugin settings. Logic Pro X allows you to automate every function in regard to mixing. Automation data is independent of audio and MIDI regions and is entirely track-based. In other words, any automation data you create applies to the individual track. Automation is often used to fade in and out of finalized projects and control necessary track changes throughout the project itself.

To view automation options, press the Show/Hide Automation button in the Tracks area's tool bar.

Automation parameters appear on each track to facilitate creating automation data (Fig. 7.18). The default automation parameter is volume because it is one of the most commonly automated values.

Before we begin automating values, it is import to discuss the type of automation you can perform—real time and offline. Real-time automation refers to automation data that is recorded while the project is being played back. For example, if a trumpet track is too loud in comparison to the rest of the other tracks, it can be lowered for the section of the project that is affected. When performing live automation, Logic Pro X provides several automation modes to read and record automation data:

1. Read—This mode reads the current automation data that exists on the track, if any. Automation data will not be recorded while using this mode.
2. Touch—When a channel strip controller is touched or moved, Logic Pro X will record the change while the parameter is adjusted. Once the parameter movement has ceased, Logic Pro X will not record any further

▶ **FIG. 7.14**

data until the parameter is adjusted again. This is the most commonly used automation mode. It is comparable to "riding the faders" on a hardware mixer board.

3. Latch—Latch is very similar to touch, with the exception that Logic Pro X will continue to write automation data at the last point of parameter adjustment. For example, if a track's volume were to be lowered by the channel strip or an external controller, Logic Pro X will continue to write the lowered volume level until moved again. Automation data latches onto the last written value and will overwrite any future automation data that is currently on the track.
4. Write—This is a destructive mode that erases automation data on the track. This mode primarily exists to provide a robust set of automation

▶ FIG. 7.15

▶ FIG. 7.16

▶ FIG. 7.17

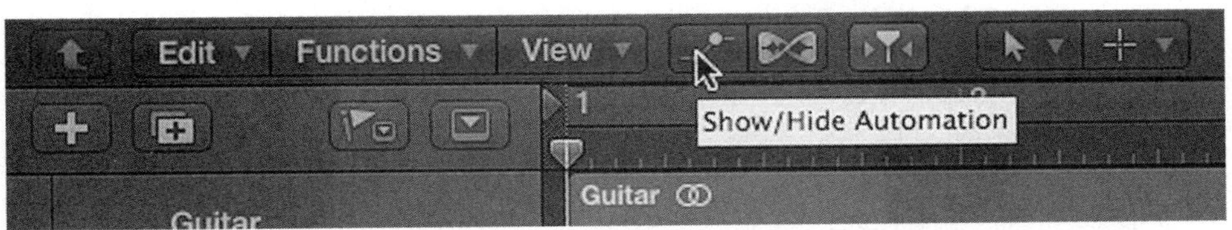

▶ FIG. 7.18

controls. It is rarely used, and if the end goal is to erase track automation data, it is far more efficient to choose Mix > Delete Automation > Delete All Automation on Selected Track from Logic Pro X's main menu.

To begin automating data, choose your automation mode from the channel strip.

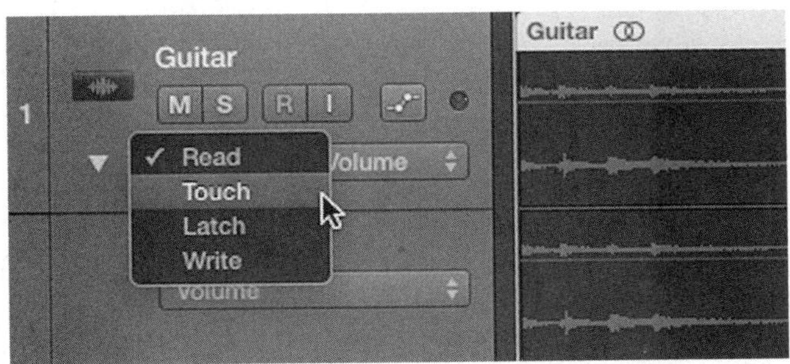

▶ FIG. 7.19

Next, choose the parameter you would like to be automated. In this case, we will automate volume. It is important to note that many external MIDI controllers and control surfaces are preconfigured to work with DAWs such as Logic Pro X, Pro Tools, and Nuendo.

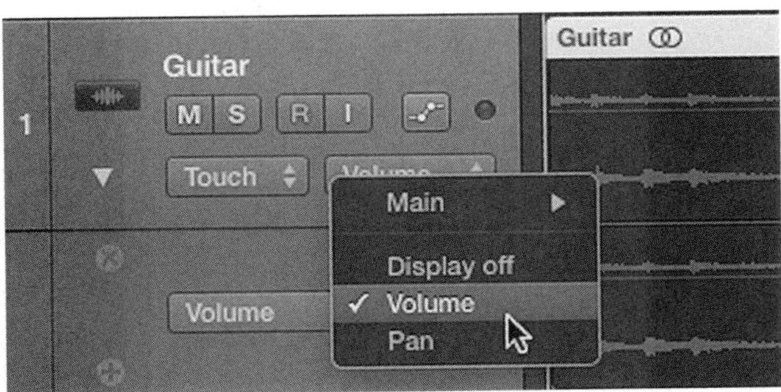

▶ FIG. 7.20

Once you have chosen your automation type and parameter, begin playback of your project and adjust either the channel strip in the Tracks area or move an external hardware fader or knob, if available. The automation data will be recorded in accordance to the automation mode selected. Automation data is written in the form of nodes.

Logic Pro X will now play back any automation data that has been recorded on the track. In this case, volume automation data will be followed during playback. The track fader will move in accordance with the automation data that was written.

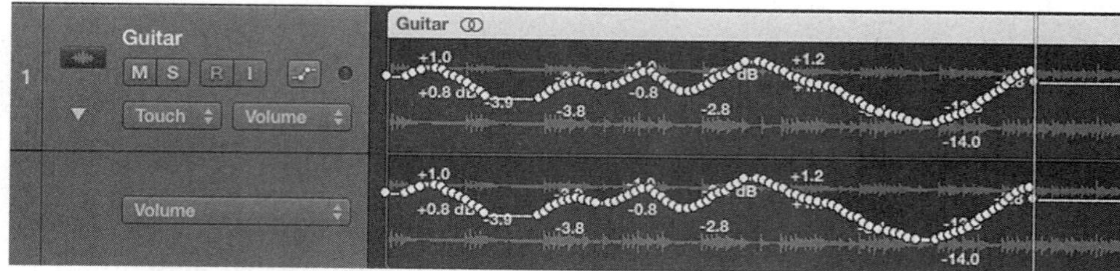

▶ **FIG. 7.21**

Another form of automation, offline automation, can also be very useful when working with musical projects. Offline automation provides the ability to input precision automation as well as automation curves in your project. When writing offline automation, it is not necessary to assign an automation mode such as read, touch, latch, or write because automation will be manually entered, rather than through the movement of a channel strip fader or knob, or external hardware controller surface. In fact, offline automation can be entered even if a real-time automation mode is enabled.

To enter automation values, simply click on the automation line that is enabled on your track. Nodes will be entered at each point where you click.

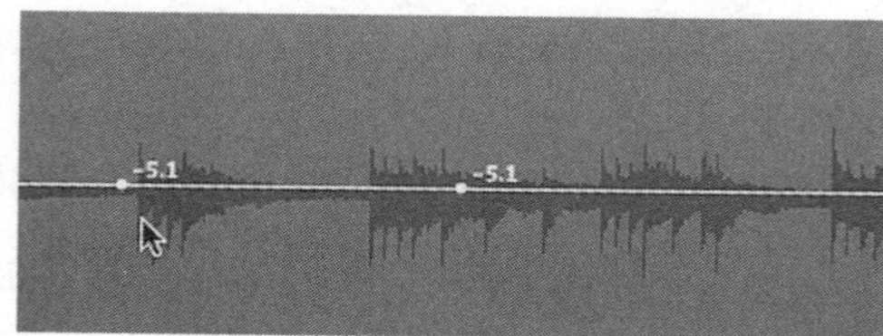

▶ **FIG. 7.22**

Nodes can be moved by simply clicking the node and dragging it to the desired level.

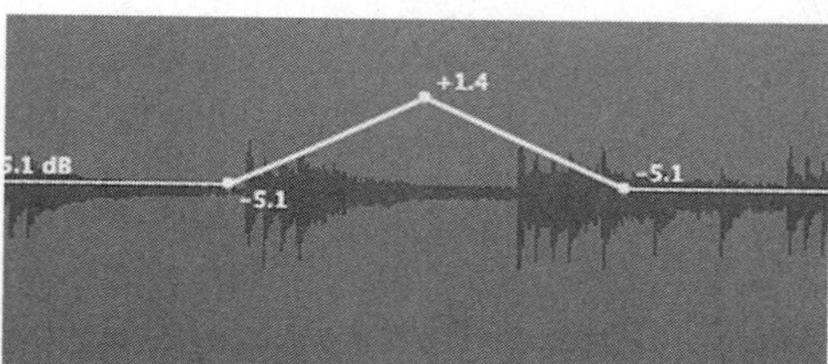

▶ **FIG. 7.23**

The volume level for this particular track will move from -5.1dB to 1.4dB and down to -5.1dB during playback. The values will be equally scaled from one node to the next during playback. This may not be the most musical approach to automation. For that reason, it is possible to automation curves between modes when using offline automation.

Automation curves can be created by using the automation tool or by using holding Control and Shift when dragging between two nodes. It is often more efficient to use the key command because you can quickly alternate between the pointer tool and the ability to create tempo curves. Dragging left to right allows you to ease the automation curve, while dragging up or down will create a parabolic automation curve.

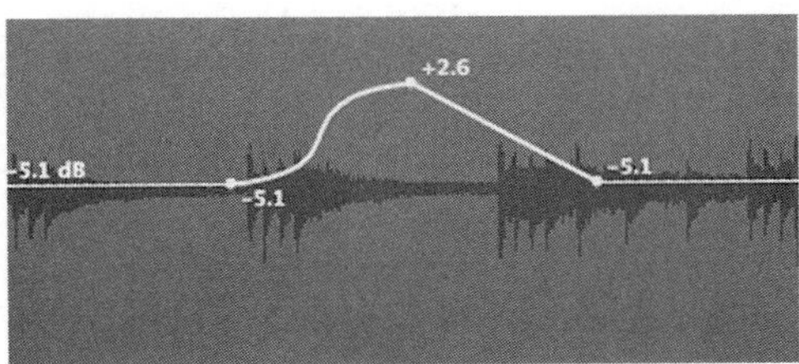

▶ FIG. 7.24

The automation curve will arguably produce results that are more musical and natural to the listener and make offline automation sound less static. Automation data can also be copied from one track to another to speed your workflow when creating automation nodes, lines, and curves. This is helpful when working with two tracks of the same instrument.

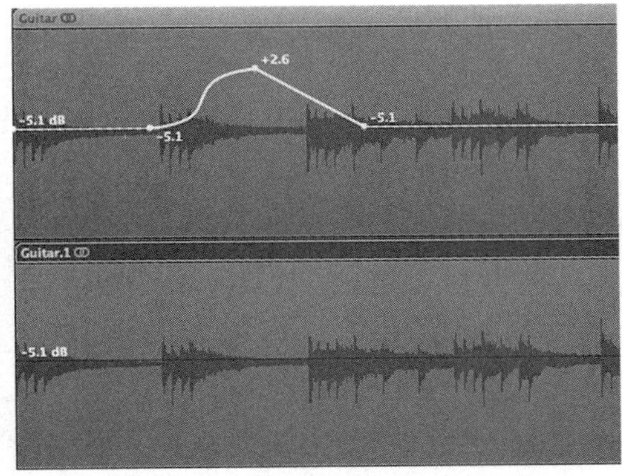

▶ FIG. 7.25

To copy automation data, hold the shift key and drag around the automation data you wish to be copied. Select the track you would like the automation to be copied to and press Command–V.

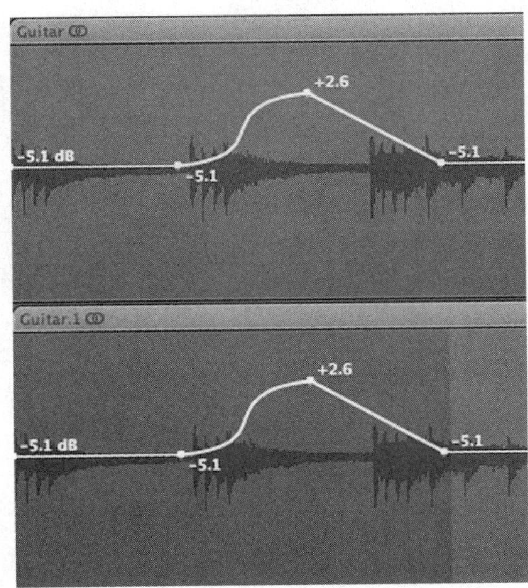

▶ FIG. 7.26

The automation data will now appear on the second track. Both tracks will be affected by the automation data.

AUTOMATING GROUPS

Track automation is a wonderful tool to augment and enhance your musical project by changing parameters in real time. That said, automating individual tracks at once could be problematic when automating an instrument that may utilize several tracks of audio data. For example, a drum set is typically recorded with several microphones that are carefully placed to capture the distinct qualities of each component of the drum set. The audio data from each microphone will enter the DAW on a separate audio track. Once the tracks are in the Tracks area, the levels of the drum tracks will need to be mixed to create a proper balance between all of the drum tracks. This way the drum set as a whole will sound balanced and create a foundation for the other tracks in the project to be mixed against. There may be times in a project where the drum set volume needs to be raised to balance the musical path of the project. It is very likely that the carefully crafted mix for the drum set that was created before will be lost

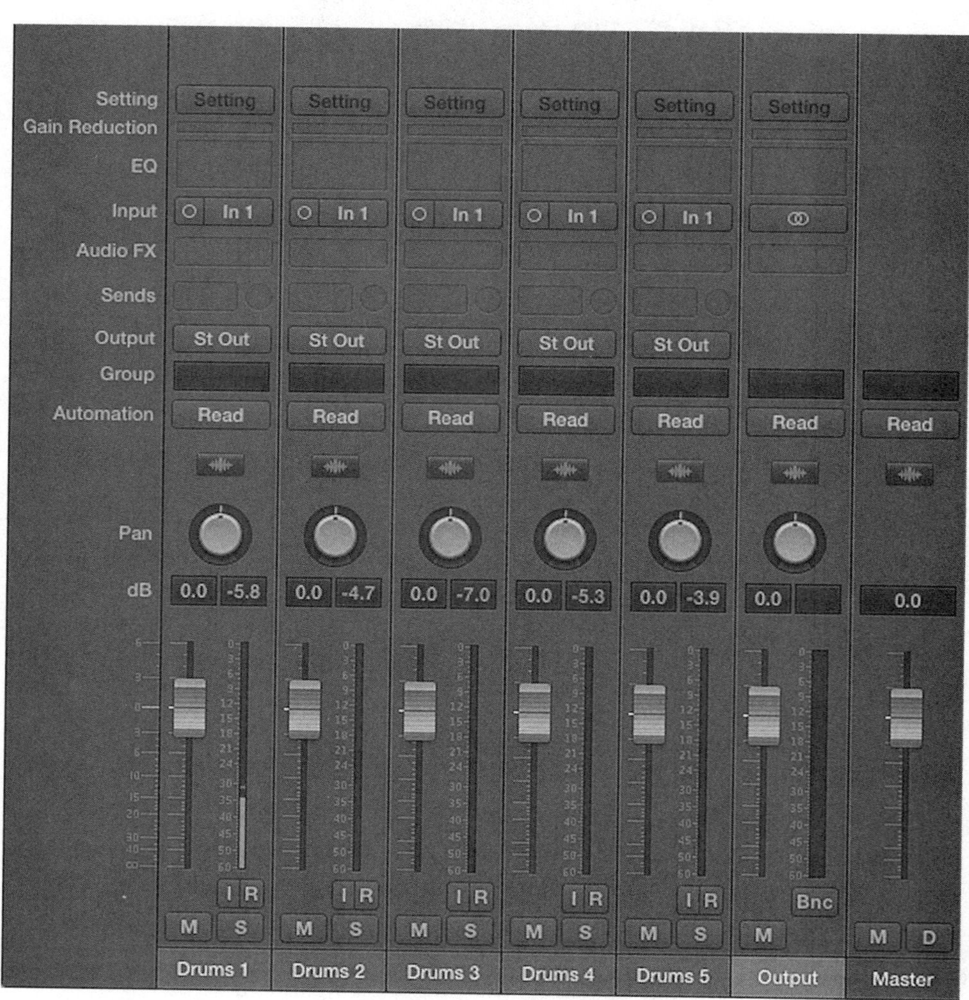

▶ **FIG. 7.27**

because each track will be required to move individually. In cases such as these it is possible to group tracks together so that the faders are locked together and move in scale.

In Logic Pro X, this functionality is known as group clutch. Similar functionality exists in other DAWs, as well. To enable group clutch, navigate to the

▶ **FIG. 7.28**

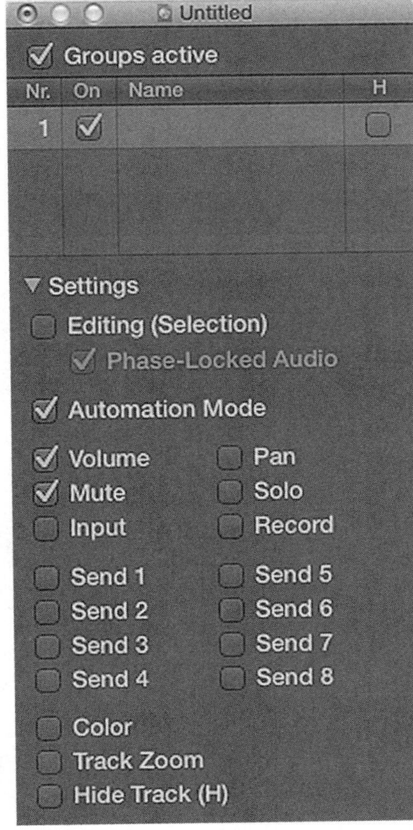

▶ **FIG. 7.29**

mixer. Notice that the drum set tracks are all set to different levels. The drum set volume levels were mixed or balanced based upon the levels each track was recorded at.

To assign these tracks to a group, simply drag left to right on the track name to select all of the tracks (Fig. 7.27). With all of the tracks selected, click and hold the group membership space directly above the volume fader and panning knob of one of the tracks. Assign it to the first group available. In this case, group 1 was is the first available groups.

Logic Pro X allows you to change the name of the group for ease of use in the event you wish to assign tracks to various groups (7.28).

To enable the group clutch functionality, simply choose Options > Disable Groups from the mixer's menu bar or press Shift–G on your keyboard (Fig. 7.29). The drum set tracks will now move to scale and ensure that the mix you created will remain intact even if you need to raise or lower the volume of the drum set as a whole.

CHAPTER 8
DELIVERY, COLLABORATION, AND ARCHIVING

It's not like... you're not handing it up or handing it down; you're handing it across. And that is just a beautiful thing.

—David Earl

... Sometimes when you're so deep and close to the music, sometimes when you're working on a big project with that amount of minutes, you just can lose perspective. Or you just start to like... I need a second opinion. So collaborating with someone that you trust is great.

—Paul Lipson

WRITING MUSIC for the moving picture comes with challenges that are solved through great creativity, determination, and, in most cases, the professional experience that inspires you to create musical brilliance. The challenges to be negotiated in a writing project are not limited to the writing process. Quite the contrary, consistently delivering drafts of music to clients in a timely manner throughout the project can be equally stressful, taxing time and valuable resources that can and should be focused on the project at hand—writing music. The goal of this chapter is to utilize technological resources and to streamline the process of delivering musical drafts and final products to clients, all without leaving your studio or workspace.

BOUNCING AUDIO

When sending musical projects to clients, it is important to export your project to a format that is playable without the use of a digital audio workstation, in other words, provide an audio format that is compatible with music playback devices such mobile devices, MP3 players, and so on. This enables your client to listen to the mockup you have prepared and provide feedback for any changes that may need to be made in a future revision.

Download the Delivery, Collaboration, and Archiving project file and unzip it to your Desktop. Open the Logic Pro X project file. From the Menu bar, choose File > Bounce > Project or Section.

Note: This project does not contain a movie. In some cases, clients request music that follows a general mood or theme that can be used as library music. Clients will often specify instrumentation, genre, general tempo, and duration that can be used interchangeably for a number of different clips.

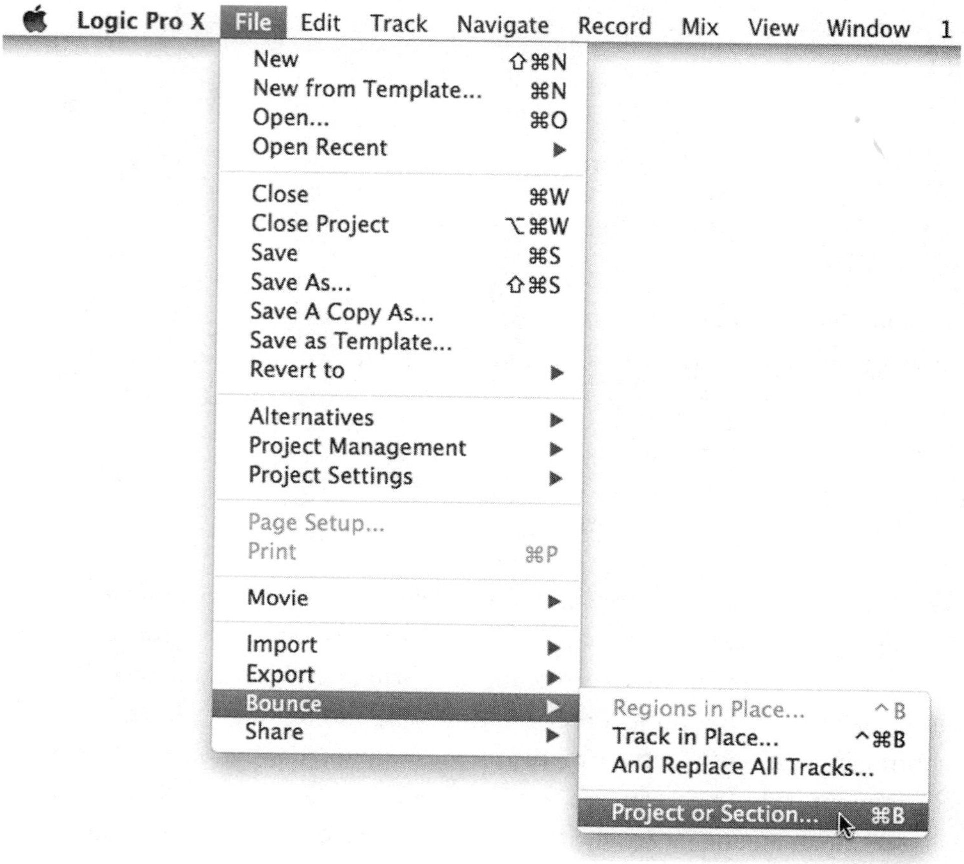

▶ **FIG. 8.1**

The Bounce dialog box opens and displays the various parameters for bouncing your music into a playable audio file. There are several available options for bouncing audio. It is possible to select a portion of the audio project to bounce, choose quality and file type, and choose if the project will be bounced in real-time or offline mode.

When a project is bounced in real-time mode the project will be bounced while the project is playing. Conversely, when a project is bounced in offline mode the tracks in the project will be quickly merged together. In most cases bouncing in offline mode is acceptable for drafts and saves a great deal of time because the project does not have to be playing during the bouncing process. Bouncing in real-time mode is advised when preparing a final music bounce for

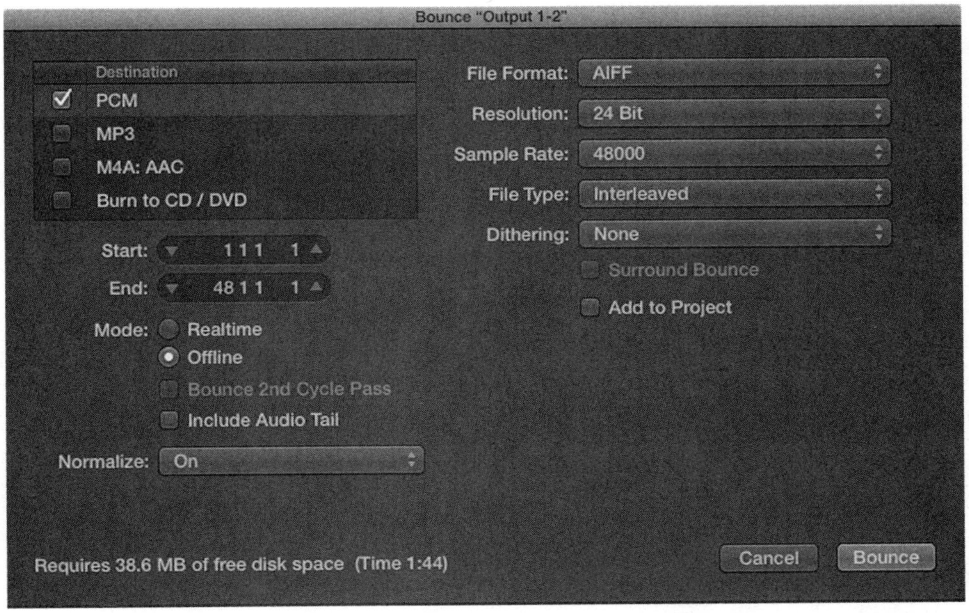

▶ **FIG. 8.2**

clients. This process allows you to listen to the final mix as it is bouncing for any possible issues that may have been missed in previous editing sessions. If a problem is detected it is very easy to quickly fix the problem and start the bounce process again. If you are using software instruments that include tail offs, real-time bouncing is always necessary. This ensures that the decay of the software instrument will be printed and included with the final audio bounce.

There are a number of options to explore in the Bounce dialog. The left side of the Bounce dialog box provides destination settings, which enable you to choose the format of the audio file that will be bounced. A destination is a simply the final file result after the musical project has been exported. Logic Pro X allows projects to be bounced as Pulse Code Modulation (PCM) files, MPEG-1 Audio Layer 3 (MP3) files, MPEG 4 Audio (MP4/AAC) files, and a burned CD. These are all common audio formats that are frequently used when delivering final project files. The project can be bounced to all four destinations simultaneously, saving a great deal of time by enabling you to provide your client with multiple versions of the audio file.

The right side of the Bounce dialog box allows you to adjust the attributes of the file type that is selected as a destination. For example, when choosing a PCM as a destination, the file format, resolution, sample rate and file type will need to be specified. Generally speaking, the default attributes are appropriate for the bouncing process. However, if the need arises, attributes can be adjusted to fit your specifications. Select PCM and MP3 as destinations with the following settings:

PCM
File Format: AIFF
Resolution: 24 Bit
Sample Rate: 48,000

File Type: Interleaved
Dithering: None

MP3
Bit Rate Mono: 320 kbps
Bit Rate Stereo: 320 kbps
Quality: Ensure "Use best encoding" and "Filter frequencies below 10 Hz" are selected.
Stereo Mode: Joint Stereo, Ensure "Write ID3 Tags" is selected.

When you have completed these actions, click Bounce.

By default, Logic Pro X offers to save your bounced audio file project in a folder entitled "Bounces" in that resides at *Your User Account Name/Music/Logic*. This is helpful because bounces are organized within your user folder. However, it is possible to change this location for quick access.

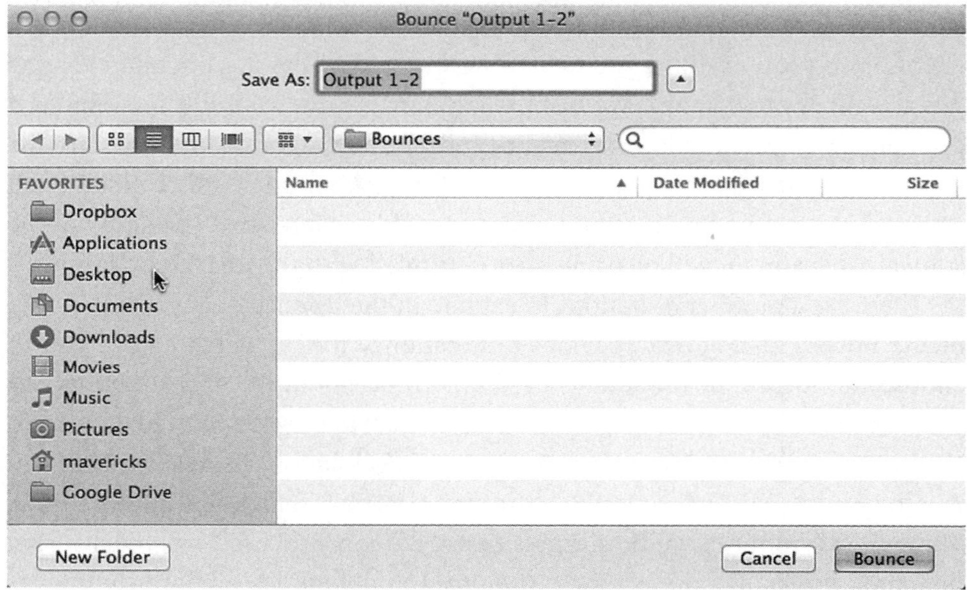

▶ **FIG. 8.3**

Select the Desktop from the left sidebar of the save dialog box. Click the New Folder Button at the lower left side of the save dialog box. Create a folder entitled "revisions" on the desktop, name your project "Revision 1," and click Bounce once again.

Once the bouncing process has completed, you should have a folder on your desktop entitled "revisions" with two audio files entitled "Revision 1.aif" and "Revision 1.mp3" inside the folder. The AIFF file is a high-quality audio file that film editors can use in any film-editing software, such as Final Cut Pro, Avid Media Composer, or Adobe Premier Pro. The MP3 file is a lower-quality audio file that can be used in handheld media players and shared more easily via email or the Web because of its smaller footprint. MP3 files are not usually suitable for final delivery to clients because they are compressed audio files that are not of the same quality of AIFF files.

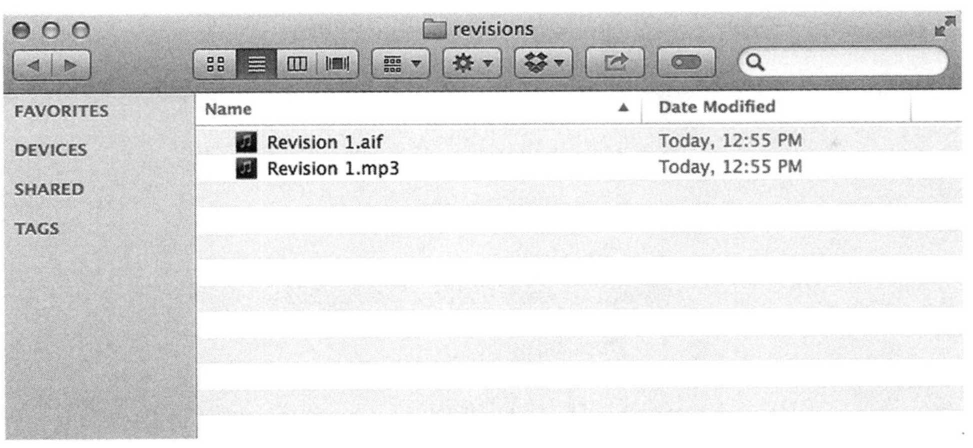

▶ **FIG. 8.4**

CREATING ARCHIVES

Archiving is the process of creating a single file that contains one or more compressed files or folders. The most common archive is the ZIP (.zip) format. There are other archiving formats such as Stuffit (.sitx) and tar (.tar and .tar.gz). They are not as commonly used as the ZIP format and can create compatibility issues if software to open the archives is not installed. The ZIP format is natively supported on OS X and the various versions of the Windows operating system. Archives can be extremely useful in backing up information, but they can also be useful when sending a group of files or folders to clients. Your various music files can be compressed into a single file that greatly simplifies sending musical ideas and mockups to clients.

Navigate to your desktop and control-click (or right-click if you have a two-button mouse) on the "revisions" folder that was created previously. Choose Compress "revisions."

Once the archiving process has completed, you will notice that a file named "revisions.zip" now appears on your desktop. The "revisions" folder was zipped into a single file. There are several benefits to this archive:

- The files in the "revisions" folder are now flattened into a single file and, as a result, are much easier to send.
- The folder and its nested files have been compressed so they occupy less space on the hard drive.
- A fresh copy of the "revisions" folder can by created by double-clicking on the archive. Think of the archive as a blueprint that can create new instances of the compressed file or folder. In other words, it is possible to create fresh copies of your archived files simply by opening the archive on your computer.

File-naming conventions are very important in terms of organization of your musical project. It is not uncommon to be dealing with quite a few drafts of a project. Multiple files and drafts can be difficult and confusing to organize,

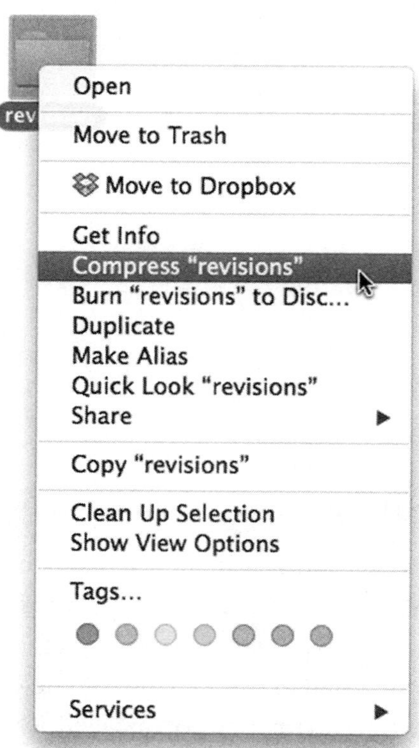

▶ **FIG. 8.5**

potentially leading to inefficient use of valuable time. To combat this issue you may want to experiment with using a file naming convention that employs dates. (e.g., 2014-1-1-myfile.zip). Using this approach, files will automatically be sorted by date rather than name.

Select revisions.zip and press the enter key to rename the file and name the file with the current date and file name.

Note: If files are going to be sent via the Internet, they should be lowercase and named without spaces in the title. This will help prevent potential issues on file servers that are case sensitive.

Once an archive has been made from a folder and its enclosed files, the archive can be easily sent to a client or a collaborator on the film and television project. There are several methods for sending files to clients. Email is one of the most commonly used methods for sending files via the Internet; however, most email providers limit the size of files that are attached to email messages. For the most part, size limitations are imposed to ration network bandwidth and server space that is being used by mail servers and to ensure that email is sent quickly and efficiently. Audio and video files are not conducive to being sent via email because of their large file size.

There are other methods for sending large files. In the following sections of this chapter, we will explore various methods of delivery and the strengths and weaknesses of the varying approaches.

FILE TRANSFER PROTOCOL

Depending on the location of the composer and the client, it is not uncommon to have drafts and revisions delivered by expensive overnight delivery options or courier. While these options do indeed fulfill the delivery, they are not conducive to quick changes that may need to be done within hours on any given aspect of a project. These inefficiencies are expensive and can add unnecessary confusion in an already complicated production timeline. To combat this issue, many industries utilize the standard file transfer protocol (FTP) service to deliver drafts and revision requests to and from clients and composers. While FTP has helped alleviate some of the inefficiencies and stress that accompanies the process of remotely working with clients, it is not without problems. Many people are confused about what the FTP service is and how it works.

FTP is a file-sharing protocol that is widely used to place files on remote servers. These files can be of any type as long as they are in a digital format—Hypertext Markup Language (HTML) files, digital photos, audio files, movie files, etc. For this reason, FTP has been the default choice of Web designers and Web developers for quite a long time. When speaking about connections to a remote server, it is common to speak in terms of two parties: the client (not to be confused with clients who hire you) and the server. The client is a computer that possesses files that need to be delivered to another location—in this case, a server. The server is a computer that is usually in a different location than the client. Servers can take on various roles that include hosting websites, storing and sharing data, and so on. The client connects to the FTP server via the FTP protocol and sends files to the remote FTP server. The server can be thought of as an intermediary data repository that you can connect to as well as any party that you specify. The time required to send a file is only limited by the speed at which you can send, or upload, to a remote server. In many cases this transfer speed is dramatically faster than express shipping and courier services.

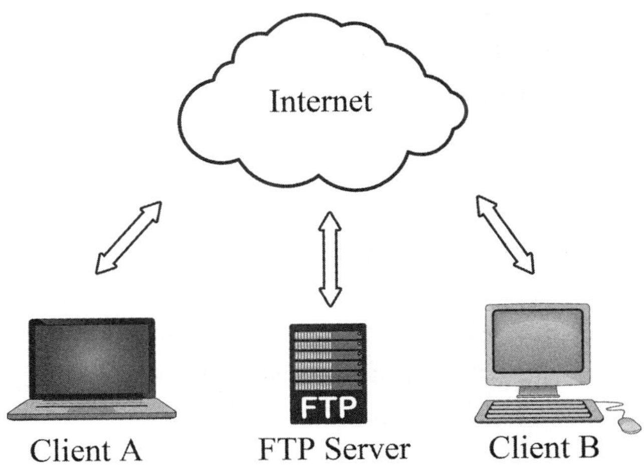

▶ **FIG. 8.6**

In a workflow that utilizes an FTP server, the FTP server acts as an intermediary between the various clients that connect to it. In the previous figure, Client A connects to the FTP server through the FTP protocol via the Internet and uploads files to the FTP server. The FTP server receives the files from Client A and makes them available to other clients. Client B connects to the FTP server through the FTP protocol via the Internet and can download any files that were made available for download.

Even though FTP has been in existence since the 1970s, many still find the process of connecting to FTP servers confusing and difficult. This is due, in part, to the steps one must complete before using the FTP service.

Client Side

- Receive a username and password to the FTP server from the administrator.
- Download client software to utilize FTP services or use FTP through the command line interface at a terminal window.
- Bridge a potential learning curve to use the client FTP software and connect to the FTP server.

Server Side

- Necessary to create a username and password for the FTP users.
- Necessary to configure access permissions to prevent unauthorized access to particular files and folders on the FTP server.

Barring potential configuration and connection issues, FTP is a good choice for musicians who need to send large files to clients without the worry or hassle of using express shipping and courier services. The use of FTP client software is necessary, as most computer operating systems have limited support for connecting to and sending files to an FTP server. OS X only currently supports read-only access to connected FTP servers. The various versions of Microsoft Windows support read/write access to connected FTP servers. Even if the operating system supports reading and writing files to an FTP server, the functionality will arguably not match that of third-party software solutions.

FTP CLIENT INSTALLATION

Panic Inc. is a third-party Macintosh software development company based in Portland, Oregon. They create well-crafted Macintosh software such as an FTP client entitled Transmit.

Download Transmit from Panic's website. Once downloaded, locate the application and unzip the file. Drag the unzipped Transmit application into your Applications folder to install it.

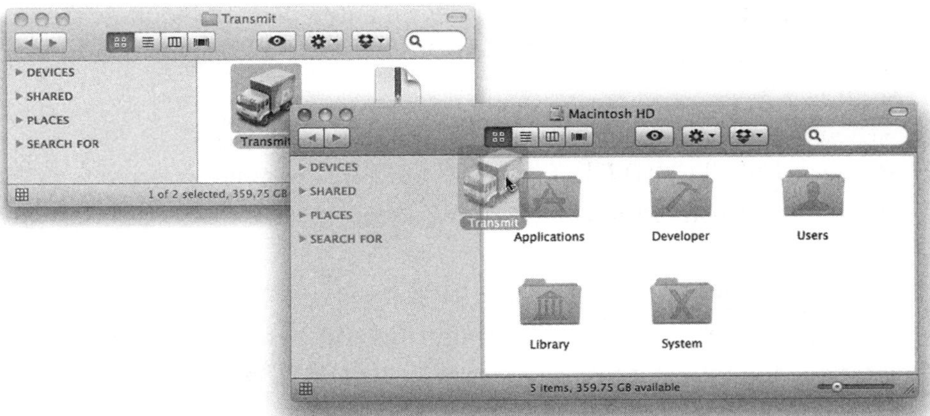

▶ FIG. 8.7

Tip: A quick way to navigate to your Applications folder is by pressing Shift–Command–A.

FTP CLIENT CONFIGURATION

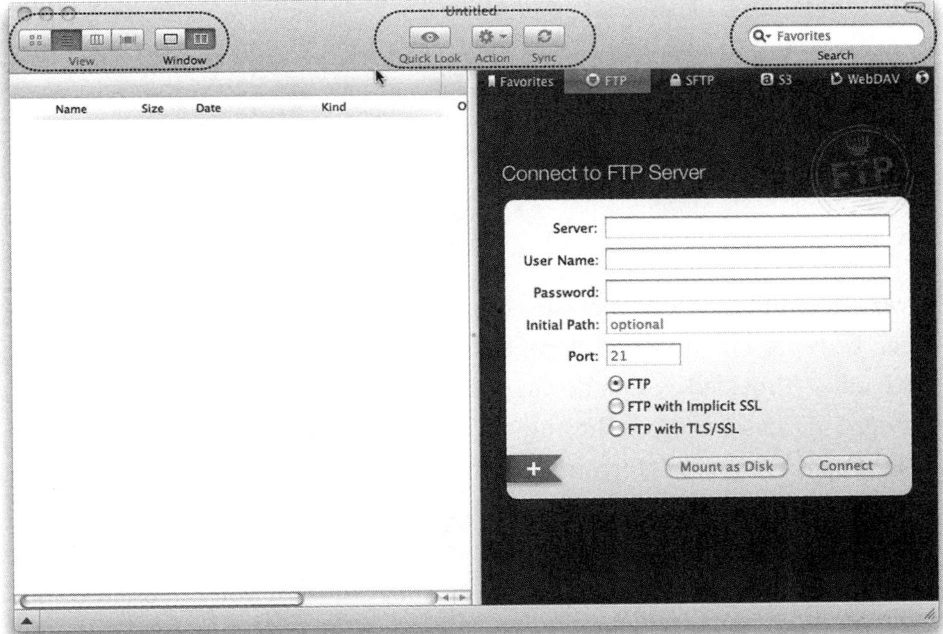

▶ FIG. 8.8

The user interface for Transmit is extremely inviting to the user, providing a great deal of functionality while maintaining an appearance that is approachable. There are several view options in the left-hand side of the toolbar: thumbnail view, list view, column view, and cover flow view. The center of the toolbar provides Quick Look functionality, an action pop-up window, and a site sync button. Finally, a search box is provided at the far right of the toolbar.

The default view for Transmit is column view, displaying two columns. The left column is currently displaying the files in the user folder for the currently logged-in user. The right column provides an authentication window for various services—FTP, SFTP, S3, and WebDAV.

FTP—File Transfer Protocol.

SFTP—Secure Shell (SSH) File Transfer Protocol. Sometimes referred to as the Secure File Transfer Protocol. Essentially, this protocol creates an encrypted tunnel between the client and the server.

S3—Amazon Simple Storage Service.

WebDAV—Web-based Distributed Authoring and Versioning. This protocol allows the mounting of a remote server as if it were a locally connected hard drive or flash drive.

Essentially, files can be opened and edited directly from the mounted WebDAV share.

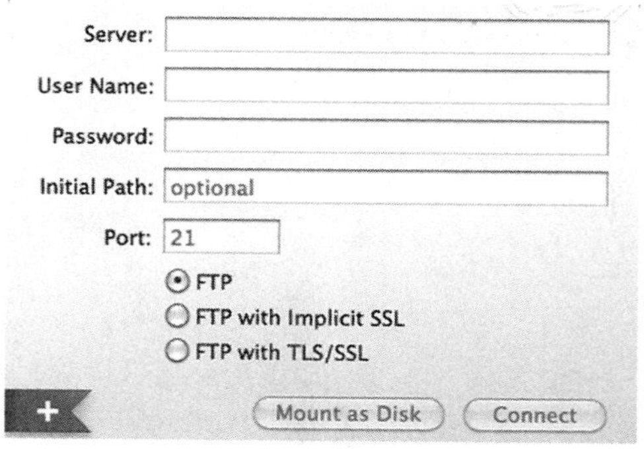

▶ FIG. 8.9

Server—Example: ftp.yourwebsite.com. In some situations the server address can be represented by an Internet Protocol (IP) address.

User Name—Provided by your hosting company or by a client you are working with.

Password—Provided by your hosting company or by a client you are working with.

Initial Path—You can determine which directory, or folder, on the server you wish to see when you log in. For example, if there is a folder titled downloads, the path will be represented as/downloads. If you leave this box empty you will see the root of the server when logged in. If you are unsure about the directory, leave this box empty.

Port—The default port for FTP is 21. If you are unsure about the port, chances are you should use the default port 21.

Enter the following credentials into Transmit, leaving all other fields empty, and click Connect.

Server: musicfilmbook.com
User Name: guestftpuser@jasongaines.com
Password: login2014!

There are two types of credentials that you may have. You may have received a user name and password from a client that you are working with or you may have your own web server that will be accompanied by a user name and password. In either case, the user name and password allow access to a specific folder (often referred to as a directory) on the server.

Note: The user name and password provided for this exercise allow access to the remote_files folder located on musicfilmbook.com.

Once proper authentication credentials have been provided for the selected service, the right column will display the contents of the connected service. The left column displays the contents of a selected directory or folder. Essentially, the left column allows you to view a folder or directory of your choosing, whether on your computer or on a remote server. By default, the contents of your user account folder are displayed in the left column.

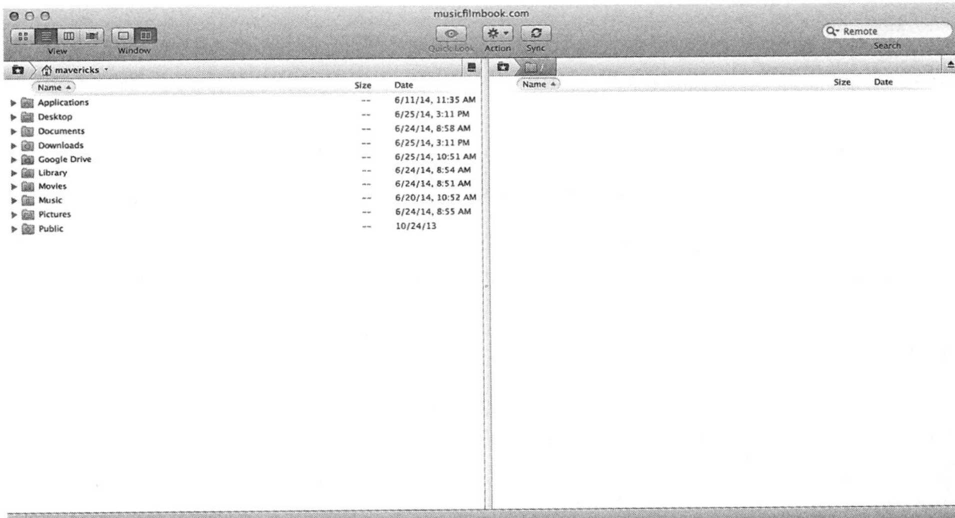

▶ **FIG. 8.10**

Notice there are folders displayed in the left column, but not the right column. This is because there are currently no files or folders located in the remote_files directory of musicfilmbook.com. This dual window interface makes the process of adding files to the connected server extremely easy. You are now ready to send musical files from your computer directly to clients.

PLACING FILES ON FTP SERVERS

In the left column, navigate to the desktop. Your archive should be in the directory. If not, navigate to the directory where your archive is located. Drag the archive from the left column to the right column.

Note: Your file will be named differently than the file seen below. It will be named with the current date.

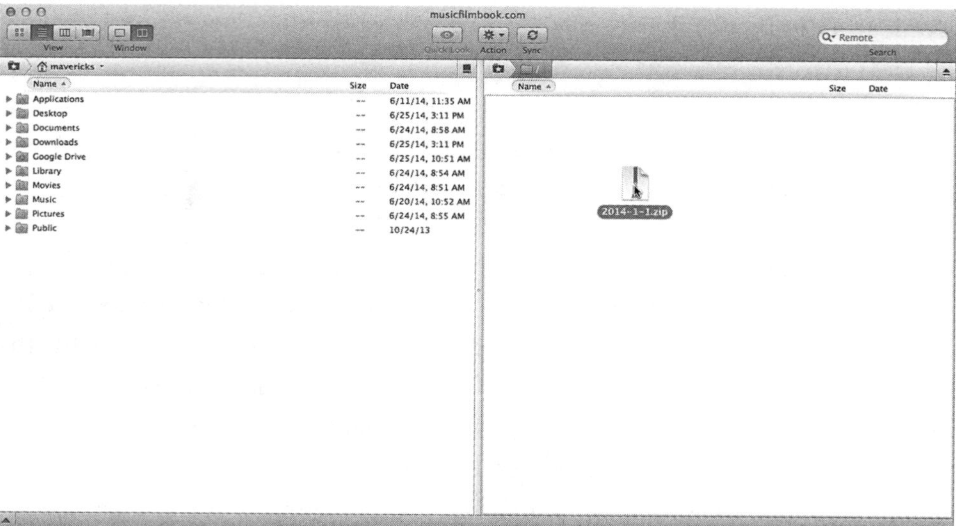

▶ **FIG. 8.11**

The upload process will begin once the file has been dragged to the right column. Depending on the size of the file, the time required to upload the file can vary significantly. Upload speed is dependent on the amount of bandwidth provided to you by your Internet Service Provider (ISP).

It is common for download speeds to be significantly faster than upload speeds.

Once your musical project has been transferred to the remote server through the uploading process, it is now available to your client for download. Direct download links (DDLs) are used to point to a file that resides on a server. In order to create a DDL, you must know the name of the file and where it resides on the server. In this case, files are being stored in the remote_files folder. Just like any computer file system, files and folders on a server are stored in a hierarchal structure. In this example, the direct download link to the file placed on the FTP server would be:

http://www.musicfilmbook.com/remote_files/2014-1-1myfile.zip

CREATING DIRECTORIES ON FTP SERVERS

The FTP user name, guestftpuser, is limited to the remote_files directory on the server. This is to protect against unauthorized access to the root level, or bottom directory, of the server. The remote_files directory resides on the root level of the server. If you have root level access to a Web server, you can create directories at root level. This can be extremely helpful when working with multiple clients. Directories can be made for each individual client. For example:

http://www.musicfilmbook.com/client1/myproject.zip
http://www.musicfilmbook.com/client2/myproject.zip

If you are restricted to a particular directory on the server, in this case remote_files, you can still make subfolders in the directory you have access to. This can be helpful when sorting files for specific projects or stages of projects.

1. Select the right pane in Transmit and choose File > New Folder.

Tip: Key commands can dramatically speed up your workflow. The key command for creating a new folder (directory) is Shift–Command–N.

2. A new folder entitled "untitled folder" will be created in the remote_files directory.
3. Select the newly created folder and press the return key on your keyboard.
4. Rename the folder in the remote_files directory with *yourfirstname_yourlastinitial* (for example, jason_g).
5. Drag the ZIP archive into your newly renamed folder in the remote_files directory.
6. Double-click into your folder. You will see the ZIP archive has been copied into the folder.

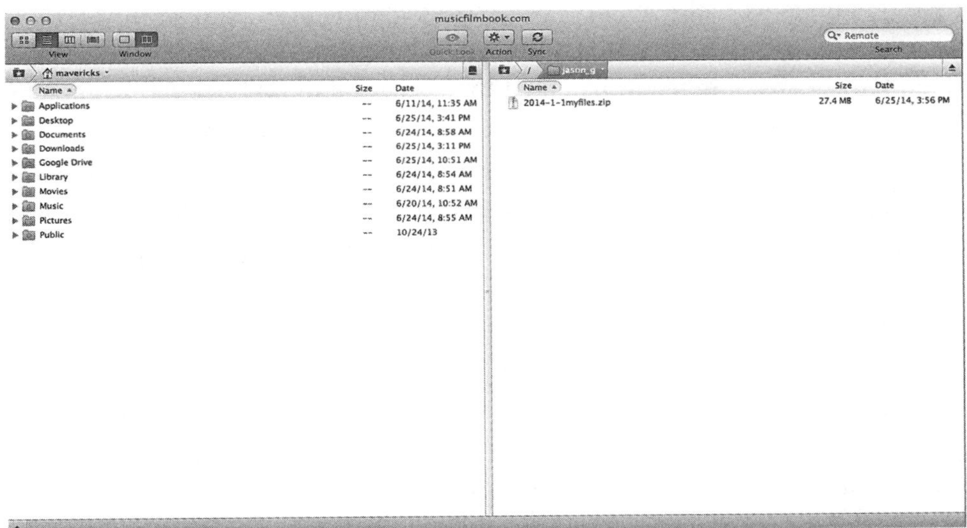

▶ **FIG. 8.12**

The direct download link to the file placed on the FTP server would be:

http://www.musicfilmbook.com/remote_files/jason_g/20141-1-1myfiles.zip

LOCAL AREA NETWORK (LAN) SHARING

Production houses in some cases invite composers to work in-house to speed production and eliminate the need to work remotely. Unfortunately, while working in-house does eliminate the need for FTP, it opens the door for potential file sharing complications. There are several file-sharing protocols to choose from: Server Message Block/Common Internet File System (SMB/CIFS), Apple Filing Protocol (AFP), and Network File System (NFS). It is advantageous to choose a file-sharing protocol that suits the needs of network users. Choosing an inappropriate file-sharing protocol can yield disastrous consequences for end users.

Before file-sharing protocols are discussed, it is appropriate to briefly mention file systems. Computer operating systems, such as OS X, are optimized to use a particular file system on a hard drive used to run the operating system as well as connected hard drives. A file system is simply a method for how your operating system organizes files and folders. There are two file systems available for Windows-based computers: New Technology File System (NTFS) for Windows XP and, later, and File Allocation Table (FAT) for computers running Windows XP and prior that possess a hard drive that is 32 GB in size or smaller. Macintosh computers use the Hierarchical File System Plus (HFS+) for startup. NTFS and HFS+ are both advanced file systems that are used by millions of people on a daily basis. Manufacturers often use FAT to format external hard drives and flash drives because both Windows and Macintosh operating systems can read and write to the file system. FAT is not used as a boot file system on newer Windows-based computers because it imposes a 32GB partition limit for operating system installations. Also, the file system cannot accommodate single files that are larger than 4GB in size. Microsoft invented the successor to FAT, exFAT, to remedy many of the shortcomings of FAT, but it has not gained wide adoption.

When working with network shares on a LAN, the sharing protocols used are generally dictated by the operating systems present on the network. It is common to have a mixture of Linux, Macintosh, and Windows systems on any given network. The systems are used in various capacities from traditional workstations to servers working in various roles. Windows environments often use the Server Message Block (SMB) sharing protocol. Linux, Unix, and Macintosh clients can connect to the SMB protocol via Samba (www.samba.org), an open source implementation of SMB. Since SMB can be used by every operating system, it is the most widely used sharing protocol. Apple has made great strides to provide seamless compatibility for Macintosh users in Windows-based environments. This makes interoperability with Windows-based and Linux-based computers possible in a relatively simple manner. Although Macintosh computers can connect to SMB shares, there are implications for using this sharing protocol.

OS X often uses "forked" files that contain two components: a data fork and a resource fork. The data fork contains the most pertinent information in the file, and the resource fork stores information, such metadata that describes the file. The HFS+ file system utilized by OS X recognizes the two separate forks as a single file. A perfect example of a forked file is an application or program. Applications on a Macintosh computer appear as single file to the end user, even though they are made up of myriad files. Single application files make application installation extremely easy—simply drag the single file to the Applications folder on the computer. Right-clicking on an application and choosing "Show Package Contents" will display the various files that make up an application.

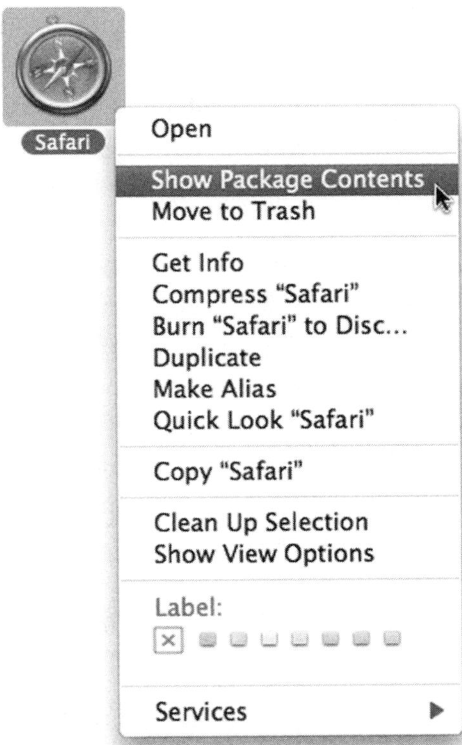

▶ FIG. 8.13

When this option is chosen, the Finder will open a new Finder window that will display the contents of the package.

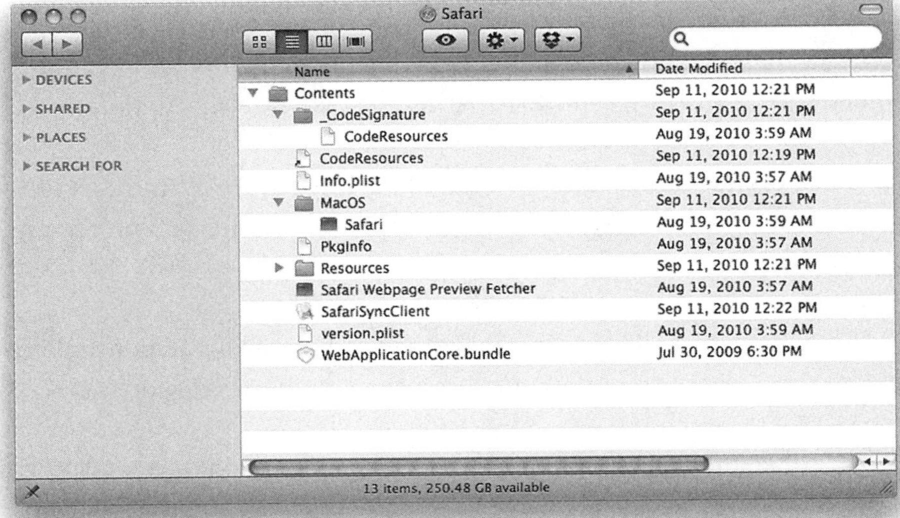

▶ FIG. 8.14

Forked files are beneficial because they offer simplicity to the end user, but this simplicity can cause problems when working in a network environment. Windows-based SMB shares do not support forked files. The file will appear as two separate files on the share—the original file name and another file that contain a "._" in the front of the file name. This file is the resource fork. Many users delete the resource fork file on the share, which can potentially destroy the file. When sharing and storing files on an SMB share point, it is advantageous to compress the file into a ZIP archive. This will flatten the file into a ZIP archiving that will preserve the forked file architecture.

The SMB sharing protocol has been widely adopted because of the large market share of Windows-based computers. Even with the wide-scale adoption of the SMB sharing protocol, there are several different file sharing protocols to choose from. Apple created its own sharing protocol that supports the specific needs of Macintosh clients, including resource forks and extended attributes. The Apple Filing Protocol (AFP) is the default sharing protocol on the OS X family of operating systems. AFP should be the file-sharing protocol of choice if the local area network (LAN) only contains Macintosh clients. Windows-based computers, by default, cannot connect to AFP shares because the operating system does not understand how to communicate with the sharing protocol. Third-party developers have come to solve this problem by creating software that will enable AFP support on Windows-based and Linux-based computers.

MOUNTING SMB AND AFP SHARING POINTS IN THE FINDER

The Finder allows users to connect to various file-sharing protocols with read/write access, assuming the user credentials allow read/write privileges. The only exception to this is the FTP protocol, which has limited read-only support. The ability to mount various sharing protocols directly in the Finder is beneficial because it provides continuity to the end user. They are already familiar using the Finder through their daily use of the computer. The process of connecting to a server share with a specific file-sharing protocol is relatively simple.

1. Click on the Finder icon in your Dock. This ensures that the Finder application has been selected and the corresponding contextual menus are available in the menu bar.
2. Choose Go > Connect to Server.
3. Enter the server address. The images shown here are for demonstration only. If required, the System Administrator will provide the server address to you.

Notice that the server addresses are identical, with the exception of the sharing protocol. When connecting to a server, you must choose the type of sharing protocol you wish to use.

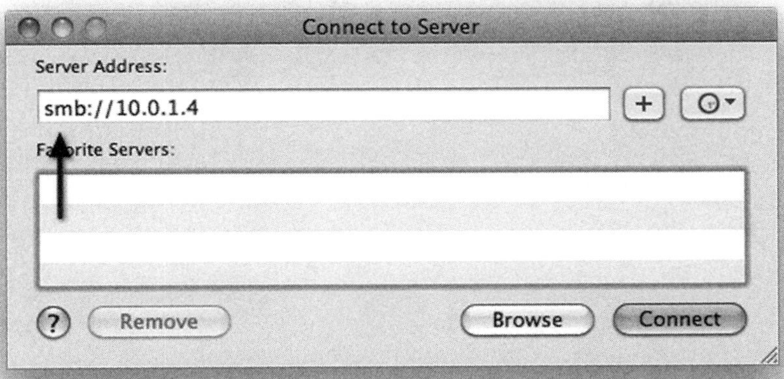

▶ FIG. 8.15

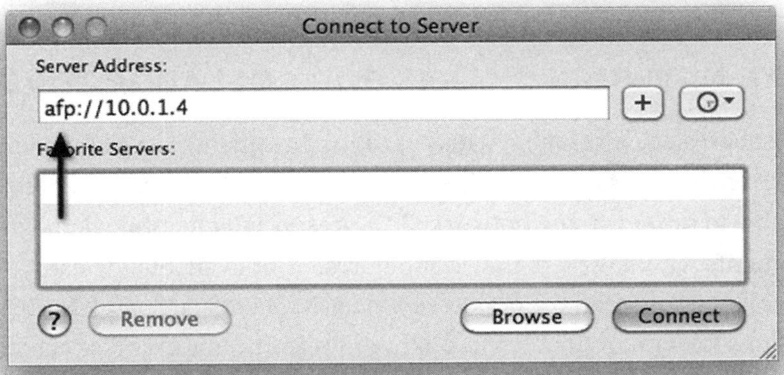

▶ FIG. 8.16

4. Click Connect.
5. Enter the credentials provided by the System Administrator. Once the proper credentials have been presented for authentication, the server shares that are available to that user will be presented.
6. Select the appropriate share and click OK.

Once the server share has mounted, it is available for use. Systems administrators provide varying levels of access to server shares. Generally, permissions are set for users or groups of users. It is common to limit the ability to write (create files and folders, edit current files and folders). This is referred to as read-only access. These types of shares are generally used to distribute content to users without the risk of those users editing the original content. When working in a collaborative environment there will likely be a server share that provides read/write access. This level of access gives the user permission to create files and folders as well as edit current files and folders that reside on the server share. Macintosh computers utilize POSIX (Portable Operating System Interface for UNIX) permissions.

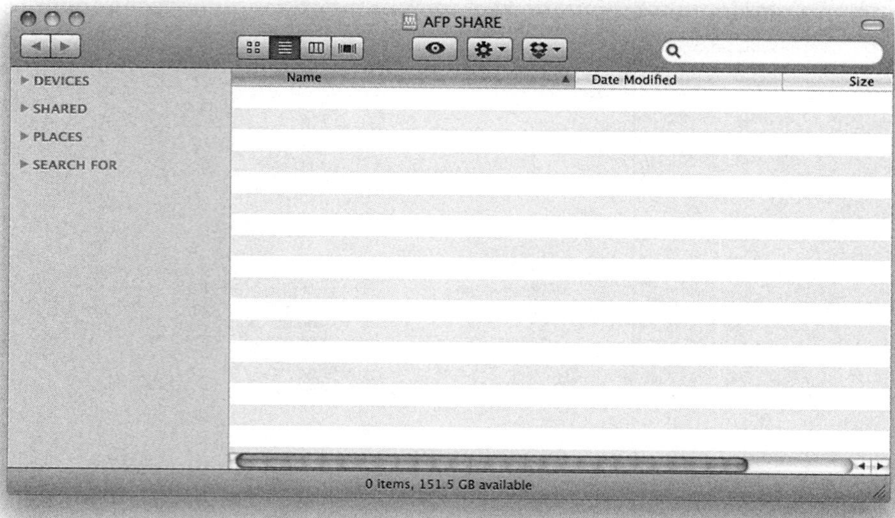

▶ **FIG. 8.17**

CREATE NETWORK SHARES FOR COLLABORATIVE USE

Network shares are invaluable when working in collaborative environments. If you do not have access to network shares, it is possible to create shares that will be available to others on the network. This is especially helpful when working in environments where servers may not be present or available for use.

Create a new folder on the desktop entitled "My Personal Share." Navigate to the Applications folder and double-click System Preferences.app and select Sharing. If it is not available, check File Sharing in the left pane of the Sharing window. Drag the newly created "My Personal Share" folder into the Sharing window.

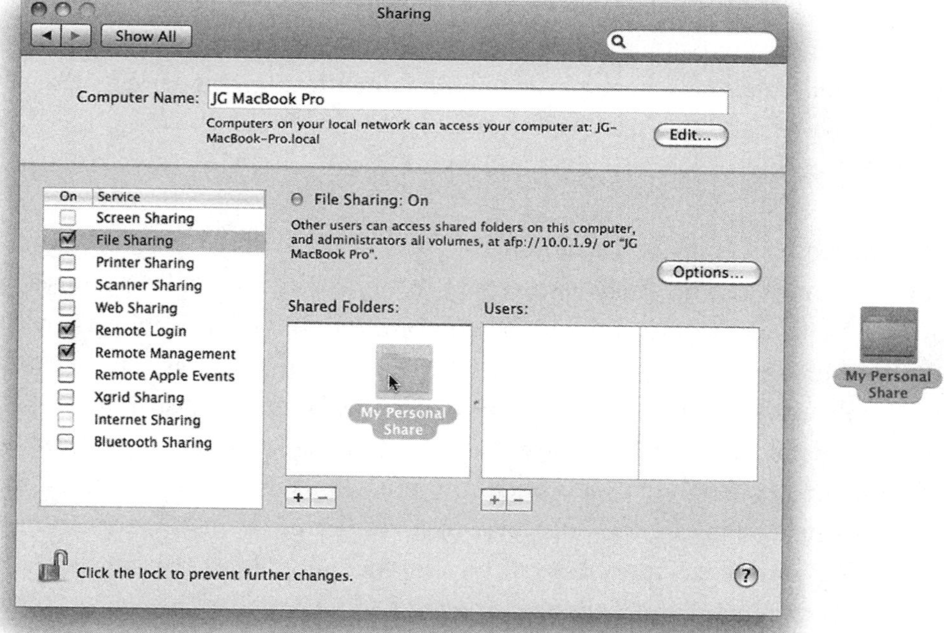

▶ **FIG. 8.18**

The server share is now active and available for use on the local network. By default, the server share has been set to provide read-only access to everyone but the user who created the share. These permissions have been set to protect the files from being edited or deleted by users who should not have access to the files or folders. However, this can be problematic if the files or folders need to be edited by others.

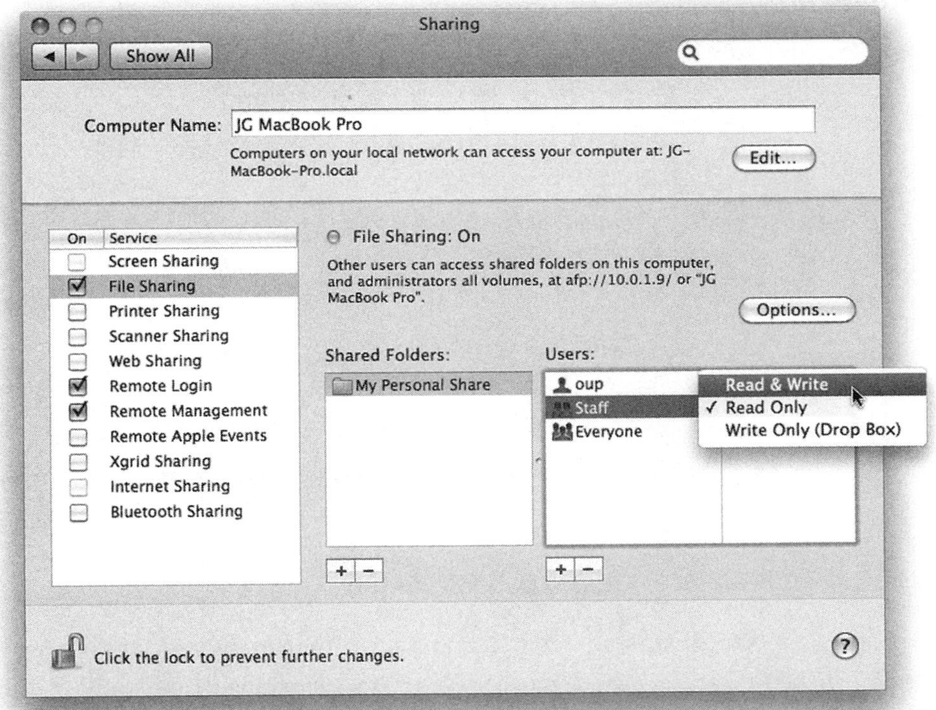

▶ **FIG. 8.19**

Change the permissions from Read Only to Read & Write for both the Staff and Everyone groups. This enables anyone on the local network to create and edit files and folders in the newly created server share.

ENABLE THE SMB PROTOCOL ON SHARE POINTS

OS X uses the AFP sharing protocol by default when creating share points. However, it is possible to allow users to connect to the share point with the SMB protocol. This will allow Windows-based and Linux-based computers to connect with the share point. It is common to interact with Windows-based editing workstations in postproduction environments and is advantageous to enable the SMB protocol if you are working in this type of environment.

Click the Options button in Sharing Preferences and select Share files and folders using SMB (Windows). Select which users will utilize SMB sharing.

You will be prompted to enter the password of each user that will utilize SMB sharing because SMB sharing requires authenticated connections. Once the credentials for the SMB users are entered, click Done.

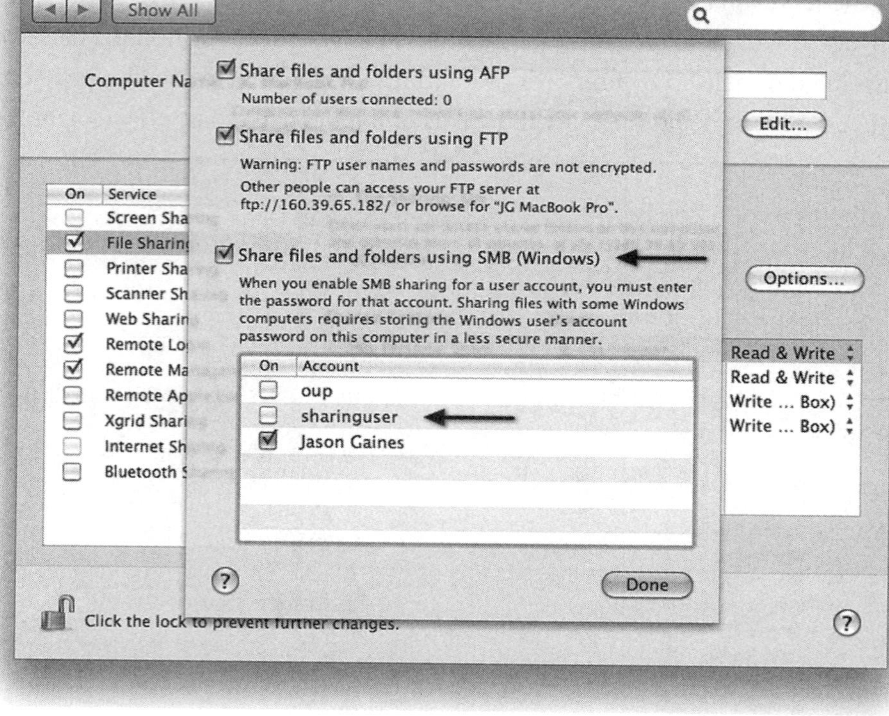

▶ **FIG. 8.20**

COLLABORATIVE CLOUD STORAGE

In recent years cloud storage has become a term that many are familiar with. While this term has become a part of common vernacular, many still do not understand what cloud storage is and how it works. At a very basic level, cloud storage refers to large networks of servers that provide access to your data from nearly any location. Cloud storage is extremely helpful because the need to be mobile has become increasingly necessary in recent years. Many users have more than one computer—work, home and personal laptops, mobile devices, and tablets. It is easier than ever to be constantly connected to our data through readily available Internet connections and remote file servers. Dropbox provides a seamless way for musicians and composers to collaborative in near real time with clients.

In light of this new trend, several companies have converged in the marketplace to provide simple turnkey solutions that provide syncing services, off-site storage and archiving, as well as collaborative sharing models. One of the most popular services, Dropbox (www.dropbox.com), offers scalable and affordable solutions to utilize cloud storage.

DROPBOX AS A SYNCING SOLUTION

At the most basic level, Dropbox is an incredible syncing solution for users who have multiple computers and mobile devices. When a file or folder is placed in the Dropbox folder on your computer, it is instantly synced to the Dropbox servers, which use the Amazon S3 server network for storage. Once the data has completed the uploading process, the files are downloaded to any other computers that may be linked to your Dropbox account. The initial process of uploading files to your Dropbox account may require a significant amount of time as upload speeds are rarely at parity with download speeds. Any future changes to files in folders inside of the Dropbox folder propagate to your Dropbox account (and other linked computers) quickly because Dropbox only uploads the portion of the file that changed instead of uploading a separate copy of the file. Conversely, changes from the Dropbox servers download to your linked computers quickly because Dropbox only downloads the portion of the file that has changed.

Your data is encrypted on the server. In fact, the System Administrators at Dropbox cannot access your data without your permission. All data transferred to and from your computer from Dropbox's servers are encrypted and use a Secure Socket Layer (SSL) connection. Unlike other services, Dropbox keeps a copy of your data on your local machine. This ensures that data is available even if the Dropbox service is not. In turn, this approach creates another level of redundancy to ensure your data is not lost. Also, there is no lost time downloading and uploading files before using them. This process happens in the background. The Dropbox folder on your computer behaves in the same manner as other folders. The only difference is that anything placed inside this folder will sync to Dropbox's servers. This is invaluable for musicians and composers because you are able to access your musical project at any time, even when an Internet connection is not available.

The Dropbox service was designed with simplicity in mind. There is no additional software to learn and integrate into your daily workflow. Dropbox simply runs as a process in the background to ensure that files placed in the Dropbox folder will be synced to Dropbox's server and ultimately to the other computers connected to your Dropbox account. Once the service has been set up there is little to no user interaction needed to maintain the basic core functionality of Dropbox. It is simple to determine files that have been synced to Dropbox's server and files that are in the process of syncing.

When files are up to date, Dropbox's menu bar status will contain a green check mark to indicate that all of the files in the Dropbox folder on your computer mirror those that are present on Dropbox's servers.

Dropbox also provides this status indication in the Dropbox folder on your computer. Every folder or file that is up to date is denoted with a green check (Fig. 8.21). This status indication comes in handy when trying to determine files that are currently in sync or files that are in the process of syncing.

When a file or folder is changed in the Dropbox folder on your computer, Dropbox instantly notices this change and begins indexing the file for changes that were made (Fig. 8.22). Once this quick process completes Dropbox begins uploading the changes to Dropbox's servers. The menu bar status icon changes

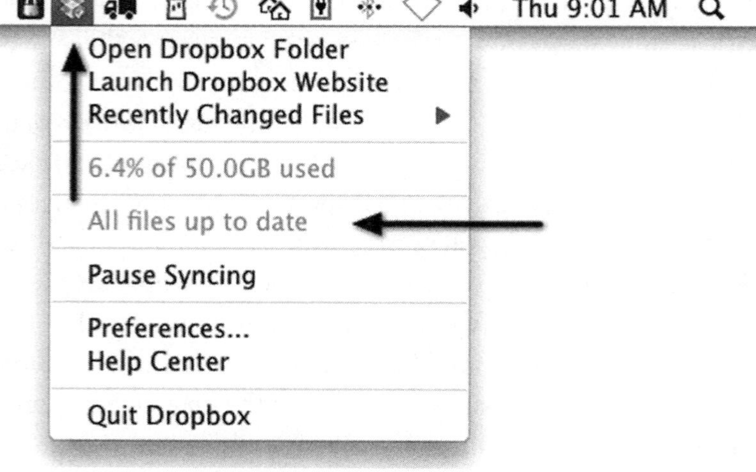

▶ FIG. 8.21

▶ FIG. 8.22

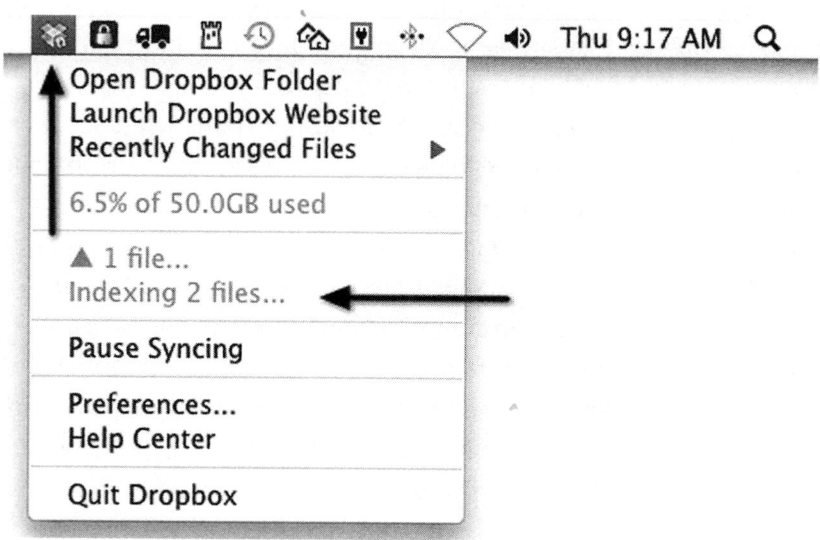

▶ FIG. 8.23

to a blue syncing icon to reflect that the syncing process has been initiated. This efficient syncing model makes your music files available much faster than they would be using an FTP server.

The status icons on files and folders in your Dropbox folder also reflect that the syncing process has begun. Folders that are up to date will be denoted with a green check icon. The files or folders that are actively syncing will display a blue syncing icon to reflect the syncing process (Fig. 8.23).

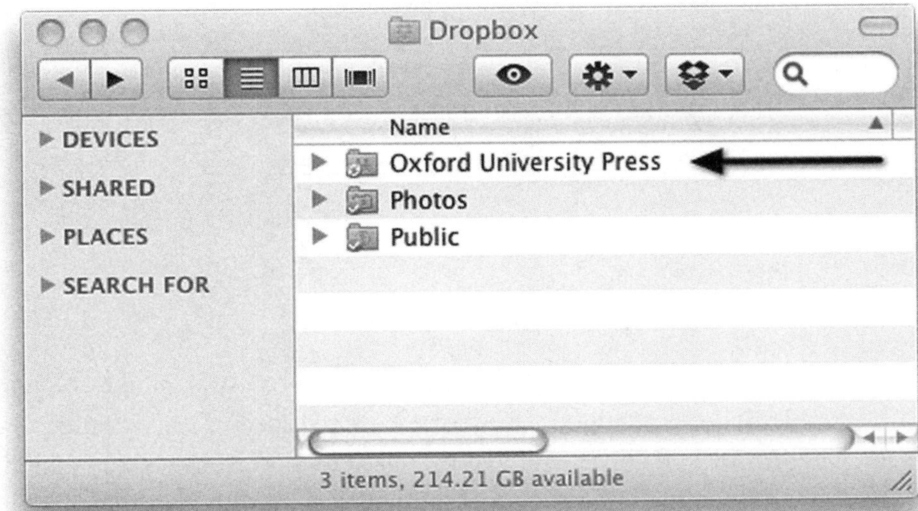

▶ FIG. 8.24

OFF-SITE PROJECT ARCHIVING

Creating backups can be a daunting task for many. There are several factors that can complicate the creation and use of backups: backup frequency, backup redundancy, and backup location, to name a few. Most people create backups that are strewn across multiple hard drives, which makes finding the backup a potentially complicated and frustrating process. Backups that exist on a single physical site are useless if the site is compromised by theft, fire, or natural disaster. Off-site backup is extremely important to protect your digital property. Dropbox is a wonderful solution for archiving off-site backups. It is simple to back up and archive your musical projects to ensure they are available for future revisions or implementation.

Open the Dropbox folder and create a new folder inside of the Dropbox folder entitled "backups."

Dropbox will sync this folder to Dropbox's servers. Anything you choose to place inside of this folder will also sync to Dropbox's servers. It is important to create archives (discussed earlier in this chapter) of your work prior to placing the archive in your Dropbox folder. This will ensure that the files are compressed into a flattened ZIP archive. Since this ZIP archive needs to be uploaded to Dropbox's servers, smaller file sizes will decrease the amount of time required to upload the file.

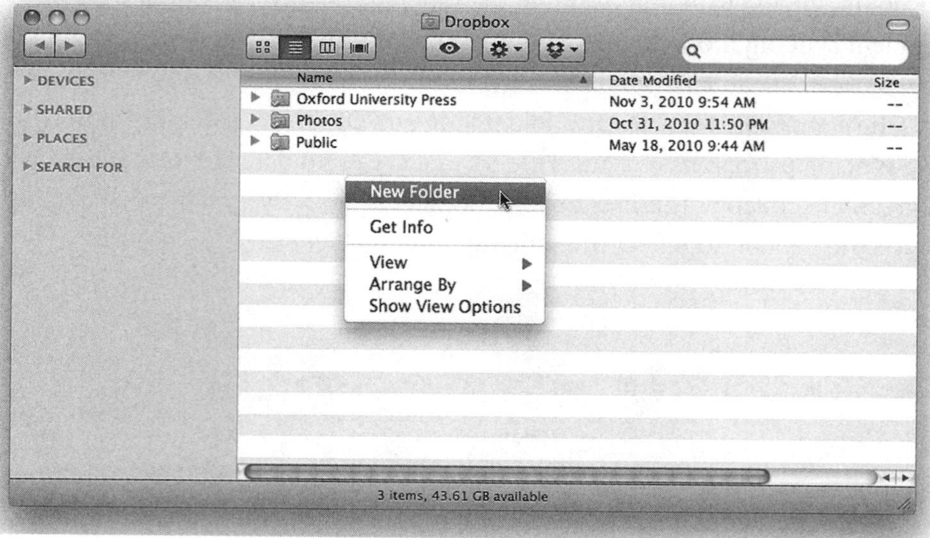

▶ **FIG. 8.25**

FILE VERSIONING AND RESTORATION

Whenever a file changes in the Dropbox folder, Dropbox only uploads the portion of the file that has changed. Dropbox keeps a record of each change that was made to the file and allows you to revert back to a previous version of a file or folder. This is invaluable when working with film and television projects. Musical changes are frequently requested during the creative process. It may be necessary to revert to a previous revision. It can be beneficial to place your active musical projects in your Dropbox folder and work on them from this location. Every change you make to a project is saved and can easily be reverted. Your projects are continually backed up during the editing process.

Open your Dropbox folder and drag the ZIP archive you created earlier in this chapter into your Dropbox folder. Once the file has finished uploading, change the name of the archive to a name of your choosing. Allow Dropbox to sync the name change and launch the Dropbox website from the Dropbox icon in the menu bar.

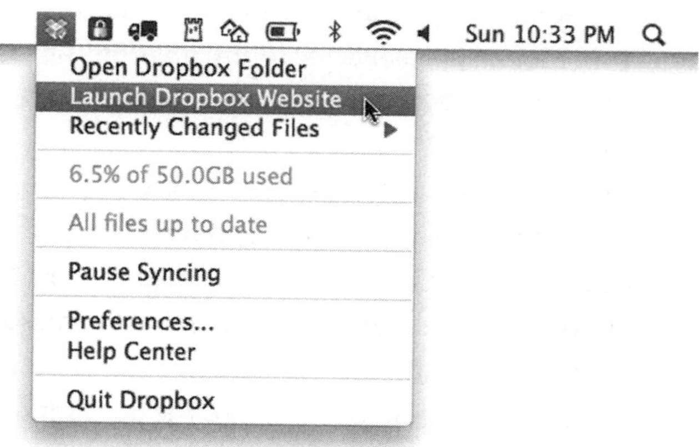

▶ **FIG. 8.26**

You will notice in the Web interface that the file and the file name change have been synced.

You can view and restore previous versions of the file by right-clicking on the file and choosing "Previous Versions."

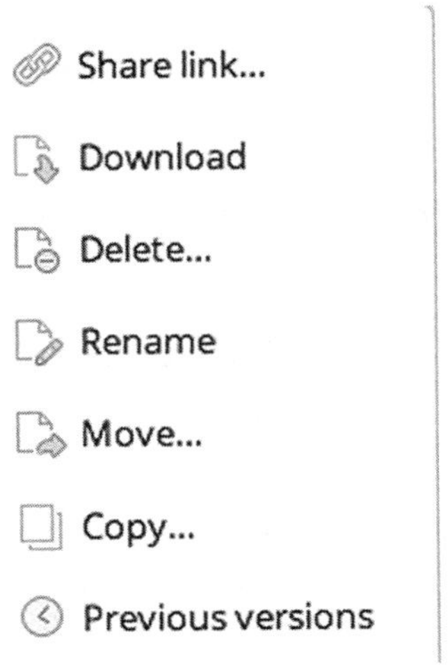

Share link...
Download
Delete...
Rename
Move...
Copy...
Previous versions

▶ FIG. 8.27

COLLABORATIVE FOLDER SHARING

FTP has long been used as a method for transporting large digital files to remote file servers. While the protocol does a decent job of moving around data on local and remote networks, it is not conducive to quick and easy collaboration. This is due to the static nature of FTP. It is only possible to "put and pull" files from the server before editing can take place. The process of uploading and downloading files before an edit can be made significantly increases the time it takes to complete and deliver changes. Musician and composers rarely have the luxury of time, so any method that can speed the delivery of your musical content is essential.

Dropbox provides users with the ability to share folders on their system with users of Dropbox on other systems. The end result is a share point, similar to AFP and SMB, which will allow users to add files and folders to the share. The main difference between a local or remote share point and a Dropbox shared folder is the core syncing functionality of Dropbox. There are local copies of the files and folders as well as a mirrored version of the files and folders on the Dropbox servers. As a result, files and folders are available even when network connectivity is not available.

Users of the shared folder receive file changes quickly because Dropbox only uploads the portion of the file that changes. This speedy file-transfer method enables efficient collaborative workflow between musician, composers, and clients even when that working environment is remote.

Open the Dropbox folder and create a new folder entitled "Collaborative Share." Right-click on the Collaborative Share folder and choose Dropbox > Share This Folder.

▶ **FIG. 8.28**

Once the folder has been designated for sharing, Dropbox will launch your default Web browser to continue the folder sharing process.

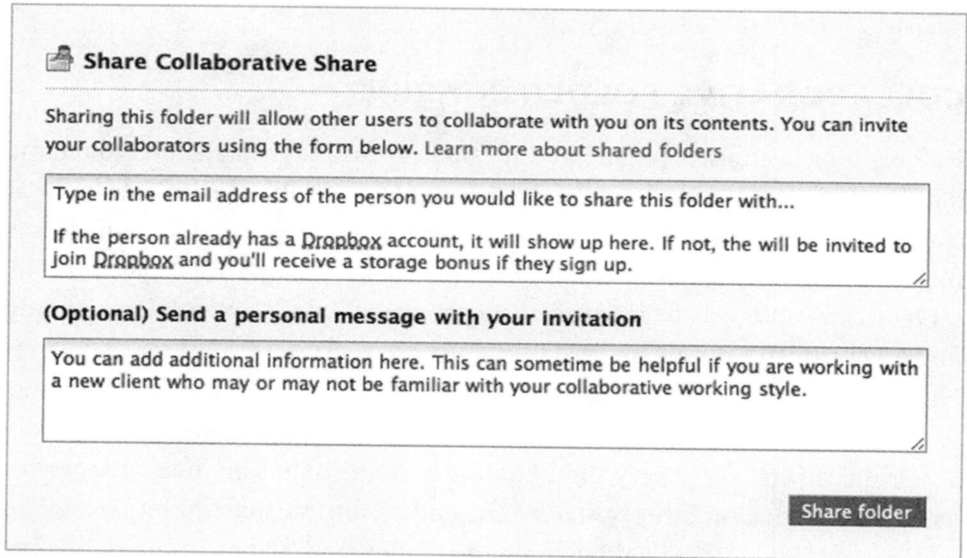

▶ **FIG. 8.29**

You will be notified via email when the user has accepted your request. Upon accepting the request, the user will receive the shared folder in their Dropbox folder.

SHARE LARGE FILES VIA PUBLIC LINKS

The FTP protocol allows for the sending of large files that are not possible to send via email because of file size quotas that may be imposed by an email provider. FTP works well but can be problematic to set up because files need to be uploaded to a static folder. Once the file has been uploaded, the user has to determine the path of the file in order to send the intended recipient a proper direct download link. This method is often too time consuming to be beneficial to musicians and composers who are on a strict production deadline.

Dropbox takes the work out of uploading musical files and creating direct download links. Once the file has been placed in the Public folder of your Dropbox folder, Dropbox is able to generate a direct download link to the file that can be copied and placed in an email message. This simple workflow allows musicians and composers to quickly send audio files to clients without the stress and hassle of uploading files to an FTP server and creating direct download links.

Locate the ZIP archive that you created earlier in this chapter. If needed, re-create the archive from the bounced Logic Pro X project. Open your Dropbox folder and drag the archive into the Public folder in the Dropbox folder. Right-click on the archive once it has been placed in the Public folder, and choose Dropbox > Copy Public Link from the contextual menu.

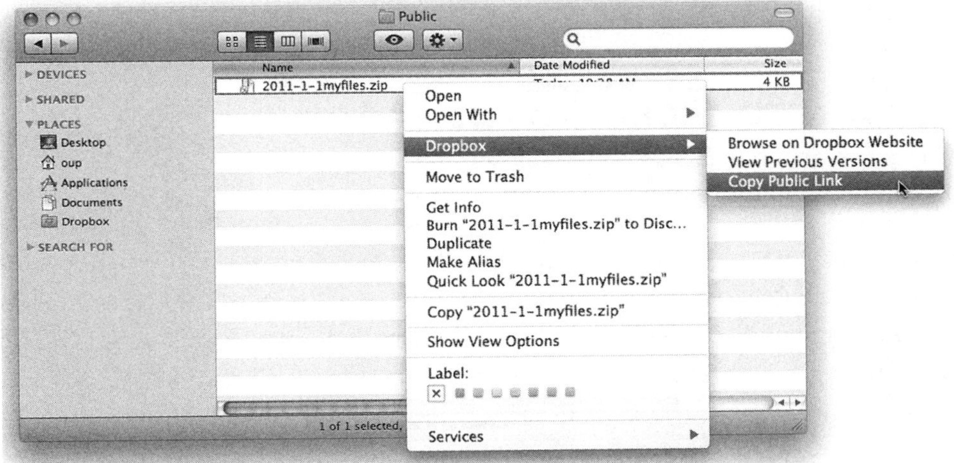

▶ **FIG. 8.30**

Dropbox will generate a direct download the link to the file in the Public folder. The link is copied to the computer's clipboard and can easily be pasted into an instant message chat window with a client or an email message. If the link is somehow lost from your computer's clipboard or needs to be sent at another time, simply repeat the above steps to regenerate the link. Dropbox allows you to create folders inside of the Public folder in order to keep files of one project separate from another. This is helpful to organize and separate files for particular clients that you may be working with. It is not uncommon for musicians and composers to be working with multiple clients at any given time.

Create a folder inside of the Public folder entitled "Music Film Book" and move the archive from the root of the Public folder into the newly created Music Film Book folder. Double-click on the Music Film Book Folder to view its contents. The ZIP archive should be listed.

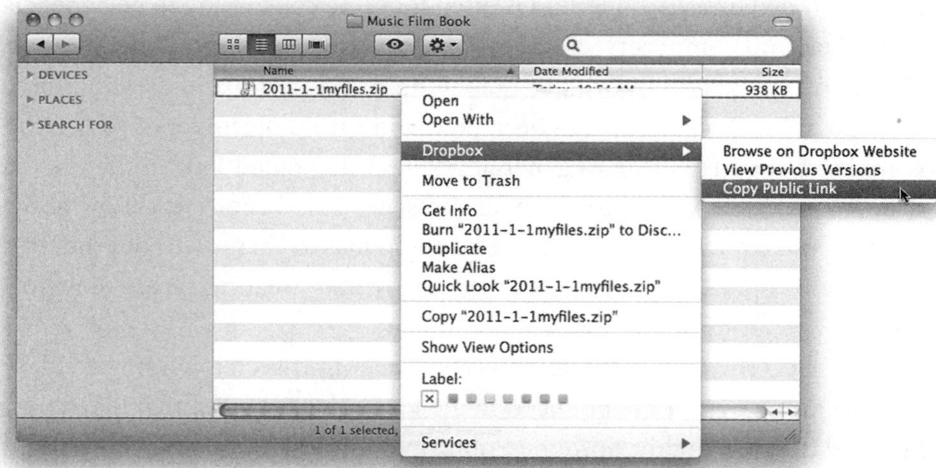

▶ **FIG. 8.31**

Right-click on the archive. Choose Dropbox > Copy Public Link from the contextual menu. The link will now point to the location of the file inside of the Music Film Book folder.

AUTOMATED ARCHIVING AND BACKUP OF LOCAL FILES AND FOLDERS

The backup process is one that is often overlooked because it is generally not automated or user friendly. Automatic backups of specific files and folders often require background daemons (processes that do not possess a user interface and require no user interaction) or CRON jobs (UNIX scheduler that executes shell scripts) to be running to ensure that files are properly backed up. The aforementioned approaches require knowledge of scripting and/or basic programming. Most musicians simply want to compose and arrange music and not worry about scripting actions via programming languages. Fortunately, OS X ships with an automation program, Automator, which provides a user-friendly interface for automating rote tasks.

INTRODUCTION TO AUTOMATOR

Create a new folder on the desktop. Choose File > New Folder from the Finder's menu bar.

Rename the folder "My Backup" and drag the archive created earlier in this lesson into the newly created folder. Once you have completed this task, navigate to Applications > Utilities and launch Automator.app.

Choose Workflow from the template dialog box. A new Automator workflow template will open.

Automator was designed with the user in mind. Apple designed an automation platform that allows developers to create Automator actions that users can combine to create complex workflows to automate rote tasks. The user interface is simple to use and has few components to complicate the automation process.

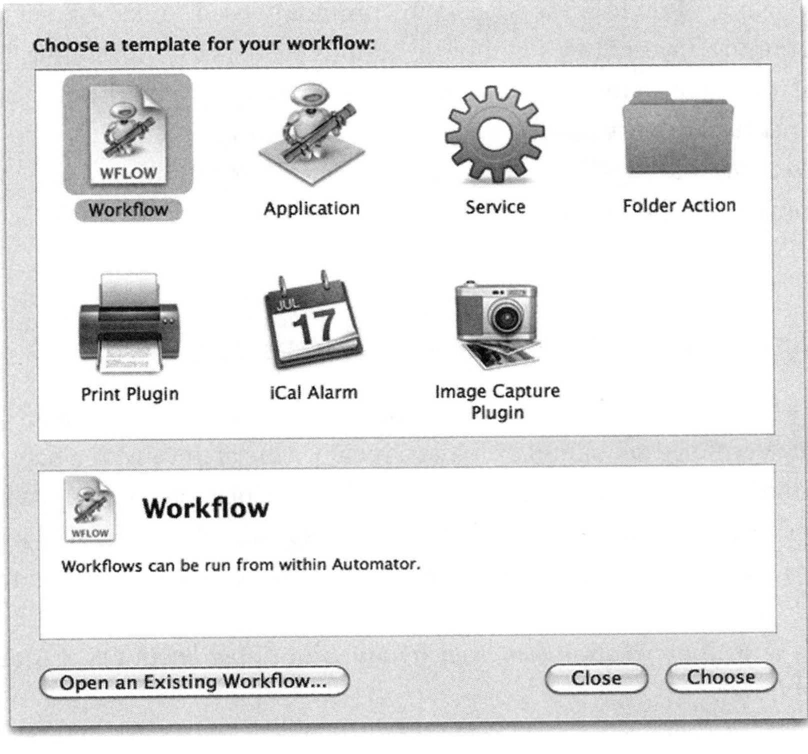

▶ FIG. 8.32

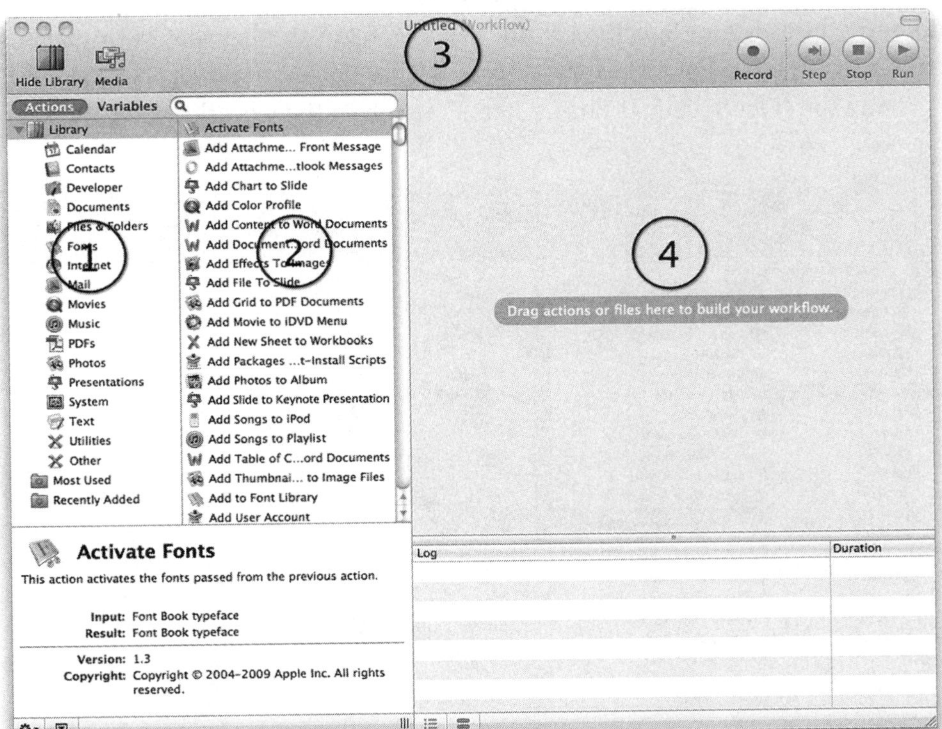

▶ FIG. 8.33

1. Application Library—Displays applications installed on the machine that can interact with Automator.
2. Actions List—Displays the Automator actions that are available for the selected program.

3. Toolbar—Provides easy access to commonly used functions, such as running a workflow. The toolbar buttons can be customized in a similar fashion to the toolbar in Logic Pro X. Simply right-click (or control-click) on the toolbar and choose "Customize Toolbar..."
4. Workflow area—This pane contains the various actions that are combined into the workflow.

CREATION OF A FILE BACKUP WORKFLOW

In this lesson, we will build a simple Automator workflow that creates an archive of a predetermined set of files or folders, renames the archive with a date stamp, and moves that archive into a predetermined backup location (i.e., off-site backup solution). This is an invaluable tool for creating backups of your musical projects. Backups can be scheduled to run at any time through Calendar application.

Note: The iCal application has been renamed to Calendar in OS X Mountain Lion and later.

From the Library in left pane of the Automator, select the Files and Folders library. Choose "Get Specified Finder Items" from the list that is propagated from the Files and Folders Library.

Drag the "Get Specified Finder Items" action in the workflow area.

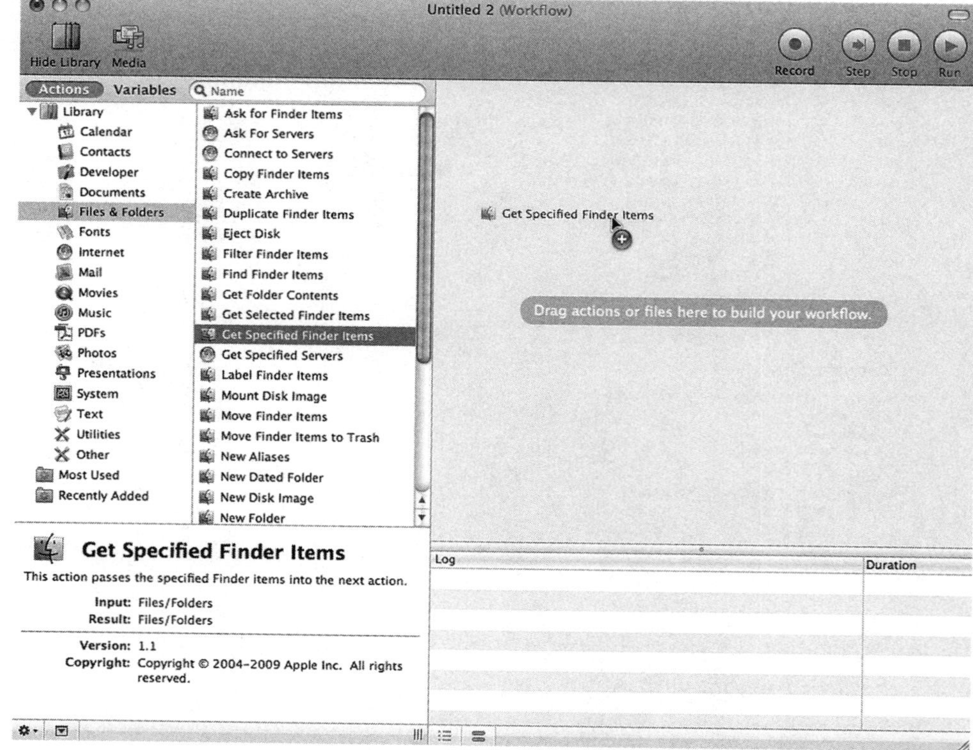

▶ **FIG. 8.34**

Download the project file entitled Automator Workflow from the companion website and unzip the project to your Desktop. Click the Add button in the lower-left corner of the newly added action and navigate to the unzipped project file.

Click the Add button to add the Automator Workflow project to the "Get Specified Finder Items" action. We will now create a location for the backup to be placed in. This can be an FTP sever, AFP, or any location of your choosing. For the purpose of this lesson, we will use Dropbox as the save location. Create a new folder inside of the Dropbox Folder. Name the folder "project backups." In Automator, select the "Create Archive" action from the Files & Folders Library. Drag the action into the workflow area underneath the "Get Specified Finder Items" action.

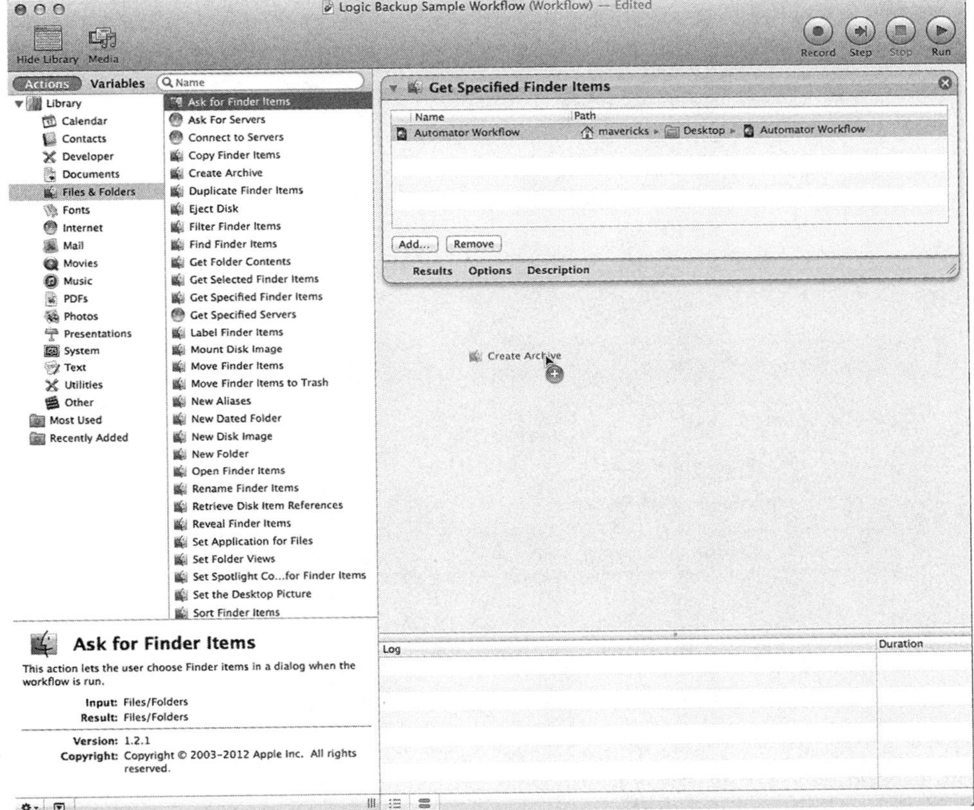

▶ FIG. 8.35

In the "Save As" box, enter the name "Logic Backup."

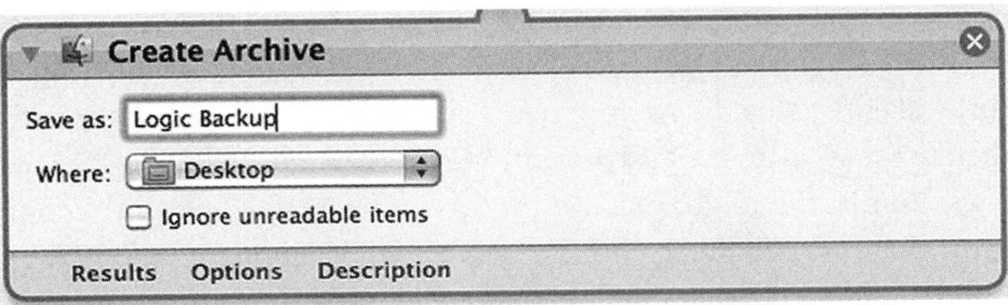

▶ FIG. 8.36

Click on the Where pop-up to choose the save location for the archive. Select "Other" and navigate to the project backup folder in the Dropbox folder.

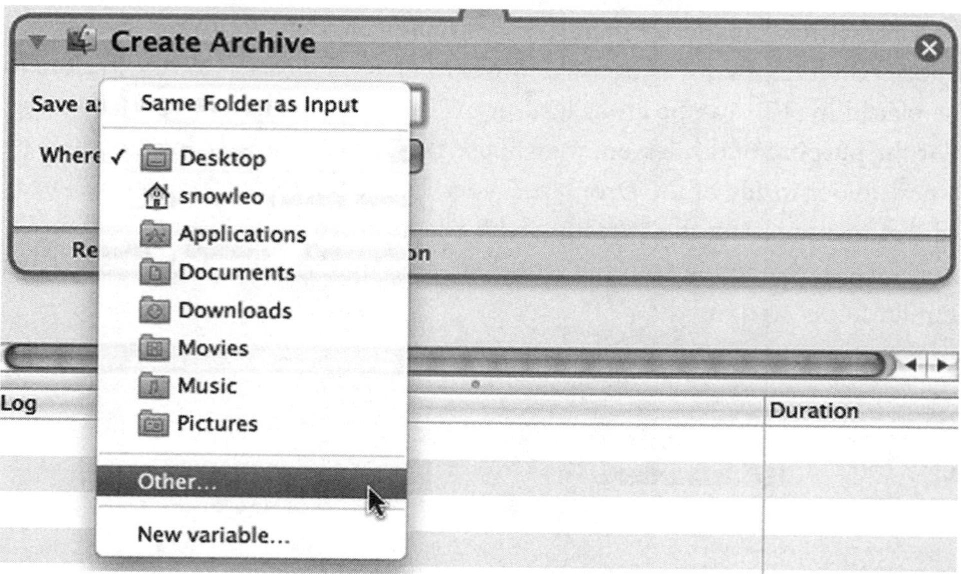

▶ FIG. 8.37

The end result should mirror the image below.

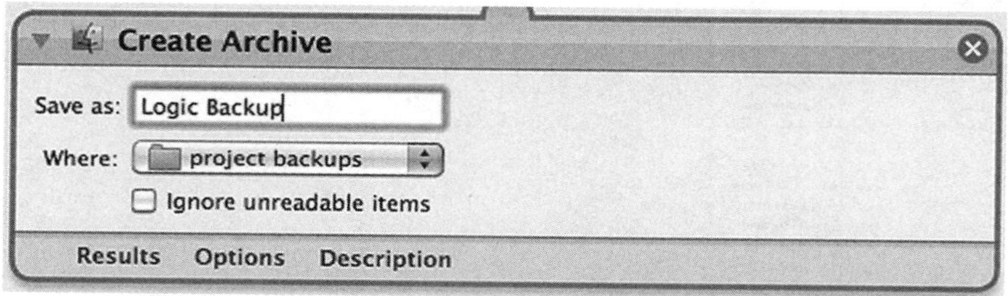

▶ FIG. 8.38

If this action is run from the toolbar, Automator will create an archive that contains the selected Logic Pro X project and save it in the project backups folder in the Dropbox folder. Dropbox will then ensure that this archive is backed up off-site. However, it is problematic to create archives with the same name every time the Automator workflow is run. This can cause naming conflicts. With one additional action, it is possible to ensure there are no conflicts with the archives created by Automator. Ideally, it is best to name each with a date stamp.

Select the "Rename Finder Items" action from the Files & Folders Library. Drag that action beneath the "Create Archive" action in the workflow area (Fig. 8.39).

Use the following settings in the "Rename Finder Options" action (Fig. 8.40).

This will ensure that the archive name is appended with the year-month-day date before the file name Logic Backup, for example, "2014-1-1 Logic Backup.zip."

Click Run in the toolbar to test the workflow. If the workflow completed properly, there will be green check marks on all of the items in the log at the bottom of the workflow area.

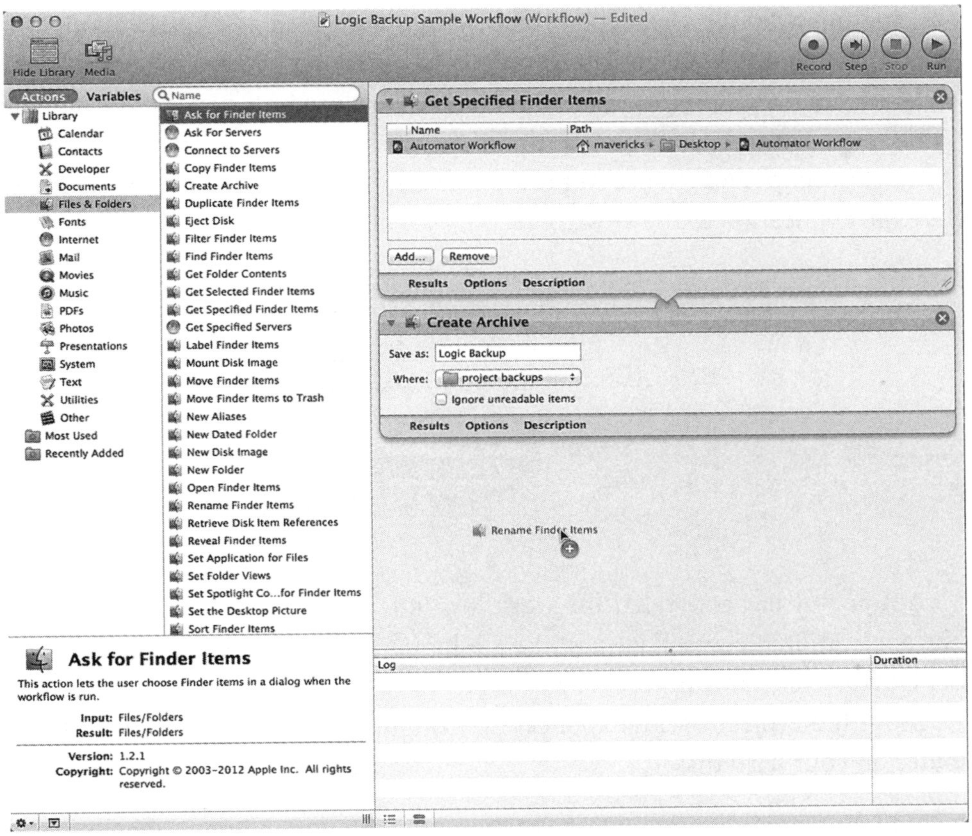

▶ FIG. 8.39

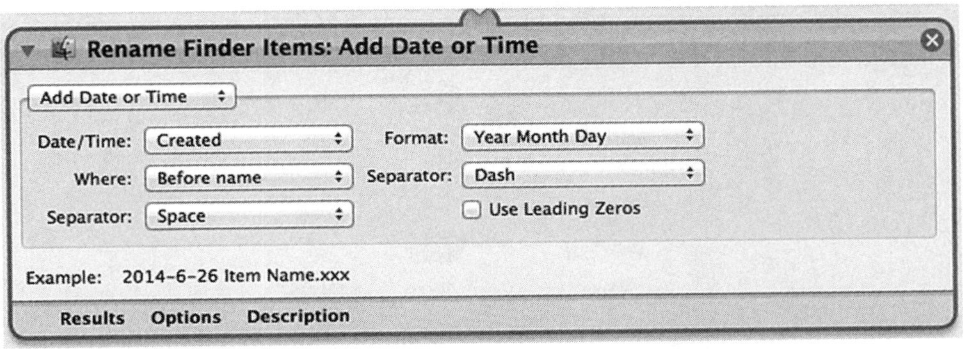

▶ FIG. 8.40

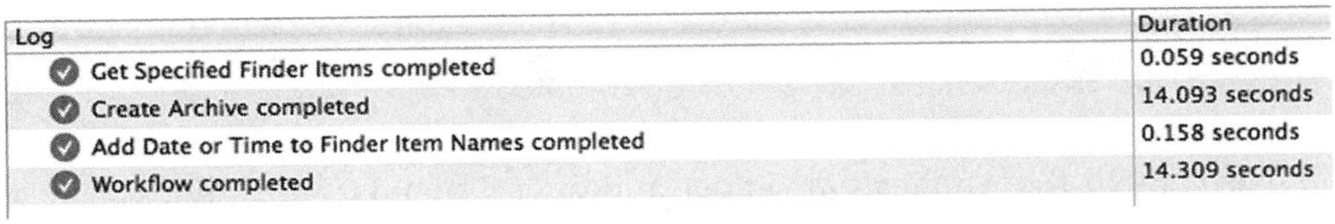

Log	Duration
Get Specified Finder Items completed	0.059 seconds
Create Archive completed	14.093 seconds
Add Date or Time to Finder Item Names completed	0.158 seconds
Workflow completed	14.309 seconds

▶ FIG. 8.41

Choose File > Save As from the Automator Menu bar and save the Automator workflow.

SCHEDULING AUTOMATOR WORKFLOWS

Creating a backup workflow does little good unless it is run consistently. This is true with all backup schemas. Fortunately, Apple provides the ability to schedule the opening of applications and files in OS X via the Calendar application. You can protect your valuable musical projects in a few quick and easy steps.

If the previous Automator workflow has been closed, reopen the Automator workflow. Choose File > Save As from the Automator Menu bar. Name the file "Project Backup" and choose Application from the File Format pop up window. Save the application to the Desktop.

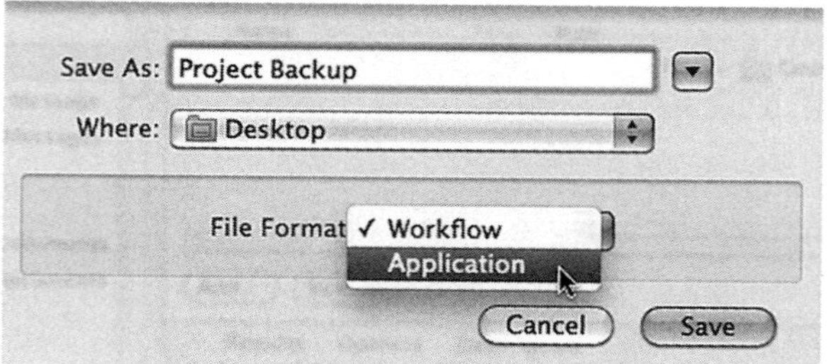

▶ FIG. 8.42

Automator has converted the workflow into a fully executable application. The application file was placed on the Desktop. Double-click the application on the Desktop to test its functionality.

Move the Project Backup application from the Desktop to the Applications folder on your hard disk.

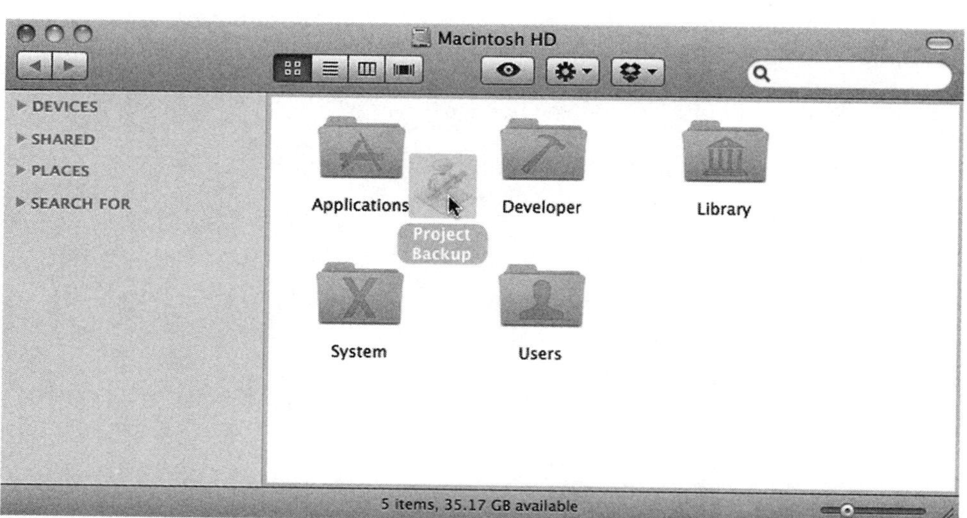

▶ FIG. 8.43

Navigate to the Applications folder and open Calendar.app. Choose File > New Calendar from the menu bar.

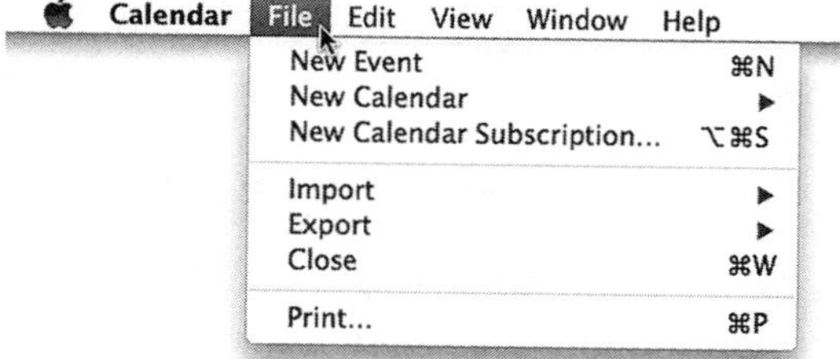

▶ FIG. 8.44

Name the newly created calendar "Backup Scheduler."

▶ FIG. 8.45

Change the view in Calendar to month view.

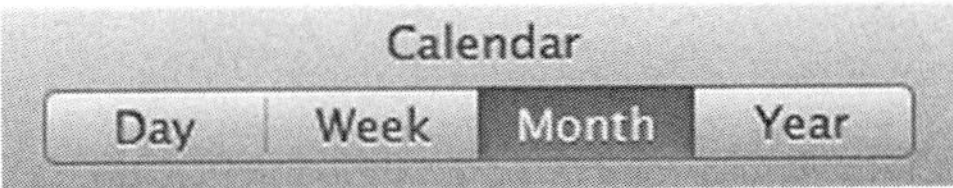

▶ FIG. 8.46

Double-click on any day in the month view to create a new event and enter the following information into the New Event window.

- Name the event "Project Backup."
- Change the repeat settings to every day. Change the end setting to never (note: this frequency can be edited to repeat at any interval).
- Ensure that the Project Backup event resides in the Backup Scheduler calendar.

Choose Open File from the alert pop-up window. Navigate to the Applications folder and choose the Project Backup application.

The Calendar event will repeat every day and open the Project Backup at the designated time (Fig. 8.47). The time settings may not be appropriate for your backup needs and can easily be adjusted. For example, it would be advantageous to schedule the backup for the middle of the night when the project will likely not be in use.

If Calendar is your time and task management application of choice, you will likely not wish to view the Backup Scheduler in-line with other calendars in Calendar application. The calendar can be easily hidden to focus your attention on daily tasks and appointments. Deselect the Backup Scheduler calendar in iCal to hide the calendar.

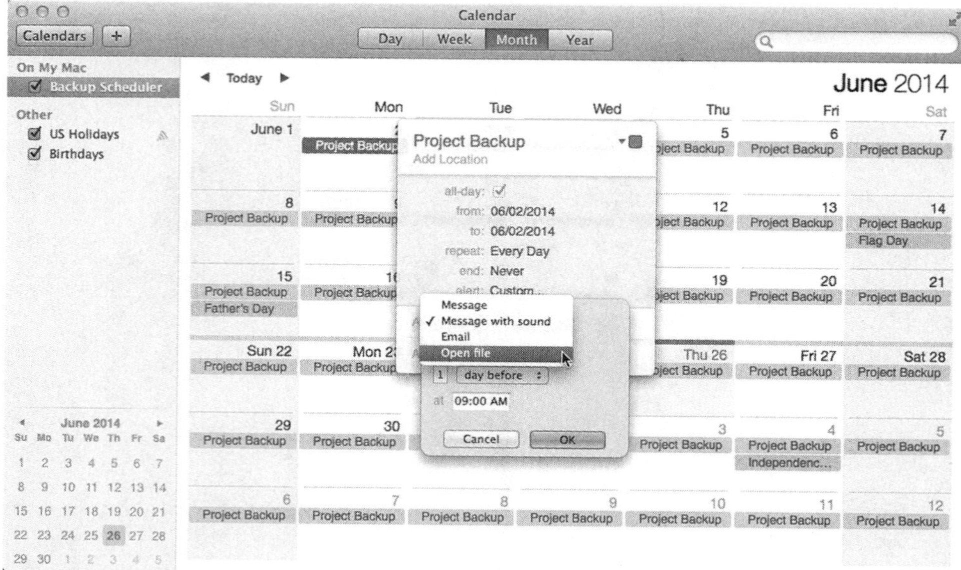

▶ **FIG. 8.47**

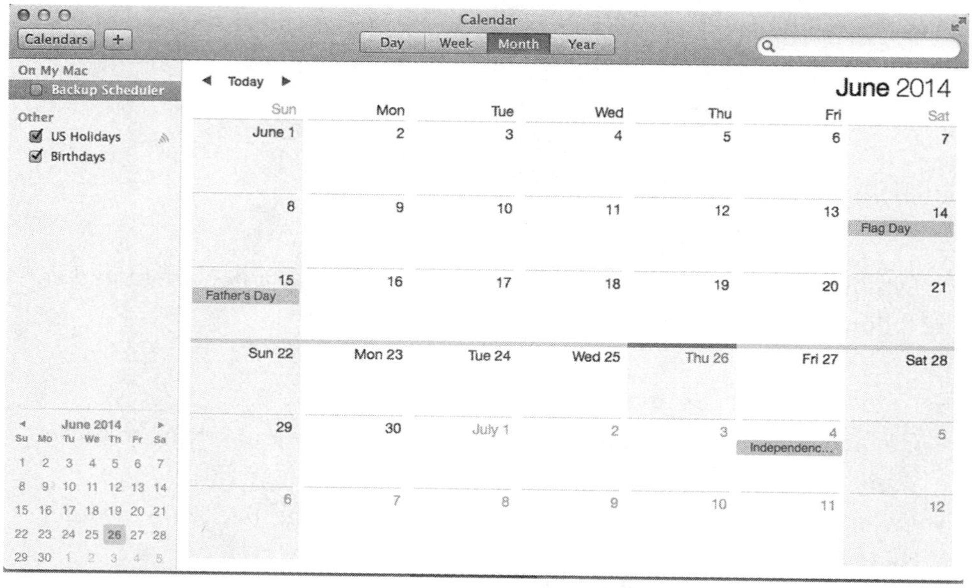

▶ **FIG. 8.48**

The Calendar application will now take care of the heavy lifting of the backup process. The Calendar application utilizes background process that will run and ensure that the Automator application will run on schedule. You now have a scheduled backup mechanism that will ensure that your musical projects are consistently backed up and available when needed.

CHAPTER 9
BEST PRACTICES AND TROUBLESHOOTING

Music is sort of revealing truth. When you compose, you're freezing pieces of truth together as best you can.... When you're composing or you're playing music, you're revealing something that is ultimately already there.

—Paul Lipson

HARD DRIVE CONFIGURATION AND SETUP

PROPER HARD DRIVE configuration is crucial to successful daily use, archiving, and recording. Although drive installation is, for the most part, relatively straightforward, there are critical steps that should be taken when using a new hard drive in your system.

Unless specifically designated by the manufacturer as a Mac or Windows formatted drive, new hard drives are generally formatted with the FAT 32 (File Allocation Table) format. This is true with most internal and external storage devices. While this format will perform adequately in most situations, it can be problematic when working with large files sizes (FAT 32 has a single file size limitation of 4GB) and files that utilize metadata. It is important to reformat the new drive before first use. Disk Utility handles this task and is arguably one of the most useful applications that ship with OS X. As the name suggests, it handles all of the maintenance operations that can be applied to a hard drive—repair, volume formatting, and restoration, to name a few.

Navigate to Applications > Utilities and open Disk Utility. Select the drive you wish to partition from the drive list in the left pane of the application. Disk Utility shows the drive name, which is denoted by the manufacturer name and model, and any volumes that exist on the drive, in this case, 1 TB WDC and the volume name, Data. Consider this analogy (Fig. 9.1). Think of a hard drive as a dresser drawer set. The dresser itself is the similar to the hard drive and the volumes are similar to drawers.

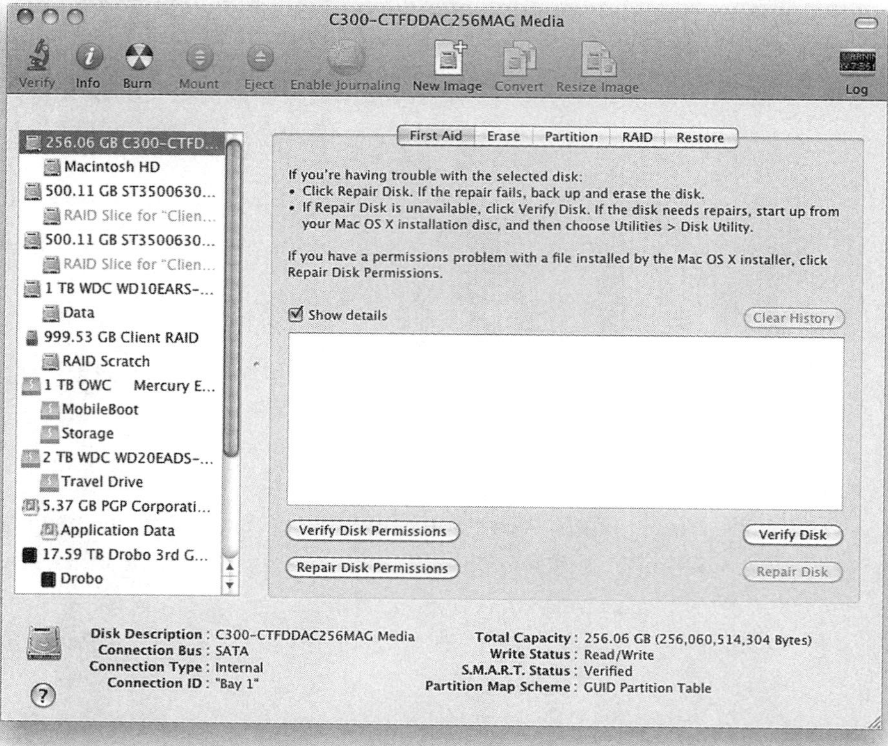
C300-CTFDDAC256MAG Media
Verify
Info
Burn
Mount
Eject
Enable Journaling
New Image
Convert
Resize Image
Log
256.06 GB C300-CTFD...
Macintosh HD
500.11 GB ST3500630...
RAID Slice for "Clien...
500.11 GB ST3500630...
RAID Slice for "Clien...
1 TB WDC WD10EARS-...
Data
999.53 GB Client RAID
RAID Scratch
1 TB OWC Mercury E...
MobileBoot
Storage
2 TB WDC WD20EADS-...
Travel Drive
5.37 GB PGP Corporati...
Application Data
17.59 TB Drobo 3rd G...
Drobo
First Aid
Erase
Partition
RAID
Restore
If you're having trouble with the selected disk:
• Click Repair Disk. If the repair fails, back up and erase the disk.
• If Repair Disk is unavailable, click Verify Disk. If the disk needs repairs, start up from your Mac OS X installation disc, and then choose Utilities > Disk Utility.
If you have a permissions problem with a file installed by the Mac OS X installer, click Repair Disk Permissions.
Show details
Clear History
Verify Disk Permissions
Verify Disk
Repair Disk Permissions
Repair Disk
Disk Description : C300-CTFDDAC256MAG Media
Connection Bus : SATA
Connection Type : Internal
Connection ID : "Bay 1"
Total Capacity : 256.06 GB (256,060,514,304 Bytes)
Write Status : Read/Write
S.M.A.R.T. Status : Verified
Partition Map Scheme : GUID Partition Table

▶ **FIG. 9.1**

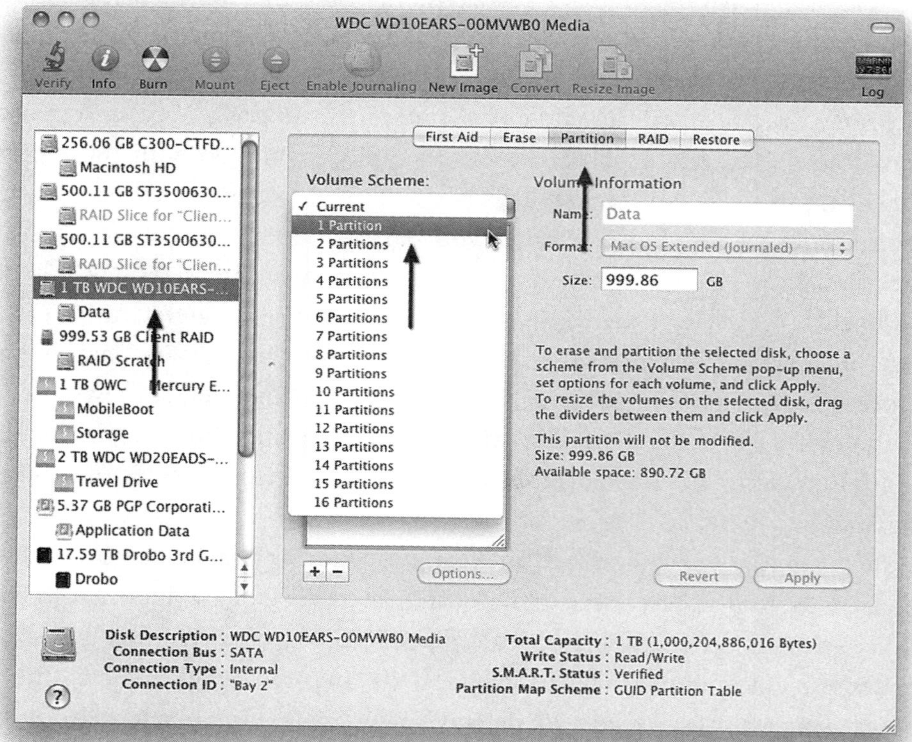
WDC WD10EARS-00MVWB0 Media
Verify
Info
Burn
Mount
Eject
Enable Journaling
New Image
Convert
Resize Image
Log
256.06 GB C300-CTFD...
Macintosh HD
500.11 GB ST3500630...
RAID Slice for "Clien...
500.11 GB ST3500630...
RAID Slice for "Clien...
1 TB WDC WD10EARS-...
Data
999.53 GB Client RAID
RAID Scratch
1 TB OWC Mercury E...
MobileBoot
Storage
2 TB WDC WD20EADS-...
Travel Drive
5.37 GB PGP Corporati...
Application Data
17.59 TB Drobo 3rd G...
Drobo
First Aid
Erase
Partition
RAID
Restore
Volume Scheme:
✓ Current
1 Partition
2 Partitions
3 Partitions
4 Partitions
5 Partitions
6 Partitions
7 Partitions
8 Partitions
9 Partitions
10 Partitions
11 Partitions
12 Partitions
13 Partitions
14 Partitions
15 Partitions
16 Partitions
Volume Information
Name: Data
Format: Mac OS Extended (Journaled)
Size: 999.86 GB
To erase and partition the selected disk, choose a scheme from the Volume Scheme pop-up menu, set options for each volume, and click Apply.
To resize the volumes on the selected disk, drag the dividers between them and click Apply.
This partition will not be modified.
Size: 999.86 GB
Available space: 890.72 GB
Options...
Revert
Apply
Disk Description : WDC WD10EARS-00MVWB0 Media
Connection Bus : SATA
Connection Type : Internal
Connection ID : "Bay 2"
Total Capacity : 1 TB (1,000,204,886,016 Bytes)
Write Status : Read/Write
S.M.A.R.T. Status : Verified
Partition Map Scheme : GUID Partition Table

▶ **FIG. 9.2**

Select the Partition tab and choose one partition from the pop up window. OS X supports 16 volumes per hard drive (Fig. 9.2).

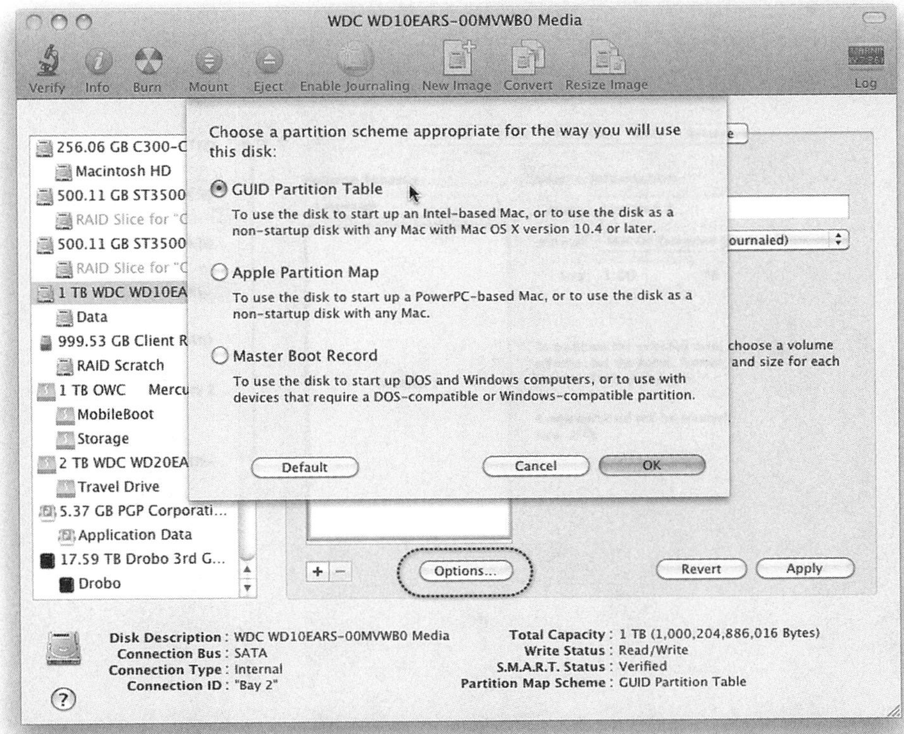

▶ **FIG. 9.3**

Click the Options button and choose GUID (Globally Unique Identifier) Partition Table (GPT). This is the default formatting scheme for Macintosh computers that contain Intel processors. Apple Partition Map (APM) was used in legacy machines that contain PowerPC processors. Windows-based machines utilize Master Boot Record. Flash drives are often formatted with the Master Boot Record (MBR) scheme in order to garner instant compatibility with Windows-based and Macintosh-based computers. OS X has native support for GPT, APM, and MBR. Windows XP-based machines only support MBR, while Windows 7-based machines (and later) support GPT.

Provide a desired name for the volume and select Mac OS Extended (Journaled) from the format pop-up window (Fig. 9.3). This is the default format type for OS X.

Mac OS X supports formatting volumes with a great deal of formatting types. It is possible to format a drive with the New Technology File System (NTFS) that is used by Windows-based machines through the installation of a third-party driver, Paragon NTFS, made by the Paragon Software Group (http://www.paragon-software.com). By default, OS X only provides read-only access to NTFS. Click Apply after the name and formatting type has been selected to complete the formatting process.

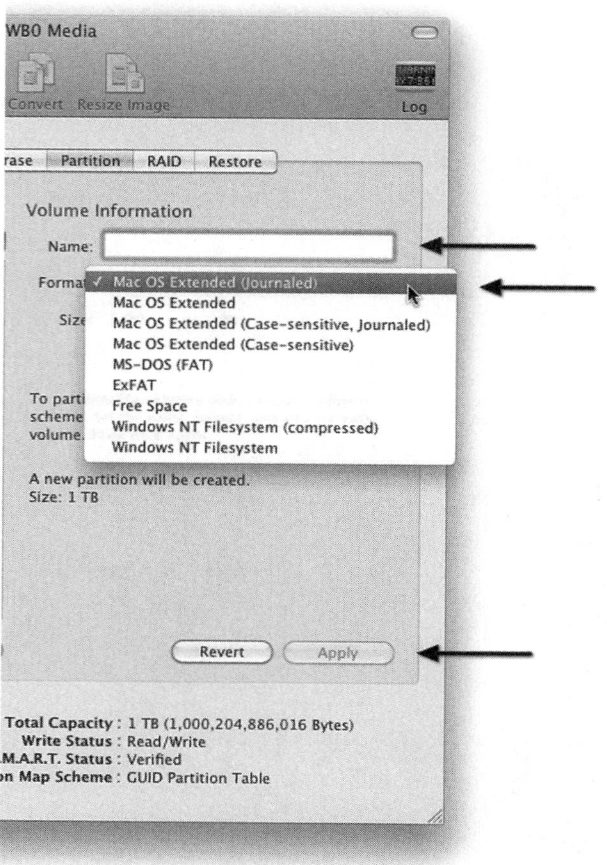

▶ **FIG. 9.4**

WRITING ZEROES TO HARD DRIVES TO REMAP BAD SECTORS

Hard drives utilize sectors to store data. Essentially, data that is copied to the hard drive is broken up into small pieces and stored in sectors typically 512 bytes in size. Like any other human-made product, hard drives are not perfect and can contain sectors that are damaged and cannot be written to. Hard drive sectors can also become damaged over time through improper system shutdown, among other factors. Manufacturers anticipate that bad sectors will be present and allocate spare sectors on a hard drive. When the operating system tries to write to a bad sector, the operating system discovers that there is a problem and remaps the bad sector on the hard drive to a new, fully functioning spare sector. This operation is performed in the background and is seamless to the end user.

Audio and video applications require a great deal of hard disk bandwidth that is steady and reliable. Bad sectors can cause problems during audio recording or video transcoding because a slight decrease in bandwidth occurs when a bad sector is being remapped by the operating system. In some cases this latency can result in write errors. To prevent this problem from happening, it is advantageous to preemptively write over every sector of the hard drive before using it in a professional situation to remap any bad sectors that may exist on the disk. This process is know as zeroing a disk and can be accomplished with Disk Utility. There are other third-party applications that perform this task, but Disk Utility performs just as well and is provided as a free tool within the operating system.

Zeroing the hard drive will thwart potential issues that arise from bad sectors, but the process also has an added benefit. Zeroing a drive sanitizes the drive and prevents deleted files from being recovered by third-party recovery tools. Essentially, when a file is deleted it is not wiped from the hard drive. It is simply not being protected from being overwritten by the operating system. The file will sit intact on the hard drive until that disk space is needed and used for another purpose. Zeroing a hard drive is recommended before donating or discarding a hard drive.

1. Navigate to Applications > Utilities.
2. Open Disk Utility.
3. Partition the hard drive with the steps previously described.
4. Select the device name, then click on the Erase tab.

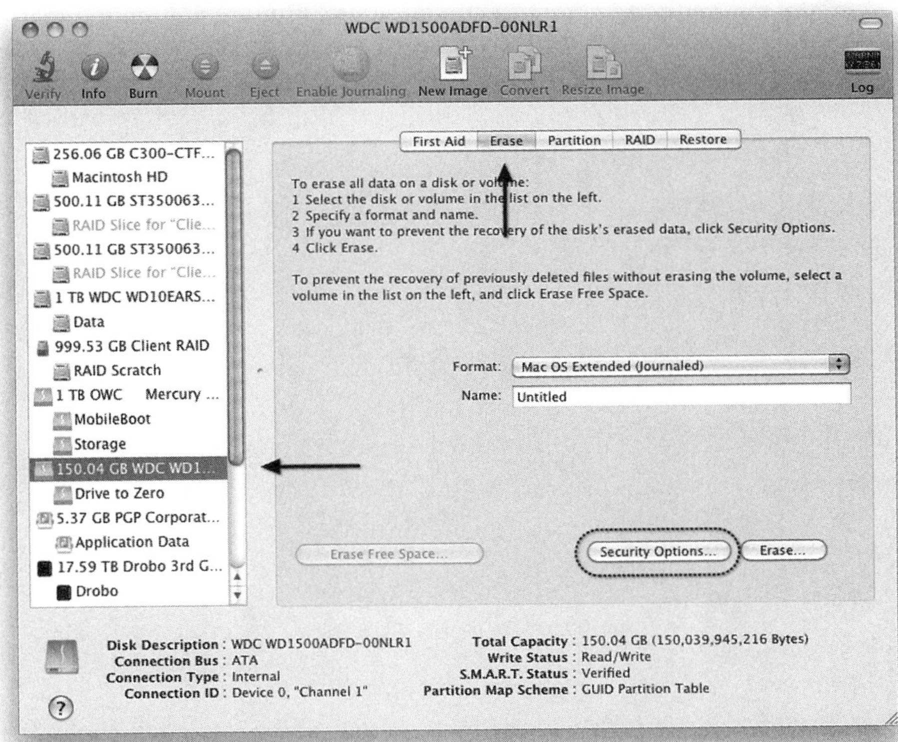

▶ **FIG. 9.5**

5. Click the Security Options button.
6. Select the option to Zero Out Data and click OK.

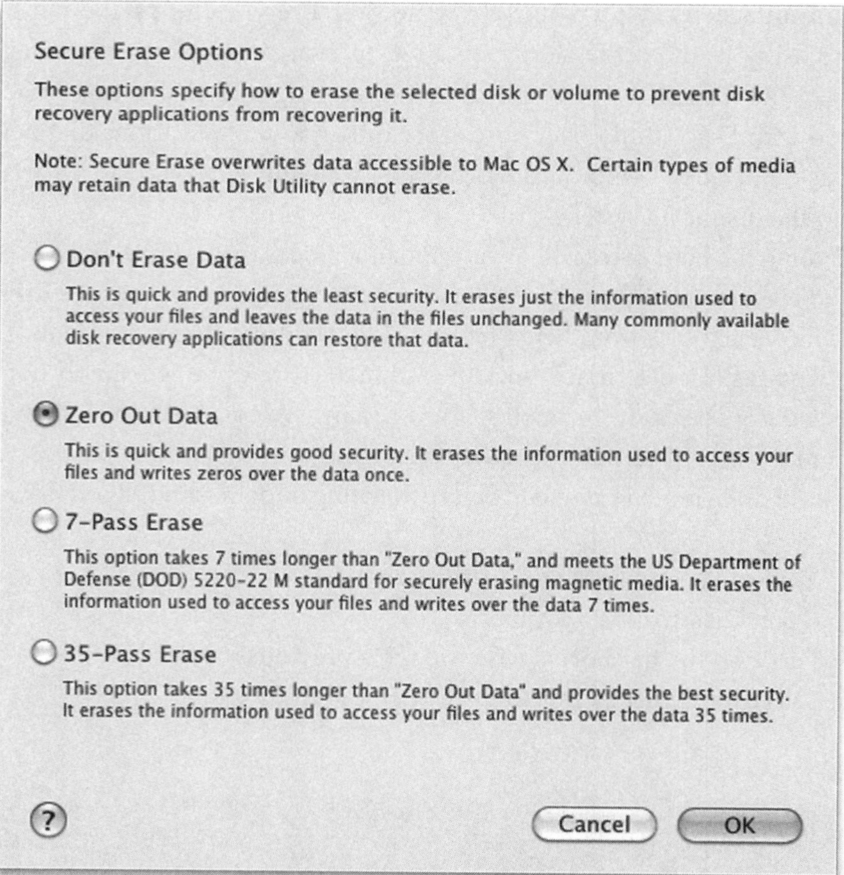

FIG. 9.6

This will write erroneous data to every sector of the drive. When Disk Utility encounters a bad sector, it will be remapped. There are options to erase the disk with varying levels of security—single pass through thirty-five passes. As you might imagine, filling erroneous data on a drive thirty-five times will require a significant amount of time. Single pass will suffice for sanitizing your drive in most cases. Even when the files are overwritten once, there may still be artifacts of the file that was overwritten (similar to recording on a cassette tape that contains previous audio information). In some cases, the previous audio can still be heard through the new recording. If performing this process to remap drives, the lengthier zeroing processes that involve multiple passes are not necessary, as the bad sectors will be remapped on the first pass.

7. Provide a new name for the volume.
8. Click Erase. This process may take some time because the whole entire drive will be filled with erroneous data. Depending on the rotation speed of the hard drive, a 1 TB hard drive can take up to four hours to be erased. This process is best run overnight or when ample time is provided to complete the zeroing task.

REPAIRING DISK PERMISSIONS VIA DISK UTILITY

OS X is a UNIX-based operating system that utilizes POSIX permissions. At its simplest form, POSIX permissions allow and deny access to files and folders on a computer. User access levels, commonly referred to as permissions, enable read-only, read-write, write-only, and no-access permissions to files and folders in the directory structure of the computer to users. There are times when these permissions settings become changed and cause problems for the operating system. For example, if OS X normally has read-write access to a folder and that access is changed to read-only, the operating system will not be able to function properly. This can manifest in many forms including undesired results when using programs, sluggish performance, and frequent program crashes.

Permissions changes can happen for a number of reasons including when application installers inadvertently change permissions that they should not. Fortunately, OS X provides the ability to repair disk permissions on the computer. In other words, OS X has the ability to change permissions back to their default state. Repairing permissions will often remedy system anomalies.

1. Navigate to Applications > Utilities.
2. Open Disk Utility.
3. Select the volume used to boot the OS X. In this case, the Macintosh HD volume is used for the boot drive.

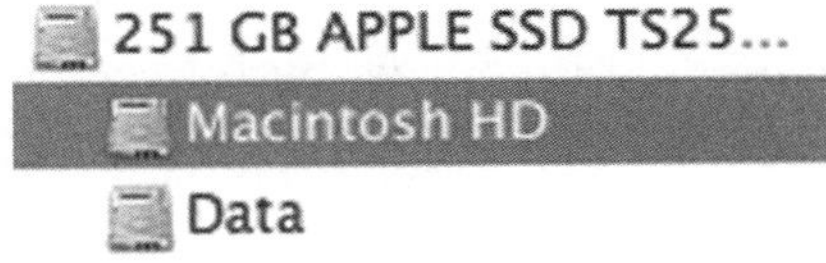

▶ FIG. 9.7

4. Click Repair Disk Permissions.

Disk Utility will restore the permissions on a startup volume to their default state. It is best to repair disk permissions from a boot CD or a recovery partition if you are using OS X Lion or later (Fig. 9.8).

RESETTING PARAMETER RANDOM ACCESS MEMORY

Macintosh computers utilize multiple sources of memory to create the most streamlined experience for users. The two most heavily used storage areas include random access memory (RAM) and hard drives. Parameter RAM, or PRAM, is a small portion of RAM that maintains system configuration settings for Macintosh computers. Over time, it may be necessary to reset the PRAM to remedy undesired system performance. Fortunately, it is simple to reset the PRAM to its default state.

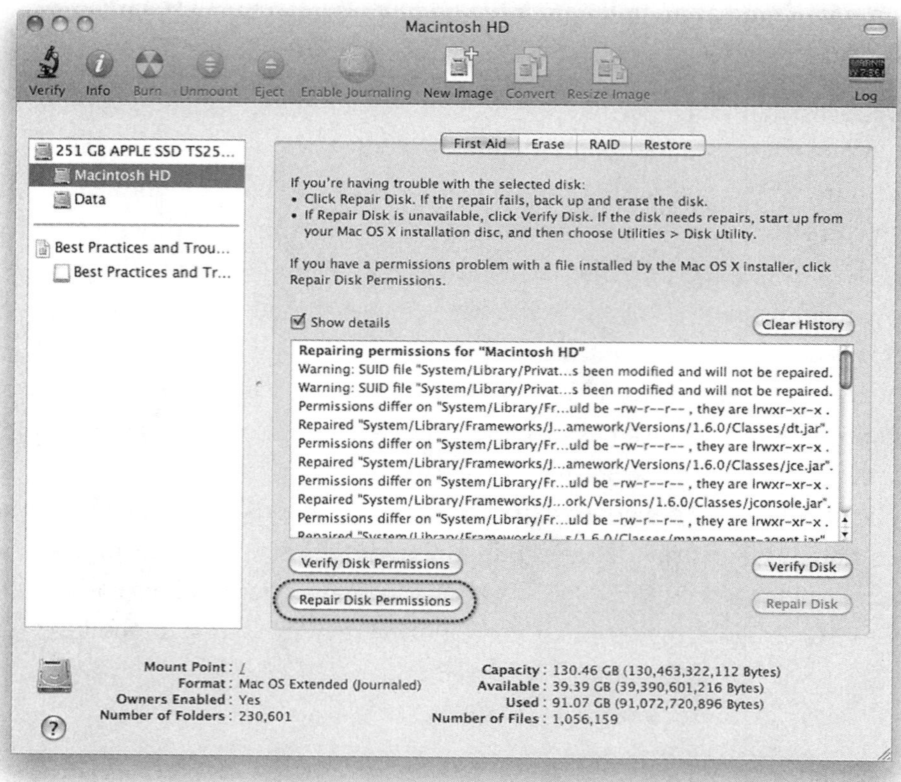

▶ **FIG. 9.8**

1. Shut down the computer.
2. Location the Option, Command, P, and R keys on the keyboard.
3. Turn on the computer via the power button.
4. Simultaneously hold the Option, Command, P, and R keys until three startup chimes are heard.

The PRAM will be set back to its default state. Some of the items that are reset include startup disk choice, memory, sound, and network settings. More information can be found about PRAM at http://support.apple.com/kb/ht1379.

TROUBLESHOOTING VIA SYSTEM PROFILER

OS X contains extremely robust audio and MIDI layers known as Core Audio and Core MIDI, respectively. These layers are the foundation for audio and MIDI on OS X. They handle all of the encoding and decoding of audio, allow the use of class-compliant Universal Serial Bus (USB) and FireWire audio interfaces, communicate with MIDI controllers, and edit MIDI in real time. Although these frameworks are extremely robust, it is necessary to understand the process of troubleshooting devices that interface with Core Audio and Core MIDI.

1. Navigate to the Applications > Utilities (Shift-Command-U via the Finder).
2. Open System Profiler.

System Profiler is an extremely helpful application that details the configuration of your particular computer. This includes the model and serial number of the machine, specific hardware information, network information, installed software, and kernel extensions (.kext files).

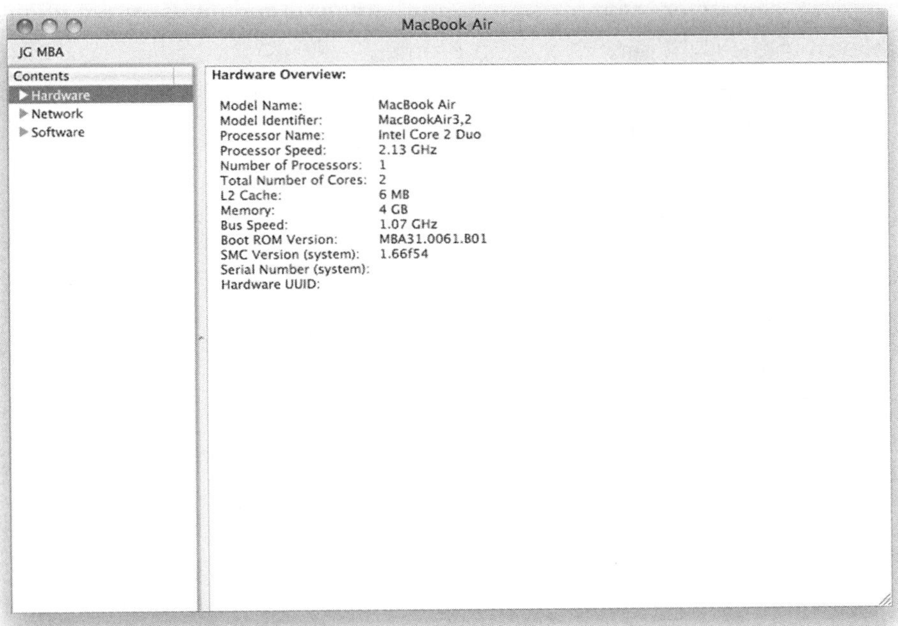

▶ **FIG. 9.9**

3. Click the Hardware disclosure triangle in the left pane of System Profiler to reveal the hardware configuration information.

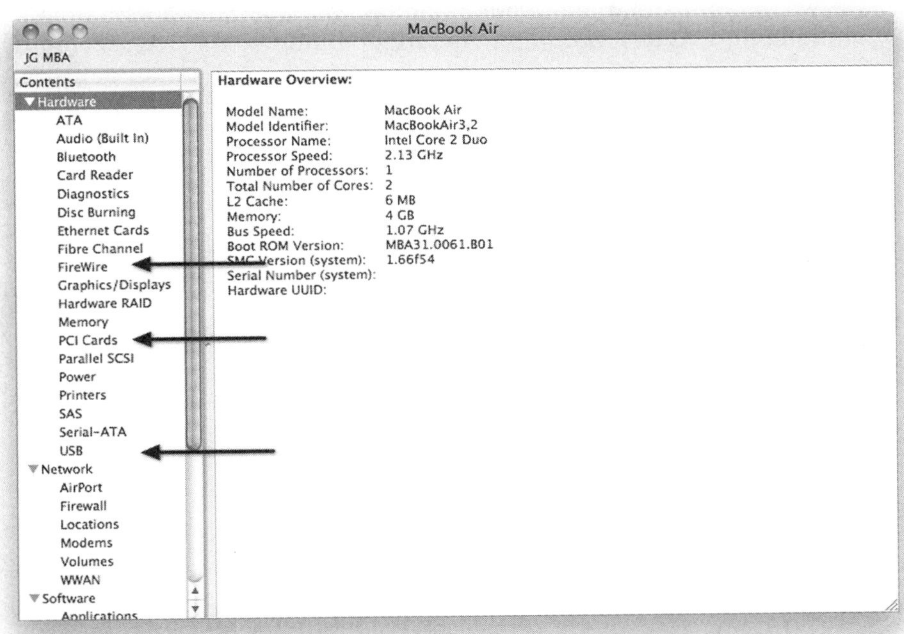

▶ **FIG. 9.10**

When working with audio interfaces and MIDI controllers, it is highly likely that you will be using FireWire, USB, or Peripheral Component Interconnect Express (PCI Express or PCIe) cards.

4. Select the USB category. You will likely see quite a few devices in the list—mouse, printer, or any other USB device that is connected to the computer. If a USB MIDI controller is connected to your computer and powered on, it will be displayed in the right pane of System Profiler.

If your device is not listed in the appropriate hardware category (FireWire, USB, PCIe, etc.) it is not being detected by the operating system at the kernel level.

Use the following steps to troubleshoot the connection issue:

- Restart the machine.
- Check to ensure adequate power is being provided to the device. All USB ports are not equal. Some USB ports provide 1.0 Amps of power, while other ports provide 2.1 Amps of power.
- Check to ensure that the connection cable is securely seated in the device and the computer. Unplug the cable at both ends and reseat it.
- Unplug all other devices on the same bus (FireWire, USB, etc.). Check the manufacturer's website to verify that you are using the appropriate hardware driver for system you are using.

TROUBLESHOOTING VIA AUDIO MIDI SETUP

Audio MIDI setup is a program that displays all of the audio and MIDI interfaces connected to your Macintosh. It is possible that devices will display in System Profiler but still not be working properly. Audio MIDI Setup can help diagnose problems with the audio interface or MIDI controller.

1. Navigate to Applications > Utilities.
2. Open Audio MIDI Setup (AMS).

Audio MIDI setup possesses a simple interface that is meant to make the management of your audio interfaces and MIDI controllers as streamlined as possible. It is divided into two views: Audio Devices and MIDI devices. The image above displays the Audio Devices view.

The left pane of the application windows lists the audio interfaces that are connected to the machine. This includes built-in audio interfaces that are specific to your particular Macintosh and third-party audio interfaces. The right pane provides details that are specific to the currently selected device.

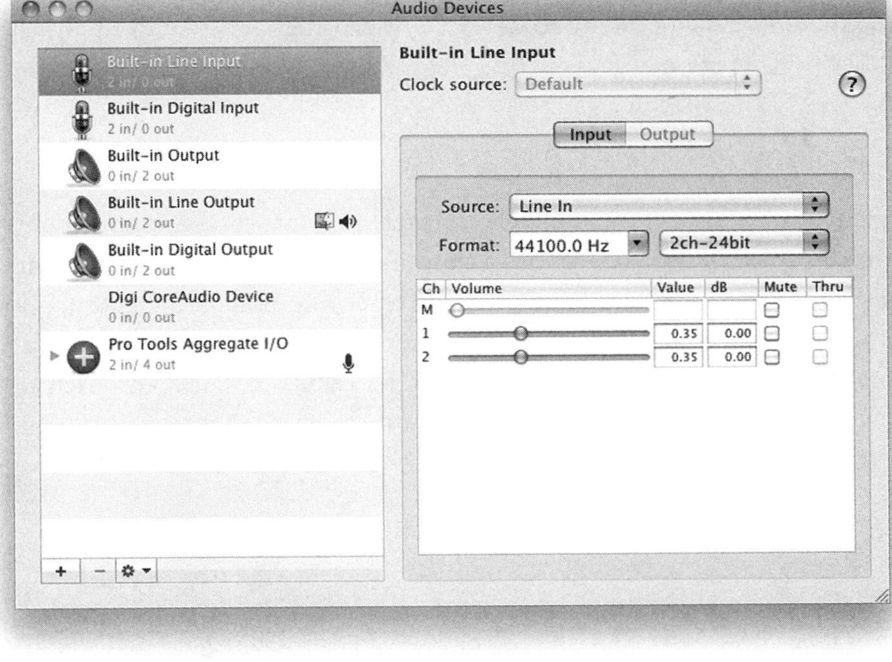

▶ **FIG. 9.11**

3. Select Built-in Line Input from the list in the left pane.

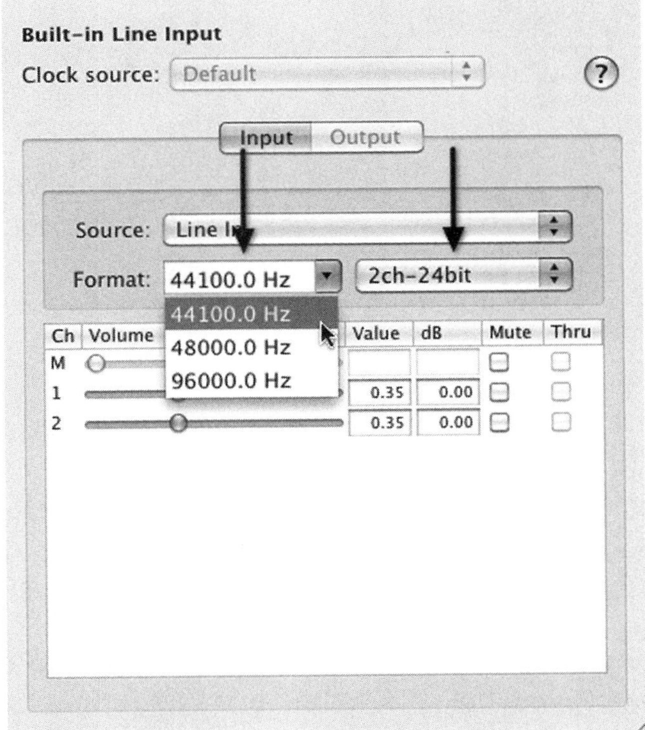

▶ **FIG. 9.12**

This right pane allows you to verify sample rate and bit rate settings. If problems arise with sample rate errors in your digital audio workstation, verify that the sample rate settings mirror those in Audio MIDI Setup for the audio interface being used. If these settings do not mirror each other, it is possible that unpredictable errors can occur.

CREATION OF AN AGGREGATE AUDIO INTERFACE

Aggregate audio interfaces can be extremely helpful when a high number of channels are needed in your audio project. Essentially, an aggregate audio interface is a virtual interface that is created when multiple audio interfaces are bound together and seen as one audio interface by the operating system and digital audio workstation. The sum of the individual channels on each audio interface will be combined into a single audio interface. Aggregate audio interfaces are managed through Audio MIDI setup.

Note: This lesson requires two or more audio interfaces.

1. Navigate to Applications > Utilities.
2. Open Audio MIDI Setup (AMS).

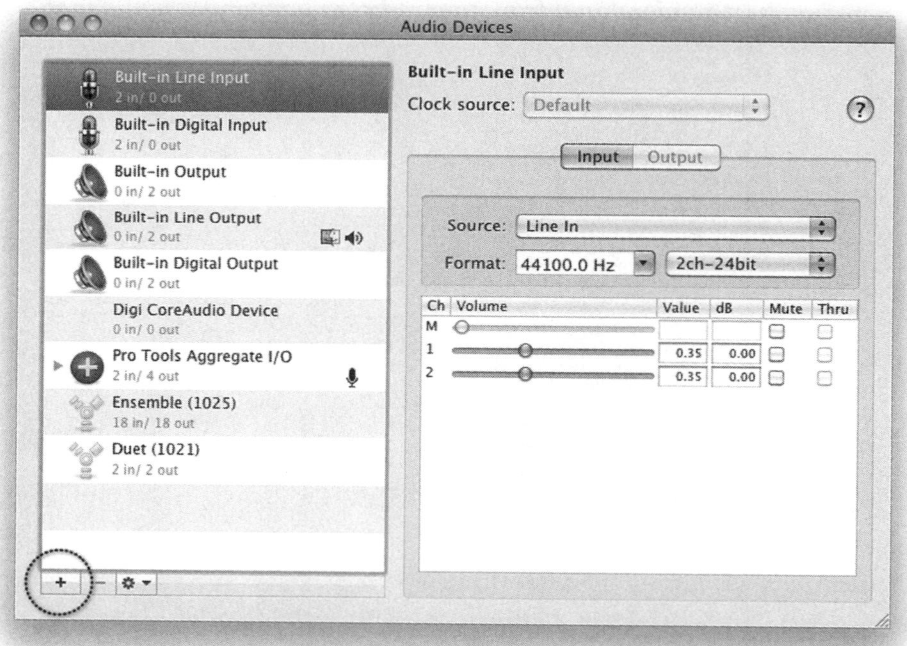

▶ FIG. 9.13

3. Click the plus sign in the lower left corner of the application window.
4. A new aggregate device will be created in the device list in the left pane.
5. Double-click the newly create aggregate device to rename it. Name the device My Agg Device.

▶ FIG. 9.14

6. Click the disclosure triangle to the left of the aggregate device name.

▶ FIG. 9.15

Notice that no devices are revealed when toggling the disclosure triangle. Also, the device says 0 in/0 out, signifying that you have no available inputs and outputs in the aggregate interface. This is because there are no devices assigned to the aggregate device.

7. With the My Agg Device selected, navigate to the right pane.

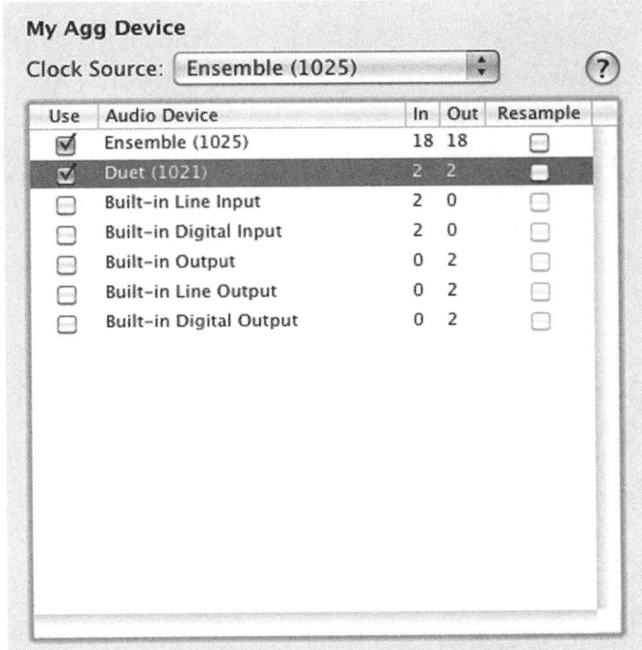

▶ FIG. 9.16

8. Select the audio interfaces you would like to add to the aggregate device by toggling the check box next to the name of the desired audio interface.

The aggregate device will display the total number of inputs and outputs from the multiple audio interfaces; in this case, 20 in/20 out. The devices used will be listed with the aggregate device in the left pane.

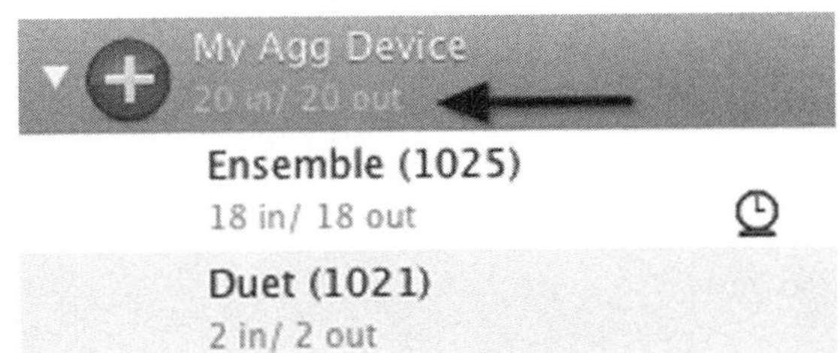

▶ FIG. 9.17

Notice that the Apogee Ensemble interface has a small clock icon to the right of its name. This icon indicates the word clock from the Apogee Ensemble will be used as the master clocking mechanism. This mechanism ensures that each device in the aggregate group uses a master sampling rate. This is important because analog signals are captured as digital information. If the sampling rates are out of sync, the aggregate device will misinterpret the analog information being captured. This misinterpretation results in errors in analog-to-digital (AD) conversion and yields poor audio quality.

All audio interfaces have word clocks built in. Generally speaking, more expensive audio interfaces contain higher-quality clocking mechanisms. In fact, many people buy dedicated word clocks to be the master clocking mechanism for multiple audio interfaces. Apogee Electronics' Big Ben clock is an industry standard and is used by audio engineers around the globe. In an aggregate device, it is advantageous to use the clocking mechanism that is the most "clean." The master clock can be changed through a pop-up window located in the right pane of the Audio MIDI Setup window.

▶ FIG. 9.18

UTILIZING AGGREGATE DEVICES IN THE DIGITAL AUDIO WORKSTATION

1. Navigate to the Applications folder and Open Logic Pro X.
2. Create an empty project via the projects dialog box.
3. Create one mono audio track when prompted by the new tracks dialog box.
4. Navigate to Logic Pro X > Preferences > Audio.
5. Select the My Agg Device aggregate audio interface from the pop-up window.
6. Click Apply Changes to utilize the aggregate audio interface (Fig. 9.19).

TROUBLESHOOTING AUDIO INTERFACES VIA THE DIGITAL AUDIO WORKSTATION

In certain circumstances audio interfaces may be visible in both System Profiler and Audio MIDI setup, but audio is not audible in the digital audio workstation, despite the presence of the audio interface. This is generally due to an issue with Core Audio. In many cases this can be remedied by toggling Core Audio within the digital audio workstation. These steps can be performed in any audio project in Logic Pro X.

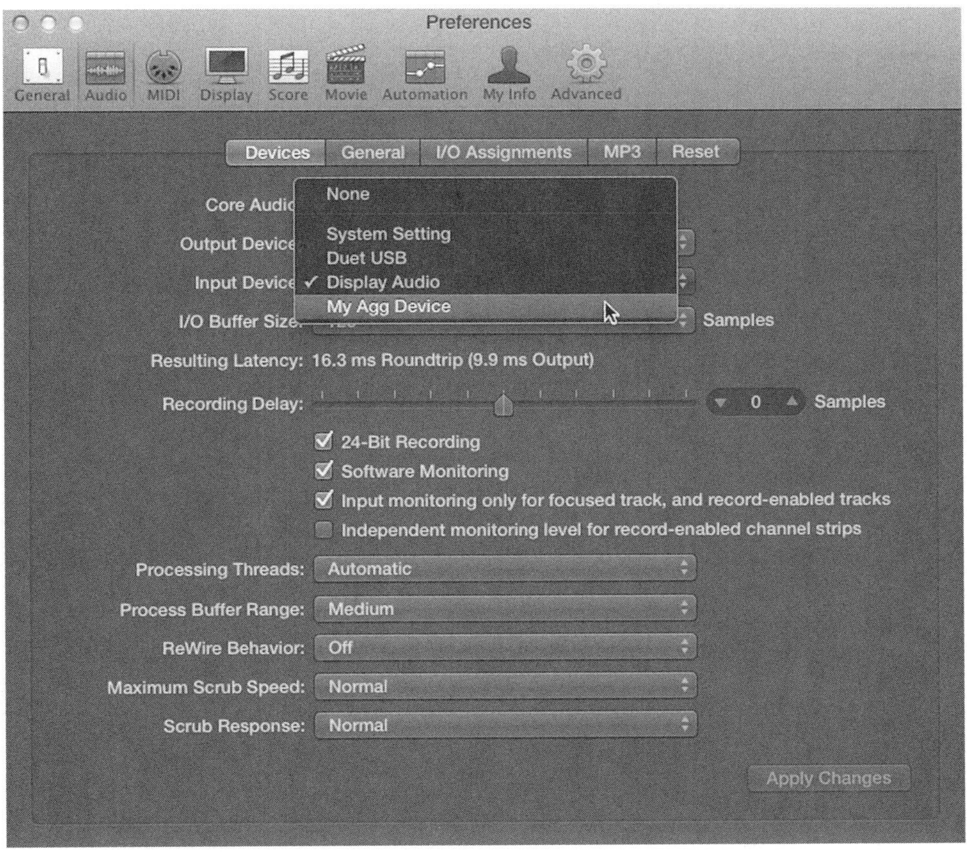

▶ **FIG. 9.19**

1. Navigate to Applications and Open Logic Pro X.
2. Create an empty project via the projects dialog box.
3. Create one mono audio track when prompted by the new tracks dialog box.
4. Navigate to Logic Pro X > Preferences > Audio.
5. Verify that Core Audio is enabled for use.

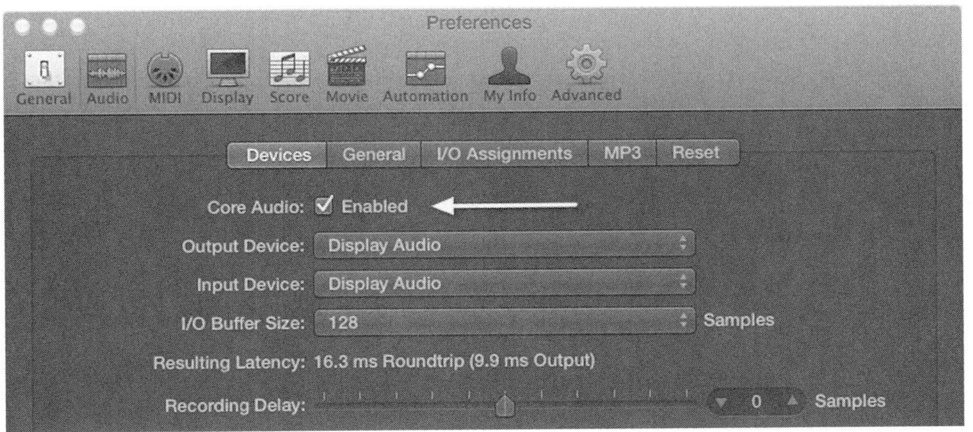

▶ **FIG. 9.20**

6. If it is not enabled, toggle the checkbox and click Apply Changes. This will likely fix audio playback issues.

7. If the box was checked, toggle the checkbox to disable Core Audio and click Apply Changes.

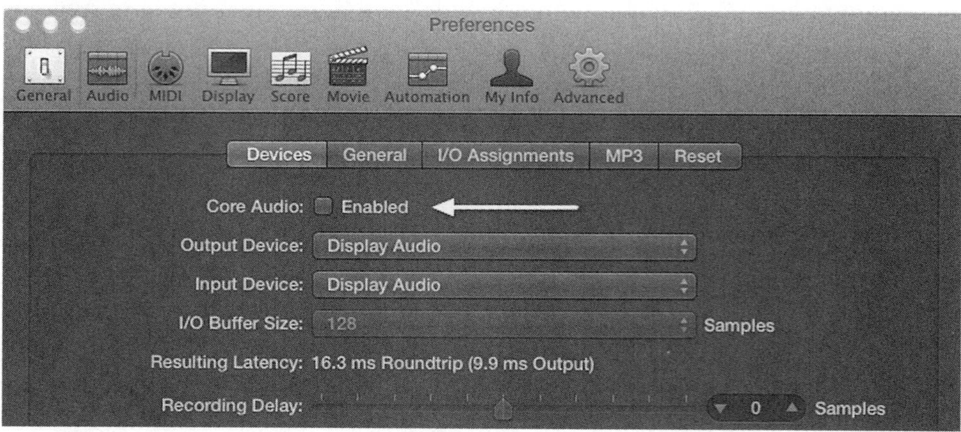

▶ **FIG. 9.21**

8. Enable Core audio again by toggling the checkbox and click Apply Changes. This will restart Core Audio.

This workflow will often remedy audio playback in Logic Pro X. If this does not restore audio playback, try the following troubleshooting steps:

- Save work and restart the machine.
- Check volume knobs on the audio interface.
- Check XLR, TRS cables, or sound system used. Verify that power is being supplied to the monitors or sound system used.
- Check to ensure that the audio interface bus connection cable (FireWire, USB, etc.) is securely seated in the device and the computer. Unplug the cable at both ends and reseat it.
- Unplug all other devices on the same bus (FireWire, USB, etc.). Check the manufacturer's website to verify that you are using the appropriate hardware driver for system you are using.

TROUBLESHOOTING AUDIO INTERFACES VIA SYSTEM SOUND

System-wide sound can be used to test problems with an audio interface. By setting your system sound to output to the problematic audio interface, it will become apparent if there is an issue with the audio project or the audio interface.

1. Navigate to Applications and open System Preferences.
2. Click on Sound in the Hardware row.

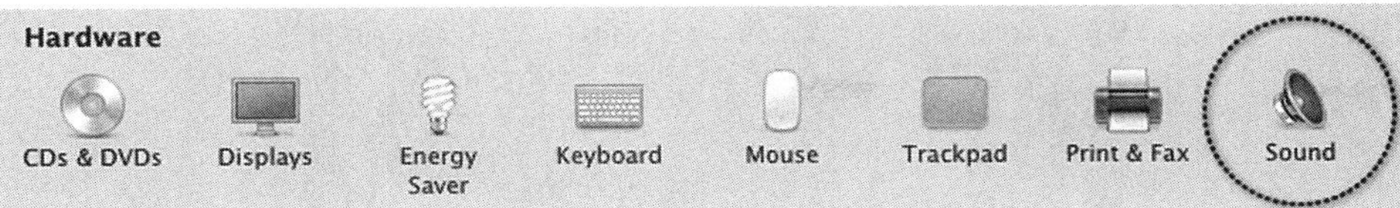

▶ **FIG. 9.22**

3. Set the output to the audio interface.

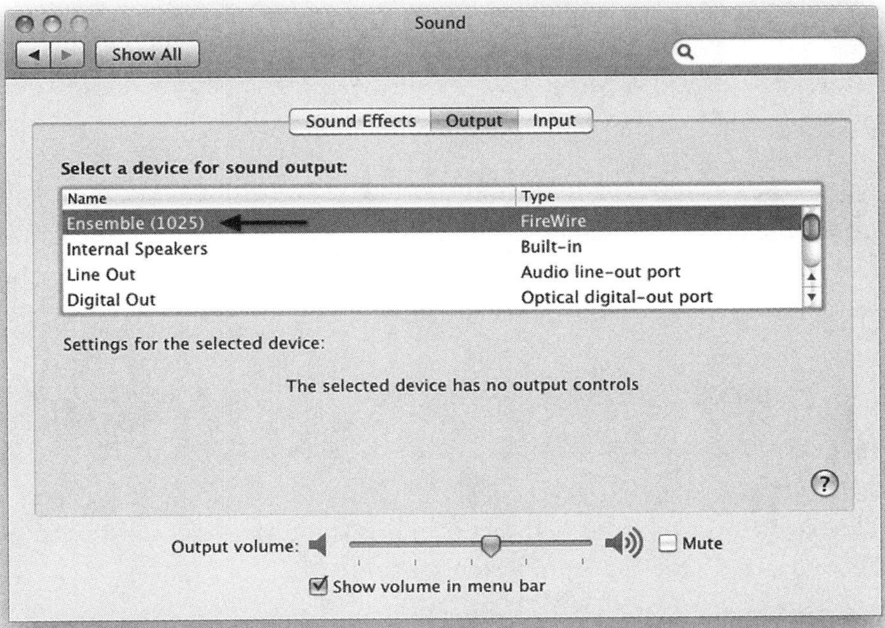

▶ **FIG. 9.23**

If system sound outputs properly through the audio interface, return to Logic Pro X and restart Core Audio by toggling the audio interface in Logic Pro X's audio preferences. If audio still does not output properly via the audio interface, try creating a new project in Logic Pro X. This will help narrow the search to the root of the problem.

TROUBLESHOOTING MIDI CONTROLLERS IN LOGIC PRO X

By and large, MIDI controllers work seamlessly with Logic Pro X and other digital audio workstations. In most cases it is only necessary to plug in the device prior to using it—no drivers required. However, there are instances where MIDI data may not be reaching the sequencer.

Ensure that the MIDI controller is connected to the computer and powered on and navigate to the Applications folder and open Logic Pro X. When prompted, create an empty project via the projects dialog box and create a single software instrument track. By default, the LCD in the transport displays Beats and Projects. To view MIDI data, click on the far left of the LCD and choose Custom.

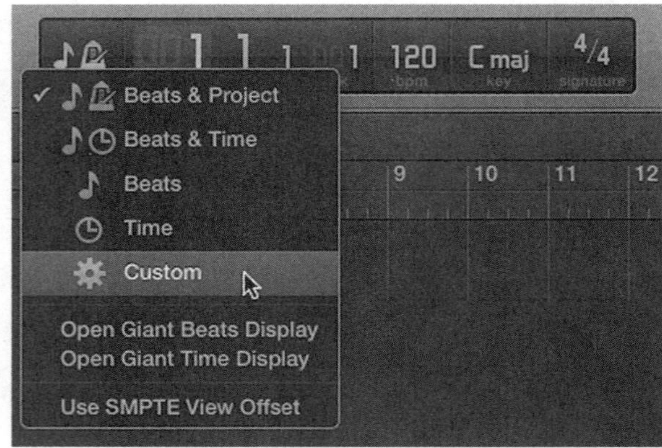

▶ FIG. 9.24

Notice there is a section in the transport LCD that displays MIDI activity. At this point the display should read No In and No Out. This is because there is no MIDI data being received from the MIDI controller because it is not being played. In other words, no MIDI is flowing in or out of your MIDI device.

▶ FIG. 9.25

Play a few notes on the MIDI controller. The display should update with MIDI data as it is received from the MIDI controller.

▶ FIG. 9.26

If the display does not update with MIDI data while the controller is being played, ensure that the MIDI controller is connected to the computer via the proper port, the proper drivers are installed (if necessary), and that the device is receiving adequate power from the connection port. As mentioned previously, some ports do not provide adequate power to bus-powered devices. Try another port and disconnect any other devices of the same connection type.

The MIDI environment is a powerful tool that allows you to view all MIDI data that flows in and out of your project. In previous versions of Logic Pro X, the environment was easily accessible from the Window menu. In the most recent version, Logic Pro X, the environment must be enabled from the advanced section of Logic Pro X preferences.

Navigate to Logic Pro X > Preferences > Advanced. Select the checkbox, Show Advanced Tools, to enable the advanced editing features in Logic Pro X (Fig. 9.27).

Choose Window > Open MIDI Environment. Click on the pop-up window at the left side of the environment window. Choose Click & Ports.

The Click & Ports layer of the environment is displayed. This view shows the signal flow of MIDI data as it leaves the MIDI controller and is brought into

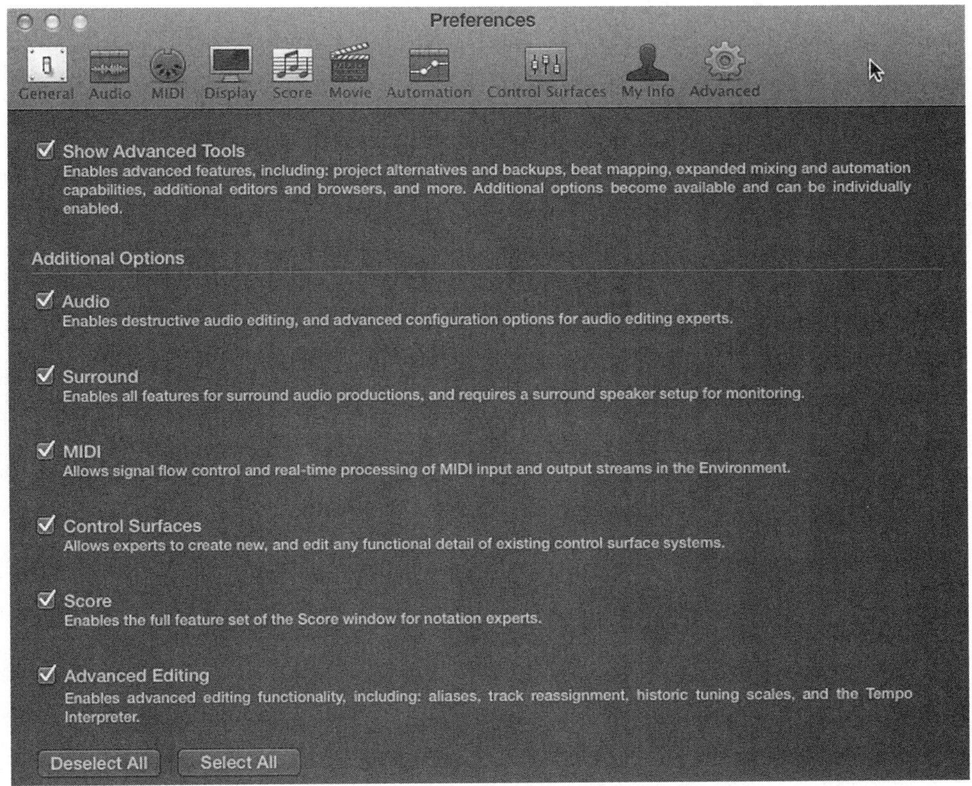

▶ **FIG. 9.27**

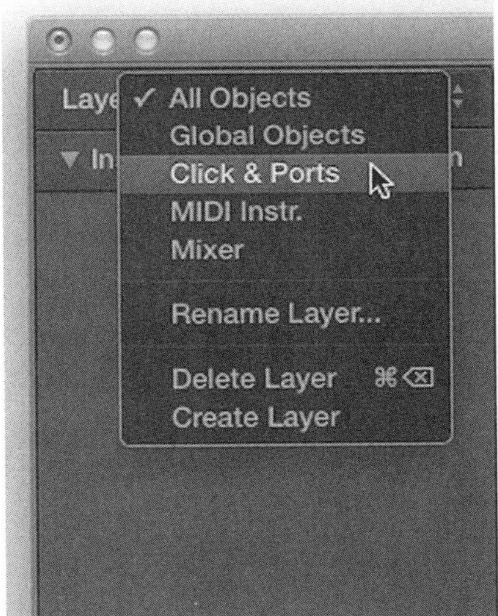

▶ **FIG. 9.28**

Logic Pro X's sequencer. This view can be extremely helpful because it will help pinpoint the point of failure in the path of MIDI data.

1. Physical Input—Represents the MIDI devices that are physically connected to computer. If your keyboard is powered on and connected to the computer, it should be listed in the physical input object (Fig. 9.29).
2. Keyboard Object—Displays the notes played on the MIDI controller in real time.

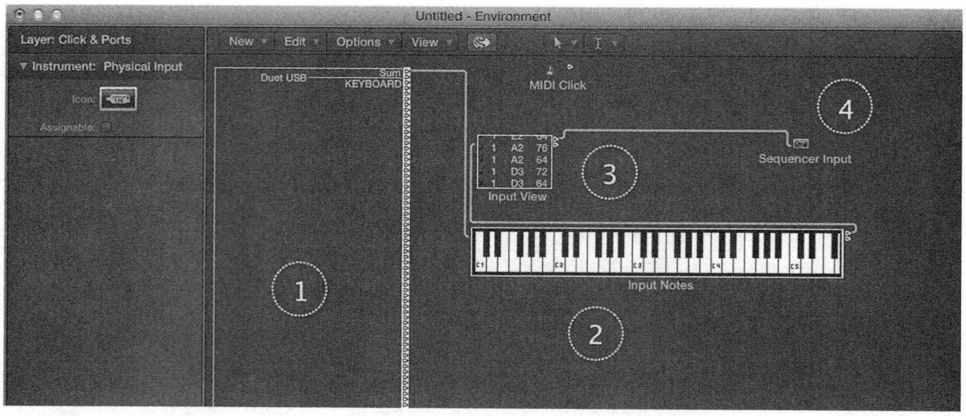

▶ **FIG. 9.29**

3. Monitor Object—Displays a line-by-line view of MIDI data as it is received from the MIDI controller in real time.
4. Sequencer Input—Brings the MIDI data in Logic Pro X's sequencer.

The image shown here represents the signal flow of MIDI data via the MIDI controller attached to the computer. The data flows through the keyboard object and the monitor object on its way to the sequencer input. This process is facilitated through virtual cables just as one would expect in a physical studio. The cables utilized in the environment act as physical cables but are known as virtual cables because they are not made by physical components—they exist in a virtual environment.

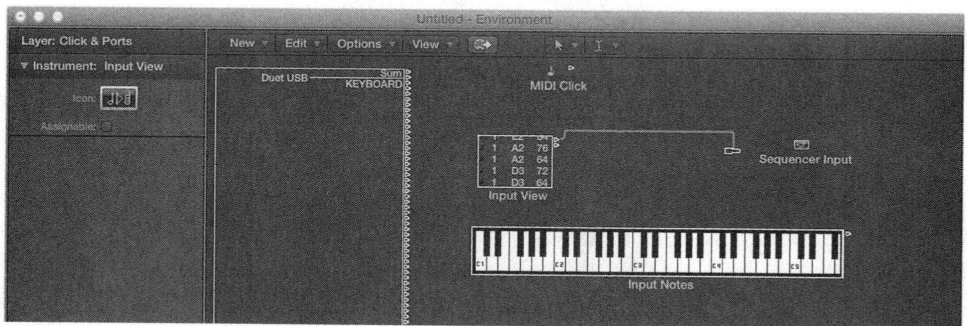

▶ **FIG. 9.30**

While the keyboard and monitor objects are helpful because they display MIDI controller data, they are not absolutely necessary in the environment. All that is needed is a physical input and a sequencer input. In other words, the MIDI data only needs to move from the physical input to the sequencer input and does not need to be displayed by the keyboard and monitor objects before reaching Logic Pro X's sequencer.

Disconnect all of the objects from one another by dragging the cables out of the objects. This is done by clicking and holding on the cable at the left side of the object. It is also possible to select the cable and press Control–Delete.

Once the cables have all been disconnected, the environment will look similar to the image shown here. Even if notes are played on the MIDI controller, no sound will emit from Logic Pro X. This is because the signal path has been disrupted.

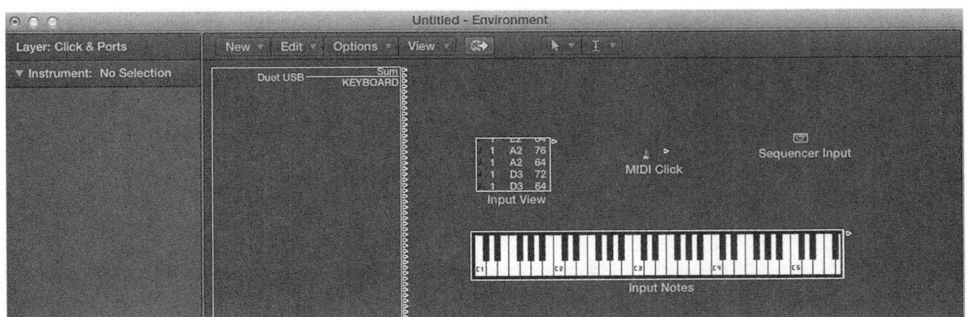

▶ FIG. 9.31

Delete the keyboard and monitor objects by right clicking on each object and select Delete.

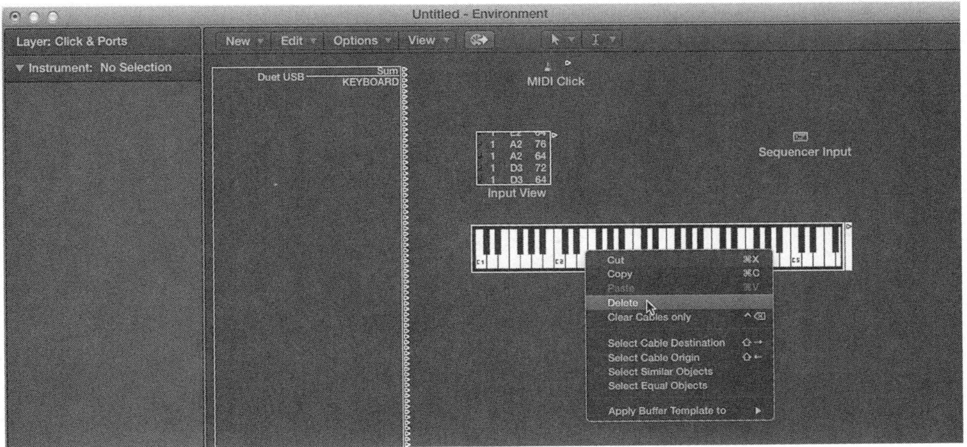

▶ FIG. 9.32

At this point, there should only be a Physical Input object, MIDI Click object, and a Sequencer Input object. Currently, they all exist in Logic Pro X's environment, but they have no way of interacting with each other because there are no cables present to establish communication between the objects.

Drag a cable from the upper right corner of the Physical Input object into the left side of the Sequencer Input object.

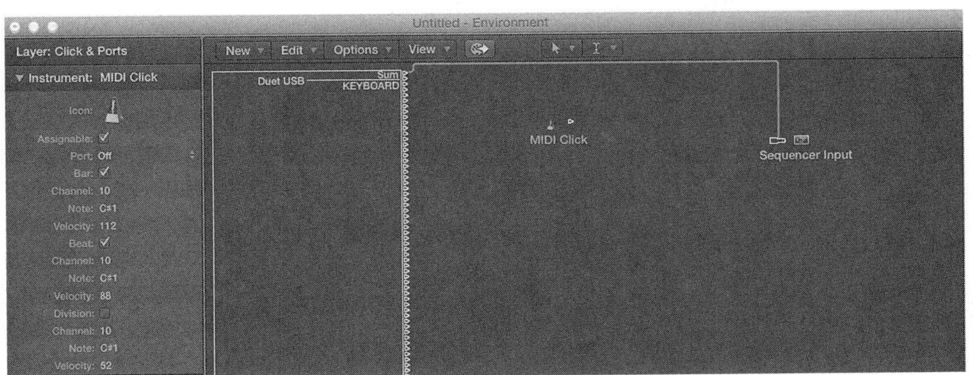

▶ FIG. 9.33

Play a few notes on the MIDI controller. Signal flow should be restored after the two objects are cabled together, resulting in MIDI data triggering a software instrument.

ARCHIVE AND RESTORATION OF PREFERENCE AND PROPERTY LIST FILES

Nearly every program that runs on the Macintosh utilizes one or more property list (plist) files. Essentially, these files store the user-specific and sometimes machine-specific preferences for a program. Over time, these preference files can become corrupted and cause program crashes and, in some cases, system crashes. Deleting plist files for Logic Pro X will not damage the installation in any way. The property list files will be rebuilt on the next launch of the program.

Locations of property list files for Logic Pro X are:

~/Library/Preferences/com.apple.logic10.plist

~/Library/Preferences/com.apple.logic.pro.cs

1. If Logic Pro X is running quit the application.
2. Navigate to ~/Library/Preferences.
3. Drag the following files to the Desktop:

~/Library/Preferences/com.apple.logic10.plist

~/Library/Preferences/com.apple.logic.pro.cs

4. Navigate to Applications and open Logic Pro X.
5. Return to ~/Library/Preferences. The property list files were rebuilt and are free of any corruption that may be afflicting the files and, ultimately, the error-free operation of Logic Pro X.

This same approach can be used to archive the property list files for future use. Further, the files can be placed in at ~/Library/Preferences on another machine or another user account to provide the same preferences as the original machine.

1. Create a new folder on the Desktop entitled “Pref Backup.”
2. Drag the following files into the newly created folder:

~/Library/Preferences/com.apple.logic10.plist

~/Library/Preferences/com.apple.logic.pro.cs

3. Right-click on the folder and choose Compress “Pref Backup.”

An archive has now been created from the Pref Backup folder. This ZIP archive can be stored for future use, copied to an external drive or cloud service, or emailed for setup on another machine.

ARCHIVE AND RESTORATION OF KEY COMMANDS

One of the most powerful features in Logic Pro X is the ability to customize key commands sets. This allows the user to create a truly unique manner of working that other digital audio workstations do not provide.

1. Reopen Logic Pro X if it is closed.
2. Navigate to Logic Pro X > Key Commands > Edit.

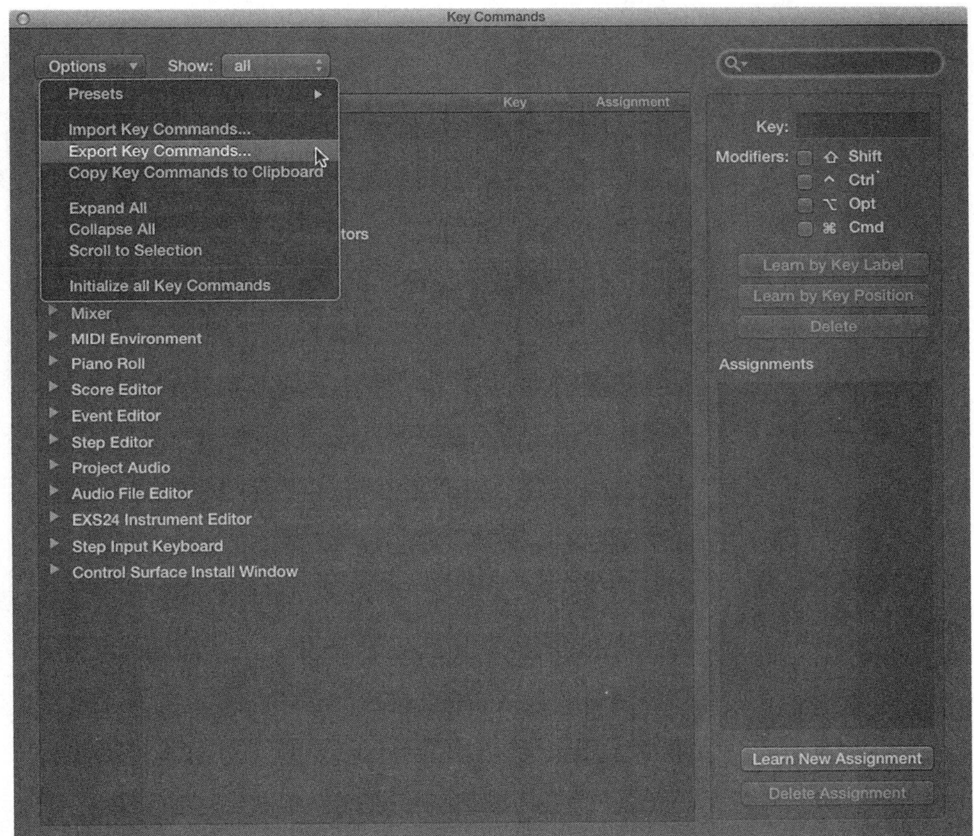

▶ **FIG. 9.34**

3. Choose Export Key Commands from the Options pop-up window.
4. Name the file with the following name convention:

   Year-Month-Day-File_Name

By default, Logic Pro X will export your personal key commands set into a flat file that resides at the following location: ~/Library/Application Support/Logic/Key Commands. This file can be used to archive your key commands for future restoration. Some composers choose to create key command sets that are specific to the current task they are working on. For example, it is possible to create a specific key command set for mixing and a separate key command set for mastering.

RESET THE AUDIO UNITS CACHE

Logic Pro X, like most digital audio workstations, can be extended with the use of plugins that can manipulate digital audio. Logic Pro X interfaces with audio units (AU) plugins and can cache these plugins for quick access. An AU cache can become corrupted, resulting in a system that may be unstable.

1. Navigate to Logic Pro X > Preferences > Audio Units Manager.
2. Once the Audio Units Manager has opened, press Command–A to select all of the Audio Units plugins.

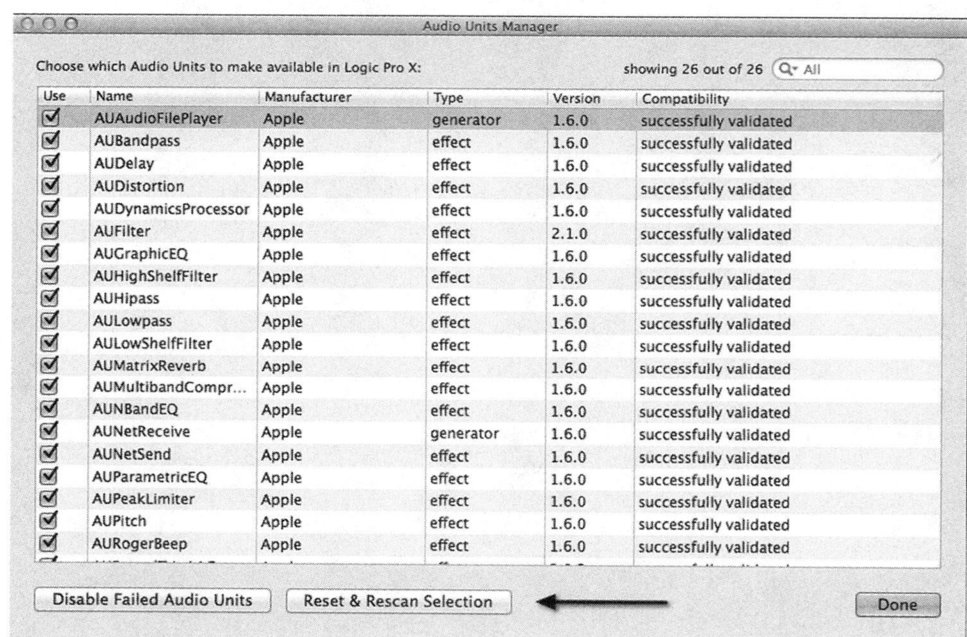

▶ **FIG. 9.35**

3. Press Reset & Rescan Selection. Logic Pro X will scan each AU plugin and attempt to validate that it is working properly and is compatible with the application. A new AU cache will be created in this process.

If an AU plugin fails to validate, it is necessary to disable the plugin from being used within Logic Pro X (Fig. 9.36). An AU plugin that fails to validate can cause system instability and produce undesirable results while using the application.

4. Sort the AU plugins by compatibility.
5. Select any AU plugins that failed validation.
6. Click the Disable Failed Audio Units button.

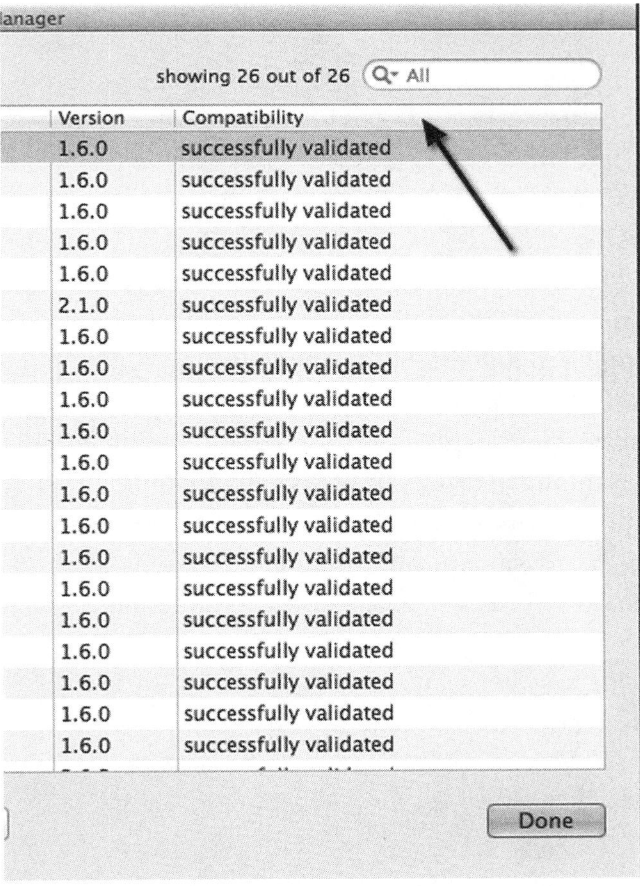

showing 26 out of 26 All

Version	Compatibility
1.6.0	successfully validated
1.6.0	successfully validated
1.6.0	successfully validated
1.6.0	successfully validated
1.6.0	successfully validated
2.1.0	successfully validated
1.6.0	successfully validated
1.6.0	successfully validated
1.6.0	successfully validated
1.6.0	successfully validated
1.6.0	successfully validated
1.6.0	successfully validated
1.6.0	successfully validated
1.6.0	successfully validated
1.6.0	successfully validated
1.6.0	successfully validated
1.6.0	successfully validated
1.6.0	successfully validated
1.6.0	successfully validated
1.6.0	successfully validated

Done

▶ **FIG. 9.36**

Audio Units Manager

Choose which Audio Units to make available in Logic Pro X: showing 26 out of 26 All

Use	Name	Manufacturer	Type	Version	Compatibility
☑	AUAudioFilePlayer	Apple	generator	1.6.0	successfully validated
☑	AUBandpass	Apple	effect	1.6.0	successfully validated
☑	AUDelay	Apple	effect	1.6.0	successfully validated
☑	AUDistortion	Apple	effect	1.6.0	successfully validated
☑	AUDynamicsProcessor	Apple	effect	1.6.0	successfully validated
☑	AUFilter	Apple	effect	2.1.0	successfully validated
☑	AUGraphicEQ	Apple	effect	1.6.0	successfully validated
☑	AUHighShelfFilter	Apple	effect	1.6.0	successfully validated
☑	AUHipass	Apple	effect	1.6.0	successfully validated
☑	AULowpass	Apple	effect	1.6.0	successfully validated
☑	AULowShelfFilter	Apple	effect	1.6.0	successfully validated
☑	AUMatrixReverb	Apple	effect	1.6.0	successfully validated
☑	AUMultibandCompr...	Apple	effect	1.6.0	successfully validated
☑	AUNBandEQ	Apple	effect	1.6.0	successfully validated
☑	AUNetReceive	Apple	generator	1.6.0	successfully validated
☑	AUNetSend	Apple	effect	1.6.0	successfully validated
☑	AUParametricEQ	Apple	effect	1.6.0	successfully validated
☑	AUPeakLimiter	Apple	effect	1.6.0	successfully validated
☑	AUPitch	Apple	effect	1.6.0	successfully validated
☑	AURogerBeep	Apple	effect	1.6.0	successfully validated

Disable Failed Audio Units | Reset & Rescan Selection | Done

▶ **FIG. 9.37**

REBUILDING CORRUPT PROJECT FILES

It is rare, but in some cases it is necessary to rebuild a project that has become corrupt and will not open. A file can become corrupt for a number of reasons including, but not limited to, errors writing the file to disk from RAM or bad blocks on a hard drive. Regardless of the cause of the corruption, it is imperative to be able to recover from it.

1. Download the project file and unzip it to your Desktop.
2. Open Logic Pro X and create a new empty project.
3. Create one stereo audio track from the new tracks dialog box.
4. Check your sample rate to ensure that it is compatible with the project you are planning to rebuild. If your current sample rate is not identical to your project sample rate, the project will not play back in the desired manner. In this case, the project sample rate is 48 kHz.
5. Navigate to the Browsers area and select the All Files tab.

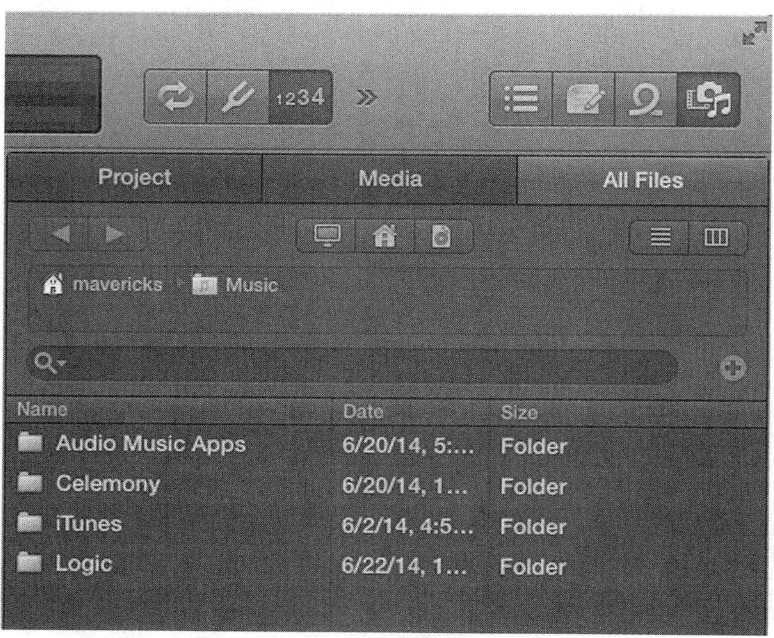

▶ FIG. 9.38

6. Select the home button.

▶ FIG. 9.39

7. The home folder view will display all of the files and folders that are currently present in your user folder. Navigate to the Desktop folder.

8. Select the Delivery, Collaboration, and Archiving project.
9. Click the import button at the bottom left corner of the Browser window. Logic Pro X presents options on what can be imported from the Delivery, Collaboration, and Archiving.logic project.

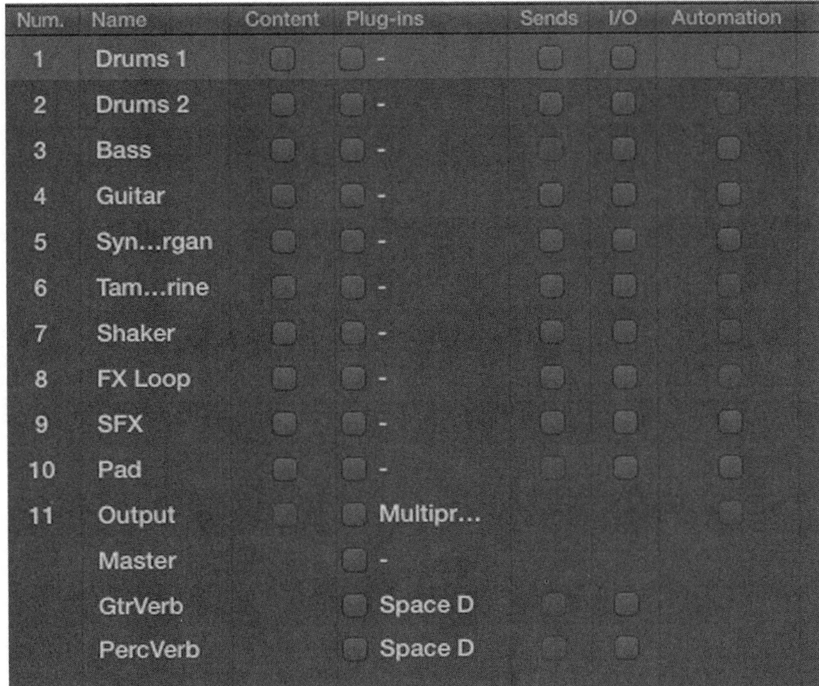

▶ **FIG. 9.40**

10. Check all of the boxes in the Content, Aux, Sends, and I/O columns.

Tip: Hold down the Option key while checking a box and all of the other boxes in the row will be checked as well.

11. Click the Add button at the bottom left corner of the Browser window. Logic Pro X will import all of the relevant information from the project into the current project.

Logic Pro X can also import project settings into the current project. Click the Import button.

Project Settings button at the bottom of the Browser window.

For the purpose of this lesson, it is not necessary to import any of these settings at this point, but this is a handy option for rebuilding projects that may have custom project settings. Once Logic Pro X has finished importing the desired tracks and various other settings, a newly rebuilt project will be available for use.

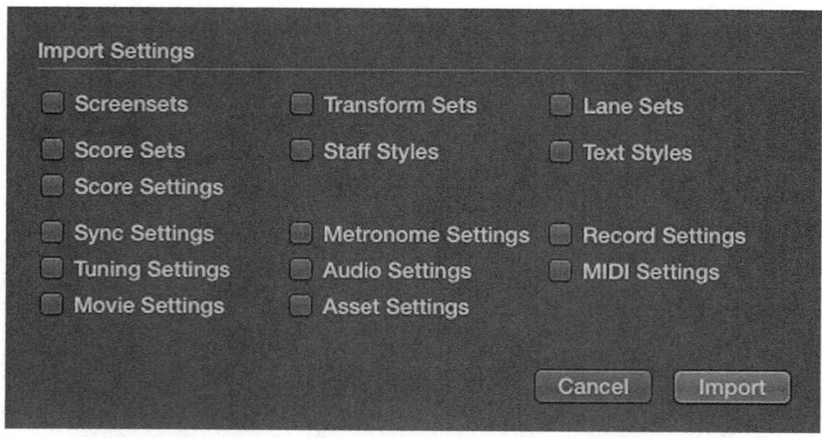

▶ **FIG. 9.41**

UNDERSTANDING RANDOM ACCESS MEMORY

RAM is one of the most useful components of a personal computer. This single component has fostered the ability for modern computers to operate multiple tasks in a seemingly effortless fashion. Essentially, RAM is extremely fast memory that is used for the temporary storage of files and folders currently being used by an application or the operating system. When reading computer specifications at the time of purchase, it is easy to overlook RAM in the long list of customizable options. Many buyers simply look at hard drive size and raw processor speed. While these components are important, RAM should be considered in the purchasing decision as well.

A common misconception is that when a program, file, or folder is opened on a computer it is running from the hard drive installed in the computer. This is true to an extent, but in actuality, the program file or folder is being copied into RAM for use. When a file is saved, it is archived back to the hard disk for long-term storage. This is due to the drastic difference between RAM and hard drive read/write speeds. RAM is markedly faster than traditional spinning hard disks. In fact, when a computer runs out of available RAM, it begins to use the hard drive as a RAM. This greatly decreases the perceived working speed of the computer because the hard drive is much slower than RAM. In environments where large media files are frequently being used and manipulated, it is advantageous to possess a large amount of RAM. The necessary amount of RAM varies depending on the demands for the application at hand. For example, working on a text document will likely require far less RAM than a video project would require.

RAM is considered to be volatile not because it is an unstable environment but because any information that is stored in RAM will be lost if the power supply to the RAM is interrupted. The information will also be lost if it is not archived to the hard disk before an operating system or program crash. The notion of saving files and projects frequently is not new, but still remains true. It is necessary to archive files to the hard disk on a regular basis. A number of programs offer autosave features, but not all.

EVALUATING RAM USAGE AND NEED

It is common to need additional RAM when working with large media projects, but it can be difficult to determine how much RAM to purchase. Adding additional RAM can be an expensive proposition, so it is important to purchase enough RAM to satisfy the balance between cost and user benefit.

Navigate to Applications > Utilities and open Activity Monitor. Choose the System Memory tab.

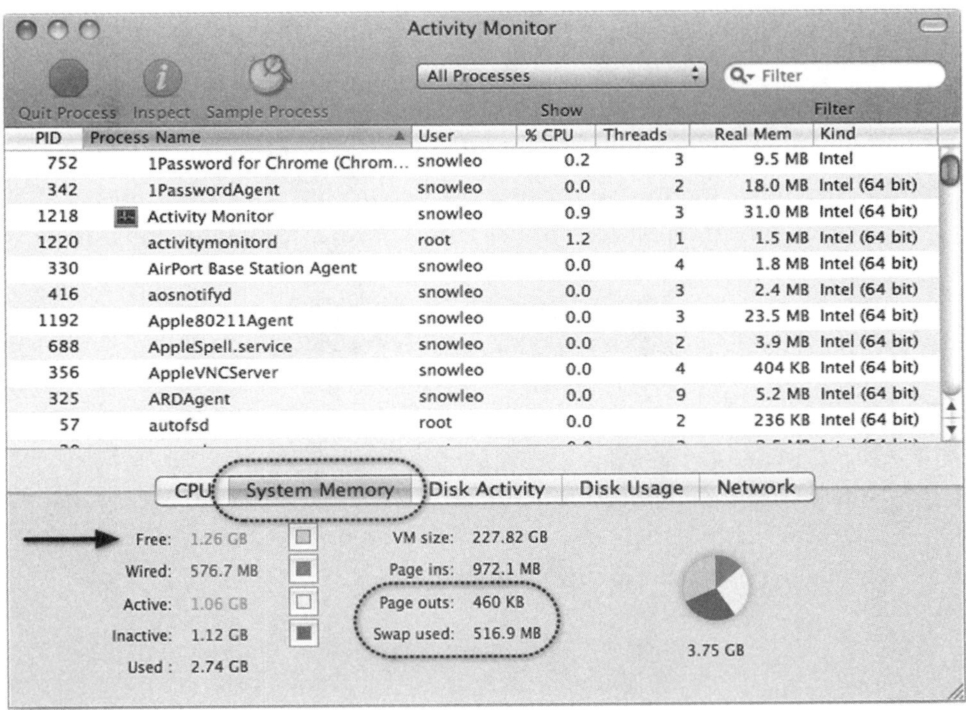

▶ FIG. 9.42

Tip: The utilities folder can be quickly opened by the key command combination Shift-Command-U.

The System Memory tab displays a wealth of valuable information in regard to RAM usage, including how much RAM is being used and how much is currently free. Activity Monitor will help you determine if the hard disk is being used for RAM.

Free: RAM that is available.
Wired: This is information that cannot be moved out of RAM to the hard disk.
Active: RAM that is being actively used by applications.
Page outs: These occur when the RAM on the machine is full. OS X will begin using the hard disk as RAM, which will greatly decrease system speed.

The general rule is that if you experience page outs, you should add more RAM to your computer.

IDENTIFYING UNSAVED CHANGES MADE IN RAM

Applications that run on the Macintosh platform provide current save status in the application window. In other words, applications allow the user to quickly see if there are document changes that exist in RAM but that have not been yet archived to the hard disk via the save command.

1. Open Logic Pro X and create a new empty project.
2. Create one stereo audio track from the new tracks dialog box.
3. Choose File > Save As. Choose the Desktop as the save location and name the project "RAM."
4. Navigate to the Media and Lists area and click on the Loops tab.
5. Focus your attention on the icon that resides at the top middle of the application window. Notice that the application icon is in full color and not greyed out. This signifies that there are no changes in RAM.

RAM - Tracks

▶ **FIG. 9.43**

6. Choose any loop from the loop browser and drag the loop into the tracks area.
7. Notice that the application icon becomes greyed out to signify that there are changes that exist in RAM that do not exist in the version of the file that has been archived to the hard drive.

▶ **FIG. 9.44**

8. Choose Save from the File menu and notice that the icon will change to full color to indicate the changes in RAM have now been archived to the hard drive. This behavior is generally consistent throughout programs that are written for OS X.

HARDWARE DRIVERS

Hardware drivers are commonly used to extend the functionality of a computer. Essentially, a driver is a small piece of software that allows a computer to interact with hardware that is attached to it. Drivers extend the capabilities of a computer to interact with hardware that it is not familiar with. Every device connected to a computer requires a driver to operation. For example, hardware drivers exist for Wi-Fi cards, Ethernet cards, and graphics cards. Audio recording interfaces typically rely on hardware drivers to allow proprietary hardware to communicate with the computer. On Macintosh computers drivers are referred to as kernel extensions (.kext files). The kernel is the core of the operating system. In order for hardware devices to interact with the operating system, kernel extensions are necessary to act as the intermediary between the device and the operating system.

Hardware drivers ideally function in the background with no user interaction required to manage the driver. The process should be seamless. Unfortunately, this is not always the case. Since drivers interact with the core of the operating system, the kernel, they can cause a great deal of instability if they do not function properly. System crashes known as kernel panics are commonly caused by hardware drivers that are not compatible with the operating system. Hardware driver incompatibilities can occur for several reasons, including system software updates that render the driver out of date. It is necessary to periodically update hardware drivers to ensure the stability of the operating system, applications, and hardware devices.

It can be difficult to determine the version of the hardware driver used on a computer. This information can be extremely valuable when checking for updated drives on the hardware manufacturer's website. Navigate to Applications > Utilities and open System Profiler.

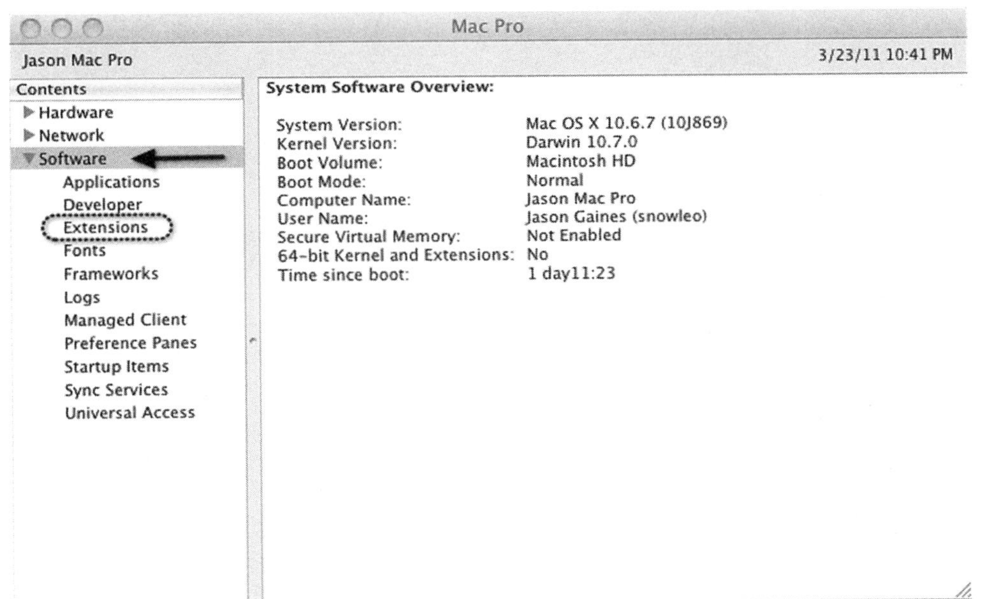

▶ **FIG. 9.45**

Click on Software in the left pane of System Profiler and navigate to Extensions. System Profiler will populate the right pane with a complete list of kernel extensions installed on the computer.

System Profiler provides some very useful information about the currently selected kernel extension—version and date modified. This information can be used to determine if the kernel extension installed is current when compared to the driver version available from the manufacturer.

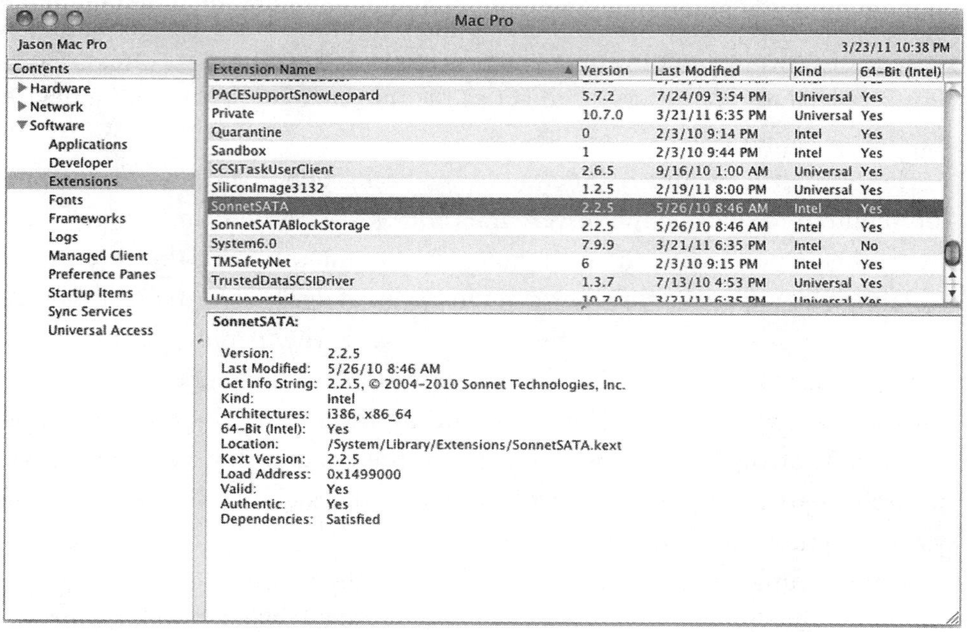

▶ **FIG. 9.46**

PART II

DISCUSSION OF PROFESSIONAL PRACTICE

CHAPTER 10
TERENCE BLANCHARD

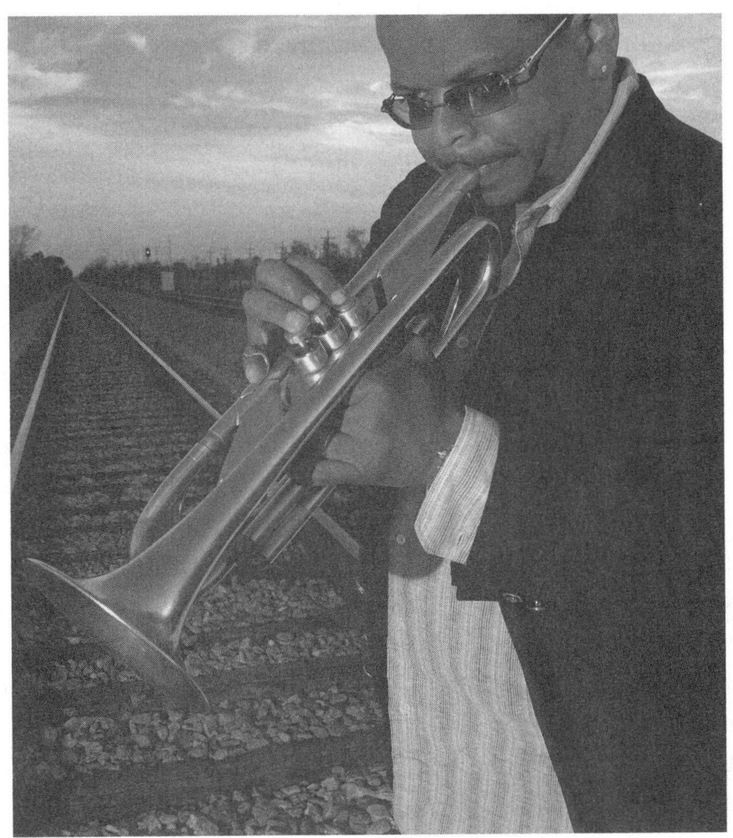

▶ FIG. 10.1

THE CRUCIBLE OF CATASTROPHE impels creative expression. Since the turn of the century, this has taken shape in manifold ways, from artistic responses to the 9/11 terrorist attacks to the war in Iraq to the pummeling of New Orleans in the wake of Hurricane Katrina in 2005. It is this latter calamity that informs Crescent City native son Terence Blanchard's impassioned song cycle, *A Tale of God's Will (A Requiem for Katrina)*, a 13-track emotional tour de force of anger, rage, compassion, melancholy, and beauty. *A Tale of God's Will*, which features Blanchard's quintet—pianist Aaron Parks, saxophonist Brice Winston, bassist Derrick Hodge, drummer Kendrick

Scott—as well as a 40-member string orchestra, is his third album for Blue Note Records. (Since signing with the label in 2003, Blanchard has released two other critically acclaimed albums, *Bounce* and *Flow*, the latter of which was nominated for two Grammys in 2006.)

"This is what we are called to do as artists," says the trumpeter, bandleader, arranger, and film score composer. "We document our social surroundings and give our impressions of events. The problem with Katrina is that the devastation is so vast that there's only been a trickle of art so far. We're all still digesting what went on and what continues to happen. It's like an unending story. For me, like so many others, it's taken me a moment to get my mind around all of this. I knew I needed to express this musically to keep the story alive, but so many important things—the safety of family members, figuring out how to rebuild my mother's house—never allowed me the time to breathe for a minute."

An important jump-start for *A Tale of God's Will* was director Spike Lee's decision to document the aftermath of Katrina on film, in what turned out to be the four-hour HBO documentary *When the Levees Broke*, which aired in 2006. Lee, who has enlisted Blanchard on numerous occasions to score his films, such as *Mo' Better Blues*, *Malcolm X*, *25th Hour*, and *Inside Man*, tapped him once again for his documentary. "That started me to make some musical statements for this moment in time," Blanchard says. "It's part of the grieving process. Once I wrote some of the music for Spike's film, I knew I could take it and expand upon it. Meanwhile, guys in my band were writing music that reflected on what happened in the aftermath of Katrina. This provided me with the perfect opportunity to bring the band all together." Four of the *Levees* tracks—"Levees," "Wading Through," "The Water," and "Funeral Dirge"—formed a nucleus of material for *A Tale of God's Will*. "Melodically and structurally, the tunes are the same, but the arrangements are different," says Blanchard, who cites as an example the dramatic piece "Levees" with its lyrical trumpeted woe. In that case, there's a long orchestral opening and interlude. "Spike had limited resources in filming the documentary, which means there was no money for orchestration," says Blanchard. He adds, "The whole idea for this piece was to show the calm before the storm that you can hear in the string arrangement, and the interlude is when the storm comes and the levees break. The second section is when people are on their roofs waiting for help, so the trumpet cries."

Recording this album challenged Blanchard, who says that he had to "contain myself, but I was so frustrated and in rage. I wanted the trumpet to scream on every track, but I feel that God is using me to speak for all the souls in New Orleans. We're all still tired, but it's almost as if things have gone back to normal for people outside while our lives here don't matter." Another tune from *Levees*, "Water," features a full orchestral plunge with Blanchard's wailing trumpet emerging. Blanchard explains that with all the floodwaters still high, it looked as if the city was cast away in an ocean. "The water was omnipresent," says Blanchard who was out of the city when disaster struck yet was watching CNN nonstop. "I was in disbelief seeing how 80 percent of the city was under water and that my old neighborhood had 12 feet of water. I remember when I was a kid and Hurricane Betsy hit New Orleans and there were a few feet of water. That scared me then and actually made me fear water." The other Lee-related tracks are the slowly loping melodic gem, "Wading Through" (also used in Lee's film *Inside Man*) and the march-beat "Funeral Dirge," a tune Blanchard says "was one of the hardest pieces for me to write. To see your city on TV with dead bodies in neighborhoods you knew was deep. It was as if it were Baghdad. This was my attempt to pay homage to the people who lost their lives, to give people a proper burial. It was intense working on these pieces that sometimes I had to take a breath, go outside and play with the kids, and then come back at it."

Other Blanchard tunes on *A Tale of God's Will* include "Dear Mom," his personal tribute to his mother who lost her home (her emotional first return to see the remains was documented by Lee in *Levees*), and a series of "ghost" tunes interspersed throughout the album: the African beat–drenched "Ghost of Congo Square," the trumpet-bass dance "Ghost of Betsy" (about the aforementioned Hurricane Betsy), and the plaintive tune sketched by saxophone and drums, "Ghost of 1927" (another flood that ravaged New Orleans). The ghost pieces were unplanned at the onset of the recording sessions, which took place in Los Angeles and Seattle.

"They just came to me throughout the recording," Blanchard says. "The ghosts represent the warnings of the past. In the first one, we added in handclaps and percussion as well as the chant, 'This is the tale of God's will.' That's what this story is about: God's will be done. We can't understand why things happened, but we can trust that we can learn something from it." The band member contributions prove to be just as potent and reflective as Blanchard's music. Park's composition "Ashé,", which was translated from the Yoruban language, means "and so it shall be." He explains that the beautiful melody "acts as a benediction: an acceptance of—and release from—past troubles and an ushering in of something new, determined and optimistic." Blanchard notes, "The emotion and melody set the tone for the album in capturing the exhaustion a lot of people felt after the storm and flood."

Winston's melancholic "In Time of Need," is buoyed by Blanchard and Scott's wordless vocals. "This tune marks a shift in Brice's artistic career," Blanchard says. "He wanted it to feature my trumpet, so I said, sure, but slowly I took myself out of the piece so that it became his feature." Winston, who spent his entire adult life in New Orleans, says he was compelled to write the tune "to express, through music, my sadness and frustration for my own family's tumultuous existence as well as for the countless people affected as a result of human ineptitude."

Scott's epic piece, "Mantra," begins with a bass feature with tablas in the mix that opens into a pensive and then dramatic soundscape. Scott says, "Our obligation is to help those who survived rebuild their lives and to rebuild their communities safer than they were before. The word mantra is characterized as a statement that is repeated frequently. My greatest hope is that this recording and this song will serve as a mantra for healing and renewal, for reflection and progression, and as an offering to touch peoples' lives for the better." Hodge says that his ultimately hopeful tune, "Over There," is about the "constant search in life" for something better. He notes, "Our present circumstances can make it difficult for us at times to see better for ourselves. Sometimes that 'Over There' may be just a song that can help us through." Blanchard explains that the song was captured on tape when the band was sound checking microphones. After subsequent takes, all agreed that the first run through was the keeper. Blanchard adds that the entire project, like Hodge's song, is about gratitude. "Requiem tells the story," he says, "that needs to heard so that people will continue to talk about what happened after Katrina."

JG: Can you state your name, please?

TB: Terence Blanchard.

JG: When and where were you born?

TB: I was born in New Orleans, Louisiana, March 13, 1962.

JG: I can imagine growing up in New Orleans that it's pretty much near impossible to avoid playing an instrument. What brought you to the trumpet?

TB: For me, music was always in the house. My father sang opera and my mom's sister, Aunt Doris, plays piano and teaches voice. Also, my grandfather on my mom's side played guitar just for fun around the house. There was always music in the house. When I was a little kid, I would play my dad's little recital performances at the church. He sang with a group called the Osiola Five, which was a group made up of these vocalists from Central Congregational Church. There were some interesting members of that group. My aunt, the one I was just telling you about and her first husband, who's passed away now—Frederick Hamilton. Also, Andrew Young and his father, Dr. Young, were in the group. There was another guy named Gully Carter. It was an interesting group of all the guys. They used to sing in church every Sunday and would also perform around the city. They went caroling around the city every Christmas.

As you can see, I was always around music—mostly operatic and classical music as a youngster, but I was hearing jazz out in the street. I was always hearing music around the house. I started playing piano when I was about five years old because of our neighbor actually. I remember trying to sit down and play the piano at my grandmother's house, but I didn't know what I was doing. I was about five years old, and my mom's neighbor taught piano. I began taking lessons from her when I was really young.

The trumpet thing didn't come into play until I was in fourth grade. I heard this guy named Alvin Alcorn, who was a local musician. He came to the school and did a demonstration of jazz performance. After I heard him play, I just focused on the trumpet. I went home and told my dad I wanted to play the trumpet. That is how the trumpet playing started, but I still continued playing piano. I changed piano teachers from Martha Francis, who was my first piano teacher, to Louise Winchester. Studying with her was revolutionary. If I recall, I was in junior high school or possibly still in elementary school. This woman was teaching me theory and some very complex subjects as a child. We also studied ear training quite a bit, alongside the piano lessons. Her lesson scheduling was interesting. My piano lesson would be on a Saturday, and then she would have these little classes right around the same time, with like four or five of us. She would just sit in her house and give us these lessons when we were really young.

From her, I went to study with Roger Dickerson, who is still a big influence in my life—he's a great composer. Roger is the guy that I try to get all these kids [Thelonious Monk Institute Students] to study with. Roger is an amazing composer, and a brilliant mind.

JG: Is he here locally in New Orleans?

TB: Yes. He studied in Vienna as a kid, and he has written a number of pieces for orchestra. He is one of our most underrecognized composers in American music. He is pretty amazing. As a matter of fact, I'm working on a piece now for the Louisiana Philharmonic, and I'm going to take it over to Roger to see what he thinks.

While I was studying with Roger, I began taking lessons with George Jenson here in New Orleans over at Loyola University in my junior year. I'd been playing trumpet, but hadn't taken any [private] lessons. Things really started to change for me at that point. Anderson Lewis was the first one who showed me how to buzz and get a sound out of the trumpet in elementary school. It's funny, I see his wife walking in the park just about every day. He has passed on now. The thing that's the most interesting about that period in my life is that in the African American community here there was a large contingency of people who were really trying to make things better for kids in New Orleans. They worked to make sure that we had more opportunities I'm the direct manifestation of all of their efforts, along with some other folks from this area. This is probably one of the reasons why I still have a sense of community, giving back to the community, because of them. Those people weren't paid a lot of money and weren't heralded as some of the greatest teachers on the planet. They just did it because they loved it. Even now there are some people here in the city that are still very passionate about education. Simply, it's all about giving a hand up. That's really what it's about. When you start to really have a sense of community and that you belong to a community, then all the other things change in your life.

JG: I definitely agree with you and it is nice to hear you say that. It is obvious that you do have a sense of community through your work in schools and especially through your work at the Thelonious Monk Institute. I'm sure it takes up quite a bit of your time, but that dedication truly shows your character. How did school shape your musical voice versus New Orleans shaping your musical voice? Which one, if any, had more of an influence on you?

TB: I think they both had an equal amount of impact, but just in different areas. I think New Orleans had a huge impact on how I relate to music because here music is a celebratory thing. It is a very communal kind of experience. You don't just go to a performance, sit down, hear someone perform, and leave. We have that, too, but my early reflections of music are very much in community-oriented events, whether it be parades, outdoor events, social events.

That's one of the things that I've learned about any type of music from New Orleans. I think what education has given me is a means, number one, by which I can break things down and learn from them, analyze them, and continue to move forward. My education gives me the ability to look at what it is that I'm learning and take aspects of it, from it, that mean something to me and use those things the way that I see fit. The hardest part was learning there are many ways to look at and learn from something. This is becoming more and more true as I become older. That's why we have styles, that's why we have individuals, that's why we have all of these various approaches to not only playing music but composing music. There's no one way to skin a cat and that is why I believe education in this city has occupied very important roles in my life—separate things are finally starting to come together. Music has to mean something to you. The thing about it is you can't just be out here for the sake of being out here. You can't just create music solely for the sake of creating music. I'm a firm believer that something has to propel you. Whether you realize it or not—that's the funny part and you may not realize it. Music can be that therapeutic kind of thing that helps you put things in perspective. I think sometimes with young musicians, they don't make that connection. I think this is normal because we all grow and we're all human. When you're younger, it's all about the theory and learning your art. It's about those things. The older you become, you start to realize those things are just a tool any artist will use to express a more profound thought.

JG: When were you first introduced to composition?

TB: Through Roger [Dickerson]. When I was sixteen years old, Roger was the one who not only brought me into composition but really made me think about it in a very profound way.

JG: You studied at Rutgers University in New Jersey. What made you move to the New York area?

TB: We were at NOCCA [New Orleans Center for the Creative Arts], the arts high school here in New Orleans. Dr. Burrell, Ellis Marsalis, along with all of these other guys, Kid Jordan, Roger Dickerson, Alvin Baptiste, were preparing us for the move since they met us. We were always taught that New York was the place to be. We were always told that, that if you want to make it in this business you need to be in New York, you need to be where all of the musicians are. I needed to figure out how I was going to get there. For me, I knew couldn't just move to New York. I saw that

Wynton [Marsalis] was going to Juilliard in New York. In school, he had a place to stay—everything was cool. I started thinking about it and I might to go to Eastman, because Juilliard didn't have a jazz program at that time, and I wasn't really a classical major. I was going to go to Eastman or I was going to go to UCLA in California. I decided to go to Rutgers because while we were here at NOCCA, Larry Ridley started telling us about this program at Rutgers and who was teaching there. Ted Dumbar, who was a great guitarist, was teaching there. Michael Carven, the great drummer, Kenny Barron, Paul Jeffreys were teaching there at the time. Paul played with Thelonius Monk. Also, Bill Fielder was there. Bill was not widely known in the jazz world, but he's a great trumpet player, great classical trumpet player. I knew that getting a chance to study with him was going to be a big honor and a big opportunity. I immediately applied to Rutgers, and ended up going there. I was 45 minutes away from New York; it was a perfect thing for me because Eastman was six hours away.

JG: And really cold. They [Eastman] have the tunnels underground to get between the buildings. I heard that and I said, "I'll go to Manhattan School of Music instead!"

TB: There weren't those options back when I was going [to school]. It was Juilliard, Eastman, or Rutgers. That was it, man. Patterson wasn't even happening back then. At Rutgers, I studied with Bill Fielder and Kenny Barron. I actually took some piano lessons with Kenny Barron, which was amazing!

JG: I can imagine that must have been pretty amazing.

TB: I was in New Jersey, and while I was in New Brunswick, man, every chance I got I'd go to New York. I wound up playing with Lionel Hampton before school even started, because of Paul Jeffrey. He took me on one of the gigs and then Lionel hired me. I was working with him on the weekends and then going to school during the week. When I had my time off, if Lionel wasn't working, I tried to go to New York, hang out and hear some music. If Freddie Hubbard was playing I was there. Woody Shaw, any of those guys were playing, I would try to be there.

That's how I got up to the East Coast. I wound up joining Art Blakey's band after that. So my progression in this business was rather quick and rather orderly in a sense. I didn't have to really worry too much, because while I was in college, in my second year at Rutgers, I'll never forget it, I'd finally gotten into the orchestra. They didn't want to let me in to the orchestra because I was a jazz major. They finally let me audition and once I made it in I got the gig with Art Blakey the night before the first concert. I'll never forget it.

JG: Let's talk about the Blakey band. That band has an amazing lineage of musicians in its history. What was that like for you?

TB: Well, I didn't think I was going to get the gig. I didn't think I was really ready for that. Wynton [Marsalis] was on the gig and he called me and he said, "man, come on up and sit in, man." Donald Harrison and I both knew it was an audition. We went up and played and the next thing you know Blakey said, "Man, you guys are going to Chicago next week." I said, "We're doing what, man?" The next week we were in the band and we played in Chicago. Shortly after, we went to Europe for ten weeks. It started rather quickly and I was only nineteen. It was right before my twentieth birthday. I turned twenty on March 13, and joined the band in February right before my birthday. We made a record in Europe, and on the record it says, "the 19-year-old drummer!"

JG: How did that shape you compositionally? I can imagine how that would shape you as a trumpet player. You're sitting in the chair that the greats before you sat in. Did you write for the band a lot?

TB: Well, I'd already been writing and that was the thing—Wynton had told Art that I could write or I had talent for writing because the first thing Art said to me was, "Wynton tells me you got a box full of compositions, you need to pull them all out." The good thing about it for me was, and I'm just realizing this now, before I joined the band I didn't try to write Jazz Messenger music. I already had compositions that I was trying to orchestrate and arrange for the band. It was good because I kept my musical identity, if I had any at that time! The thing that was really cool about Art was he used to talk to us about finding our sound for the group. It was interesting because we'd always wanted to play some of the great arrangements that we listened to on records—Caravan and others. There were a lot of tunes that we wanted to play with the Messengers that we had learned from recordings. Art's whole thing was "No, you guys need to find your own sound." He'd allow us to play some of those things like "This is for Albert," that's what it was.

He always encouraged us to find our sound. The funny part about it was that his personality was so strong that it just kind of shaped everything we did anyway. His personality musically was so strong that it was hard for us to hear outside of the [Jazz] Messenger, three-horn kind of sound. Even with that, we all kind of found our way through that because if you go back and you listen to a lot of those compositions, Donald's compositions, Jean Toussaint, Michael Miller, myself, they all had their own style and vibe to them. Art was great because he allowed us to do that. He could have just rested on the history of his accomplishments that he had made up until that point. He said, "No, you guys need to find your own thing for the school."

JG: Blakey was known for playing with young, up-and-coming musicians. I look at the bands that you have worked with recently and you seem to follow a similar path. You have musicians such as guitarist Lionel Loueke and pianist, Aaron Parks. Both are incredible, young musicians. I remember going to school at the Manhattan School of Music when he was 14 and we were all in our twenties! He's obviously very talented. It didn't surprise me to see him in your band a couple years later. It seems you approach your band roster in much the same way as Art [Blakey]. What are your thoughts on this?

TB: Oh, yeah. Definitely. Art used to say, who knows how much of it's true or not, but he believed that hiring young musicians pushed him and made him play differently. He could always go out and get some older guys to play, but those are the guys he'd already played with. Who knows? We were cheaper, too! That probably played a role in it. I notice that with the guys I hire to play in my bands always bring something to the table that I don't think about. It is always a little uncomfortable at first because you're so used to playing with certain guys. I got accustomed to playing with Aaron, and then all of the sudden here comes Fabian. Fabian is totally different. It keeps me in a forward movement in terms of my thinking.

They bring freshness and new ideas to the music. For me as a bandleader it is important not to ever step on it, to never say whatever you're doing is wrong—unless it is extreme. I don't want to give the impression that people have free will; it's not that. But as long as they're making music and they're bringing something to the table, I'm not going to squash anybody's ideas. And listen, man, I went on tour with Herbie Hancock a couple of years ago, and he's just turning seventy this year! I was expecting him to talk to me about what it is I should do, etc. He didn't do any of that. He said, "What you got?" I realized then—that's what I do to guys in my band.

JG: I think that's why your records have a fresh sound.

TB: I feel very fortunate because I've had some young talented guys in the group. Kendrick. Leno. The bass players, Brandon Owens.

JG: How did you make this transition into writing for film? I've read interviews where you said everyone you know in the business fell into it backwards.

TB: Most of the people that I know as friends in the business wanted to be musicians. When I say musicians, I really mean performing musicians. But the thing is, being a composer involves a desire to expand and express yourself through your expansion. So all of us have had this thing that I can't really describe. It's like playing is not enough. It's kind of like being a chemist in a weird way, in a musical sense. When the opportunity came for me to write something for Spike [Lee], I jumped at it. I looked at it at the time as a one-time experience, because I thought he just needed me to write some music for one scene.

JG: How did that happen? Did he just call you up and say, "Terence, I want you to write for me?"

TB: No, no. We were doing *Mo' Better Blues* and we had to do all the prerecording for the movie. He heard me playing a tune at the piano that I was working on for a solo album, and he asked me, "Man, can I use that?" I said, "Sure." We recorded it just with the trumpet at the time because it was supposed to be for a scene with Denzel [Washington] playing on the bridge in the movie. Luckily, he set up this recording before the scoring began because his father was writing the music. Spike's father wanted to add strings to it. So I guess his father said, "Why don't you get him to do it?" His father could have done it. Spike asked me to write the strings for it. I wrote the string section and his father said to me, "You wrote it, you conduct it." I had to get up there and conduct, too, which was great!

JG: That must have been an intense experience.

TB: Yeah, I was scared to death, but it was cool. I was nervous. When we finished doing it, Spike came over to me and said, "Great work. You have a future in this business." He called me to do *Jungle Fever*. It's funny; you can see the pattern in my life. I just jump into things. I don't get a chance to . . .

JG: Think about it?

TB: Yeah. Whether it's playing with Lionel Hampton, whether it's playing Blakey, whether it's the film thing, I just kind of seem to be thrown right into the situation, which is probably the best for me because if I thought about it too much, I'd probably not do it.

JG: What kind of artistic license did he give you musically?

TB: Oh, Spike gives me more room than anybody.

JG: Do you think that helped you? I can imagine you were definitely a strong composer at that point, but that's certainly a different approach to writing for film.

TB: There was a bit of that, too, but that's when I started to write using technology. That helped me a great deal. For me, I feel like you figure it out as you go. That was the reason why I got a computer to begin with. I got a computer and I got Master Tracks Pro. There were two programs, Master Tracks Pro and there was another program called Q that a lot of people used to use. When I figured out that Q could help me find timings and could actually print out measures, I knew I could use this program a great deal. I would map out all of my scenes and then I'd print out a grand staff or something to write a general idea.

JG: There's so much new gear these days.

TB: That's funny, because I think about 16 channels. Now, man, if you have 64 channels of orchestral samples, that's not enough.

JG: What's your favorite digital audio work station now? What do you use?

TB: Now I use Digital Performer. I've been using that for a number of years. I tried Logic Pro but after working with DP for so long, it's a different animal. I got Logic 8, but I didn't get the new one [Logic Pro 9]. Every now and then I open it up and I say, "You know what, no, let me just go back to what it is that I know." I have three computers that I use. I have two Intel Macs with Komplete on it with Ivory and some other plugins. The other one just has some of my East West orchestral sounds on it. I have a laptop that has Giga Sample on it. So I have all of those things, and I only have three hardware boxes. That's funny, I actually have four, but I don't use it. I have a Roland 5080 and a Roland Visa. I have a slew of plugins. In my Intel machines, I have all of the Spectrasonic stuff. Then I also have Native Komplete in there. Also, I have Alchemy, which is kind of going to replace what I use my 5080 for. Oh, boy, what else? I can't remember. The thing that I'm trying to say is that all of my computer stuff is starting to dwindle because I'm not using the Giga Library and the third Mac Pro so much. It's just the two; the Intel is mostly what I'm using. My focus has really been on sound design.

JG: You might like Logic then for Sculpture.

TB: Well, people say that, but I use Peak a lot for editing sounds. I try to upgrade my audio equipment so on my Intel with all Apogee stuff—the Symphony 64. I have two cards. I used to have a whole bunch of stuff, man, but it's all dwindling down. And now the focus has really been on the audio quality. I have some decent microphones, a few decent mics, 414s and a couple of Neumann mics, also, the Taylor 49, but I really want to get some really great microphones. That's my next goal.

JG: They're like lenses on a camera. That's what it's about.

TB: Well, the engineer that I work with, Frank Roth, tried some stuff in my studio. He brought his C12s. I had a percussionist coming here from Miracle and we recorded some stuff up in my room, and it's just some funny stuff when you've recorded in your room for a while and a guy brings great microphones and your room sounds different!

JG: I find the more gear I buy the more I want to get rid of it now. I used to carry a rolling bag with all the other gear in it. When it comes to your musical approach with technology, what role does it play in your workflow? Are you just using MIDI mockups or are you actually going to the studio, or both?

TB: The MIDI mockup thing is over with for me. We still do that, but that's not the sole intent for having all this gear. For me it's actually to do production work. I'm actually thinking about getting a machine, because what I've been doing now is I've been stockpiling sound design and grooves for a lot of various situations.

JG: You're building a library?

TB: Yes and the thing is I've been going through this thing up in my studio of creating some loops and creating some sounds. They're in files, and what I've been looking at about Machine, what attracts me to it, is to have something that you can call up quickly and just kind of monitor and go through all of those things. What I've done is a little arduous. When I created some of these loops, I've made rex files and put them in the style sheet, which is OK, but there's something about being able to mix and match all of the stuff inside them. I haven't really touched Machine, but from what I see, being able to mix and match all this stuff rather easily is one of the things that attracts me to it. See, my viewpoint is that the technology has always been marketed through the eyes of people in the pop world, because you want to sell it! You want to sell a product and I understand that, but I see other ways of using it. I remember Roland used to have this box out called a VP-9000. A friend of mine, T. J. Hudson, told me about it when he used to work at Roland. I remember when I got it, I was excited because it was the first thing that could create loops, chop the loops, and you could have them right there. I had a stockpile of loops. Later I started using it for creating pads. The thing I hate about certain pads is that they evolve over a certain period of time, but then you play them in another register they evolve quicker or slower depending on the register. I started getting into sound design with a VP-9000, and it was funny. I was talking to T. J. on the phone about it and he said, "You're the only dude [there first]." Apparently, everybody was using it for loops and using it in other ways. That was one of the times where I started to think about sound design with the VP-9000. You could see where it's limitless. It's all about what your creative output is all about. Herbie [Hancock] will sit down and deal with some stuff, and Herbie's ridiculous!

JG: I feel that technology is an instrument. People argue technology is making the musician less relevant. I don't agree. How do you feel about this?

TB: That is an issue, but I do think that it is a large issue. You see, that's one of the things where for me where guys like Harry Gregson Williams and Thomas Newman have inspired me. I really love their work. One of the reasons I love their work is because they seem to understand the strengths of everything. And they use them for those strengths. They never try, at least in my mind from what I hear from what they do, to get one thing to replace the other. I think that's where the problem comes in when young musicians get involved in the technology. They say, "Oh, this is great that it can do this, this is great that it can… blah, blah." It's like a film person who doesn't know what film editing is about. They get into Final Cut Pro and they just say, "Oh, I can move this around and move that around." They don't understand that there are certain things you just don't move around because of the technical aspects. The technical aspects force you to make other creative decisions. In the music world, I think it's important for everybody to study composition, because one of the things I see with some of the students at the Monk Institute have not. They are really talented and creative, but not too many people have talked to them about composition. When we [faculty members] expect them to evaluate certain things musically, you can see the light bulb go off. For me, it's about finding the balance between all of it. One thing is not going to take the place or be the end-all.

JG: I suppose it is like cooking in a way. At least I see it that way. There are many spices to cook with, but one is no more important that the other.

TB: Even before the proliferation of plugins, while I had a lot of gear, I never had a slew of gear because it didn't make sense to me to have a mass amount of gear. One of the things that I said about ten years ago now was that I don't want to be the guy to have a bunch of stuff and not know how to use it. For me it's about having a few good pieces that I take my time and learn how to manipulate. I just got the H-8000 and I haven't really gotten into that thing heavy yet, but I know it's amazing with some of the things that it can do. Just going through the presets has been amazing. I want to be the dude to say, okay, that's great but I need to tailor it for me. That's one of the reasons why I like Alchemy. You can create your own library and not rely on the sources.

JG: You're a composer, you're a film composer, you're a performer, you're all these musical things and you're a technologist, too. How do you take that to the Monk Institute in your educational pursuits? Is technology part of the Monk Institute?

TB: Technology is not a big part because the thing that I'm trying to focus on for them over there is the fundamentals of compositional approach. For me it's about performance and composition with them. On the other hand, with that in mind, I have one class where the guys started bringing a bunch of technology into the scenario on their own. I thought it was brilliant because I didn't say anything about it and it wasn't something that I was against. For me, I think once we get people thinking about all of the possibilities that are in front of you and how to manipulate them that is a great step. The big thing about what we try to do at the Monk Institute is not force anyone to something in a particular way. One of the things that we do try to show them is how their compositions and their solos don't have to be branded. They can be in an orderly kind of approach to creating composition. There can be an orderly and very systematic approach to taking an idea and making a composition out of it or taking any idea and creating a solo based on it. We work with them so their solos aren't just a bunch of random musical ideas that don't really make any sense. So that's basically what we try to do, and there are certain techniques and things that we do to get these guys thinking that way. Once we get you going down that road, for me, your sound sources are up to you. I'm not going to sit here and say that technology is going to replace musicians. You see with these kids, they already have a passion for playing an instrument. They already have that. I don't have to give that to them. They come to the scenario wanting to play an instrument. I'm not trying to say, hey, man, you should think about playing saxophone. I'm not doing that. These guys already have that. And what we do is to try to show them the plethora options that are before them.

JG: That is interesting. In my opinion, one of the problems with technology in education is that many people think the use of technology is all or nothing. To me, it's just another tool.

TB: That's stuff that we've been doing with the band, but that's the second thing. One of the things that we do over here, it's not a heavy technology-laden kind of environment. But, we do have a number of workstations and a computer room where these kids can go in and use Finale or Sibelius, which is on all the systems. They can sit in there and when they're writing their compositions, they can listen back, they can work on their stuff. We also have a Pro Tools rig in the band room. We can record rehearsals; we can do a lot of things. Technology still exists in that realm. One of the things that I think has always been a missed opportunity for some people is to use it as a practice vehicle. But, I think a lot of these kids are up on that and I think they do some of that on their own. I don't know about this class [of Thelonious Monk Institute students], but some of the other classes we've had the kids do that. They created scenarios on their laptops to help them learn tunes, to help them be able to practice certain new compositions from the guys that have been on their own, at their own pace.

Technology has been great in that regard. I think for us, being that we call ourselves a jazz institution, it's more geared toward performance. The thing for me is that, and I learned it from Art Blakey, is that composition was the means by which you find yourself. And he always used to tell us that. So for me while we're geared towards performance, my thing is to show them or have them find themselves through their compositions. We've got one student over there now, man, it's kind of funny. It's interesting because he's going through this thing where I'm trying to make him make the connection. He plays a certain way and he has these interesting things that he plays, but then when he writes he says, oh, I'm a composer but things have to be—

JG: A certain way.

TB: He doesn't write anything like the way he plays. And it's really interesting to see that disconnect, and I'm trying to get him. He's starting to see it now. People think they have to a performer or a player. I say no to that. Roger opened my eyes to that. When I got excited about being a film composer I remember him telling me, "That's great that you're getting that experience doing that, but you have other things you need to work on and accomplish." Going with that he said, "You know jazz is a very viable and great art form that needs to be documented for orchestra in a certain way. The problem has been most people who write for orchestra don't understand how to write phrasing." Finally, he said, "Your experience as a composer that you're gaining in the film world could make you be one of the persons to kind of bring everything together." He changed my thinking—I'm not writing for orchestra, I'm taking my ideas, these ideas, and who I am as a person and taking that and sculpting it for this ensemble that has a multitude of different colors that I can choose from. It turned my whole way of thinking around.

JG: How do you approach composition then? Do you write at the DAW? Do you write to paper?

TB: All of the above, because it all comes from different things. The stuff I was telling you I was doing, the loop-based stuff, that's all technology. I'm sitting up there creating sounds among whatever, but then there's moments where I sit down at the piano and I just start writing and I have to have paper in front of me because it's not a computer. I have to have paper in front of me so that when I get an idea, I can just start scribbling ideas really quickly and put things down on paper. But the thing is, it's really about the manipulation of ideas—that's what it is. That's the thing that I try to tell students—you're never going to run out of ideas. Ideas are not the problem. You're going to hear certain things and know how to manipulate them. One of the big issues we always have with our kids is that as soon as they write something, I'll say, "Oh man, that's a great idea! How did you come up with this part of the tune?" They inevitably say some version of, "Oh, man, I just got to it and I couldn't figure it out so I just hear something." I usually respond, "OK, well, that's good, but that doesn't relate to this. There's no relation between the two. So your composition doesn't have any type of cohesion."

I'm going to tell you what it is with jazz musicians. Jazz musicians are so used to learning how to improvise and learning how to play long extended lines. We hear these stories about so-and-so could play for twenty minutes without repeating themselves and because of this we don't want to think of a reoccurring idea. In a jazz musician's mind a reoccurring idea is kind of sacrilege in way. All these things need to evolve, but you need to have some cohesion. Wayne Shorter's tunes have cohesion. I often use his tunes as an educational tool because when you look at how he takes you through the harmony, the shape of the melody is the idea, not the actual intervals. It's the shape. You see the relationships of how those intervals change based on how you use the harmony around them. Sometimes he plays one of them in reverse to make it ascending instead of descending, but it's all coming from that first idea which gives the tunes cohesion. Once you start to get these guys to see that, a light bulb goes off. I see it in all of them, all of them, all of the students. I don't tell them what to write, I just want to see that go down. Some of these kids come up with some amazing stuff and I mean that literally. They come up with some amazing stuff, and it's proof to me that it's all about showing people how to manipulate an idea. I'm not giving them the ideas; I never give them the ideas. The only idea I may give them is we may write a tune based off of some innovative stuff we create in a class. I'll go around, give me a number from 1 to 8, give me a number from 1 to 8, and that becomes the degree of the scale that put up, and then everybody has to write a composition based off of that. But other than that, I'm not giving them ideas.

JG: When you talk about a composition, what do you like to share with musicians and composers?

TB: Well, that's where the fundamentals come into play. I think when you have this idea of a discussion between technology and not technology; I think that's probably at the core of it—fundamentals. That's the thing that I talk to my students about; the idea that fundamentals are going to carry you in a lot of different directions because science is science. Let's just break it down. Frankly, the fundamentals may not have much to do with music. A perfect fifth always resonates a certain way. You're not going to change that. You don't have to. A minor third resonates a certain way, major third resonates a certain way and so on. When you learn those fundamentals, and then you get a job, when somebody says, "Oh, man, it needs to be a little more this, [snaps fingers], that registers a certain thing in my mind." Then you go from there, and you start to build a working relationship and build a dialogue. But, if you don't have the fundamentals under your fingers, you won't be comfortable creating something that both of you want.

JG: How has your identity shifted as a film composer when compared to your work as a jazz composer and performer?

TB: It doesn't shift. See, that's the thing. It doesn't shift; it just grows. It's funny that you say that because that's also one of the things that make people kind of hesitant about doing certain things in life. As soon as a certain thing is questioned, you say, "Wait a minute, man. That's me and my identity." You have to learn that it's not all of you; it's just a part of you. One of the things that I've noticed as I grow older was that I would get very defensive when I was younger. If someone questioned me I'd feel like saying, "How dare you? I spent time on this blah, blah, blah." If they're not relating to it, they're not relating to it. It's nobody's fault because some people have legitimate reasons for that, others obviously not. What happens is that when you start to accept that the idea may not be working, you have to find something else. It makes you expand and it makes you grow, but it doesn't change you musically. It doesn't change your identity because there are certain things that make you who you are as a musician. I remember I was in situations where I did some things and I thought, "Man, I can't believe they didn't want this!" They just couldn't agree with me. After the changes were made, I then listen back to it and realize it still sounds like me. It doesn't sound like anybody else. It's still my musical identity throughout it. I don't look at those situations as situations that diminish who I am. They may change me, but in a good way. It's never going to change the fundamental core of who I am as an artist. I think that'll always be there.

JG: I've spoken to many colleagues who say that their early career labeled them in a certain way that followed them into their later career. You obviously did a lot of work with Spike Lee and continue to do so. Does that relationship label you? Do you feel as an artist that you've been labeled in that sense?

TB: Two things—working with Spike and being a jazz musician have labeled me. I still get questions when I'm up for movies like, "Can you write for orchestra?" Which is kind of insulting. At a certain point you think, "Wow, should I work with you?" If you really don't know that much about music in general, let alone who I am as an artist, should I work with you? Then there's the Spike Lee thing, man. I've heard opinions that are positive and negative. Positive things like, "I love what you guys do! I want to have that kind of sound for my movie." My first reaction to those statements is that your movie may not require that type of sound. It may require something else. On the negative side of things, one person said to me once, "Oh man, I love your music, I just don't like Spike's movies." Then I don't get hired. So it runs the gamut, but that's part of the thing you have to bear. Look at Elmer Bernstein, man. His career pays homage to that very notion. At one point he was the only dude who could write westerns. Then at another point in his career, he was the dude who only could write romantic comedies. And you say, "Goddamn!" Just look at the breadth of all of his stuff!

JG: I look at you and your career, and even as a kid growing up listening to your records, I knew that you were and are an amazing trumpet player. Then you look at your career and say, all right, now he's also this film composer. I've always kind of wondered if that relationship has been an issue for you.

TB: Oh, yeah, it's an issue. It's been an issue when I was up for a few films. It always amazed me when people would make a comment like, "Oh yeah, man, I would love to have him write the score but we just don't want trumpet." I think to myself I'm not a dude that writes trumpet in all of my stuff! Truth be told, man, there's been a few films where when I get into compose mode and frankly I don't touch my horn as much as I should because I'm trying to make that deadline. I've got to write an hour's worth of music—It's got to be done in a certain amount of time. I get up every day and I get into a routine, just working, working, working. Playing the music for directors. It's happened a few times, where you get to that and it's close to the session time, and then all of a sudden the director says, "You're going to play on this, right?" Then I start loosening up, practicing more and more and playing exercises. It goes both ways.

JG: That's interesting that you bring it up. As you grow older, these become naturally more fragmented. How do you balance this?

TB: It's managing your time, bro. Managing your time. It's all about managing your time. If there's one thing that this multi-career pronged attack that I have to my life has taught me, it's that it's about managing your time—even the time resting you have. Truth be told, we make time for things we really want to do. I should say the things that we get excited about doing. There are some things that we do that we deem as being necessary, not necessarily exciting. That's part of life, but you have to manage that as well. You've got to manage. It's a weird thing to say, but you've got to manage your expectations. I hate using that phrase, but you have to understand that, okay, I need to do this because I'm not going to have time to do this later, so I should do this now. I know I don't feel like doing it, but doing this now I'm going to feel comfortable later on for having done it. So you play this mind game about everything. I know I'm playing a gig this weekend, putting time in on my horn, practicing a certain amount of time every day—it's a must. While I'm sitting there doing this thing I told you about earlier. It's all about learning how to manage your time, because if you don't, you'll become overwhelmed and you'll start to say, "Oh, man, I don't have enough time." That's not true. It's simply not true. You may not have enough time to do all the things you want to do, but you'll have time for the important things. That's how I guide my life.

CHAPTER 11
MARC SHAIMAN

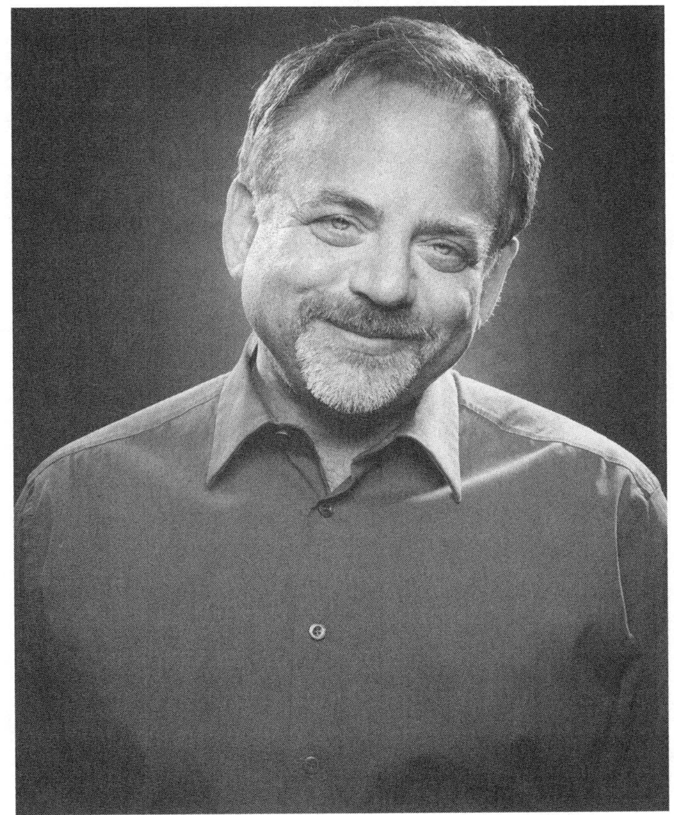

▶ **FIG. 11.1**

MARC SHAIMAN ENJOYED COMPOSING the music and co-writing the lyrics for *Hairspray* with Scott Wittman. For their score, the pair won the Tony, Grammy, and Olivier awards. Their next Broadway score was for *Martin Short—Fame Becomes Me*, for which they won absolutely nothing.

As a composer and arranger, Marc's film credits date back to the silents and include *When Harry Met Sally, Beaches, Misery, City Slickers, The Addams Family, A Few Good Men, Sister Act, Sleepless in Seattle, The First Wives Club, Patch Adams, The American President, George of the Jungle, South Park: Bigger,*

Longer & Uncut, and The Bucket List. He has been nominated five times for an Oscar and lost every time.

Marc is currently Emmy-nominated (for musical directing and co-writing this year's Oscar telecast), was Emmy-nominated for writing on *Saturday Night Live* (the Sweeney Sisters), and won an Emmy Award co-writing Billy Crystal's medleys for The Academy Awards. His arrangements for *Harry Connick, Jr.* resulted in two Grammy nominations, as did the *Hairspray* soundtrack.

Marc has worked with many artists, including Will Ferrell, Jack Black, Eric Clapton, Kristen Chenoweth, Jennifer Holliday, Jenifer Lewis, Patti LuPone, John Mayer, Barbra Streisand, Rob Thomas, and Raquel Welch, although not all at the same time.

As her music director and co-producer, Marc brought his longtime partner Bette Midler the Grammy-winning songs "The Wind beneath My Wings" and "From a Distance," but it is their collaboration on her Emmy Award–winning performance for Johnny Carson's penultimate *Tonight Show* that will always remain a dream. He auditioned but was not chosen to play himself on her sitcom.

Marc and Scott co-wrote the original Broadway musical based on *Charlie and the Chocolate Factory* (directed by Sam Mendes) as well as collaborated with Steven Spielberg on a scripted series for Showtime about the goings-on behind the scenes of the creation of a Broadway musical.

JG: Can you please state your name.

MS: Marc Shaiman.

JG: When and where were you born?

MS: New Jersey. Born in north New Jersey, grew up in Scotch Plains, New Jersey.

JG: When were you born?

MS: October 22, 1959.

JG: What kind of role did music play in your upbringing? Was it something that ran deep in your house, or were you the only musician?

MS: It wasn't in my house at all, and I was really the only musician. My mother had taken piano lessons and could only play one piece. [He plays piano.] She had all her kids take piano lessons, like suburban parents do. My sisters wanted to quit, so she asked the piano teacher if I was too young to start, just so she wouldn't have to look for another piano teacher in two years. I guess I was in first grade, which is maybe earlier than most. Anyway, the teacher took me on. I have no memory of playing the piano before that. But once I started, it was kind of creepy.

JG: Were any of your friends doing music, or was it just you?

MS: No, it really wasn't until I was a teenager. There was a family who lived across the street and I was friends with one son, but became closer to his brother who played the guitar and wrote songs. He was kind of my only friend for a while. We had a shared interest in music. I have no recollection of any music programs or anything musical ever available in my elementary school.

JG: Was that in Newark?

MS: No, that was in Scotch Plains, New Jersey. I even remember once taking something called the melodica, it has a keyboard, but you blow into it. I played it in school, I guess it was my way of showing off since there was not a musical outlet for me to participate in. In the summer before junior high school, a friend, I wonder how she knew, brought me to audition for these two women who had a summer music theater program for kids of any age. I went with her, and I said, can I audition to play piano? They said, "well, sure, play something." I played, and when I finished, everyone was very quiet and staring at me, which I guess I liked a lot. I've told this story now enough that I wonder have I made it up? But I do actually think I remember it, and from that moment on, that was the beginning of the whole life for me. School work fell by the wayside because all I did was study Broadway musicals. I guess I sort of knew of them the way anyone hears about stuff, but I wasn't obsessed until that moment. My musical experience wasn't just with kids. The woman who ran that theater workshop also directed community theaters around the whole area. She started taking me to adult community theaters. The adults would look at her like, "Are you insane? Who is this pimply little thirteen-year-old, or twelve?..." I don't remember how old I was, thirteen, fourteen. And she'd say, "Marc, play!" I'd play and they'd say, okay, fine, because I was like a freak. Like a child prodigy with show business and theatrical playing and accompanying. I just got it.

JG: I've known your work from all the films that you've done and the television work that you've done. I've always kind of wondered how you made that jump from being a musical director and being in the New York City scene for theater and then making that jump over to film. Is that where you would credit your early years of learning music?

MS: Yeah. It all took kind of a natural jump from piano player/accompanist, to working as a musical director. Community theater was my music school, because we used the full scores, not just the vocal selections you buy in the music store. I had access to scores with trombone parts and the string parts, just within the small notes on the music but you can now listen to your cast album and go, "oh yeah, look," those are clarinets making that sound, or those are trombones. And getting the much more textured chords than just what's in the simplified music. Everything I learned, I learned from doing those years of community theater and studying those scores.

I moved to New York and was doing the same kind of stuff. It was through theatrical people in New Jersey that I started wanting to move to New York. It's a long story how it all happened, but I was playing piano for people and then became their musical director. One of the acts I directed were the Harlettes, they were Bette Midler's backup singers. They were in her act called the Harlettes, and they wanted to do their own act when not on tour with Bette. I became their musical director through a very long story of being in the right place at the right time, but I was a Bette Midler fanatic. While still living in New Jersey, I met Scott and a bunch of other friends and started staying with them in New York City on the weekends. One of the Harlettes lived across the hall from him.

I was thinking about it, and it's like I often find myself... what have I learned? I learned that it's luck because I can't ever tell anyone what I did to achieve this life. I happened to meet some people one day and they happened to live across the hall from my idol's backup singer, who happened to be looking for a cheap musical director. I knew the harmonies they wanted from studying Bette Midler's records and from studying the records that the Bette Midler records led me to, such as The Andrews Sisters and other girl groups from the 60s, or Busby Berkeley musical stuff.—your basic gay musical mind. I became the Harlettes' musical director, and then they took me with them when they went back with Bette, and I was suddenly working with Bette Midler as an accompanist.

JG: How old were you when that happened?

MS: It was all dizzying. It all happened within a year of moving to New York.

JG: You're young.

MS: I was crazy young. I was always for a long time the youngest person in the room.

JG: You're young now.

MS: Compared to what?

JG: Well, you're roughly fifty years old, right?

MS: I just turned fifty-one. I wouldn't call it young.

JG: It's relative, right?

MS: Yes. From that time that Judy called, the lady who would take me to the community theaters to.... Up until around thirty I guess, I was always a little freakishly young compared to the other people I was working with. Then suddenly it leveled off. But then suddenly working with Bette was a big schooling of arranging and being around her band rehearsals and doing other musical directing gigs in New York—cabaret gigs. That led to meeting people who worked at *Saturday Night Live* and then getting called to write funny stuff or arrange stuff, just freelance. Then I finally got hired for a full year. During one of my freelance years at SNL I became friends with Billy Crystal, Martin Short, and Christopher Guest. The point to all that was that through Bette Midler and Billy Crystal, working with them on their acts, I was just working with them a lot when their movie careers took off. Bette asked me to help choose the songs for *Beaches*. There's also a long story there leading to that about how I got my first movie scoring job by helping her out on another movie called *Big Business*. No one had helped her. She had a scene where she was supposed to yodel in front of a steel drum band in New York. No one had prepared anything except they hired an actual steel drum band and they gave her a cassette of things they play. She called and she said, "Help! I need to yodel over this. Can you figure out what I need to do?" I sort of saved the day that day on the film.

JG: Were you in LA at the time?

MS: No. It was here in New York, and it reminds me of that other story I told you about where I said, "How do you audition to score a film?" They laughed. You don't really audition, but something stuck with them and a few weeks or months later, they said you know what, we're going to send you some footage from the movie and you can audition and write some music to it. To make a long story short, I got the job. Then to make a really long story short, I got taken off the job when Jeffrey Katzenberg found out that they had hired an unknown, inexperienced composer to score a huge-budget movie. It's a much more textured story, and I guess it's part of what you're writing about in your book.

JG: Yes, it is important to talk about.

MS: It has to do with this stuff actually.

JG: Yes, it does.

MS: So I didn't know anything about click tracks or anything. I just knew how to write music that fit a moment in life, whether it's someone walking in the room and playing something funny, or whatever. They sent me this footage and I would say, okay, I know by the time that she puts that pencil down on the desk, I better be on the down beat on a B-flat six chord. I went through this over and over again making sure I could play the music while hitting all the signposts in the film. I wrote three scences this way and sent it in. I went in to the studio with a drummer and a bass player to record the music. The poor guys; they had to follow me. In the end, I amazingly got the gig, but only if they also hired Ralph Burns, who was an experienced, brilliant arranger, film scorer, a real old hat, old hand. They believed we could really do it as a team, which seemed like a great idea at the time. I was thrilled. So I moved to LA and rented a place. It was just when this technology stuff started appearing for me. I went to the guitar center because Ralph Burns set me up with someone who just helped him get his technology setup. Now, Ralph Burns, I don't know if you know who he is?

JG: Yes, I do.

MS: Legendary jazz arranger, didn't need to use this stuff [technology] to sit at a score pad and create music, but he was very much trying to stay current. He was getting all this stuff, and he set me up with this guy, Larry, at the Guitar Center. I got my first Kurzweil and I still actually use it.

Well, maybe not the same one. They're so out [of style]. If it breaks, I'm dead. If any of this breaks, it'll be impossible to try to replace it because I just don't like the new plug-ins as much. I've yet to hear the sounds that are as good as a lot of the stuff that are in these boxes.

JG: That brings me to an interesting question for you. I've listened to your scores for years. They're lush, beautiful scores. You can also write very playful music for films like *South Park*. Have you felt pressure to scale back the orchestration for budget considerations and use more software instruments?

MS: My film scoring career was really at a time when orchestra use was at its highest. Luckily downscaling didn't happen a lot. People weren't saying we could do this for a lot less if you just did it all with your synths. Nowadays I'm sure that happens a lot more, but I'm not scoring movies like I did then that I'm coming up against the need to downscale. The few movies I've scored in the last few years that were budgetarily extremely frightening, I just chose to score them in a way that didn't require a huge orchestra.

JG: I've done TV work where they want you to bring back the budget because they are so limited in funds.

MS: I was lucky in that I got to ride the magic carpet in the sense that a big orchestra was booked for every movie.

JG: That must have been amazing. Did you conduct everything as well?

MS: No. I learned early on through the work on the Bette Midler records, Harry Connick, Jr. records, which resulted from *When Harry Met Sally*, that my conducting skills were not, I felt, good enough at the sessions to get the best job done. It became clear I that I had to get better at this. I realized soon that it was because I'm such an accompanist at heart that I would start following the orchestra. Instead of that bizarre thing where you just have to be in front of them, meaning ahead of them. I couldn't do it. I would follow them! Then on the first big scoring job I got, *Misery*, they said, oh, you know, the orchestrator can conduct. Do you want to conduct? Do you want to stay in the booth? I was like, I have a choice? Someone else could conduct for me? I'll do that, because it's my first movie. I'd much rather just be thinking about the composition and the orchestration. And from thereon in, I just got lazy and spoiled and just felt I did a better job not conducting. Now, of course, there are great composers who probably would think I'm a hack for not conducting. But the music's written, you can express what you want to the musicians when you're rehearsing, and I often just like to stand next to the conductor and make all the faces. But film conducting is so much about just being really good at bringing them in on the streamer or making things exact, and I'm just not exact enough. I often say my autobiography should be called *Marc Shaiman, the Sloppy Perfectionist.*

JG: I don't know if I would consider you to be sloppy. Let me ask you, going back to when you were working in theaters here, was film something you had always wanted to do? Or were you more interested in staying in theater and caberet productions?

MS: I think it was everything. I just loved music and show business. But I didn't as a kid listen to film scores and think "Who's writing that music?" and I'd like to do that some day. I would listen to Broadway cast albums and go, gee, I can imagine working on Broadway, whether it was playing piano or writing my own stuff. If I had any kind of fantasies at all, which I don't really remember, it was more towards Broadway and songwriting, theatrical songwriting. So the movie stuff kind of fell in my lap.

JG: A lot of people have said that. You're not the first.

MS: Yeah. In the circle of modern film composers, Danny Elfman, Mark Isham, people like that, James Eaton Howard, it all kind of came to them.

JG: Your career has been very interesting for me to study. I was first exposed to your music through Harry Connick, Jr. records and various cast recordings of Broadway orchestras. As I studied your career more deeply, I became aware of the films scores you had written. It all began to make sense. I think your process is very different from others. I think the movies that your music is in take on the role of a character.

MS: [Jokingly] For better or for worse.

JG: I would say for better, personally.

MS: But if I think of anything that made my writing different than others it's that I never became slave to the click track and slave to one steady tempo playing throughout a whole cue or a whole scene. Now, I've learned that was also bad sometimes when I watch my scores and go like, "Oh, Jesus, calm down! Or stick with something." Then I go see movies like the kind of movies like Thomas Newman really became like the king of, where there's this one steady textured groove that really makes sense.

JG: Well, the rhythm is a character.

MS: I'm just a Broadway songwriter at heart, and all my film scores were basically melodies and themes that I was writing words for in my head. And they didn't necessarily mean anything more.

JG: But if you think about it, with the music that you've written, it really feels as if it takes on a character in the movie. Some of the other scores that I've listened to and studied just feel stock. I don't think films like *City Slickers* or any of the Rob Reiner movies would have been as good without your music. I just don't know if those films would have been what they were. Maybe that's because of the career that you had in Broadway. In my opinion, you're one of the few composers I can think of that really has that old Hollywood sound—the showmanship in their music. It doesn't sound stock to me when I listen to your music.

MS: Oh, thank you.

JG: It doesn't. Even the funny skit you performed with Jack Black in California for Prop 8. That was hilarious. There's a playful kind of feel to your music. Where do you think that came from? Do you think that came from all of your experiences in Broadway?

MS: I was born with it. Then my experience in New York with comedians and theatrical people just helped it blossom. But that's something you're born with. It was just something in my blood, or soul, that has that theatricality. Who can explain it?

JG: You're right. When I listen to your music, the same thing with the Harry Connick, Jr. records. Correct me. You wrote *We're in Love.*

MS: No.

JG: You wrote parts of it, right?

MS: I only wrote one song on that. I did all the orchestrations on that.

JG: Did you do anything for *Blue Light, Red Light*?

MS: No. I did all the orchestrations on *When Harry Met Sally*, which actually I think was only four orchestrations on that album. I co-produced the whole thing with Harry. Then the second one, I co-produced most of it and orchestrated I think almost all of it. Then that was it. Harry started doing his own orchestrations. When it comes down to it, "A Wink and a Smile" was the only other thing with Harry that I orchestrated after that time, from *Sleepless in Seattle.*

JG: You have such a wide musical vocabulary. Like I said before, you've done everything from Broadway shows such as *Hairspray* to slapstick movies such as *South Park 2.* You have this wide vocabulary of musical ideas and approaches. How do you distill those ideas? What is your process for sketching an idea for a cue when you are given it? Everyone is a bit different in this.

MS: Content dictates form—isn't that the expression? The movie or the project itself just lets you know. I'm trying to think if there ever was a project I was handed where there was truly, oh my God, I could go this way or I could go that way. Something like *City Slickers*, you pretty much know the style you're going to be writing in. The one kind of movie I didn't get to do a lot of, and the best version of it that I did get to do, was *The American President.* That kind of austere type of film score.

JG: A lot of people have their own style of writing. Composers will often get hired for that style. But looking at your work, it ranges everything from theater all the way up through huge large-budget motion pictures. Your ability to write across the board is pretty impressive considering that most other composers don't have as wide of a vocabulary.

MS: I'm sure any composer doesn't like when they are classified as just being able to do one kind of score, like Danny Elfman who score after score is brilliant. He can keep doing certain things that are his style unmistakably, but it's always unbelievable. But I'm sure he would also like, as he has had a chance over his career, but probably not as much as he'd like, to have done other kinds of stuff that are not at all recognizable as, oh, that's a Danny Elfman, *Edward Scissorhands* style of voices. I was lucky for a while there to be offered a lot of projects that allowed me to show the fact that I just love all kinds of music and just never understood why anyone would not want to explore all of it.

JG: Which style of music do you feel more comfortable with?

MS: I think it's clear now—Broadway-style theatrical. And *Hairspray* gave me the opportunity to explore two genres, which is both theatrical, but then 60s pop music. Probably because I grew up in the 60s—I found myself constantly being involved with projects that were about or full of 60s pop music. By the time *Hairspray* came along, well, by the time *Sister Act* came along, I was so versed in every note of every arrangement, of every Phil Spector, every girl group, every Motown, from these gigs I had that I was the perfect guy to do that movie. Then when *Hairspray* came, I was able to write songs that were timeless. It's always a compliment when people say, "this sounds like songs that were on the radio at one time." Then hopefully also still make them feel that they were of the period without ripping off that period. There certainly are many tips of the hat in our score to *Hairspray* to specific songs of the period, but never so much that legal departments would come after us. You can't ignore the building blocks of a certain sound.

JG: When you listen to that music, it just kind of feels like we're still in that time period and that you're a new artist who came out in that time period.

MS: That was the goal.

JG: It came off that way. Walking in, I didn't know the role of technology in your workflow. Obviously, now I do [wall flanked with audio recording equipment]. Do you still like to write to score, or do you mainly spend most of your time at the DAW?

MS: It's all on that [pointing to Mac Pro tower]. In those formative years of writing for cabaret acts, I would write all the charts out myself for a sax, a trumpet, a bass, or a guitar. My lines were perfect. I was totally into writing that music. But then once I got to the movies I just started writing into the computer, the computer spitting out the music. It used to be much more horrific. Then I got to the luxury of film scoring and be able to send what I was writing in the computer, someone else would then transfer to manuscript. Which was often a big problem financially on movies. They would always be angry that there was this guy, or guys, who had to be paid to make the music readable to the orchestrator. Because as you know...

JG: You needed a copyist.

MS: A guy named Nick used to do most of it. He would call it "excretions, musical excretions." Writing it out so when the orchestrator saw it it looked like an 8th note, not a 64th note. And the spellings, F-sharp versus G-flat. Just everything you can do to make it look like what it would have been in a millisecond if I was just writing it by hand. So it's ironic that all this other time and expense had to now be accounted for. They think that writing to this stuff [computers] was cutting costs, but in reality it was adding costs. I'm finding writing it to the computer, there's no time to give them these fully orchestrated cues.

JG: Do you have a copyist that you work with all the time now?

MS: As a matter of fact, I sort of do. JoAnn Kane Music Service in Los Angeles became my copyist of choice through their brilliant work. Not that the other copying music libraries aren't also. They're all great in Hollywood. But JoAnn Kane's office is filled with brilliantly perfect people, how they think of things, how they've taught me. Thinking about this more, all I can is they're just really good. And now I have one lead guy there named Russ who has been working on shows now. Besides movies and stuff, he's down here working. We're just starting rehearsals for *Catch Me if You Can* on Broadway. Scott and I have written a musical of *Charlie and the Chocolate Factory*. Because they want to come to New York, they've been making Russ available to be here, and he's literally with me every day at rehearsal so the music can keep getting updated as changes happen. He just is always listening. He says, oh, I heard you made a change at measure 89, do you want to put that in music? I'll say, not yet, they're probably going to change it again tomorrow. Having him around, he is literally my right-hand man, because he's literally doing what my right hand would have been doing in previous years. Once again, producers ask, "What's this expense? Why? Why aren't you just writing it out for the musicians at these readings?" And I say, "I'm sorry, I'm spoiled, I'm still spoiled from all that time in Hollywood." But then they say, my God, that reading of the music sounded so [slick]. I hate the word slick. It's always used as a bad thing. So right—how's that for a word? Gee, the music sounded so right, or the demos are so perfect. I'll say, well, that's because I am the perfectionist side of the sloppy perfectionist and Russ helps to make it be exact. Not just head charts.

JG: That's fantastic. So your copyist is almost your assistant orchestrator in a way.

MS: To an extent. Every now and then I actually have had to say to them, here's the string parts, "Can you guys use common sense and write this out as to what's the violins, what's the violas?" I would say that's probably happened three times in the space of 25 years or something. But as to what comes between me and the orchestrator, they are invaluable, not to mention everything else that they do. Copyists, that's a whole other area that didn't exist in the old days.

JG: Like I said, you'll say relatively young but I will still call you young. Your career really grew as technology grew in the industry. How do you think technology has shaped you as a musician? Do you think technology has shaped you as a composer and orchestrator?

MS: It definitely has. For better or for worse. I learned so much from sitting here [at the computer]. When I think of brilliant guys, whether it's Beethoven, Ralph Burns, or Nelson Riddle [who was writing on the score pad on the way to sessions in the back of a car], how they literally hear it in their head and have the confidence to just write it. Now, I hear music in my head all the time, but I don't have the confidence of the the exact orchestration. I go back and forth a million times with this stuff, and it allows me to have a finished product that I'm happy with. But on the way to that finished product is an endless amount of experimentation. If I do a string line, then I go do the brass parts, and then that starts to affect the string line and you have to change that. I think to myself, my God, what would have happened if I'd written that with ink on a score pad? How did those guys do it? They were just brilliant.

JG: Yes, there was a composer I studied with at Manhattan School of Music. When he was younger and on the road, he would just be at the back of the bus and would write directly to score. I could write a simple big band chart in a couple of days, but he could do it in 35 minutes at the back of a tour bus. It comes out and it just sounds great.

MS: I'm more of a pecker.

JG: You labor over it until...

MS: Oh, my God. It's probably to the point of it might be better if I didn't, but I'll never know and I don't care. I'm happy to have this stuff, and I'm happy to spend those hours doing that. I love that part of it.

JG: Do you have the luxury now to peck around or have you just become really fast in your writing over the years?

MS: I can create something pretty fast on that [computer]. But even the other day, on a thing with *Catch Me If You Can* for the demos, we decided to cut a verse. So I had to go from [plays piano] A-flat to C. I suddenly had to go to the bridge in C. So I finally settled on [plays piano]. Something that sounded like it's lifting off. But then first it was [plays piano], but then little by little [plays piano]. So the A-flat that had already been recorded on the demo didn't end until one. That's a fun puzzle, too. I already remember once with Bette Midler, the very first orchestration I ever did was in a concert where she wanted to sing in G-flat, which was kind of too low for her, but she insisted on this key because the last note would be [plays piano]. She would hold that note as long as she and the backup singers could together. And they had to figure out how to go into the next song in C. I'm patting myself on the back now, but I'm literally playing [plays piano]. I wanted to figure out how to make an orchestra now go from G-flat to C, holding a G-flat as long as possible, and also be hopefully a stunning moment [plays piano].

JG: Beautiful.

MS: It's fun when you have to...

JG: That's a harsh transition, G-flat to C.

MS: I love that stuff.

JG: But when you just played, G-flat to C, that's a really harsh transition. It's a pretty large jump harmonically? That was a beatiful, interesting harmonic transition. A lot of other composers don't do that. They'll probably go to a different key so it's a very easy transition, but I think maybe that tension that you use is what sets you apart from a lot of other people. I really do. I don't really know that many other people who will do or pull off that same kind of transition.

MS: Also, there's not much place. I'm lucky that I have fallen into a lot of gigs that, because I'm sort of one of the few people doing it, who want to do it. And it's also, of course, probably costing some other jobs where people only think of me now as this one thing.

JG: That's interesting. There's been some other composers that I've spoken to who kind of feel that they've been typecast.

MS: They are. Everyone is.

JG: Do you kind of feel that your career has gone that way as well?

MS: Yeah. It went that way. Like we were talking about a few minutes ago.

JG: What do you think you're locked into now?

MS: Rob Reiner for a few years. My work with him, when I did *When Harry Met Sally*, *Misery*, first scoring job, a psychological thriller, I didn't understand the music at all. So that's got tension, psychological crazy tension music and sustaining tension. I didn't know from that at all. That was really jumping into the deep end for me. Then I got to do, through him, or his company, *City Slickers*, *A Few Good Men*. Then I also got to do the *Adams Family*. So at that time in my life, every movie was quite different. And although I maybe brought a theatricality to it, they were really different genres. Then by the time *Sleepless in Seattle* came along, having done *When Harry Met Sally* and *Sleepless in Seattle*, and the soundtrack recordings also becoming big successes, then it was just romantic comedies, one after another. I literally heard myself literally writing the same music to the point where, whether anyone else was noticing, I was embarrassed and got into a real rut. Outside of *The American President*, it gave me a chance to write that kind of beautiful music that isn't with jazz hands. And although I got nominated for an Oscar for that one, I still didn't beat the perception of me, which is understandable because it's my personality also, still was not leading me to other jobs like that. This was depressing, because I really thought *The American President* and the Oscar nomination for it would have led to more gigs like that.

Then luckily, just when I was really getting sick of it all, the phone call to write the musical of *Hairspray* for Broadway came. It was my salvation and probably changed my life.

JG: It's theatrical but with an interesting 60s sound. So it certainly isn't a romantic comedy sound. But I don't even know if you were writing that romantic in *When Harry Met Sally* and *Sleepless in Seattle*. They are romantic comedies, but even those soundtracks are quite diverse. There is some great variety across the board on the soundtracks.

MS: For around five years, I really was lucky to get a lot of diverse stuff.

JG: How did you then get into kind of writing for the Oscars?

MS: Through Billy Crystal. First he hosted the Grammys for two years, and then he did just one little bit on one Oscars. Then they asked him to host the show, and this idea of spoofing the cheesy opening numbers. Now some people, they think of Billy Crystal as too old school and his opening numbers as, oh, that thing he does. But it's ironic that we did it as a spoof, and then some people think it's spoofable now. At any rate, that's a huge thing. Then I got to do that a lot in my career, which is also why what I was saying, my personality, and the other things I do, I understand why people kept thinking of me in a certain way. Because even in the year I scored *The American President*, I also did a medley for Billy Crystal at the Oscars, showing lyric writing and comedy and show business. But always ironic show business stuff, kind of spoofing it at the same time. Even with Harry Connick, Jr., I went on the road with him and did Broadway after that first album. So there's always a kind of flashier kind of side of music. I think I forget the question!

JG: I think you answered it. When you come down to writing these projects, when you do get a project coming in, do you have the liberty now of having a lot of time? Or do they put pretty tight constraints on you?

MS: I don't really score much stuff anymore.

JG: Even the projects, any kind of project that comes in, do you at least have the luxury to write, or do you feel like you're under the gun?

MS: Well, Broadway has an as-it-needs-to-be pace more than a movie. Having said that, on *Charlie and the Chocolate Factory*, when we had our second reading recently, we did one reading and we only wrote the first act. Then the second reading, six months later, was to do the first act and the second act, which Scott and I had to write a whole other act. But then from the first reading, we had two or three spots in the first act we wanted to redo. Then out of the blue, I got the call to work on Mariah Carey's new Christmas record. Because of what we're talking about, Randy Jackson thought of me. He was trying to think who's like the modern Nelson Riddle to give Mariah Carey a Nat King Cole-ish kind of vibe on a cut or two, or whatever happens if I put them together. So that literally went like, what, Mariah Carey? Okay, go. So I got to do some stuff on her new record that is full old-school orchestral kind of stuff, and also got to work with someone of her stature in pop music and really hit it off with her. The only reason I brought that up was that we suddenly had no time to write for the second reading of *Charlie*. We even wrote to the producer and director, guys, we really gotta push the second reading. They're like, we can't push the second reading, too many people have booked flights based on the studios. Warner Bros. is the producer of it because they have the film rights. Anyway, to make a long story short, there is a moment where, oh my God, we are literally under the gun to write theater songs, which we weren't quite as used to having to do. In the end we got more written than we thought we could.

JG: Do you ever send anybody MIDI mockups?

MS: I was at the beginning of that, which is actually the story I was telling about Ralph Burns. Him having to do MIDI mockups was both insulting and just insane. But because of the MIDI mockups and what they had me doing, which ironically on this movie *Big Business* that I got hired to do, I wrote late 50s-style women in the big city stuff that I actually got to finally do in a movie called *Down with Love* twenty years later. They hired me based on that, and then they only wanted me to write like Harold Faltermeyer, who had just done *Beverly Hills Cop* and *Fletch*. I was like, guys, this isn't at all what you hired me to do. They're like, yeah, well, what we hired you to do showed you were talented, but this is the music we need this movie to have to be current. I didn't really agree with this choice, and neither did Ralph Burns. It all blew up, Ralph Burns didn't feel like he should have to do MIDI mockups and the ones he did send in sounded old-fashioned to them because it wasn't at all what he or I thought the movie should have. And that's when Jeffrey Katzenberg said we can't have this situation, and I got taken off of the project.

JG: A lot of the composers that I've talked to who are at a pretty high level like yourself, they've had to send MIDI mockups. Have you had to do this type of audition? For me, if you've got somebody of your caliber, I know what style of music I want to hire you for. I know your work. Thoughts?

MS: Just recently someone said to me, someone from the studio—I can't remember their name. They said, oh, I just heard your score for Rob Reiner's movie *Flip*, I had just scored and it only came out in two theaters. Anyway, I wrote literally five minutes of score in the most simplistic fashion, because that's what the movie called for. I bring it up because I realized they had been sent there to hear what Marc Shaiman is up to lately. That's insane to me. It's sort of like what you're talking about. It wasn't me auditioning, but it was using my CDs to audition in effect when my agent says think about Marc. Then they say send over his latest thing so we can all talk about it in the music department or play it for the director. I'm like, I cannot believe it. On the other hand, the only good part would be if someone only thinks of me as Broadway and if my agent were to send over *The American President*, it might make some go, oh, it could be this kind of more stirring kind of film score. So it's good and bad.

JG: It's interesting because I never thought that typecasting would be present in your life.

MS: Yeah. I can't even believe that—they have to do a synth version to get the gig.

JG: And even in TV work, you're having to do that all the time.

MS: There's no doubt that everything is always an audition in life. But every day that you do a synth mockup on a cue and play it for the director or producer, it's an audition. It's a double-edged sword though, because with all this stuff [pounting at computer] I learned how to write music in a certain style and orchestrate and got to figure it out at my house instead in front of an orchestra. I didn't have to fail miserably in front of an orchestra. I got to work it out at home. So without all this stuff and the synth mockups that we were suddenly expected to create for the director or producer, I don't know how I would have survived without it.

JG: You use a lot of different third-party software instruments, like Vienna Symphony Orchestra or…

MS: Everything. All this stuff, everything that's in that. I have people who work with me who I can't even list it all for you because I remain blissfully above knowing every single library's name. But it's all in there, and they keep trying to get me to—

JG: Upgrade to the newest one, right?

MS: Yeah. But I still hang on to certain things. It's what I'm used to, and it's amazing how certain libraries just have a certain sound of the room. I'm like, well, that's great for a specific cue, but I can't use that library on every single thing I do because there's too much reverb on that.

JG: Exactly.

MS: So I'm still kind of amazed sometimes.

JG: Do you get to do a lot of session dates with real orchestras anymore?

MS: Yeah.

JG: I feel like you're one of the lucky ones that still gets to do that.

MS: Well, like the Mariah Carey album was nice that I got to do that with a real orchestra.

JG: Did you guys record it in LA?

MS: Yeah.

JG: I know a lot of people are going to other countries to record.

MS: I've never done that. I burned a few bridges in my time film scoring by refusing to do that. For being a union man, and also because I was too scared. The idea of having to bring all my equipment and be in a hotel room somewhere else. It never seemed to me like how much money are you going to save. I know it's more and more and more. I'm surprised it didn't come up with Mariah Carey, because they were freaking out budget-wise. Ironically, Mariah Carey, for her TV special where she did a few of the cuts with the orchestra, they didn't want to pay for the re-use.

And, when they called and said can you help us figure out some way to do this, I'm like, figure out what? Then I realized, I guess I could fluff up my synth demos and make it sound even better, because I made them sound good but I could make them sound even better knowing that they're going to now be on TV.

JG: So they wanted it to basically to be karaoke style?

MS: Then, of course, by saying that they realized, oh, wait a second, we already have that, you already sent us that stuff. Because as I did each thing, I would send it over to Mariah to hear what I was doing. So they did have all my synth stuff, and they were like, this sounds great! I'm like, yeah, I didn't make it to be played on TV though. I'd really love to hear the woodwind patch is just a woodwind patch, it's not flutes and clarinets. I could make that sound better. Meanwhile, it was taken out of my hands. There was nothing I could say.

JG: I know you have some other obligations today, so I'll finish it up with where do you see yourself? Where do you see where you want to change and evolve and move musically?

MS: It's very unhealthy to say, I don't want to change or move at all. I want to keep doing exactly what I'm doing till I die. I couldn't be happier if I got to be doing just what I'm doing right now, which is for the most part Broadway musicals. I wish there was more chance to work with orchestras in that. Luckily on *Catch Me If You Can*, it's written in the style of Nelson Riddle, so the orchestrations are very important. The band is onstage, and although it's way cut down—it's like 17 pieces—they're like, Marc, we've given you this huge orchestra! I'm like, are you kidding? It's like nothing.

JG: I used to do Broadway for a long time as a trumpet player, so every couple of years the pits would start shrinking and shrinking.

MS: So me, I have a co-orchestrator on it.

JG: Are you using a lot of synth?

MS: Yeah. Our job now is to figure out how to make it work, and that's the problem with this stuff [referring to synth], especially when it comes to Broadway, is I make these demos that are full-fledged albums. Then on *Hairspray*, the job for the orchestrator was taking what I had done and figuring out how to make it be able to be played by the orchestra. Along with adding his own artistry to it. On *Catch Me If You Can*, I chose to remain billed as a co-orchestrator, and Larry Blank is my co-orchestrator. It's our job now to take everything I've done over the years and just figure out, okay, how are we going to make this sound good with just 17 players? Because my demos sound like an 80-piece orchestra.

CHAPTER 12
STEVE HOROWITZ

▶ **FIG. 12.1**

STEVE HOROWITZ IS A CREATOR of odd, but highly accessible sounds and is a diverse and prolific musician. Best known for his original soundtrack to the Academy Award–nominated film *Super Size Me*, Steve also composed the music for MTV's hit reality show *I Bet You Will* and Spike TV's *Casino Cinema*. Steve has worked extensively with Nickelodeon Digital, where his groundbreaking work in interactive entertainment has garnered him both Webby and BD awards. Horowitz also received a Grammy Award for Best Bluegrass Album in recognition of his engineering work on the 1996 multi-artist release, *True Life*

Blues: The Songs of Bill Monroe [Sugar Hill]. Steve records and tours with his band, The Code International, year-round and has released sixteen albums of mind-altering original sounds to date.

Steve Horowitz's career integrates his experiences as a bandleader with his explorations as a multifaceted composer. Horowitz possesses a large catalog of music for traditional and unusual ensembles. Steve studied composition with Morton Subotnik, Mel Powell, and Stephen "Lucky" Mosko at the California Institute of the Arts and has received performance underwriting and commissions from numerous ensembles and organizations. A frequent guest lecturer at schools around the globe, he has spoken at New York University, California Institute of the Arts, Expressions College, and SAE and teaches a course in sound for interactive media at the Academy of Art University in San Francisco.

Specific performance underwriting as well as commissions have included Meet the Composer Fund, The Kitchen, Red Cat, the Amsterdam Fund for the Arts, the American Music Center, Gravy Train Dance Company, the Alternate Currents Ensemble, the Sonus Imaginorem String Quartet, Composers and Schools in Concert, Music at the Anthology (executive producer Phillip Glass), and Yamaha.

Touring projects in the United States Europe have helped to form Horowitz's unique perspective and voice. Steve and his music have appeared at the Great American Music Hall in San Francisco, The Bim Huis in Amsterdam, The Miller Theater and The Kitchen in New York, and the Red Cat Theater in Los Angeles, to name a few. Steve frequently collaborates with other artists—joining forces with an eclectic variety of musicians such as Elliott Sharp, Fred Frith, Henry Kaiser, William Winant, Lenny Picket, Dan Plonsey, Steve Adams, Michael Moore, The Clubfoot Orchestra, Glen Spearman, and many others.

Over the years, Steve's music has explored some persistent musical themes: the intertwining of electric and acoustic instruments, new forms, extended techniques, interactivity, music for picture, theater, and live performance. Drawing on a finely honed sense of humor, Horowitz looks deeply into the sociological filter and re-examines pop culture's presentation of "truth" as entertainment. Additionally, Horowitz has been featured in *Bass Player* magazine (May 2007) as well as the books *The Art of Digital Music* and *The Guerilla Guide to the Music Business.*

JG: Can you please state your name?

SH: Steven Horowitz.

JG: When and where were you born?

SH: I was born in Brooklyn, New York, October 3, 1964.

JG: Growing up in Brooklyn, what role did music play in your upbringing? Was music present in your house?

SH: I lived in Brooklyn until I was 5, but we moved to Miami when I was 5 years old. Music really started for me in Florida. The earliest memories I have are of my mom and involve a recording of *The Fox* by Harry Belafonte. It's one of my earliest musical memories. I can still remember playing that recording and over and over again. The Bards, a family who lived next to us in Florida, ran a music shop called the House of Melody. My sister had guitar lessons, but she didn't like them very much. When I was 6 I took over her guitar lessons. I did group lessons with the Bards for a couple years, and I did group lessons, didn't like it so much and subsequently stopped the lessons. I revisited private lessons when I was 8 and fell in love.

JG: That's interesting. Were you the only musician in your family?

SH: In terms of my immediate family, yes. There's a super strong art and music gene, or combination of both, in my family. My brother's a fantastic photographer—he has work in the Corcoran. He is beautiful fine art photographer. My sister's a fantastic painter, although she doesn't really paint that much anymore. When she was in high school she did a complete, perfect copy of Rembrandt. Her teacher said she should go to art school and she said surprisingly, "really?"

In terms of the music ability in my family, my grandfather was a concert-level pianist and violinist. The story goes that he was actually offered a music position by patron who was willing to pay for him to go to Europe to study for his career. In the end, he didn't go because of the family. He needed to stay and support the family. I feel he extremely bitter about it because he never talked about it. He died when I was very young, but he was extremely bitter about it. My uncle is a great drummer and my niece is a singer/songwriter—she's amazing. Certainly, there is a very strong music gene. In my immediate family I was the one who got it, but it travels through the line.

JG: Growing up in Florida, what role did schooling play in your musical voice, or not very much at all?

SH: In terms of music education, that didn't start until we moved. My parents moved to Berkeley, California, and I went to Berkeley High. That's when music education became very serious for me.

JG: Up to that point, were you essentially studying on your own?

SH: Right. I started guitar lessons in Florida, and continued my lessons when I moved to Berkeley. I discovered that my school, Berkeley High School, had an amazing jazz program.

JG: That's very interesting. I know of Berkeley High School well. I went to Rio Americano High School in Sacramento. Berkeley High School was one of our chief rivals.

SH: Right! When I got to Berkeley High in tenth grade, the band director gave me a chance to audition for the lab band. He's said, "What do you want to play?" He mentioned there was an opening for a bass player and I decided to give it a try. I was given an electric and an upright bass and was told to go home and learn to play. The band director showed me how to play walking bass lines and that was it. I had found my instrument. I switched. I'm a bass player. I was playing rock and was studying a little bit privately. This is when music education really took hold of me.

JG: What style of music do you feel personally closest to?

SH: Well, these days mostly I play my own stuff. I have my own group and I play my own music. If I am working on a particular musical project I dive into it.

JG: When were you first exposed to composition?

SH: When I was in high school my ears were wide open. I'd go to the library and listen to Stravinsky and other composers, check out scores and study. I went through modal counterpoint and orchestration books on my own. I read an interview with Frank Zappa, and he mentioned that some of the best learning happens out of school on your own. Simply, you can just go to the library and get a book. To me that made sense and sounded like a great idea. While a number of my friends were diving into the typical high school experience, I was checking out books, working through exercises, and furthering my own education.

JG: You actually went through modal counterpoint on your own for fun?

SH: Absolutely. When I finally decided to go to Cal Arts later on I was ahead of the game and passed out of a number of courses. I deeply experimented with writing and arranging while I was at Berkeley High. Jason, since you're a trumpet player, you'll appreciate this composition I wrote for the brass ensemble. It was entitled, "The Spit Valve Drains Red." The ensemble played it and that was a great experience for me. I was writing quite a bit in high school and I came out of those years as a working writing and busy performing musician. I was playing a lot of jazz on both the electric and upright bass. I had my own band and my own ensemble. I reached this point where I feel as if I hit a wall—I needed more information. In a lot of ways, I was self-taught and audited a number of classes at UC Berkeley with Andrew Embry. I also audited some classes at Hayward State where they had orchestration class that they let me join and sit in on. I had a 30-second orchestra piece played by the Hayward State Orchestra and stuff like that. That experience was extremely helpful because it provided direction to me in the form of musical questions that I personally needed an answer to. That's when I started looking around and found Cal Arts. In the end, I decided to attend Cal Arts.

JG: How did you find Cal Arts?

SH: Cal Arts started in the late 60s or early 70s. When I got to Cal Arts, the music school was quite well established. I don't remember exactly how I found out about it. I think it was just through word of mouth through friends of friends. I was 24 years old and was really was going for specific reasons. I think if it hadn't been for Cal Arts I might not have gone to music school. I remember going on a trip down there and was completely blown away. I had never experienced musicians of that caliber before.

JG: Was Morton Subotnick still around when you were down there?

SH: Subotnick was there at the time. I studied with Mel Powell, as well. The music program was amazing.

JG: Cal Arts uses technology throughout the curriculum, is that where you were first exposed to technology, or was technology something you were experimenting with before?

SH: It's interesting because during the years between high school and Cal Arts, I ran a recording studio with some friends of mine here up in the Bay area. We had a friend who had a half-inch eight track. He had a really nice [recording] room over in Oakland. Another buddy of mine, Danny, was working there and knew Mark. Mark got into real estate and wasn't using his studio, so we camped out and made it our home away from home. I did a ton of recording and, in the end, taught myself. I truly learned by doing. Literally, I recorded hundreds and hundreds of hours of my band, as well as other bands. From the beginning I was hooked and loved multi-track recording, music technology, and all of the things that go along with it.

JG: It's so interesting you say that, because most everyone I know is self-taught. For me, I feel the musicians and composers who actually understand the technology on a deep level are the people who actually had to dive right in and discover the technology on their own.

SH: Exactly. I taught at SAE for a while, the School for Audio Engineering, and I would always ask the students, "What do you want to do?" They often said, "I want to be a producer!" What does that mean? In my own learning, I remember recording bands early on. I actually feel so bad for some of those early projects I recorded because I really did not know what I was doing. You work with and are mentored by people, although it's not formal. I remember the way we used to learn a room or the way you'd learn a board is messing it up. My friend Danny was more advanced than I. We'd be in the studio and he'd say, "okay, turn your back." Then he would set up the board and mess it up, and he'd say, "Figure out what's wrong." I'd have to sit there and go through the signal path and figure out what was wrong. I literally learned by doing thousands of hours of recording. No school can take that much time and can't take the place of that experience. I used to tell the students at SAE that I think the school environment is great! They were able to learn things in a classroom that I never had the opportunity to learn. The students are gaining a great theoretical foundation of knowledge, but that doesn't take away the need to go and spend a thousand hours recording music, if that's what you want to do. I would tell them, "Start now, because taking a class won't replace that."

JG: How did you first get introduced to writing for film and media?

SH: I went down to Cal Arts, studied there for a few years and was presented with an opportunity to open up a recording studio with some friends back up here in the Bay Area. I did that, and while I was living up here [in the Bay Area], my cousin came to town. His girlfriend at the time was really good friends with a fellow named Mark Miller, who I'm still good friends with today. Mark had a company that created music for video games and different, interactive projects. This is the early 90s and the height of the CD-ROM boom. I remember meeting Mark, and he said, "Have you ever thought about making your living writing music?" I said, "No! Never." After Cal Arts I figured I'd make some weird sounds and die poor! Mark really got me my start writing music for interactive and adaptive audio. I started out doing game scores with him, some of the early scores for Rocket Science Games. That was during the Siliwood time—the meeting of Hollywood and Silicon Valley. These projects were big console games. Anything from companies that were going to do Dante's Inferno on CD-ROM to companies that were creating video games and interactive books. There was a vast spectrum of project types. It was through this experience with Mark that I truly got my start scoring for visual media.

JG: How do you approach orchestration across all of the various media fields you work in?

SH: It depends. First of all, it depends on what the project is and what format it's for and who the producer is. I approach game scores and film scores differently.

JG: Let's take a game. Console games ship on a static piece of media that only has so much storage. For example, say an 8GB DVD. How do you personally negotiate those barriers? Are you going to record audio or are you going to strictly use MIDI and hope that you have General MIDI (GM) sounds that are going to be good enough? What is the first thing that comes into your mind in this type of situation?

SH: Nobody's using MIDI anymore for GM sounds in games. Maybe on some mobile phone apps, but the paradigm shifted. Even if you're creating Web games, it's all digital audio. The question really is how adaptive is it actually going to be if you're creating it in Flash, creating an iPhone game, creating a downloadable game or a console game. Each one of those platforms has an arcane set of musical rules that you can use. In many ways the platform dictates where everything is going to start. When I start a project I ask a million questions. "What's the delivery format, what program are you developing this in, what [game] engine are you using?" Once some of the technical questions are answered, some of the logistical questions surface. "What's your budget for audio? How much sound do you need?" Once all of that is worked out and I have a picture of what the project is, then I'd like to see some kind of mockup. It always starts for me by looking at what they're creating and what the graphics and images are. As you probably know in games, the game can and likely will be in various states of completion throughout the contract. Sometimes the game creators will ask if I can work from a design draft document. Usually I'll advise against it. I'll say, "Music is tempo related so I can, but once things are moving forward it would help if I could just see a little bit of something moving or some graphics. It'll help to inspire me."

I found out years ago that I had a talent for writing music to picture. I look at picture and if it resonates with me, I start to hear music and I want to develop it. I always like to see a sample of something, if I can, to get a feel of what's happening and needed in the project. In games it depends. For example, I'm working on a project now for Nickelodeon Digital and it is a great experience because I'm able to go in, go through all the levels, go through the rooms, see what's happening, make sure the tempos are good, and make sure it feels right. That involvement puts me way ahead of the game.

JG: You bring up an interesting point about tempo. How do you negotiate writing music for something that is going to have to scale to tempo, potentially as the intensity of the game play increases? I think the process of writing for a medium that is constantly changing to engage the user is fascinating.

SH: That is really the crux of it right there. This has been an ongoing debate in the game community, I feel, since the beginning of games. How interactive and how adaptive is your score going to be? If you're talking to people like Paul [Lipson], they're dealing mostly with AAA titles. They are dealing with the state of the art. The question is—does you client need or want that type of musical interactivity? The challenge that you're asking exists on the best and most fun projects. When I get a producer who wants to push the envelope, making a game that has an interactive environment that adapts on the fly it is a fantastic and fun challenge. That's the difference between really scoring an interactive piece of entertainment and scoring a film that is linear by nature. The reality is those projects are so much fun and do not come along often.

You're following a character, and if the character is doing better in [health] or they go to the left instead of to the right, then the music can adapt and it can change. A good portion of that inert activity consists of fully mixed stems with dynamic muting. That approach isn't necessarily that interactive. Often what you're doing surrounds writing full pieces of music, breaking them out into their individual component parts [drums and percussion, bass lines, melodies] and you're delivering those. Much like TV work, you're counting on a music program or an audio program to trigger those sounds in the way that you want them to be triggered. You issue a music design document. Then they have to take it, make it adapt to the game, and trigger it the way that you want.

JG: Fascinating!

SH: The great thing about creating scores like that is that there's a specific craft of game scoring that's just starting to scratch the surface now that deeply ties in with the New York school of composers—John Cage, Martin Feldman, and Earl Brown. In regard to the art and craft of game audio and game scoring, we're just at the beginning of this era and it is going to start to get really interesting.

On some of the larger projects if you're lucky, just like in TV or in film, you'll actually hear the music if it hasn't been buried by an editor! Sometimes it can be difficult for the music to compete with all of the other sounds that are triggered. Game audio education now is becoming more and more prevalent. We're finding this new generation of students who are entering the industry and they're studying these pieces of software and middleware. When they get to these game companies, they deeply know how to use it. I really have a lot of hope for the next generation of the art and craft of game scoring and game audio.

JG: I think so, too. It's interesting that you bring all this up, because I believe the pioneers of this medium understandably didn't really know what to do. You can't blame them, right? But now there is this new influx of students who are actually growing up engaging with this from beginnings of their studies. They're actually approaching composition specifically this way. I think that is the key. Unfortunately, I feel few people wish to discuss writing music in an adaptive way—in a nonlinear way. Admittedly, a number of musicians and composers were trained to study composition and performance in a linear way.

SH: There are a lot of programs and systems, like I said, that are being developed that help to make that happen. The technology will also be there more and more to help the musician. For example, audio programs that understand weightings and based on that weighting, switch key or register.

JG: Certainly. This particular industry seems to have tremendous growth. Games are everywhere—they're on mobile devices, they're on handheld devices, they're on consoles. It's everywhere and it's a billion dollar industry, whereas I don't know if that could be said for television anymore. Switching gears for a moment, when you're working on projects how do you foster creativity throughout long projects to ensure your music still sounds fresh?

SH: Well, that's a good question, and that's something that I have been doing for Nickelodeon Digital for over ten years now. It is something I constantly deal with. Sometimes projects will show up and I'll say to myself, "Wow, this is really similar to something I've done in the past!" It starts to feel the same. For me, it's a challenge that you need to approach by internalizing what are you actually seeing on the screen, what are you actually hearing, and trying to push yourself as a musician to not rewrite or imitate yourself. You have to constantly question your musical choices and be willing to explore new approaches. The good thing about working with picture games, films, and TV is that the experience is often a collaborative process. To that end, the collaborative nature helps because there are other people in the room [the producer, the director] who can guide things in the right direction.

JG: In what way has technology influenced you as a composer?

SH: Hugely. I used to write with a pen and paper all the time. I still do occasionally for my own work, my ensembles or for a film score, depending on what's happening. I work in the box [DAW] more and more. You can put incredible sounding mockups together and then go into a studio with one string player and have them create a large section via overdubs. The technology yields quick edits and internalization of what's really happening in the studio.

JG: Do you feel pressure to replace live musicians with virtual instruments?

SH: No, I wouldn't put it that way. Production budgets vary a great deal from project to project even though the work list may be similar. I often do not have control over the budgets that are presented, but first and foremost I always strive to give the picture, film, or game what it needs musically. There are times when budget will impact that and you can't hire live musicians. I always try to hire live musicians as much as possible. Yes, budgets always influence what you can do.

JG: Some composers, myself included, have felt pressure to bring down the size of their orchestration through the use of technology and replace live musicians with decent software instruments. I still don't feel the end result is the same.

SH: No, absolutely. If you're doing a lot of TV scoring, that's definitely the name of the game. I think it's almost the other way in game scores these days. Producers will often say, "Oh, it would be cool to have exotic sounds or this or that." I find myself hiring more live musicians because of this.

JG: It's interesting you say that, because many of the videos games I have played or seen played possess such lush, orchestral scores. Contrast that with television writing where the music is often there to fill space and not much more.

SH: On the TV side, I saw the current trend coming down the road years ago. Generally, what you're being hired to do on a lot of shows these days is to create a library for them. Budgets have been decimated. The only good side about TV is that you still have a royalty stream. Every time it's played, you're going to see revenue. But as I said, the budgets on the front end have been decimated because producers know they can get it cheaper. It's less and less about scoring the picture and more about producing libraries, custom libraries that producers can use.

JG: When you're working with a client, how often do you create MIDI mockups?

SH: Oh, all the time! Absolutely. It's gotten to the point where people want to hear nearly finished product at the mockup level. The live musicians who are often added later become the icing on the cake.

JG: That seems to be in line with others I have spoken to. I have found that most composers are still creating MIDI mockups. What do you think about technology as an instrument? There are people on both sides of the debate. Some say we're taking away the musicality of students by giving them a tool that's "easy to use" and stripping musicality by just playing around with sounds on a computer. What are your thoughts on this?

SH: Well, there's a long history of technology replacing humans, especially in music. This has been something that I have put a lot of thought into over the years. Imagine living in New York City where you are now, in the 20s, and you were gigging as a musician. You'd be going uptown to do symphony stuff, you'd be going downtown to play jazz, and you'd be going on the radio and television when the medium just started. That's all gone, and that's all replaced by new technology. Musicians have been forced to adapt to new technology across the board more so than any other industry. Now, on one side you understand the loss and it's sad, and on the other side it is an evolution of music. I don't accept the notion that technology is not music I don't accept that. Technology simply provides new tools. It is up to your own musicality to decide what you want to and can create. If you just want to play trumpet, you can play just trumpet. There are still trumpet players. You can get a MIDI trumpet, too. I don't accept the notion that it's not music anymore; that it's just playing with sound. I think that sound has been freed because of technology in a way that it never has been before. Technology has caused interesting problems and brought created interesting implications for how music is sold to people and how they digest it. I was at CMJ last year to present, and there were a couple of young guys who were developing iPhone apps and iPhone games. Their musical point of view surrounded the notion that they don't listen to music that's not attached to interactive experiences. That's a real paradigm shift when you have a whole new generation of kids whose ears are so tuned into new technology and the many ways that media is going to be delivered to them. You can close yourself off to it, but I think the fact is there's a lot of interesting work going on and there's a lot of interesting changes that are happening.

JG: Do you think your career and musicality, as it relates to technology, was colored by the rich, cutting-edge environment at Cal Arts? Do you think you were better prepared for your career, as it needed to shift, especially in regard to technology, throughout your life because of that experience?

SH: Yes, but I think it also had to do with the type of person that I was. Cal Arts is where I first used a computer to write music and produce scores. I dove into technology because of the type of person I am. I didn't shy away from it—I embraced it.

JG: In closing, what advice would you give for musicians who are building a new career in music?

SH: It's the same advice that I always give—I'm asked this question a lot when I'm lecturing at conferences or working with students. Simply, follow your heart. That is really the bottom line. There are a lot of options in regard to careers in music. Focus on whatever your passion is. Put all of your time into learning and experimenting with your craft. For example, I never thought about having a career scoring films, games, or writing music for picture in general. The opportunities presented themselves and they were interesting to me. I got lucky—right place at the right time and good things happened. If you're doing something that you love to do, and something that you want to do, it'll be a whole lot easier in the end. You will get much farther following something you love to do than chasing something that you do not.

CHAPTER 13
NATHAN BARR

▶ FIG. 13.1

NATHAN BARR HAS SCORED all four seasons of HBO's Emmy-winning and fan favorite series, *True Blood*. Barr, who worked extensively with Hans Zimmer in the past, has composed music for more than twenty-five feature films in addition to his television experience. The Topanga Canyon–based composer has worked with some of the most highly respected directors, including Alan Ball and gore-horror master Eli Roth. So far, Roth and Barr have collaborated on five films: Dimension Films and Vivendi Entertainment's *Grindhouse*, Screen Gems and Lionsgate's *Hostel*, *Hostel 2*, *Cabin Fever*, and Lionsgate's *The Last Exorcism*.

Barr composed original music for Lionsgate's comedy *The Wedding*. The film starred Robert De Niro, Amanda Seyfried, Katherine Heigl, Robin Williams, Topher Grace, Susan Sarandon, and Diane Keaton.

Barr scored IFC Films' *The Ledge*, a drama/thriller starring Liv Tyler and Terrance Howard, directed by Matthew Chapman, which premiered at the 2011 Sundance Film Festival. Barr's other credits include 20th Century Fox's *Shutter*, Warner Bros.' *The Dukes of Hazzard*, and Film for Thought's *Hood to Coast*, a documentary that follows four teams on their epic journey to conquer the world's largest relay race.

Barr began studying music in Tokyo at 4 years old. He grew up surrounded by eclectic music ranging from Kabuki Theater to the sounds of his mother performing on the koto and piano and his father playing the banjo, guitar, and shakuhachi.

In addition to writing scores, he performs all of the instruments heard in many of his compositions and is skilled in many styles and genres ranging from orchestral to rock. Barr is also known for his collection and inclusion of rare and unusual instruments from around the world, such as human bone trumpets from Tibet, dismantled pianos, a rare Glass Armonica, and gourd cellos, among many others. All are kept in his garage-turned-studio—just steps away from his home, which makes Barr officially have the shortest commute in LA.

His interest in the art form was further influenced by extensive travels around the world, where he experienced music ranging from Bali's Kecak Orchestras to China's Beijing Opera. Barr went on to study at Skidmore College and toured Italy and Switzerland with the Juilliard Cello Ensemble in the summer of 1993. Barr was among a group of prolific composers who attended the renowned and respected 2011 Ubeda film Festival in Spain. He also joined twenty-four film, TV, and video game composers in the Symphony of Hope to raise money for the victims of the earthquake in Haiti. The related recording was released in September 2011 and became one of Amazon.com's top-25 new classical releases.

JG: Can you please state your name?

NB: Nathan Barr.

JG: When and where were you born?

NB: 1973, New Rochelle, New York.

JG: What role did music play during your upbringing?

NB: One of my fondest memories is of coming home from school in the afternoon and walking in the front door to hear my mother playing Bach on the piano. Another early memory is my mother asking each of us children to hum an A at the breakfast table. We would each have a try and then she would pull out a pitch pipe to see if we were correct. The guitar and the cello were my escape, my inspiration, my joy, my frustration, and my daily means of processing the world. Jimmy Page and YoYo Ma were my greatest musical inspirations. I spent countless hours memorizing and trying to replicate every nuance in their many brilliant performances, whether it was a Bach Cello Suite or the closing guitar outro of The Rain Song. My brother also used music to process the world, and no sooner had his book bag hit the floor each day then was he up in his room for hours banging on the upright. Sometimes melodies would float between our bedrooms, and the occasional similarity led to battles over who wrote what.

JG: What role did your schooling play in the shaping of your musical voice?

NB: I played cello in my high school and all-state orchestras as well as guitar in several bands that I formed. Both experiences involved making music in a group and were invaluable in forming my musical interests and identity. However, one of the most important influences in my life was my cello teacher Maxine Neuman. As all great teachers, she brought life into the lessons, and the lessons into my life. My interest in cello increased a thousand-fold when I began studying with her in the summer of 1989 at The Bennington July Program at Bennington College. Her emotional and intellectual approach to cello performance was mind-opening for me, and to this day I owe much of my musical identity to her. Schooling helps to form one's musical identity only when one's teachers are brilliant and inspiring, and Maxine was a true blessing for me.

JG: Which style of music is most comfortable for you to express yourself with?

NB: One of the best parts of being a film composer is the sheer variety of musical styles one is asked to explore on a daily basis. Therefore it would be hard for me to single out a style of music I am most comfortable expressing myself in. I think all I strive for is to have my own unique musical identity. I know that my work on *True Blood* feels like a fairly pure expression of who I am musically, but that show allows me the opportunity to explore many different styles.

JG: When were you first exposed to music composition?

NB: One of my earliest exposures to composition was watching a contemporary classical composer named Michael Torke perform one of his ballet works on piano at the Yaddo Artists Colony in Saratoga Springs, New York. A dancer from the Boston Ballet danced to his performance, and this put into my head the idea that composers actually lived and walked among us, wrote beautiful music, AND made a living doing so! This happened during my freshman year of college when my experience composing was secondary to my interest in becoming the best guitarist and cellist I could possibly be. I had the opportunity to compose a couple of very rudimentary works during college, and this planted a seed in me which would resurface several years later when I took up an assistant job with Hans Zimmer.

JG: Was composing for media and film something that had always interested you?

NB: I was always a fan of film music but can't say I always aspired to be a film composer. My obsession with film and music certainly made this career choice a perfect fit, but growing up, my interests were more on the performance side of music.

JG: How do you approach orchestration and arranging with technology?

NB: Technology has completely changed the scoring process in the past two or three decades. Pre-sequencer and -synthesizer, one's traditional composition chops had to be tops in order to even consider a career in film music. Pen and paper and stopwatch were mandatory, and today these three items are near obsolete depending on one's particular process. Arranging and orchestrating are much more accessible with the excellent instrumental samples available today. A good orchestrator is still necessary in order to competently translate score from the computer mockups to playable sheet music. I do most of the actual arranging work during the mockup/composing phase. That having been said, my excellent orchestrator Penka Kouneva brings her own ideas to the table as she works through translating my midi files into score.

JG: How do you foster and maintain creativity throughout long composition projects?

NB: It took me a long time to understand that the time I spend away from composing during a project is as important as the time I spend actually composing. My mind is always working through ideas whether I know it or not, and what on one afternoon seems an insurmountable problem is often easily fixed that evening after some time away from the studio. Some of my early mentors had an entirely different process, and it took me years to figure out that it was not the right fit for me. Once I found my own pace and working methods, the job became infinitely easier. That having been said, it can be very difficult to maintain my creative interest and spirit on projects that drag on endlessly. With unending picture changes and/or a director who is unable to express them or doesn't know what he or she wants, the job really becomes a job. At this point, I just hunker down and slog through the work. Fortunately, I have been blessed with few of these experiences.

JG: How do you approach varying projects that include film and television?

NB: In my experience the craft of writing music for picture, whether it be television or film, is the same. The biggest difference is in format. When I am working with themes in a film, I need to develop the themes in such a way that they have been as fully explored as possible by the time the film ends. With a show like *True Blood*, when I introduce a theme for the first time, I know I have an entire season, and maybe even a couple seasons within to explore that theme to its very fullest. Oftentimes when I arrive to the end of a season and listen to a particular character's theme, I am surprised by how much it has developed and changed since I first introduced it. Upon initially writing the theme, I often can never guess where it may end up down the road, and this is exciting—having the space to let it find itself.

JG: Do you prefer one format to another?

NB: Television has taken an enormous leap forward over the past decade in terms of the quality of shows that networks and cable are producing. *Mad Men, Dexter, True Blood, Breaking Bad, Game of Thrones, Boardwalk Empire, Rome*—the list goes on and on. In many cases, I find myself enjoying these shows more than I enjoy many of the movies I see in theaters these days, which seem so hit or miss. *True Blood* is my first multi-season foray into television, and it has been one of my most rewarding experiences to date. *True Blood*'s creator Alan Ball has given me that great gift of freedom to musically explore the world of Bon Temps. The series format also allows me as a composer to explore themes in a million different variations. I love scoring films as well because my work is heard through a giant sound system if it is released theatrically, so there are great things about both formats.

JG: In what ways has technology influenced your musical voice as a performer and composer?

NB: Technology has opened up a universe of sounds that I don't necessarily hear in my head. If I find myself with writer's block, I can often overcome it by starting to sift through the thousands of samples I have in my system. Oftentimes I will stumble on a sound or instrument I hadn't thought of for the composition and it can take the music in a completely different direction than I had originally anticipated.

JG: Do you use a digital audio workstation or software instruments?

NB: My primary sequencing program is Logic and in conjunction with Logic I use the EXS24 sampler and all sorts of samples.

JG: Do you use MIDI mockups?

NB: Whether I use MIDI mockups or not depends entirely on the instrumentation of a particular score. If it's orchestral, then MIDI mockups these days are all but expected. They are an invaluable tool in allowing a director to hear a close approximation of what the recorded work will sound like. They also help me as a composer understand more exactly early in the process how the music is going to interact with the dialog, sound effects, etc.

JG: How often do you hire musicians to perform your compositions?

NB: On *True Blood* I perform the entire score myself with the exception of Lisbeth Scott, who lends her beautiful vocals to the music. I try and use very few samples in order to give it an organic feel, which I think has helped to create a unique atmosphere. If I don't play the instrument I hear in my head, then I can dip into the enormous pool of incredible musicians right here in Los Angeles and bring them in to perform a particular work.

CHAPTER 14
TREVOR MORRIS

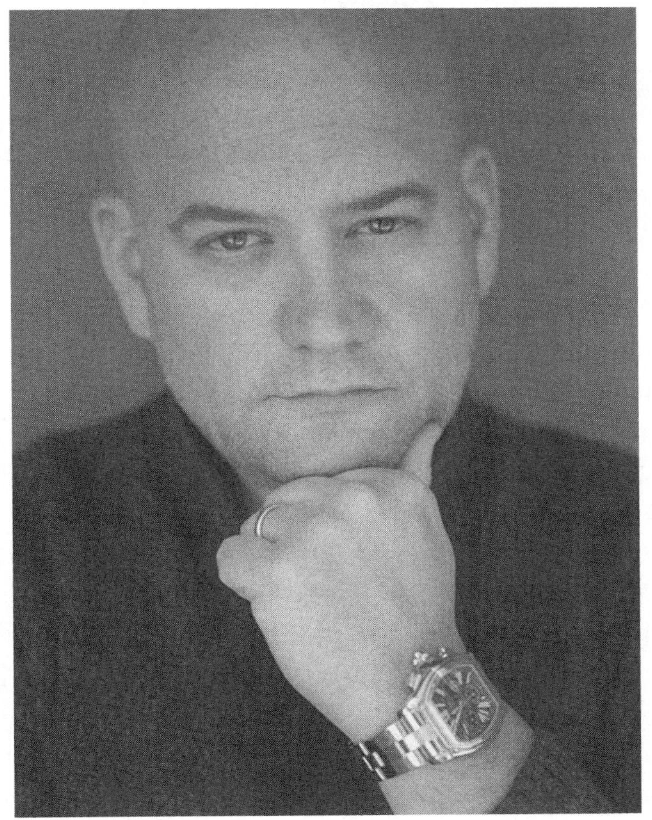

▶ **FIG. 14.1**

TREVOR MORRIS HAS EARNED multiple Emmy and Gemini nominations and awards for his work on Showtime's *The Borgias* and *The Tudors* and Starz Entertainment's *The Pillars of the Earth*. He won two Emmy Awards for Outstanding Original Main Title Theme Music, the first one in 2007 for *The Tudors*, the second one in 2011 for *The Borgias*. Morris won two Gemini Awards in 2010 and 2011 for Best Original Music Score for a Program or Series for *The Tudors*. In addition to Trevor's Emmy and Gemini wins in 2011, Trevor was also nominated for an Emmy Award for Outstanding Music Composition for a Miniseries,

Movie or a Special for *The Pillars of the Earth* and was nominated for two Gemini Awards for *Best* Original Music Score for a Dramatic Program, Mini-Series or TV Movie for *The Pillars of the Earth* and Best Original Music Score for a Program or Series for *The Borgias*.

Morris's music has also been heard in films and TV shows such as Disney's *Pirates of the Caribbean: Dead Man's Chest*, Fox Atomic's *The Hills Have Eyes II*, Columbia and Warner Bros.' *Something's Gotta Give*, Disney's *Pirates of the Caribbean: The Curse of the Black Pearl*, NBC's *The Chase*, CBS's *Moonlight*, CBS's *Miami Medical*, NBC's *Kings*, and Fox's *Justice*.

The Canadian composer was born in London, Ontario, a few hours outside Toronto. At 13 years old, Morris was commissioned by his school, St. Mary's School of the Arts, to score an original composition piece in honor of Pope John Paul's visit to Canada. He was paid $50, and it was performed on piano and by a four-part choir at St. Mary's Cathedral. Later, Morris attended Fanshawe College's Music Industry Arts program, Canada's most prestigious school for recording and production. Graduating at the top of his class, he moved to Toronto to work in music production. Morris eventually turned away from production and began to focus full time on composing music for television commercials.

Morris moved to Los Angeles in 1999 to score for films and television. He has collaborated with some of the best directors in the business, including Jerry Bruckheimer, Neil Jordan, and Tony and Ridley Scott.

JG: Can you please state your name?

TM: Trevor Morris.

JG: When and where were you born?

TM: I was born in London, Ontario, Canada, in 1970.

JG: What role did music play during your upbringing?

TM: I went to elementary school for the arts as a child where we studied strings and choir every day, so I was very much involved in music as a child and grew up with it. I took piano lessons as well, so really my, the base of all that I do really started at that age. I was very young, so it was an all-encompasing life choice at that moment to be involved in a music school, if you will. In high school, I sort of abandoned music for a little while and started to get back into it after high school during college. I continued from there. Music has gone through a few different phases of my life, but it's always been with me.

JG: Do you come from a musical family, or are you the only musician?

TM: I come from a family that has strong artistic genes. We have a couple of photographers in the family, but I'm the only one in music. My grandmother is the one I credit exposing me to music. My first memory is sitting on the piano bench with her when I was old enough to barely get up on the piano bench. She would play songs for me on the piano. I always credit her as the one who introduced me to music.

JG: When your musical activities diminished in your younger days, what inspired you to return? Did schooling play a role?

TM: Well no, that's the reason I left music. By the time I reached high school, everyone in my class was a very accomplished musician. They had been studying their instrument for a long time—whatever that may be. A lot of people were starting to take up a band instrument of sorts, and I really wasn't on the same level, and they wouldn't advance me to the senior band. I went a different way and started to become a rebellious youth and got away from the classical world of music and more into the rock-and-roll fun side of music (laughs) you know, working at a music store, a musical instrument store, embracing that side of me. It wasn't until after high school and into college that I started to reconnect with my roots in classical music.

JG: Where did you go to school?

TM: I went to a school in Canada called Fanshawe College, which is a program for the recording arts. It is similar to Berklee College of Music in the United States. It has a program that features engineering and production technique. I got accepted to university, which is, I know the nomenclature is different in Canada. University is the four-year bachelor degree and college refers to a more vocational setting. I was accepted into university, but I decided not to attend because everyone I knew who went to university to study music became a music teacher. That is not what I wanted to do, so I entered the recording studio arts world through a program called Music Industry Arts (MIA). It is probably the most prestigious program in Canada. That became my indoctrination into the world of recording studios, which really set me on the path that I am on now.

JG: Would you consider yourself an engineer's engineer or are you a composer who approaches technology through composition?

TM: You know that's a complicated question that has a rich answer. Before college, I was really knee-deep in the synthesizer generation. I bought my first synth when I was 16. I chose to forgo playing sports in high school so I could work a job at night to afford to buy instruments. I was already buying as much technology as I could afford long before college. I had a strong base with sequencers. When I went to engineering college it only reinforced that base. It has been a huge benefit to my career as I've progressed in my career.

JG: Which style of music do you feel most comfortable with to express yourself?

TM: I'm so focused on TV and film music—that's sort of what I do. If I play the piano for enjoyment, which is not that often because I work so much, I like to play Bruce Hornsby music. He was my generation's Billy Joel or Elton John. There are only so many people who have reinvented the piano. Elton John was one and Billy Joel was one. For me, Bruce Hornsby was my generation's guy. I play that kind of style music, but largely what comes out of me now is cinematic material.

JG: When were you first exposed to music composition?

TM: As I mentioned, I didn't go to school for composition like some people do. After I graduated from college, I moved to Toronto and got involved in the recording studio world. The core business in Toronto surrounds jingles and advertisements. Everybody works on jingles. The whole industry was centered on commercial production in Toronto and still is in a way. I would go into sessions and watch the composers come in, and they would run the sessions and hang with the musicians. I started to look at the process with some fondness in that it was more interesting to me than what I was doing, which was recording. I left being an engineer to go be a junior, you know, helper at a jingle music production facility. That's where I started to segue into composing. I started to revisit that idea and decided that I wanted to be a jingle composer because these guys were producing record-quality tracks even though they're 30 seconds long or 60 seconds long. They did this every day. They would go in and record drums, bass guitar, B-3, and choir. You name it. They were producing music and it seemed very appealing to me. That's really where I got back into composition, to answer your question. It was the time where I cut my teeth to be a film and TV composer. I did jingles for five or six years in Toronto—recording, writing, composing and producing inside the production world of advertising.

JG: While you were in Toronto did you ever consider moving to the United States? Was that something on your radar? How did you end up in Los Angeles?

TM: I love Toronto and still do. It's where I am from and always will be from. Once I decided to get into TV and film, I had a very hard time breaking into that circle—even with student films. I love Toronto and it's my home, but it's a tough nut to crack—tougher than Los Angeles in some strange way, so I didn't have a lot of success with my ambition of trying to become a TV and film composer. I got my first gig as kind of a really gracious favor from an existing and veteran composer. He took me under his wing and helped me do my first television show, which we co-composed. If it weren't for him, I would have never done anything. It just occurred to me at a certain point that you need to go where the work is being done and that is Los Angeles. So, if they made TV and film in Dallas, I would have moved to Dallas. If they made it in Vancouver, if that was the hub of the world, I would have moved to Vancouver. I was in my late 20's at this point and Los Angeles was the inevitable outcome. I just decided to do it while I still could before I got to a position in life where it would have been tougher. That was it, just sort of binary thinking. I thought, "Yes, I want to do TV and film music. That's where they do it. That's where I'm moving to."

JG: You're obviously working on a lot of great projects right now. How do you foster and maintain creativity throughout these long projects?

TM: You know, it's a learned skill. The one thing I find is that learning how to maintain sustained workflow is part of the learned skill set that you don't get in school. It's not talent, it's work ethic—work ethic is a huge part of it. A lot of people are not prepared for how hard it is or how many hours are involved or how constant it [work] is. Long days, seven days a week, no days off for months, sometimes. You just get good at it, or you don't I guess. You adapt to the work and you make it the center of your universe. TV is especially hard and unrelenting in regard to schedule, and that's what separates people who can do it from people who can't. There are more talented composers than me out there, but no one can deliver on a deadline as well as any of us. The people who are working, myself included, always deliver. You never miss a deadline. You always get it done and it's always good—that's the job. You can compose like Brahms, but if you can't deliver on a deadline, you don't have any business being in the film and television world; that's sort of the harsh reality. So you just adapt—it's just a Darwinian kind of a thing, isn't it?

JG: Exactly. You've got a pretty diverse portfolio that spans film, television, and even some gaming. Do you prefer one format to the other? What's your favorite format to write for?

TM: I don't. I get asked this a lot and I always respond the same way, which is, I'm a horrible songwriter. To grab a guitar, you know start at the window and think what I should write a song about doesn't speak to me. But give me something to look at, a visual to connect with, a story to tell, and the ideas start to flow almost immediately. I've been really lucky to work on very high-level television stuff. I mean all television is great, but shows like *Tudors* are like little movies. I'm always looking for the best story I can work on, the best story I can tell through music. I've been lucky to work on very rich television projects that allow me to express myself. I want to tell the best story I can.

JG: Do you prefer to write to score or a digital audio workstation?

TM: I use Cubase, which is my music vehicle of choice. I work in the score editor and the main editor, which takes on an Escher-like quality to it after a while. It's like Neo "seeing" the Matrix. I can see counterpoint and harmonic structure through the piano roll editor very well.

JG: In what ways has technology influenced your musical voice as a performer and a composer?

TM: I didn't grow up in the pencil and paper generation, like Jerry Goldsmith. I am part of the computer generation. I had my first Mac, the Macintosh SE, when I was a teenager. I've always composed at a computer. You know what I mean? I composed at the piano for melodic stuff, but the execution of my ideas has always stemmed from working with technology—from experiencing my first synth when I was in high school, the Super Jupiter, and exploring those colors. That has been a huge influence on what I write and how I write, what kind of music I listened to and what kind of film score composer I wanted to be. Now it's just evolved continuously from that point to now. I don't know how many computers I have in my studio now, but it's a lot! There's got to be a dozen. The technology has become my medium of expression; it's how I get my ideas out. More importantly, it's how I get my ideas to be realized in some way so that I can play them for the director because long gone are the days of play them the tune at the piano and they'll visualize the scoring stage. Today, it has to be fully demoed, fully marked up, fully realized, so that they can "feel it" and decide whether it's for them or not. There are a lot of composers who begrudge this process, and I'm exactly the opposite. I like it—I like the idea of getting my ideas to sound the best they can in a technological form. TV and a lot of smaller films don't provide a budget for an orchestra, so what happens in your studio is the final product. This is where my engineering background really helps because I have sort of an affinity for high-level audio.

JG: What is your digital audio workstation of choice?

TM: Cubase for composing, and Pro Tools for "mixing" and printing. They work great together and make a killer combo.

JG: Which third-party software instruments do you prefer to use?

TM: I use them all! Seriously I think I own everything out there. I cherry-pick through them to see what suits my point of view, but obviously Kontakt as a sample playback engine. I used GigaSampler before that. VEP as a 64-bit sample host has changed the game for me. It is the new backbone of my entire studio since I loathe PCs. I refuse to use them—I only use Macs.

JG: Do you create MIDI mockups when working with a director or client?

TM: That doesn't even begin to describe it. I create what I consider near final product as a mockup, the "no excuses" sound. My mockups sound very close, at least emotionally, to what my intentions are.

JG: How often do you hire musicians to perform your compositions?

TM: As often as possible, and often more than I should. Meaning, generally more than the budget allows. I very often pay for musicians to the point that I don't make any money. I thank them in every liner note of every CD I have put out and their invaluable contribution to my music.

JG: There are some who argue that technology is hindering the musical growth of young musicians through the use of loops and library music. Others argue that technology is in fact a new musical instrument. What are your thoughts on this subject?

TM: I can only speak intelligently about how it affects me, which is very positively. I'm not an educator so I'm not qualified to answer beyond my own experience.

JG: What role, if any, has technology played in the working relationships with your clients?

TM: It has changed it forever, both good and bad. There is no difference now between a client that is down the block and across the world in terms of delivery, but I always fight, ask, request, and near demand that my clients and I sit together in a room to talk about music, as opposed to any digital medium. I can't do it without the human interaction, which is what music is really all about in the end.

INDEX